AN INTRODUCTION TO JURISDICTION IN THE AMERICAN FEDERAL SYSTEM

by

LEA BRILMAYER
Professor of Law
Yale University

with

Jacob Corre
Elizabeth Henderson Esty
Jill Fisch
John Firestone
Sarah Barringer Gordon

Jim Huttenhower
Niki Kuckes
Margaret Marr
Kathleen Paisley
Ava Clayton Spencer

THE MICHIE COMPANY
Law Publishers
CHARLOTTESVILLE, VIRGINIA

This Book is Dedicated
to the Yale Law School,
in spite of itself

* * *

Royalties from this book
are being used to support
the Public Interest Loan Deferral
and Forgiveness Program for
Yale Law School Alumni

Acknowledgements

It is hard to write acknowledgements for a book of this sort. The writing of this book was communal in the best sense. Each chapter was drafted by an initial author and then assigned to another contributor to edit. A third person would enter additional changes in the process of checking for substantive accuracy. Each chapter was therefore shaped by many hands. The primary responsibility for initial drafting was as follows:

Personal Jurisdiction	Jim Huttenhower
Jurisdiction of the Federal Courts	Niki Kuckes
Case or Controversy	Sarah Gordon
Sovereign Immunity	Elizabeth Henderson Esty and Niki Kuckes
Refusal to Assert Jurisdiction	John Firestone
Abstention	Sarah Gordon
Judgments	Jim Huttenhower
State Choice of Law	Clayton Spencer
Substance and Procedure	Jill Fisch
Constitutional Limits on Choice of Law	Elizabeth Henderson Esty
International Law	Jacob Corre
Criminal Law and Domestic Relations	Margaret Marr
Jurisdiction to Tax	Kathleen Paisley

Many other individuals helped with this project. Some help on the initial stages was provided by Steve Hibbard, and Laurie Wallach generously helped us check the cites. The law school community supported us spiritually, in particular Dean Guido Calabresi who cares so much about everything that goes on at Yale. Bill Horne made us chicken cacciatore, and Dan Esty helped us eat it.

Finally, if there is one person who made the project possible, it's Cathy Briganti. We drove her wild with draft upon draft, and still she kept us organized, sane, and more or less on schedule. Most acknowledgements in books praise the secretary for accurate typing and unfailing good humor. Cathy can outclass them all on both counts, with her tremendous capacity for hard work and her snarling charm.

Preface

This book grew out of a year-long course that combined material from two different parts of the curriculum: federal jurisdiction and the conflict of laws. This is probably not a very common curricular offering. Yet it does seem that the two areas have a lot in common, and a lot to offer each other. Some of the more obvious parallelisms have been noted in the literature, such as the parallel differentiations between substance and procedure. The next logical step seemed to be to introduce the similarities into the law school curriculum in a more deliberate way. Thus, *Jurisdiction: State and Federal* (the course) was born. The year after this course was first offered at Yale, its professor and a group of its distinguished alumni and converts banded together in seminar form to try to reduce the results to writing. *An Introduction to Jurisdiction in the American Federal System* is the happy result.

The book also grew out of a series of scholarly articles that worked at making some of the less obvious analogies between the two fields explicit. For instance, it seemed that state legislation depriving local courts of jurisdiction over foreign causes of action (either federal or state) had something in common with congressional legislation depriving federal courts of jurisdiction over causes of action that Congress did not create.[1] It seemed that the "state sovereignty" rhetoric in federal jurisdiction ought to bear some relationship to "state sovereignty" rhetoric in the conflict of laws.[2] And that federal recognition of state judgments had something to do with state recognition of sister state judgments.[3] This series of articles eventually came to seem sadly piecemeal. It wasn't enough to point out similarities. It was more important to try to unify the whole subject, from the ground up.

A third motivation for this book came from numerous requests by students for a clear and simple source that they could consult on basic issues. Students, especially first year students, wanted to be able to find out the basics of the "lay of the land" without having to fight through interminable detail or profuse case discussion. Equally important, they wanted to find it all in one book. Experience suggests that students perceive the analogies between conflicts and federal jurisdiction very clearly, and recognize the relationship of both to first year civil procedure. Perhaps first year students are too naive to recognize the overriding importance of academic specialization.

---

1. Brilmayer & Underhill, *Congressional Obligation to Provide a Forum for Constitutional Claims,* 69 VA. L. REV. 819 (1983).

2. Brilmayer & Lee, *State Sovereignty and the Two Faces of Federalism,* 60 NOTRE DAME L. REV. 833 (1985).

3. Brilmayer, *State Forfeiture Rules and Federal Review of State Criminal Convictions,* 49 U. CHI. L. REV. 741 (1981).

Finally, even practitioners occasionally need something simple. This is especially true in the choice of law context, where modern academicians have developed what was already an arcane specialty into a quagmire of jargon, pretention, and manifest silliness. The ideal introduction here would be a neutral survey of what to expect in this strange domain. Neutrality is perhaps too much to hope for.[4] But it still ought to be possible to do the field the service of setting out some basic outlines, with appropriate references to the leading combatants in the field.

A word on references. This is not a reference book. The reader who already knows the basics of these areas is quite unlikely to come across citations with which he or she is unfamiliar. There are excellent hornbooks dealing with the various topics addressed here. While applauding these heroic efforts, this book in no way tries to imitate them. It simply isn't possible to be far reaching, detailed, readable and short.

Instead, this book is what it claims to be: an introduction. Jurisdiction is a very important field. Is there a lawyer in the country who doesn't need to know about it, or a law student who can ignore the subject without jeopardizing hopes of graduation? Surely judges spend a lot of time (perhaps too much) addressing jurisdictional problems. This enterprise is at the same time grand and humble, like roasting the perfect chicken.[5] We hope that students of all varieties find it helpful.

---

4. One of us has taken strong positions on these issues. *See, e.g.,* Brilmayer, *Interest Analysis and the Myth of Legislative Intent,* 78 MICH. L. REV. 392 (1979).

5. J. CHILD, L. BERTHOLLE, S. BECK, MASTERING THE ART OF FRENCH COOKING 249 (vol. 1):

You can always judge the quality of a cook or a restaurant by roast chicken. While it does not require years of training to produce a juicy, brown, buttery, crisp-skinned, heavenly bird, it does entail such a greed for perfection that one is under compulsion to hover over the bird, listen to it, above all see that it is continually basted, and that it is done just to the proper turn.

Summary Table of Contents

Table of Contents

A THEORETICAL OVERVIEW

The American law of jurisdiction reflects the basic political principles that structure the relationships among the states and between the states and the federal government. In this respect, it is like any other nation's law of jurisdiction. Jurisdictional reasoning is a process of justifying a particular political division of authority. To show why there is jurisdiction is to show why some political institution has a right either to regulate directly some happenings in the real world or to instruct another political institution how to decide conflicts. Such rights cannot exist without a political theory to rationalize the entire system.

This philosophical outlook may strike some readers as mistaken, or at least controversial. It is possible to argue that jurisdiction is based on nothing more than naked exercise of power, rather than on legitimacy or justification. Indeed, jurisdictional issues are frequently highly politicized, and may be used merely to disguise the true considerations that motivate a decision. For instance, conservatives might favor decentralized decisionmaking by the states over centralized decisionmaking by the federal government. This preference might be caused not by a genuine preference for decentralized decisionmaking but by an expectation that the states are more conservative than the federal government. And liberals are equally adept at such maneuvers.

This book, nevertheless, takes jurisdictional justification at more or less face value, and explains the jurisdictional doctrines that courts and commentators commonly cite. This outlook is not necessarily naive; it does not deny that political motivations and naked power are at work. Even if political motivations are at work, the theoretical exercise is valuable clarification of the ideals alluded to by hypocrites and power brokers to justify their positions. Even a hypocrite manipulating popular opinion would choose convincing ideals for rationalizations, since unappealing rationalizations would not serve their intended purpose. Clarification of underlying principles should be interesting even to those disposed only towards manipulation. And those who have a sincere interest in jurisdiction would, a fortiori, find the identification of underlying principles a compelling concern.

This theoretical overview of the federal/state jurisdictional system describes the basic actors and their roles in the jurisdictional drama. The material in this chapter may be too elementary to need repeating. But an introduction to jurisdiction has to start with elementary premises. First, some readers without extensive background in American law might prefer to see these premises restated. Second, there is value in making clear which assumptions the subsequent development relies

1

upon. Which features of the federal/state system are central in jurisdictional reasoning, and which are peripheral or irrelevant? We encourage readers with adequate background and/or scant theoretical interest to turn directly to the more doctrinal material which follows in later chapters.

Jurisdictional problems fall into several categories, because there are different types of division of authority that give rise to jurisdictional issues. One important question is whether the institution exercising authority is part of the state or of the federal government. The second important question is whether we are speaking of the power of courts or the power of legislatures. The first half of this book deals with the power of courts, state courts first and then federal. The second deals with the power of legislatures.

Most books and law school courses treat only some of these jurisdictional issues but not others. For instance, Conflict of Laws discusses the power of states vis-à-vis one another. Federal Jurisdiction discusses the power of the federal courts, vis-à-vis the states and also vis-à-vis other federal courts. Some books treat both state and federal jurisdiction together, but only discuss adjudicative jurisdiction, that is, the power of courts. They leave out legislative jurisdiction, or "choice of law." This in turn, is the primary focus of other analytical treatments.

Because there are common issues throughout, this book addresses all of these issues, although in an elementary way. The emphasis is on broad outlines, and conceptual similarities and differences, rather than on detail. In this introductory material, we first discuss the role of the states, then the role of the federal government, then the differentiation of authority between federal legislatures and federal courts, and then the reasons that federal courts have simultaneously the most powerful and the most limited role of all.

The Role of the States

As a historical matter, the states came first. Each had to be equipped to handle any legal problem that might come along in a relatively complete and autonomous manner. When the federal government was established, certain issues were removed from the reach of state power and vested with the federal authority. But the federal government's powers, so defined, were enumerated and limited. The power of the states was residual; it did not have to be specifically granted, but consisted of any issue not deliberately granted exclusively to the centralized authority. Unless there is an affirmative reason that a state may not exercise power, its authority is assured.

2

One of the issues left to the states was how to structure their legislative and court systems. There are few constitutional limits on the state's choice of domestic political processes.[1] By state law, each state apportions jurisdiction among its courts and decides whether to exercise jurisdiction at all. For this reason, every question of the jurisdiction of a state agency has a state law component to it. Furthermore, unless this division of authority or decision whether to exercise authority runs afoul of specific federal law, it is solely within the discretion of the state itself.

Roughly speaking, there are three ways that state law may run afoul of federal standards. First, the federal Constitution places numerous substantive restrictions on the states. For instance, the Bill of Rights, made applicable to the states through the fourteenth amendment, prohibits states from interfering with free speech or searching an individual's house unreasonably.[2] The fourteenth amendment prohibits the states from discriminating against racial minorities.[3] Similarly, the states are forbidden to impair the obligation of contract.[4]

These individual rights limitations are part of the study of substantive constitutional law. They give rise to jurisdictional problems primarily because they increase the power of the federal courts at the expense of state legislatures. However, these limitations are motivated by substantive, not jurisdictional concerns. The two other types of limitations on the states are motivated more directly by jurisdictional considerations. The American federal system gives rise to jurisdictional problems because the country is divided into states. Even where the states do not violate any particular substantive limitations imposed by the Constitution, application of a valid local law or exercise of adjudicative authority may have effects on other states. The federal Constitution protects other states from undue interference.

This protection can be accomplished in either of two methods. First, the Constitution may limit a state's ability to exercise its authority in cases where doing so would impact unduly on other states. Thus, this second type of federal limitation consists of the limits on the state's authority when extending its law or adjudicative procedures into the interstate arena. For instance, a state may constitutionally authorize

---

1. One exception is the guaranty of a republican form of government in art. IV, § 4 of the Constitution. The judicial enforceability of this provision is in doubt unless a challenge based upon it is linked to an equal protection claim. Baker v. Carr, 369 U.S. 186 (1962).

2. These limitations arise out of the first, fourth, and fourteenth amendments to the United States Constitution.

3. "[N]or shall any State . . . deny to any person within its jurisdiction the equal protection of the laws."

4. Article I, § 10.

its court system to hear certain types of interstate issues but not others. It may validly grant its courts the power to hear automobile accident litigation arising out of accidents within the state. Or, it may have a rule authorizing application of forum law to such cases of local auto accidents.

Whether a state decision to assert either legislative or adjudicative jurisdiction over interstate cases is constitutional depends primarily upon the due process and full faith and credit clauses. Sometimes the problem is that the state seeks to extend the reach of its courts, or its laws, too far. For this reason, state-court adjudicative jurisdiction over interstate cases is scrutinized under the due process clause. Ironically, at other times the problem is that the state does not extend its laws or its courts quite far enough into the interstate arena. For instance, the full faith and credit clause may be offended where the state refuses to lend its courts to the enforcement of legal rules or judicial judgments from other states. The Constitution prohibits such discrimination against foreign laws or judgments.

The second solution to jurisdictional problems is substantive; the federal government simply supplants the multiplicity of state rules with a uniform federal rule. These areas of federal preemption form the third set of limitations on the states. This third type of federal limitation is a substantive response to a jurisdictional difficulty. An entire area of substantive regulation may be removed from the reach of state power because, as a practical matter, the law must be uniform. There might be nothing wrong with the state law, in and of itself, yet practical problems would arise if fifty states adopted fifty different laws on the subject. The fact of fifty different jurisdictions provides the rationale for federal regulation; but the federal regulation takes the form of preempting substantive local law, and not just invalidating its application to interstate occurrences.

There are many grants of federal power which are based upon a practical need for uniformity. These are binding on the states because of the supremacy clause, which invalidates state laws which conflict with federal law.[5] Such areas of practical uniformity include: bankruptcy, coining money, foreign affairs, and interstate commerce.[6] Contrast this category with the first category of individual rights. There, the foremost goal is to preserve particular substantive rights, and uniformity throughout the nation is merely a byproduct of centralized

---

5. U.S. Const. art. IV.

6. Article I, § 8. The states are forbidden to coin money, and enter agreements with foreign nations by art. I, § 10. *See also* Zschernig v. Miller, 389 U.S. 429 (1968) (limits on states engaging in foreign relations). They are also prohibited from interfering with interstate commerce. *See, e.g.,* Gibbons v. Ogden, 22 U.S. (9 Wheat.) 1 (1824).

authority. Here, the foremost goal itself is uniformity. No particular substantive rights are constitutionally protected; Congress creates whatever substantive rights it wishes.

The study of state jurisdiction consists of two things: first, the law the state has developed to define the jurisdiction of its courts and legislatures; and second, the federal limitations on such jurisdictional rules. These limitations are the second type of federal limitation just described. The first and third categories of federal limitations on the states — substantive constitutional limits and federal substantive limits motivated by a need for uniformity — are less directly relevant. They do give rise to certain sorts of jurisdictional problems, because as federal laws they expand the scope of federal power at the expense of the states. But their solutions to these jurisdictional problems are substantive, and because the solution adopted is substantive preemption, by Constitution or by statute, they are not addressed below. We are here concerned primarily with jurisdictional solutions to jurisdictional problems.

The Role of the Federal Government

The states are basically equivalents of one another, complete and separate sovereigns. The federal government is a different sort of creature altogether. It presupposes the existence of the states. It is not a complete government in and of itself; it corrects the defects of a totally decentralized administration without supplanting decentralized spheres of authority in their entirety. Federalism is a compromise solution.

While the states have residual authority over any issues not specifically denied them, the federal government has power only when explicitly granted. The field/ground relationship, in other words, is reversed. To find out what powers are granted to the federal government, one asks which powers are denied the states. The states' limitations, conversely, are precisely the sources of federal authority.

The categories of constitutional limitations on state power are for this reason also the categories of grants of power to the federal government. Each functional deficiency of decentralized authority results in vesting power with the central administration. Thus, federal law gives substantive solutions to substantive problems, jurisdictional solutions to jurisdictional problems, and substantive solutions to jurisdictional problems. The first category includes the substantive limitations on what states may do in regulating internal matters, for reasons having to do with individual substantive rights. On normative matters not supposed to depend on the vagaries of positive state law, federal protection is in order.

The other two sources of power are jurisdictionally motivated. This includes both substantive and jurisdictional solutions to jurisdictional problems. As already noted, there are some issues as to which there is no unique constitutionally correct answer, although it is important that the answer not vary from state to state. Thus, bankruptcy, foreign affairs, and the coining of money are reserved for federal regulation. This is a substantive solution.

Finally, the federal government rather than the states is empowered to scrutinize the interstate consequences of otherwise valid state laws. This is a jurisdictional solution to a jurisdictional problem. The states are not the final arbiters of whether they may assert jurisdiction over interstate disputes, or apply their own law. Nor may they determine whether they wish to enforce one another's judgments.

Figure A.

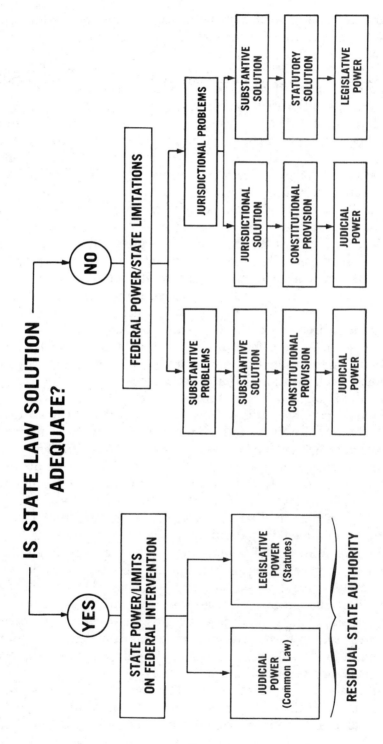

Federal Courts Versus Federal Legislation

In the division of authority between the state and federal governments, the difference between courts and legislatures becomes crucial. Some of the functions just mentioned are typically carried out by the federal courts, and some by Congress or administrative agencies. Of the different sorts of federal power, what determines which branch of government is allocated authority to exercise it?

An important functional constraint is that courts are ordinarily given the job of putting into effect the norms that other institutions have created. Under the traditional view of the judicial function, the function of the federal courts is the application of preexisting norms. "Preexisting," of course, is not the same as "mechanically ascertainable" or "unambiguous." When a court interprets the Constitution, it is very likely that there will be differences of opinion about what the Constitution requires. It may also be argued that a court has some discretion in choosing between interpretations that seem equally good, or that the court may identify and constitutionalize rights created by natural law. On this controversial issue, we prefer not to take a position. Yet still, in such cases, it makes sense to say that the court is attempting to recognize rights created by another source.

For this reason, the federal courts become most involved in those situations where a legal norm already exists. The courts thus enforce substantive constitutional limitations such as the Bill of Rights and the jurisdictional limitations imposed by constitutional provisions such as the due process clause. However, where the Constitution has signalled the desirability of practical uniformity without specifying the unique solution, the courts play a less active role. Typically, they become involved in such issues only to the extent that there are statutory directives to enforce. In order to implement this role of enforcing preexisting federal law, the federal courts are vested with "federal question" jurisdiction. Federal statutory or constitutional norms can thereby be enforced in federal court.

The implementation of preexisting rights is not, of course, necessarily limited to preexisting federal rights. Another example of federal courts implementing preexisting rights is the federal courts' diversity jurisdiction. The preexisting rights are created by state law, but the case involves parties from different states. The original reason for vesting such cases with the federal courts was that the local courts of a state might tend to discriminate against nonlocals. This falls under the second category of federal power, namely monitoring the extension of state law into the interstate arena. The state law itself is valid, but its manner of application to interstate cases is potentially suspect. Diversity jurisdiction is a jurisdictional solution to a jurisdictional problem.

While the federal courts implement preexisting norms created by the Constitution or by state or federal statutory law, Congress and the administrative agencies further the goals of a federalist system through the creation of norms themselves. As noted above, the main types of federal power are protection of individual rights, limitation of state jurisdictional rules in the interstate context, and supplanting state law where practical uniformity so requires. Congress plays only a limited role where the Constitution has already supplied a norm protecting individual rights or limiting state law on jurisdictional issues.

This is in part because the whole point of constitutionalizing certain norms was to make certain individual rights invulnerable to popular political pressure. Since the popular pressures that cause state legislatures to attempt to override constitutional guarantees may afflict Congress equally, the congressional role in defining the scope of individual rights must be limited. There are nevertheless certain situations in which Congress is invited by the text to play an active role in implementation of the rights the text creates.[7] An example is the enforcement power granted by section five of the fourteenth amendment, although the scope of this enforcement power is controversial.[8]

Moreover, when the constitutional text speaks to interstate jurisdictional issues, as opposed to individual rights, the reasons for invulnerability to popular pressure are inapplicable to Congress. Where one state overreaches or discriminates against another state, the political pressure accounting for the state's action is unlikely to have much influence in Congress. Congress is thought to be sensitive to the needs of the states, and more important, equally sensitive to the needs of all states. Thus, if Congress authorizes the states to take action that would otherwise be suspect for considerations of interstate harmony, it can safely be assumed that the benefits nationwide outweigh the costs.[9]

Congress' premier role lies in those areas where the Constitution does not specify a unique right answer but simply indicates that a uniform answer might be desirable. In such situations, the role of the

7. The full faith and credit clause provides one interesting example. Although it requires, as a constitutional matter, that states respect each others laws and judgments, it also invites Congress to take an active part in determining what credit is owing to the laws and judgments of other states.

8. For the views of one of the authors, see *The Human Life Bill, the Bill of Rights and the Congressional Enforcement Power Under Section 5 of the Fourteenth Amendment: Hearings on S.158 Before the Subcomm. on Separation of Powers of the Senate Judiciary Comm.*, 97th Cong., 1st Sess. (1981) (statement of Lea Brilmayer, University of Chicago).

9. Wechsler, *The Political Safeguards of Federalism*, 54 COLUM. L. REV. 534 (1954); J. CHOPER, JUDICIAL REVIEW AND NATIONAL POLITICAL PROCESSES 177-84 (1980).

federal courts has been fairly modest, since the courts typically limit themselves to implementing preexisting rules. This function, it is often said, is better filled by Congress. And article I vests Congress with legislative power over many such issues. Interstate commerce, foreign relations and defense, copyright and patents, and bankruptcy are issues delegated to Congress (and in some cases the executive) under the constitutional plan on the theory that a single federal answer on such issues is necessary and proper, but that no single federal answer is constitutionally compelled.

State and Federal Courts Contrasted

This division of labor between courts and legislatures relies upon a traditional and modest view of the judicial role. The appropriateness of such a modest role, however, is certainly open to question. The Constitution itself does not explicitly limit the judicial function in this way. Furthermore, the fact that the function of state courts is perceived rather more broadly suggests that there is nothing inherent about courts, per se, that requires this division of labor.

Unlike federal courts, state courts have broad common-law powers to create law in such areas as torts, domestic law, and contracts. The fact that these bodies of law existed even before legislatures became involved in codifying or defining them clearly demonstrates that they are judicially created. Under the modest view of the judicial function, federal courts in contrast are supposed to have only the most limited role in creating federal common law. One wonders why the judicial function is perceived so narrowly in the federal context when the state courts so clearly enjoy much broader powers.

The federal courts are different from state courts in several important ways. First, they are created and their powers are defined by article III of the Constitution. That the federal courts are defined by the Constitution suggests that there are principled limitations on what their role should be. In contrast, there are fifty different states, which suggests that they may have different ways of defining the judicial function. Perhaps for this reason the states need not be bound by any particular definition.

Furthermore, the federal courts are part of the federal government. As such, they share the limitations of Congress to exercising only enumerated, specifically granted, federal powers. In contrast, the power of the states is residual, rather than enumerated. Such residual power cannot be limited to state legislatures; it must be shared by state courts. The state courts share this residual power because where there is no preexisting state or federal norm, the court must still resolve the litigation somehow. Where there are no preexisting norms, state courts necessarily create new ones.

10

Moreover, it is not just a matter of the limits of federal authority to particular enumerated powers. Federal courts have narrower powers even than the federal legislature. The federal government typically does not even exercise all of the power that it might. For instance, Congress could probably choose to supplant all of state contract law under its power to regulate interstate commerce, but it has not. A fundamental assumption (if perhaps a subconstitutional one) is that the enumerated federal powers are ones that the federal government *may* exercise, but ones that need not all be exercised at once.

The decision about how much to exercise of the potential power that the federal government possesses is typically thought to be a prerogative of Congress, and not the courts. Or, in other words, if Congress chooses not to address an issue as to which there is potential federal power, then the courts should follow suit. The general prohibition against development of federal common law protects state authority from the federal courts. This prohibition is reflected in the Federal Rules of Decision Act — which requires federal courts to follow state law unless an applicable federal statute, treaty, or constitutional provision exists — and in the doctrine of *Erie Railroad*.[10] The absence of federal statutory law is taken, so to speak, as a federal legislative determination that state law should be left uninterrupted. Where there is only potential federal power but no constitutional or statutory norm, it is apparent that such a congressional decision should be controlling.

There are good reasons even aside from the Rules of Decision Act to interpret legislative silence as a deliberate choice not to exercise federal power. A court must address all issues necessary to resolve the case before it, or else give principled reasons why addressing the issue is inappropriate.[11] The judicial tendency, for this reason, is to expand power to the limits of where it can give a principled reason to stop. Whether to preempt state law is, however, an essentially political decision. Perhaps one year it seems unnecessary to intervene, but the next year changing political coalitions or empirical conditions might make intervention more desirable.

A court cannot decide whether to decide without creating precedent, but Congress can. If the goal is a simple decision as to whether creating federal law is sensible now, without a determination whether creating federal law on the issue would ever be acceptable, then the decision

---

10. 28 U.S.C. § 1652; 304 U.S. 64 (1938).

11. The Supreme Court has a largely discretionary docket, and need not create precedent when it declines to hear a case. However, this leaves the lower court decision intact, and this judicial determination of rights does establish a precedent. It can fail to establish precedents only because it has no responsibility to resolve cases; in this sense, it resembles a legislature.

must come from Congress and not the courts. The courts are well equipped to declare that, as a matter of principle, some topic is beyond the federal sphere of authority. But they are less capable at simply refusing to exercise power without creating a requirement of silence for the future.

Federal Court Limitations Vis-à-Vis Majoritarian Processes

There is a second limitation imposed upon the federal courts by traditional notions of the proper judicial function. That is the constitutional restriction to making decisions in the context of "cases or controversies." The language is taken from article III, which defines the federal courts; thus the basic outlines of the restriction (if perhaps not its precise contours) are constitutionally compelled. It limits the federal courts in their abilities to review legislation for substantive constitutionality. It represents a jurisdictional solution to the jurisdictional problem of allocating power between the elected branches and the courts.

This set of jurisdictional doctrines contains what would otherwise be a very far reaching grant of federal judicial power. By restricting the occasions for constitutional adjudication, it limits judicial intrusion into the spheres of authority of state and federal legislatures. Furthermore, it limits the ability of one court to tie the hands of its successors through the operation of the doctrine of stare decisis.[12] Decisions in concrete cases are more easily limited to their facts through the process of distinguishing factual situations. The limitation to cases or controversies means that power is distributed among various courts according to the rate at which issues arise in the outside world.

This restriction is necessary because of the federal court system's peculiar omnipotence. When the Supreme Court interprets or declares federal law, its pronouncements are binding on the states by virtue of the supremacy clause. In addition, when the Court exercises its powers of constitutional interpretation, its pronouncements are binding on the other branches of the federal government as well. Indeed, through the doctrine of precedent, the Court's holdings are fairly authoritative even in later Supreme Court cases. This puts the Court, when it speaks, at the apex of power. In order to contain such peculiar power, there must be restrictions on the appropriate occasion to speak. While it seems that the limitation to cases or controversies protects primarily

---

12. *See generally* Brilmayer, *The Jurisprudence of Article III*, 93 HARV. L. REV. 297 (1979).

legislatures from having their statutes declared unconstitutional, the limitation also protects other courts in the court system, and later litigants who may wish to argue their issues without having to confront too heavy a burden of prior law.

The entire scheme can be roughly diagrammed as follows.

Figure B.

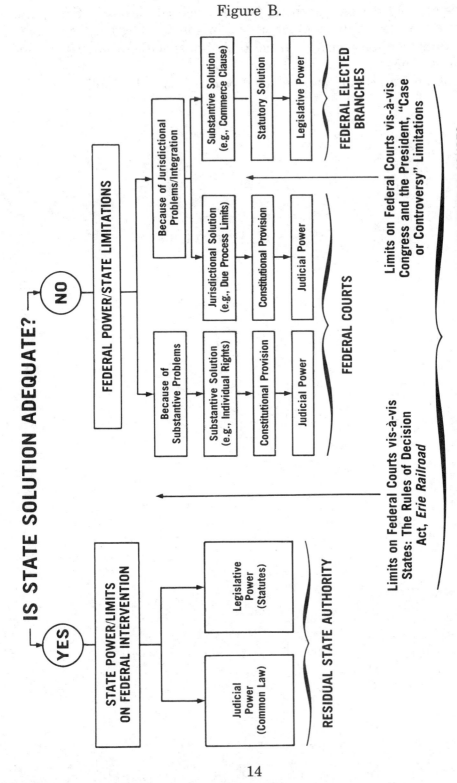

Balance

Overall, one can see a common pattern in these allocations of power. Some institutions have a very wide range of powers, but are easily preempted by other institutions. For instance, state courts deal with any issue whatsoever, but are preempted by any valid regulation created by state legislatures, Congress, or the federal courts. Their broad powers can be exercised only in the context of silence of the state legislatures and of federal law. Conversely, there are institutions such as the United States Supreme Court which are highly authoritative, but only on a specialized range of issues. Limitations on the powers of such decisionmakers are determined by the issues they may address, since they are authoritative when they do speak.

The balance of power consists of keeping within bounds the product of an institution's range of competence and its ability to overrule other institutions. If any decisionmaker had power both to review every other decisionmaker and to address every issue, it would have preempted the total legal authority. The system would be out of balance. State power in our present system is balanced because each state addresses the same issues but none can hierarchically review any other. The federal/state system is balanced by allowing review by federal courts and legislatures but only on a limited set of issues. State courts address more issues than state legislatures because they have to answer every issue in a case; but state courts are easily preempted. Federal courts, which are hard to preempt on constitutional issues, develop strict self limitations on the occasions on which they speak.

It is this delicate balance that makes jurisdiction such a fascinating topic, particularly in a complex federal system. The discussion below treats the legislative/judicial dichotomy as the main division. Accordingly, it first addresses judicial jurisdiction in Part I, and then legislative jurisdiction in Part II. Part III deals with special problems at the intersection of these two types of jurisdiction. Within each part, we see the constant interplay of federal actors and state actors, and state actors vis-à-vis one another. We see statutory, constitutional, and judge-made discretionary doctrine from both state and federal sources. For any grant of power, there is a countervailing limit that demonstrates the true meaning of "checks and balances" in the American federal system.

15

PART I

ADJUDICATIVE JURISDICTION

Chapter 1

PERSONAL JURISDICTION

State courts have broad powers compared to their federal counterparts. Unlike the federal courts whose powers are granted by Congress and the Constitution, state courts have the authority to hear almost any matter without the need for an affirmative grant. This schema is appropriate given that the states and their judicial systems predate the federal government and form the background for a federal government of limited powers.

Regardless of this residual authority, the power of state courts is limited in certain ways. The most important limitation derives from constraints on the ability of a state court to exercise authority over certain parties. A related constraint concerns limits on a court's ability to apply its substantive law to a controversy. These two limits ultimately derive from the federal Constitution, which established a national government of limited powers but superior authority, and are grounded in the due process and full faith and credit clauses.

This chapter discusses state courts' authority over certain parties — particularly defendants located outside the boundaries of the state — and the constitutional limits on that authority. The chapter begins with a description of the basic concepts and terminology, followed by a discussion of the history and current status of the limits imposed on state courts by the due process clause.

I. Basic Concepts: The State Law of Jurisdiction

To adjudicate an action, a court needs to possess two types of jurisdiction: (1) jurisdiction over the subject matter, which means that the court is empowered to hear a controversy of this type; and (2) jurisdiction over the person or property involved, which means that the court has the authority to enter a judgment binding on these parties in relation to this property. The absence of either type of jurisdiction deprives a court of adjudicatory authority. The outer boundaries of each type of jurisdiction thus limit a court's power.

A. SUBJECT MATTER JURISDICTION

Subject matter jurisdiction generally is not an issue in the context of federal limits on state court authority. State courts can be vested with authority to hear almost any matter. One limit does exist, however. The federal government can vest the federal courts with exclusive jurisdiction over particular areas of law, such as bankruptcy, and thereby deprive state courts of the power to hear such disputes.[1]

Subject matter limitations of another sort are meaningful in the state law context, however. These limits relate to a state's own decision to allot adjudicative responsibilities among various judicial bodies. These decisions are analogous to the federal doctrines discussed in Chapter 2, that allocate cases among the federal courts. Some state courts are known as courts of general jurisdiction and thus have authority to hear almost all cases.[2] States have given other courts original jurisdiction only over certain types of cases. This allotment can occur, for example, according to the monetary value of the controversy,[3] the type of remedy requested,[4] or the nature of the action.[5] The subject matter allotment also can be based on the stage of decisionmaking the litigation has reached (i.e. trial versus appellate court).[6]

B. JURISDICTION OVER PERSONS OR PROPERTY

Unlike subject matter jurisdiction, limits on jurisdiction over persons or property are an important constraint on state court power. Two conditions — basis and process — must exist for a court to exercise valid jurisdiction over a person or property. Basis refers to the relationship between a party and the sovereign (the state) from which the court derives its power. Process refers to the procedural steps prescribed by the sovereign to connect the party with the court: that is, process requires sufficient notice to the defendant. Most of the discussion in this chapter concerns questions about basis, rather than process. Process is not really a jurisdictional concern; there are notice requirements even in purely intrastate disputes.[7] This requirement of due process is a substantively protected individual right.

---

1. 28 U.S.C. § 1471 (1982).

2. *See, e.g.,* 42 Pa. Cons. Stat. Ann. § 931 (Purdon 1981) (granting to courts of common pleas unlimited original jurisdiction of all actions, unless specifically assigned to other courts by statute or by the Supreme Court).

3. *See, e.g.,* 42 Pa. Cons. Stat. Ann. § 1515(a)(3) (Purdon Supp. 1985) (granting district justices jurisdiction over certain claims where the amount at issue does not exceed $4,000).

4. *See, e.g.,* 42 Pa. Cons. Stat. Ann. § 1515(a)(2) (Purdon Supp. 1985) (granting to district justices jurisdiction over certain landlord-tenant matters).

5. *See, e.g.,* 42 Pa. Cons. Stat. Ann. § 762(a)(2) (Purdon Supp. 1985) (granting Commonwealth Court exclusive appellate jurisdiction for criminal matters).

6. *Compare* 42 Pa. Cons. Stat. Ann. § 742 (Purdon 1981) (granting Superior Court exclusive appellate jurisdiction over most appeals from courts of common pleas) *with* 42 Pa. Cons. Stat. Ann. § 741 (Purdon 1981) (no original jurisdiction in Superior Court except in certain extraordinary matters).

7. *See, e.g.,* Lambert v. California, 355 U.S. 225, 228 (1957) (failure to register as a convicted felon may not be punished under due process clause, "[e]ngrained in our concept of due process is the requirement of notice").

Historically, jurisdiction was separated into three categories: personal, in rem and quasi in rem jurisdiction. First, a court could have personal (or in personam) jurisdiction over a party, meaning that the court has the power to adjudicate a controversy, and can obligate the party to comply with its orders to the full extent of his or her assets. Traditionally, only three conditions were sufficient to confer personal jurisdiction in a court: domicile (or residence) in the forum, physical presence in the forum, or consent.[8] These conditions made it difficult to obtain personal jurisdiction over defendants located out-of-state. The requirement of personal jurisdiction also applies to corporations and other organizations; conditions analogous to the three bases mentioned above were required for a court to have personal jurisdiction over a corporation.

In recent years, the state law definition of what constitutes an adequate basis for personal jurisdiction has expanded. All states have enacted long-arm statutes, which allow their courts to gain jurisdiction over out-of-state defendants on the basis of certain connections with the forum. These long-arm statutes contain guidelines for determining when a state assertion of jurisdiction is proper. For example, in addition to the traditional bases of domicile, physical presence, and consent, jurisdiction could be predicated on engaging in tortious conduct within the state.[9]

The second and third varieties of jurisdiction — in rem and quasi in rem — involve property located within the forum. In essence, the court's power (the basis) rests on the location of a defendant's tangible or intangible assets within the state. An action in rem is a lawsuit that establishes a party's ownership of property against the claims of all others. An example of this sort of action is a suit to quiet title to a piece of real estate, which purports to be binding on the world. The quasi in rem suit is similar to an in rem proceeding. Quasi in rem actions adjudicate claims of specified persons to property. Mortgage foreclosures are an example of this type of action.

A different type of quasi in rem action has questionable current status for constitutional reasons that will be discussed below.[10] In such cases, the court also derives jurisdiction over a party on the basis of property located in the forum. The claim asserted by the plaintiff, however, is a personal one; it has no relation to the in-state property, which is merely an excuse to get the defendant into court. Although the plaintiff's claim is essentially personal, any judgment against the

---

8. Pennoyer v. Neff, 95 U.S. 714, 720 (1878).
9. *See, e.g.,* N.Y. Civ. Prac. Law § 302(a)(2) (McKinney 1972 & Supp. 1986).
10. *See infra* Section IIA1.

defendant is limited to the value of the in-state property, which is then subject to attachment proceedings.[11]

As this example illustrates, a purported basis for jurisdiction will not necessarily be related to the cause of action. The same is true when in personam jurisdiction is sought, with the basis being the defendant's in-state activities rather than his or her property. Thus, a defendant domiciled in Florida might go to California on vacation and get involved in an automobile accident there. The plaintiff might choose to sue in Florida, and would obtain jurisdiction over the defendant by virtue of his Florida domicile. The Florida domicile has nothing to do with the automobile litigation. Nevertheless, it would be both convenient for the defendant and fair to require him to defend in Florida.

In an influential article in 1966 by Professors Von Mehren and Trautman,[12] this sort of jurisdiction was denominated "general" jurisdiction, because the defendant's contacts with Florida gave the state jurisdiction over any cause of action in which he or she was involved.[13] In contrast, "specific" jurisdiction was jurisdiction only over some particular piece of litigation.[14] In the above example, Florida would have general jurisdiction over any litigation brought against the defendant, while California would have only specific jurisdiction over the defendant in the automobile litigation. California would not have adequate contacts for general jurisdiction and therefore could not adjudicate litigation, say, between the Florida defendant and his Florida employer in a contract suit arising in Florida.

II. Constitutional Limits on State Court Jurisdiction

Recently, the traditional framework for state court jurisdiction outlined in the preceding section has changed a great deal. Within the last decade the Supreme Court has narrowly redefined the constitutional checks on state court jurisdiction. Consequently, states have expanded their assertion of jurisdiction far beyond these traditional categories. State long-arm statutes now set out broad guidelines for state assertions of jurisdiction, and fall into two basic types. First, enumerated act statutes list certain kinds of acts (such as committing a tortious act in

---

11. Attachment is the act of seizing property under judicial order and bringing this property into the custody of the court to secure satisfaction of any judgment ultimately entered in the action. BLACK'S LAW DICTIONARY 115 (5th ed. 1979).

12. Von Mehren & Trautman, *Jurisdiction to Adjudicate: A Suggested Analysis,* 79 HARV. L. REV. 1121 (1966).

13. *Id.* at 1136-44.

14. *Id.* at 1144-63.

the state or transacting business within the state) that will subject a person to jurisdiction.[15] Second, general statutes simply state that courts can exercise jurisdiction on any basis that is not unconstitutional.[16] Some states have added a general provision to their enumerated act statutes.[17]

The relevant constitutional checks are embodied primarily in the due process clause,[18] but also to some extent in the full faith and credit clause.[19] The original due process limit was based on the finite power of the state court: the forum had no power to adjudicate a matter unless the person or property was somehow physically present. To act without this physical power was to violate due process. The discussion below will show how the Court has gradually abandoned this power-based notion of due process in favor of a theory relating to the "fairness" of exercising jurisdiction over the defendant, based on the level of his or her connections with the forum state. Furthermore, under the most recent decisions, the Court has explicitly recognized an additional component to due process, relating to state sovereignty.

Although most constitutional litigation over personal jurisdiction involves the due process clause, the full faith and credit clause also serves to limit state court power, perhaps in a more fundamental way than due process. The full faith and credit clause provides that the judicial proceedings of one state shall be recognized and enforced in every other state.[20] It has been implemented by federal statute.[21] The clause allows a litigant who obtains a judgment against an opponent in one state to go to another state, where the opponent is now located, and have the judgment enforced there. Full faith and credit prevents the party against whom enforcement is sought from relitigating the merits of the original suit.

However, if the opponent claims in a subsequent proceeding that the original court did not have jurisdiction over his or her person or prop-

---

15. *See, e.g.,* Ill. Ann. Stat. ch. 110, § 2-209 (Smith-Hurd 1983); N.Y. Civ. Prac. Law § 302 (McKinney 1972 & Supp. 1986); Del. Code Ann. tit. 10, § 3104 (Supp. 1984).

16. *See, e.g.,* Cal. Civ. Proc. Code § 410.10 (West 1973); Wyo. Stat. § 5-1-107(a) (1977).

17. *See, e.g.,* 42 Pa. Cons. Stat. Ann. § 5322(8)(b) (Purdon 1981); Me. Rev. Stat. Ann. tit. 14, § 704-A(2)(I) (1980).

18. U.S. CONST. amend. V; amend. XIV, § 1.

19. U.S. CONST. art. IV, § 1.

20. *Id.* "Full Faith and Credit shall be given in each State to the public Acts, Records, and judicial Proceedings of every other State. And the Congress may by general Laws prescribe the Manner in which such Acts, Records and Proceedings shall be proved, and the Effect thereof."

21. 28 U.S.C. § 1738 (1982).

erty, then the original judgment may not be entitled to full faith and credit and can be challenged.[22] State court jurisdiction was thus a matter of federal constitutional significance even before the Fourteenth Amendment due process clause was enacted, because lack of jurisdiction was a valid ground for refusing to enforce judgments from sister states.

Such collateral attacks on a state court have been an important (although potentially risky) way to challenge a state court's jurisdiction. Basically, the defendant does not appear in the original suit in Forum A to present a defense or even challenge jurisdiction. Instead, he waits until the plaintiff attempts to get her judgment enforced in Forum B, where the defendant is located. The defendant then claims that the first judgment is invalid because the Forum A court lacked jurisdiction over him. If this challenge is successful, the judgment is given no effect. If the attack is unsuccessful, however, the defendant is precluded from litigating the merits of the original suit and may have sacrificed what might have been a winning argument on the merits.

The full faith and credit limitation is discussed at greater length below in our discussion of judgments.[23] Since the adoption of the due process clause, however, that provision has governed most issues of adjudicative jurisdiction. Following a discussion of the history and current status of the due process analysis, other possible constitutional limitations on a state's ability to exert jurisdiction will be mentioned briefly.

A. DUE PROCESS CLAUSE

1. Supreme Court Development

Any discussion of the due process clause and personal jurisdiction must begin with *Pennoyer v. Neff*,[24] the foundation of Supreme Court discourse on the subject. Although the case's current relevance is largely historical, it still casts a shadow over current decisions, and its reasoning is responsible for the strange contortions in the cases discussed below.

In *Pennoyer,* Neff brought a suit in federal district court in Oregon which, in effect, challenged a judgment previously rendered in Oregon state court. Neff claimed that the federal court had no obligation to give full faith and credit to that judgment because the state court had

---

22. D'Arcy v. Ketchum, 52 U.S. (11 How.) 165 (1851) (New York judgment not enforceable in Louisiana because defendant had never been served with process in New York action).

23. *See* ch. 5, sec. IIC *infra.*

24. 95 U.S. (5 Otto) 714 (1878).

not had personal jurisdiction over him. Neff was not an Oregon resident at the time of the state court action, and the only notice provided was by publication. The Supreme Court upheld Neff's argument, focusing on the territorial limits of the state's judicial power.

The Court held that a state had "exclusive jurisdiction and sovereignty over persons and property within its territory,"[25] but only had jurisdiction over non-residents to determine obligations relating to property owned by them within the state. In keeping with this territorial view, the Court found that personal jurisdiction over a nonresident defendant required personal service within the territory; and a judgment rendered in the absence of jurisdiction need not be given full faith and credit by another court. In dictum,[26] the Court then discussed the applicability of the due process clause to the situation, finding that due process is violated when a court enters a judgment without proper jurisdiction over the parties. Thus, not only is a judgment entered without proper jurisdiction unenforceable outside the state of rendition, it is constitutionally unenforceable in the rendering state as well.[27] The Court suggested that due process limits the personal jurisdiction of state courts to three bases: consent, presence, and domicile.[28] This three-fold basis for the assertion of jurisdiction became the accepted view.

Pennoyer severely limited the ability of plaintiffs to obtain personal jurisdiction over out-of-state defendants. The decision left intact in rem jurisdiction based on presence of property,[29] but such jurisdiction was of limited utility. It depended on the presence of some asset of the defendant's within the jurisdiction, and any judgment was limited to the value of that asset. To get around the strictures imposed by *Pennoyer,* two schemes developed over time to increase the effective reach of state courts adjudicating personal claims. The first was expansion of the definitions of such approved bases as consent and presence, and the second was the increased use of quasi in rem jurisdiction of the second type to get defendants into court on essentially personal claims. Reconciling the actual effects of these expansions of personal jurisdiction

---

25. *Id.* at 722.

26. The discussion was dictum because the fourteenth amendment, which made the due process clause applicable to the states, had not been ratified at the time of the state court judgment against Neff.

27. This made the due process standard the equivalent of the full faith and credit standard announced in *D'Arcy, supra* note 22.

28. *See* 95 U.S. at 720.

29. The *Pennoyer* court stated that a court's in rem powers could be invoked only by seizure of the property or some equivalent act. *Id.* at 727. The property thus not only provides the basis for the court's power, but the seizure of the property is deemed to provide the defendant with notice of the action.

with the original power theory required the development of convoluted legal fictions.

The first type of fiction in which courts engaged to obtain jurisdiction over out-of-state defendants was an expansion of the definition of such traditional jurisdictional bases as consent and presence. For example, states passed statutes declaring that any nonresident using roads in the state consented to jurisdiction for claims arising from such use.[30] In addition, a corporation, by doing business in a state, could be deemed to be "present" in the state and thus subject to personal jurisdiction.[31] Similarly, the act of doing business could be deemed to constitute implied consent.[32] These fictions were necessary to reconcile the assertion of jurisdiction with the limited theoretical basis on which jurisdiction had to rest. The Supreme Court generally upheld assertions of jurisdiction based on these fictions.[33]

In *International Shoe Co. v. Washington*,[34] the Court moved beyond such fictions, and attempted to set up a more rational system of adjudicating the question of personal jurisdiction. The case concerned an attempt by the State of Washington to impose an employment tax on a Missouri corporation and to collect the tax in its courts. The corporation employed salesmen in Washington, but their activities in the state were not sufficient to constitute "doing business" under previous case law.[35] The Court held that Washington did not violate the due process clause by asserting jurisdiction over the corporation, and announced a new standard for determining the constitutionality of a court's assertion of jurisdiction:

> Historically the jurisdiction of courts to render judgment *in personam* is grounded on their de facto power over the defendant's person. . . . But now . . . due process requires only that in order to subject a defendant to a judgment *in personam*, if he be not present within the territory of the forum, he have certain minimum contacts with it such that the maintenance of the suit does

---

30. *See* Hess v. Pawloski, 274 U.S. 352 (1927) (upholding Massachusetts nonresident motorist statute).

31. *See, e.g.,* Philadelphia & R. Ry. v. McKibbin, 243 U.S. 264 (1917) (in personam jurisdiction over corporation only valid if corporation transacts business within state); Mutual Reserve Fund Life Ass'n v. Phelps, 190 U.S. 147 (1903) (insurance company doing business in Kentucky subject to personal jurisdiction there).

32. Pennsylvania Fire Ins. Co. v. Gold Issue Mining & Milling Co., 243 U.S. 93 (1917) (state may validly imply consent to personal jurisdiction in return for privilege of doing business in the state); *but see* Flexner v. Farson, 248 U.S. 289 (1919) (mechanism of implied consent cannot be used to gain jurisdiction over nonresident natural person).

33. *See supra* notes 30-32.

34. 326 U.S. 310 (1945).

35. Mere solicitation of orders within the state did not constitute "doing business" under prior case law. *See, e.g.,* Green v. Chicago, B. & Q. Ry., 205 U.S. 530 (1907).

not offend "traditional notions of fair play and substantial justice."[36]

The Court found that the corporation carried on systematic and continuous operations in Washington, in the course of which it received the benefits of the state's laws. In addition, the dispute arose directly out of the corporation's activities in the forum. These factors made it reasonable to subject the corporation to suit in Washington.

The second scheme to expand state court power to hear personal claims involved increased use of quasi in rem jurisdiction. Through this mechanism, a court could attach any property — tangible or intangible — a defendant had within the state in order to compel him or her to appear and defend. Property, for this purpose, was defined quite liberally. For example, if a defendant's debtor was present in the forum state, the debt constituted property and could be used as the basis of a quasi in rem proceeding by one of the defendant's creditors.[37] In a more modern example, plaintiffs in auto accident cases would use the quasi in rem device to garnish the obligation owed to the defendant by his or her liability insurer. The insurer owed the defendant an obligation to defend the litigation, and this constituted "property" wherever the insurance company was present.[38]

Shaffer v. Heitner[39] effectively eliminated this form of quasi in rem jurisdiction, requiring instead that "all assertions of state-court jurisdiction . . . be evaluated according to the standards set forth in *International Shoe* and its progeny."[40] *Shaffer* involved a suit in Delaware court alleging mismanagement of the Greyhound Corporation, a Delaware corporation, by a number of its officers and directors. The activities leading to the suit primarily occurred in Oregon, and none of the officers or directors sued was a Delaware resident. To obtain quasi in rem jurisdiction over the individuals, Heitner obtained an order of sequestration based on the location of their stock in Delaware.[41] The defendants argued that use of sequestration to obtain jurisdiction violated *International Shoe* because the claims asserted and the defendants had no relation to Delaware.

The Supreme Court accepted the defendants' argument. The Court pointed out that jurisdiction in rem is not simply jurisdiction over a thing, but jurisdiction over the interests of persons in the thing. There-

---

36. 326 U.S. at 316 (quoting Milliken v. Meyer, 311 U.S. 457, 463 (1940)).

37. Harris v. Balk, 198 U.S. 215 (1905).

38. *See, e.g.,* Seider v. Roth, 17 N.Y.2d 111, 216 N.E.2d 312, 269 N.Y.S.2d 99 (1966).

39. 433 U.S. 186 (1977).

40. *Id.* at 212.

41. Under Delaware law, Delaware is the situs of all stock in a Delaware corporation. Del. Code Ann. tit. 8, § 169 (1975).

fore, conditions equivalent to those used to justify jurisdiction in personam must exist to justify jurisdiction in rem, where personal interests are equally at stake. In cases such as *Shaffer,* the property on which jurisdiction is based is only a vehicle to get the defendant into court. "[I]f a direct assertion of personal jurisdiction over the defendant would violate the Constitution . . . an indirect assertion of that jurisdiction should be equally impermissible."[42] The Court rejected the fiction that jurisdiction over property is somehow distinct from jurisdiction over the owner of the property as "an ancient form without substantial modern justification."[43]

Turning to the facts in *Shaffer,* the Court found nothing to support Delaware's exercise of jurisdiction. It found no physical contacts between the defendants and Delaware and no aspects of the disputed transaction that had occurred in Delaware. In addition, the Court held that the mere fact that the defendants were officers or directors of a Delaware corporation was insufficient to convey jurisdiction over a shareholder's derivative suit. Finally, the Court found that the defendants had not purposefully availed themselves of the privilege of conducting activities within Delaware such that they could reasonably have expected to be sued in a Delaware court on the basis of these activities.

Three years after *Shaffer,* the Supreme Court again emphasized that quasi in rem jurisdiction could not be used to establish jurisdiction absent compliance with *International Shoe* standards. In *Rush v. Savchuk,*[44] the Court ruled that Minnesota had violated the due process clause by exercising quasi in rem jurisdiction over an out-of-state defendant in a car accident case through garnishing the obligation owed the defendant by his liability insurer. This mechanism has been called *Seider* jurisdiction, after *Seider v. Roth,* the first case to use it.[45] Although the insurance company did substantial business in Minnesota (probably sufficient to allow Minnesota to exercise general jurisdiction over it), the individual defendant had no contacts with Minnesota and the accident had not occurred there. The Minnesota Supreme Court had distinguished *Shaffer* by finding that the cause of action and the insurer's obligation were closely connected, whereas no connection had existed in *Shaffer* between the stock and the cause of action.

The Supreme Court reversed, finding that the named defendant had more than a nominal stake in the case and that the insurance policy was not closely enough related to the cause of action to support juris-

---

42. 433 U.S. at 209.
43. *Id.* at 212.
44. 444 U.S. 320 (1980).
45. 17 N.Y.2d 111, 216 N.E.2d 312, 269 N.Y.S.2d 99 (1966).

diction. The Court found that the effect of *Seider* jurisdiction was to shift the minimum contacts/due process inquiry from a focus on "the relationship among the defendant, the forum, and the litigation to that among the plaintiff, the forum, the insurer, and the litigation."[46] This shift violated the due process standard set forth in *International Shoe* and its successor cases.

Although both *Shaffer* and *Rush* struck down overreaching by state courts, neither decision presents insuperable barriers to expansion of state court jurisdiction. In both cases the Court suggested that if the state had chosen to exert jurisdiction in similar fact situations through more direct means, jurisdiction might have been upheld. In *Shaffer* the Court hinted that Delaware could lawfully get jurisdiction over the defendant officers and directors by passing a statute making the officers and directors of a Delaware corporation subject to Delaware jurisdiction for suits arising out of their corporate responsibilities.[47] Delaware took the hint and passed such a statute.[48] Likewise, in *Rush,* jurisdiction over the insurance company might have been upheld if Minnesota had passed a so-called "direct action" statute making the insurance company rather than the individual defendant the appropriate party to sue.[49]

This does not mean, however, that careful or specific drafting will cure all jurisdictional defects. In the cases following *Shaffer,* the Supreme Court has articulated two limits on state court jurisdiction over out-of-state defendants, even if the defendant has some contacts with the forum state and the statute is specifically drawn. One limitation is a requirement that the defendant's contacts with the forum somehow result from his or her purposeful conduct. The second limitation, an aspect of federalism, prevents individual states from infringing on the coequal rights of their sister states. The Court has not clearly defined either limitation, and may already have retreated from the federalism standard.

The requirement that a defendant must have purposefully availed himself of the privilege of conducting activities within the forum state before the forum can lawfully exercise jurisdiction over him had been

---

46. 444 U.S. at 332.

47. 433 U.S. at 214-15 ("If Delaware perceived its interest in securing jurisdiction over corporate fiduciaries to be as great as [plaintiff] suggests, we would expect it to have enacted a statute more clearly designed to protect that interest.").

48. Del. Code Ann. tit. 10, § 3114 (Supp. 1984). The constitutionality of the statute was upheld in Armstrong v. Pomerance, 423 A.2d 174 (Del. 1980).

49. *See* 444 U.S. at 331 n.19 (citing Watson v. Employers Liability Assurance Corp., 348 U.S. 66 (1954) (upholding constitutionality of direct action statute)). Whether *Watson* would have supported jurisdiction in *Rush* is not clear, given that in *Watson* the injury had transpired in the forum. This factor was not present in *Rush.*

foreshadowed in prior case law. A complicated and confusing opinion from 1958 first suggested this "purposeful availment" requirement.[50] However, *Shaffer* and two cases following it lifted this doctrine from relative obscurity and made it an important requirement for a state's exercise of jurisdiction.[51] The "purposeful availment" requirement does not mean that a defendant's conduct must occur in the forum; out-of-state actions are sometimes sufficient. For example, if the defendant intends to cause an effect in the forum state from which the litigation stems, the requirement is probably satisfied. The outer reach of this reasoning is unclear, however, given that people normally are thought to intend all the foreseeable consequences of all of their deliberate acts.

With the growing nationalization of commerce, almost anything might be viewed as foreseeable. *World-Wide Volkswagen Corp. v. Woodson*[52] indicated that mere foreseeability did not establish purposeful availment. In that case, the New York purchasers of an automobile drove the car to Oklahoma, where a traffic accident occurred giving rise to a products liability claim. The purchaser sued in Oklahoma, but the Supreme Court found the exercise of jurisdiction improper because the New York defendant could not reasonably have anticipated being haled into court there.

Unfortunately, the sort of activity that gives rise to a reasonable expectation of being haled into court is no clearer than what constitutes purposeful availment. Presumably, the defendant must expect the possibility of this kind of suit in this forum, and this foreseeability might be demonstrated in different ways. One factor might be the relevant state law. For instance, *Shaffer* distinguished between suits over stock ownership, which Delaware law allowed and might therefore be foreseeable, and suits over a director's fiduciary duty, which were not foreseeable.[53] In the alternative, a contractual clause specifying that the law of a particular state be applied in any subsequent disputes can contribute to a party's expectation of facing suit in that state.[54] In addition, the precedents suggest that if the defendant en-

---

50. Hanson v. Denckla, 357 U.S. 235, 253 (1958).

51. Kulko v. Superior Court, 436 U.S. 84, 94 (1978) (California does not have jurisdiction to adjudicate child support claim over New York defendant, since defendant had not purposefully availed himself of benefits of California laws). *Cf.* World-Wide Volkswagen Corp. v. Woodson, 444 U.S. 286, 297 (1980) (defendant's connection with forum state must be such "that [defendant] should reasonably anticipate being haled into court there").

52. 444 U.S. 286 (1980).

53. *Shaffer,* 433 U.S. at 216.

54. Burger King Corp. v. Rudzewicz, 105 S. Ct. 2174, 2187 (1985).

gages outside the forum in commercial activity that regularly affects residents of the forum, the test would be met.[55] However, if the defendant's conduct only caused an effect within the forum because of the actions of the plaintiff or a third party, this unilateral activity does not amount to the necessary "purposeful availment".[56]

The second limitation on state court power relates to notions of federalism. The decision in *World-Wide Volkswagen* stated that due process, in terms of the minimum contacts necessary to satisfy *International Shoe*, has two components. In addition to the fairness analysis described previously, due process also requires that the states "do not reach beyond the limits imposed on them by their status as coequal sovereigns in a federal system."[57] This federalism component has some basis in language from older cases,[58] but *World-Wide Volkswagen's* emphasis on the importance of state lines suggests a return to territorialist notions that *International Shoe* seemingly discredited. The Court indicated in dicta that federalism limitations might be sufficient to prevent a state from exercising jurisdiction even where it would not be inconvenient to litigate the matter in the forum, or where the forum had a strong interest in applying its law.[59]

The *World-Wide Volkswagen* Court did not explain the limits that the state sovereignty idea imposes on personal jurisdiction, and reaction to the idea has been mixed. It has been argued that the federalism idea is wrong and has no place in the due process analysis, which in other areas pertains only to the relationship between the government and the individual.[60] The Court itself, in a subsequent decision, suggested that federalism components of due process ultimately derive from fairness to the individual.[61] It conceded moreover that if the sovereignty component were truly based on federalism, it couldn't be waived by the defendant as jurisdictional limits can be.[62]

---

55. *See, e.g., Kulko,* 436 U.S. at 96; *World-Wide Volkswagen,* 444 U.S. at 295. *See* cases cited *supra* note 48. *See also* R. CASAD, JURISDICTION IN CIVIL ACTIONS ¶ 2.05 (1983) [hereinafter cited as CASAD].

56. *See* CASAD, *supra* note 55, at ¶ 2.05.

57. *World-Wide Volkswagen,* 444 U.S. at 292.

58. *International Shoe,* 326 U.S. at 317 (contacts with a state that make it reasonable "in the context of our federal system of government" to require the defendant to defend against a suit there); *Hanson,* 357 U.S. at 251 (restrictions on the personal jurisdiction of state courts are "a consequence of territorial limitations on the power of the respective States").

59. *World-Wide Volkswagen,* 444 U.S. at 294.

60. *See, e.g.,* Redish, *Due Process, Federalism and Personal Jurisdiction: A Theoretical Evaluation,* 75 Nw. U.L. REV. 1112 (1981).

61. Insurance Corp. of Ireland, Ltd. v. Compagnie des Bauxites de Guinee, 456 U.S. 694, 702-03 n.10 (1982).

62. *Id.*

2. The State of the World Today

Because the recent Supreme Court decisions in the area have been complicated and somewhat confusing, the doctrinal end result is areas of relative clarity interspersed with areas of uncertainty. We summarize the clearer topics first, then list some important open questions.

a. Areas of Relative Clarity

Property-based jurisdiction. — As the *Shaffer* decision pointed out, a state's ability to exert jurisdiction based on property related to the cause of action[63] will not be much affected by evaluating such actions under *International Shoe* standards.[64] In situations where the property located in the forum is a significant factor in the litigation — i.e. the property is the source of the dispute — a state would almost automatically have sufficient contacts with the matter to obtain jurisdiction over a nonresident.

Domicile. — Systematic and continuous activity or connection with a state — such as domicile/residence for an individual, and incorporation for a corporation — allows a state to exercise jurisdiction over a defendant for any cause of action, even one unrelated to the forum connections.[65] However, the question of what constitutes "continuous and systematic" activity, regarding a corporation, has no easy answer. The Court did not provide a clear standard of decision in the one recent case that addressed this issue,[66] and any determination probably must be fact-specific.

Consent. — Consent as a basis for personal jurisdiction is one area that has remained relatively untouched by the leading Supreme Court decisions in the field. Implied consent has little current utility, because *International Shoe* removed the need for states to invent such fictions

---

63. That is, in rem jurisdiction and quasi in rem jurisdiction of the mortgage foreclosure variety.

64. *Shaffer,* 433 U.S. at 207.

65. Perkins v. Benguet Consol. Mining Co., 342 U.S. 437 (1952) (Ohio has personal jurisdiction over foreign corporation that maintains continuous and systematic contacts with the state); Helicopteros Nacionales de Colombia, S.A. v. Hall, 466 U.S. 408 (1984) (hereinafter cited as *Helicol*) (contacts such as sending chief executive to state to negotiate contract, opening bank account, and receiving training for helicopter operators in state, do not rise to "continuous and systematic" level).

66. In his dissent in *Helicol,* Justice Brennan argued that the majority opinion mistakenly disregarded the recent expansion of personal jurisdiction, and the cases that emphasize "traditional notions of fairness," such as *International Shoe* and *World-Wide Volkswagen.* Brennan maintained that the majority should have considered any contacts "related to" the underlying cause of action, rather than whether the defendant engaged in continuous and systematic business activity within the forum. 466 U.S. at 419-28 (Brennan, J., dissenting).

to gain jurisdiction over out-of-state defendants. The same result can now be achieved through long-arm statutes. As for explicit consent, one party to a contract generally may require the other party to submit to the jurisdiction of a designated court for resolution of disputes relating to the contract.[67]

A particular type of express agreement fixing jurisdiction — commonly called a prorogation agreement or forum selection clause — has also received Supreme Court approval. Under such agreements, the parties agree that a designated court shall hear any action arising out of a particular transaction or relationship. If action is brought anywhere other than the designated court, the forum court should dismiss the case. Such clauses traditionally were disfavored as an attempt to oust the otherwise proper jurisdiction of the forum.[68] However, the Supreme Court in *The Bremen v. Zapata Off-Shore Co.*[69] stated that a court confronted with a forum selection clause should enforce it unless one of the following conditions is present: (1) enforcement of the clause would contravene a strong public policy of the place where suit is brought; (2) the chosen forum is seriously inconvenient for trying the action; or (3) the clause was part of a contract of adhesion.[70] The Court emphasized that, on certain occasions, "selection of a remote forum to apply differing foreign law to an essentially American action" might contravene the public policy of the place where suit is brought.[71]

The extent of this exception to *Bremen* is uncertain. *Bremen* involved an agreement to submit to the jurisdiction of a foreign tribunal. However, the above-quoted language could justify a state court's refusal to enforce a clause selecting another state as the place of litigation, where the state of enforcement has a particular interest in trying the case. Moreover, it is not clear that a state court must enforce such clauses. *Bremen* may have only established rules for federal court jurisdiction rather than a due process right of the defendant not to be sued elsewhere. Furthermore, it is unclear whether even a federal court would follow *Bremen* if it were applying state law in a diversity suit.

---

67. National Equip. Rental Ltd. v. Szukhent, 375 U.S. 311, 315-16 (1964) (parties to a contract may agree in advance that a particular state will have jurisdiction over any disputes arising out of the transaction).

68. *See* cases collected in Annot., 56 A.L.R.2d 300, 306-23 (1957), and Later Case Service (1967).

69. 407 U.S. 1 (1972).

70. *Id.* at 15-17. *See also* Mitsubishi Motors Corp. v. Soler Chrysler-Plymouth, Inc., 105 S. Ct. 3346 (1985); Scherk v. Alberto-Culver Co., 417 U.S. 506 (1974) (enforcing forum selection clause for arbitration of international agreement).

71. 407 U.S. at 17.

Persons as to whom jurisdiction must exist. — A court generally need not worry whether the plaintiff in a lawsuit has minimum contacts with the forum. The plaintiff's voluntary act of choosing the forum in which to sue means that he or she has consented to its exercise of jurisdiction for all purposes relating to the suit.[72] Involuntary plaintiffs, such as absent out-of-state class members in a class action suit, however, are a different matter. They are entitled to some protection under the due process clause, although not as much as out-of-state defendants. The Supreme Court held recently that such plaintiffs are entitled to minimal due process protection, including notice, an opportunity to be heard and participate in the litigation, an opportunity to opt out of the case, and the right to have a named plaintiff who will represent their interests adequately.[73] While these rights are available to absent class members in the intrastate setting, the opportunity to opt out takes on special meaning in the interstate context. It guarantees that an unwilling class member cannot be forced into the adjudication by a forum with which he or she has no minimum contacts.

b. Open Questions

At this point, there are almost more open questions than there are settled areas.

Presence. — Although many cases in which jurisdiction is based on a defendant's "presence" in a state are also covered by the domicile basis discussed above, one area of uncertainty remains: transient jurisdiction. Transient, or "tag," jurisdiction involves a situation where the defendant happens to be travelling through the state at the time he or she is served with process. The quintessential example is the defendant served while flying in a plane over the state seeking to assert jurisdiction.[74] *Shaffer* stated that all assertions of state court jurisdiction must be evaluated by the standards of *International Shoe*.[75] This could mean that jurisdiction based solely on the physical presence of the defendant in the forum, absent other contacts, would violate due process. After all, how "fair" is it for a state to subject a person to suit merely because she spent half an hour there on her way to somewhere else?

This complete abandonment of the physical power theory of jurisdiction is not necessarily warranted, however. Some language in *International Shoe* suggests that physical presence may be sufficient by itself

---

72. Adam v. Saenger, 303 U.S. 59, 67-68 (1938) (plaintiff submits himself to courts jurisdiction "for all purposes for which justice to the defendant requires his presence").

73. Phillips Petroleum Co. v. Shutts, 105 S. Ct. 2965, 2975 (1985).

74. Grace v. MacArthur, 170 F. Supp. 442 (E.D. Ark. 1959) (upholding jurisdiction of Arkansas courts based on service of process on commercial aircraft).

75. *Shaffer,* 433 U.S. at 212.

and that the minimum contacts test is relevant only where the defendant is not present in the state.[76] Furthermore, even if the minimum contacts test *is* relevant to transient presence, it was relevant even before the *Shaffer* decision because transient jurisdiction was in personam; thus, *Shaffer* may not alter the analysis.[77] "Tag jurisdiction" has come to be accepted over time and, whatever compelling fairness reasons may exist to eliminate it now, it may very well simply be allowed to continue.

Jurisdiction by Necessity. — Beyond the categories of jurisdiction discussed above, it is possible that a state may constitutionally exert jurisdiction if it is impossible for the plaintiff to bring the suit anywhere else. Such jurisdiction would involve recognition of the existence of a due process-related right of plaintiffs to be able to bring suit somewhere, regardless of the level of the defendant's contacts with the forum. Examples of situations when jurisdiction by necessity questions might arise include cases involving multiple defendants who do not all have minimum contacts with a single state; cases where an alien defendant does not have minimum contacts with a single state; cases where the plaintiff would be confronted in alternative fora with adverse choice of law provisions or statutes of limitations; or perhaps even cases where the plaintiff cannot afford to travel to a forum where the defendant has minimum contacts. A related argument, that of "reciprocal contacts," suggests that a plaintiff should not have to travel to sue in a forum with which he or she has no minimum contacts.[78]

The Supreme Court has not rejected the possibility of jurisdiction by necessity, and statements in several cases seem to support the concept. In *Mullane v. Central Hanover Bank & Trust Co.,*[79] involving settlement of a common trust account with both in-state and out-of-state claimants, the Court said that the state that created the trust had such a strong interest in being able to close out the account as "to establish beyond doubt the right of its courts to determine the interests of all claimants, resident or non-resident," provided that adequate notice is given.[80] But minimum contacts probably existed in this situation, and this statement may therefore be dictum.[81] In addition, in a footnote in *Shaffer,* the Court explicitly reserved the question whether the pres-

---

76. *International Shoe,* 326 U.S. at 316 ("due process requires only that in order to subject a defendant to a judgment *in personam, if he be not present within the territory of the forum,* he have certain minimum contacts with it . . .") (emphasis added).

77. Brilmayer, *How Contacts Court: Due Process Limitations on State Court Jurisdiction,* 1980 SUP. CT. REV. 77, 82 (1980).

78. *Id.* at 110.

79. 339 U.S. 306 (1950).

80. *Id.* at 313.

81. Brilmayer, *supra* note 77, at 102.

ence of a defendant's property in a state is sufficient to give that state jurisdiction when no other forum is available to the plaintiff.[82] In the recent *Helicol* case, likewise, the Court declined to consider adoption of a jurisdiction by necessity doctrine without a more complete record, suggesting that the argument might have been more persuasive if the plaintiff had been able to show that all defendants in the case could not have been sued in a single forum.[83] It also, however, characterized the doctrine as "a potentially far-reaching modification of existing law."[84]

Although the due process argument in favor of jurisdiction by necessity sounds appealing, and the Supreme Court has not rejected it, some of the necessity scenarios described above may not actually merit special consideration. For example, necessity arguments based on a short statute of limitations or adverse choice of law rules should not be accepted. What the plaintiff wants is not a chance in *one* forum, but a chance in *two,* because he finds the rules of the first forum adverse to his interests.[85] A forum is still a forum, even if it would not allow recovery. Such a situation is inherently different from one where no one state has minimum contacts with all the defendants, and it is the due process clause which operates to deprive the plaintiff of any place to bring suit.

The closest existing analog to jurisdiction by necessity is the federal interpleader statute.[86] Interpleader is available where the plaintiff has an asset owing to one of the other parties, but needs a judicial determination of which of these claimants to pay. If the plaintiff cannot secure a determination of all parties' rights in one proceeding, he or she faces the possibility of being forced to pay twice. In such situations, federal courts enjoy nationwide service of process.[87] While one state court has argued that states should be free to exercise nationwide jurisdiction in comparable cases,[88] this argument has not generally been accepted.

Corporate Affiliation. — We have seen that jurisdiction over corporations can be exerted on the basis of systematic and continuous activity in the state. Affiliation with another corporation over which jurisdiction exists may count towards satisfaction of this standard. More gen-

---

82. *Shaffer,* 433 U.S. at 211 n.37.

83. *Helicol,* 466 U.S. at 419 n.13.

84. *Id.*

85. *See* Brilmayer, *supra* note 77, at 109-10. *But see* Keeton v. Hustler Magazine, Inc., 465 U.S. 770 (1984), where plaintiff brought suit in the one state where the statute of limitations had not run against her. The Court stated that the inquiry into personal jurisdiction was not concerned with the length of the limitations period in the forum or in other states. *Id.* at 778. This suggests that the Court might be receptive to the idea of jurisdiction by necessity in situations involving adverse procedural rules.

86. 28 U.S.C. § 1335 (1982).

87. 28 U.S.C. § 2361 (1982).

88. Atkinson v. Superior Court, 49 Cal. 2d 338, 344, 316 P.2d 960, 966 (1957).

erally, it can be argued that corporate affiliation with a business entity over which jurisdiction exists is sufficient to establish jurisdiction. For example, a parent corporation might be amenable to jurisdiction in the forum because it has a subsidiary located there.

Some commentators have argued that jurisdictional requirements are satisfied where the appropriate close corporate ties exist.[89] The Supreme Court has suggested that corporate affiliation is not automatically sufficient, and that minimum contacts with the absent corporation must still be shown.[90] This does not automatically mean that the parent/subsidiary relationship is irrelevant, however, because it might still tend to show either related contacts or systematic and continuous business in the forum.

The Relationship to Choice of Law. — The due process minimum contacts standard is superficially similar to the due process test for applying forum law. The Supreme Court has noted this similarity, but has also stressed that the two inquiries are nevertheless different.[91] The question is, precisely what relationship governs? Which test is harder to satisfy?

One author argues that since choice of law is more crucial to the outcome of the litigation, it should have a stricter test.[92] This argument neglects the fact that in the choice of law inquiry, the personal jurisdiction test has already been met. Thus, a relatively easy test for choice of law might be appropriate since it is coupled with satisfaction of a more stringent threshold for assertion of personal jurisdiction.

General and Specific Jurisdiction. — The difference between general and specific jurisdiction has become more important since *Shaffer v. Heitner.* Since *Shaffer,* property will not necessarily provide a basis for jurisdiction when it is unrelated to the controversy.[93] Property can still be used to show specific jurisdiction, but a single item of property will not establish jurisdiction unless the controversy arises out of it. The distinction is also important because *International Shoe* suggested

---

89. Brilmayer & Paisley, *Personal Jurisdiction and Substantive Legal Relations: Corporations, Conspiracies, and Agency,* 74 CALIF. L. REV. 1 (1986).

90. *Keeton,* 465 U.S. at 781 n.13.

91. *See, e.g.,* Hanson v. Denckla, 357 U.S. at 254 ("[t]he issue is personal jurisdiction, not choice of law"); *Shaffer,* 433 U.S. at 215 (applicability of one state's law to a dispute does not automatically confer jurisdiction over the disputes on the courts of that state); *Keeton,* 465 U.S. at 778 (application of one state's statute of limitations to a claim has nothing to do with jurisdiction of state courts to adjudicate the claim).

92. Silberman, *Shaffer v. Heitner: The End of An Era,* 53 N.Y.U. L. REV. 33, 87-88 (1978).

93. 433 U.S. at 207-08. Thus, the second type of quasi in rem jurisdiction, discussed *supra* in text accompanying notes 36-46, has been virtually eliminated as a valid form of adjudicative jurisdiction.

that jurisdiction based on the defendant's activities is more likely to be permissible when the cause of action arises out of the forum activities.[94] Again, the standard for showing specific jurisdiction is lower.

What does this distinction mean? It has been argued that contacts or property are related to a suit only if they are relevant to the underlying substance of the cause of action.[95] This idea finds some support in *Rush v. Savchuk,* which noted that the insurance proceeds asserted to support jurisdiction were not part of the "operative facts" underlying the controversy.[96] The idea has also had ambiguous support in more recent Supreme Court precedents[97] and resembles tests adopted by some state courts.[98] To this point, no other test has been suggested for differentiating related from unrelated contacts.

The Relationship Among Fairness, Convenience, and Sovereignty. — At different times, the Court has relied upon the different considerations of fairness to defendants, convenience in litigation, and sister state sovereignty to determine the limits of state court jurisdiction. These considerations might all point, however, in different directions. For example, a defendant in a border town in one state might be called upon to defend in litigation instituted just across the state line. The fact of state lines may implicate state sovereignty considerations. Aside from possible choice of law problems, however, the defendant cannot seriously claim to be inconvenienced by suit in the other state. "Fairness" is more difficult to determine than either convenience or territoriality. Admittedly, the defendant could be forced to defend in a distant part of the same state without giving rise to constitutional concerns. Can it then be called unfair to compel him or her to defend much closer to home? Is fairness to the defendant an issue of conve-

---

94. 326 U.S. at 317, 320.

95. Brilmayer, *supra* note 77, at 82-84.

96. 444 U.S. at 329.

97. *Helicol,* 466 U.S. at 415-16 n.10 (declining to reach issue of whether substantive relationship between contacts and dispute is relevant to jurisdictional analysis); *Keeton,* 465 U.S. at 775-76 ("fairness of haling respondent into . . . court depends to some extent on whether respondent's activities relating to [forum] are such as to give that state a legitimate interest in holding respondent answerable on a claim related to those activities"); Calder v. Jones, 465 U.S. 783, 789 (1984) (upholding jurisdiction in California courts because "California is the focal point of the [activity] and of the harm suffered").

98. *See, e.g.,* Peters v. Robin Airlines, 281 A.D. 903, 120 N.Y.S.2d 1 (App. Div. 1953) (activity within forum must be causally related to accident outside New York for New York courts to have jurisdiction); Kingsley & Keith (Canada) Ltd. v. Mercer Int'l Corp., 500 Pa. 37, 456 A.2d 1333, 1338 (1983) (Nix, J., concurring in reversal) ("the cause of action must arise from defendant's activities within the forum state"); Dufour v. Smith & Hamer, Inc., 330 F. Supp. 405 (D. Me. 1971) (Maine law requires that alleged negligence has taken place within state for Maine courts to have jurisdiction over out-of-state corporation).

nience, an issue of a sovereign state's boundaries or something else altogether?

It has been suggested many times that the Supreme Court ought only to inquire into convenience and practicalities.[99] Obviously, some fora are more convenient places to hold the litigation than others. Convenience typically depends on the location of the parties, the physical evidence, and the witnesses. Such considerations rarely implicate state lines; the defendant's travelling two hundred miles is the same regardless of whether a state line has been crossed or not. Furthermore, modern travel and communications systems have reduced such inconvenience.[100] In all fairness, however, if the defendant is now less able to raise convenience defenses because of modern communications, the plaintiff should not be able to elicit sympathy based on his inconvenience if he cannot obtain his chosen forum.[101]

This approach might be called the "interstate venue" concept because it resembles the way that federal courts apportion venue.[102] The federal venue rules seek to identify convenient places to hold the trial, without being unduly hampered by the location of state boundaries.[103] The approach remains controversial. While it may be appropriate in a single governing unit, such as the federal judicial system, it is less clearly acceptable in a system composed of independent state sovereignties.[104]

The opposite approach takes territorial boundaries seriously. Fairness and state sovereignty, under this view, are closely linked.[105] It is simply unfair for a state to exert authority over an individual who has not purposefully assented in any way. This approach relies on argu-

---

99. *See, e.g.,* Weintraub, *Due Process Limitations on the Personal Jurisdiction of State Courts: Time for Change,* 63 Ore. L. Rev. 485, 527 (1984) (jurisdictional rules should focus on fairness to defendant); Clermont, *Restating Territorial Jurisdiction and Venue for State and Federal Courts,* 66 Cornell L. Rev. 411, 451-55 (1981) (reasonableness should be sole constitutional test for territorial authority to adjudicate).

100. *Cf.* McGee v. International Life Ins. Co., 355 U.S. 220, 223 (1957) ("modern transportation and communication have made it much less burdensome for a party sued to defend himself in a state where he engages in economic activity").

101. *Cf.* Brilmayer, *supra* note 77, at 111: "If modern transportation makes it easy to defend suits in a distant forum, surely modern transportation is of equal utility to plaintiffs."

102. Hazard, *Interstate Venue,* 64 Nw. U. L. Rev. 711 (1979).

103. The federal venue rules are found at 28 U.S.C. §§ 1391-1412 (1982 & Supp. 1985).

104. *Cf. World-Wide Volkswagen,* 444 U.S. at 293 (constitutional principles of federalism make state lines relevant to determination of court's jurisdiction).

105. *See* Insurance Corp. of Ireland v. Compagnie des Bauxites de Guinee, 456 U.S. at 702-03 n.10 (discussing relationship between state sovereignty and due process minimum contacts test); Brilmayer, *supra* note 77, at 84-85 (same).

ments of principle, rather than convenience. Although it may be hard to see what is at stake, the due process clause has often been used to protect citizens against de minimis injuries.[106] Furthermore, American constitutional law recognizes clearly the fairness claims of individuals being subjected to government intrusion without their political participation or consent.[107] Under this view, even if the harm is slight or the inconvenience minimal, jurisdictional rules may not cross boundaries set by the due process clause.

B. OTHER LIMITS ON STATE COURT POWER

In addition to the important limits on state court jurisdiction posed by the due process clause, several other doctrines limit state court power over out-of-state defendants.

Commerce clause. — In a line of cases decided between 1923 and 1932, the U.S. Supreme Court applied the commerce clause to invalidate a state's exercise of jurisdiction over railroads, whose only contact with the forum state was limited solicitation of business.[108] Each case involved a claim based on activities occurring outside the forum. The Court ruled that the forum's exercise of jurisdiction in such situations was an unconstitutional burden on interstate commerce. There was no discussion of the due process clause. This line of reasoning has not been employed by the Supreme Court since the 1930s, but is occasionally still invoked by lower courts.[109]

First Amendment. — Special concerns relating to free speech arguably should enter the jurisdictional analysis when a plaintiff seeks to obtain jurisdiction over an out-of-state publication on a libel claim. Because of the possible "chilling" effect on first amendment rights, some courts, particularly the Fifth Circuit, required a higher level of

---

106. *See, e.g.,* Fuentes v. Shevin, 407 U.S. 67 (1972) (state seizure of goods worth $500); Shiadech v. Family Fin. Corp., 395 U.S. 337 (1969) (garnishment of wages to satisfy claim of $420); *but see* Ingraham v. Wright, 430 U.S. 651 (1977) (due process clause does not require notice and hearing prior to paddling of junior high school students).

107. *See, e.g.,* Goldberg v. Kelly, 397 U.S. 254 (1970) (due process requires that welfare recipients receive evidentiary hearing before termination of benefits).

108. Davis v. Farmers Coop. Equity Co., 262 U.S. 312 (1923); Atchison, T. & S.F. Ry. v. Wells, 265 U.S. 101 (1924); Michigan Central R.R. v. Mix, 278 U.S. 492 (1929); Denver & R.G.W. R.R. v. Terte, 284 U.S. 284 (1932) (invalidating jurisdiction as to one defendant, upholding it as to the other). The Court found the commerce clause argument inapplicable in the following cases: Hoffman v. Missouri ex rel. Foraker, 274 U.S. 21 (1917); International Milling Co. v. Columbia Transp. Co., 292 U.S. 511 (1934).

109. *See, e.g.,* White v. Southern Pac. Co., 386 S.W.2d 6 (Mo. 1965). *But see* Scanapico v. Richmond, F. & P. R.R., 439 F.2d 17, 25 (2d Cir. 1970) (en banc) (jurisdiction of New York courts based on sales solicitations in state satisfies "minimum contacts" due process standard, and does not violate commerce clause).

contacts between the forum and the publication in order to sustain personal jurisdiction in such libel actions.[110] Furthermore, it seems that the First Amendment would clearly be offended if a state applied a different long-arm statute to Republicans than to Democrats, or a longer one to defamation cases than to personal injury cases. The "chilling effect" reasoning never received widespread acceptance, however, and a recent Supreme Court decision explicitly rejected the idea that First Amendment concerns were relevant to the personal jurisdiction analysis.[111]

International treaties. — Treaties with foreign nations may also limit state court jurisdiction if the defendant is outside the territory of the United States at the time the state court seeks to exercise long-arm jurisdiction. Unless process is served in the manner prescribed by the treaty, notice is defective and jurisdiction does not attach.[112]

Immunity. — Various types of immunity have limited a state's ability to exercise jurisdiction over certain defendants, even if the defendant is physically present in the state or the exercise of jurisdiction is otherwise lawful. For example, persons such as witnesses or parties to a lawsuit, who enter the forum solely for the purpose of participating in litigation, were traditionally viewed as immune from service of process.[113] The special appearance device, in which a defendant appears in the forum solely for the purpose of challenging the court's jurisdiction, without consenting to that court's jurisdiction for adjudication of the merits, is a form of such immunity. The mere act of making an appearance does not vest jurisdiction. This immunity is probably not of constitutional stature, however, so that states may abolish it if they choose.[114] In addition, some courts have held that persons who other-

---

110. *See, e.g.,* Walker v. Savell, 335 F.2d 536, 544 (5th Cir. 1964) (jurisdictional contact requirements should be stricter for foreign newspapers than for ordinary commercial corporations); New York Times Co. v. Connor, 365 F.2d 567, 572 (5th Cir. 1966) (same); Margoles v. Johns, 333 F. Supp. 942, 946 (D.D.C. 1971) (same), *aff'd,* 483 F.2d 1212 (D.C. Cir. 1973).

111. Calder v. Jones, 465 U.S. 783, 790 (1984): "We . . . reject the suggestion that First Amendment concerns enter into the jurisdictional analysis. The infusion of such considerations would needlessly complicate an already imprecise inquiry . . . . Moreover, the potential chill on protected First Amendment activity stemming from libel and defamation actions is already taken into account in the constitutional limitations on the substantive law governing such suits."

112. *See* CASAD, *supra* note 55, at ¶ 2.06[3]; Kadota v. Hosogai, 125 Ariz. 131, 608 P.2d 68 (Ct. App. 1980).

113. *See* CASAD, *supra* note 55, at ¶ 1.06; Stewart v. Ramsay, 242 U.S. 128 (1916).

114. *Cf.* Lamb v. Schmitt, 285 U.S. 222, 225 (1932) (immunity for witnesses is a rule of convenience for courts, not a right of defendants); York v. Texas, 137 U.S. 15 (1890) (state need not allow special appearance).

wise could constitutionally be subject to long-arm jurisdiction are ineligible for this immunity.[115]

Conclusion

The likely reason that the minimum contacts standard has proven so difficult to define precisely is that it is concerned with fundamental issues of political fairness. Under what circumstances is a state justified in asserting power over an individual? What factors support such political obligations?

Such questions are highly controversial as a matter of political theory. Furthermore, translating general theories about fairness into rules with specific applications is no easy matter. The highly fact-specific case law that we see in this due process context should be no surprise, nor should the Court's inability to formulate precise standards.

---

115. *See, e.g.,* In re Arthur Treacher's Franchise Litig., 92 F.R.D. 398 (E.D. Pa. 1981) (if defendant over whom court could validly exercise personal jurisdiction for purposes of giving testimony in other litigation, he cannot claim immunity, which is rule of convenience for courts rather than defendants); Severn v. Adidas Sportschuhfabriken, 33 Cal. App. 3d 754, 109 Cal. Rptr. 328 (1973) (traditional immunity for witnesses has been statutorily abolished in California, allowing service on witnesses if service is made in manner permitted by California law).

Chapter 2

JURISDICTION OF THE FEDERAL COURTS

As the preceding section has explained, state courts are courts of "general" or "residual" jurisdiction, broadly empowered to hear a wide variety of cases without the need for a statutory grant of jurisdiction. The subject matter of the cases that state courts may hear is almost limitless, and the most significant bounds on their power are those imposed by constitutional due process limits on the courts' personal jurisdiction over the parties — limits which have become less and less restrictive under evolving Supreme Court doctrine.

With the discussion of federal jurisdiction, the focus shifts to a contrast between the power of the federal courts and the power, not of a particular state court, but of the whole system of state courts. For alongside the state court system exists a parallel federal court structure which offers an alternative, separate track for many of the cases state courts may hear.[1] The issue in many cases thus is not simply which state's courts should hear the case, but also whether the case can or should be heard in state or federal court. Although it might seem easy to divide cases into "state" and "federal" ones, allocating each to its respective system, this is not so. First, state courts have always played an important role in applying federal law, and federal courts have been called upon regularly to apply state law. Second, and even more important, in many cases elements of federal and state law are closely intertwined. There are large numbers of cases which might be heard in either federal or state court, and the two court systems effectively compete for judicial business.

It is in this context of overlapping power to hear cases that federal courts are described as courts of "limited" jurisdiction, a term which summarizes many of the differences between the state and federal systems. The idea that the federal system is one of limited powers is a central principle that pervades not only the federal judicial power, but also the power of the federal government in general. The Constitution establishes that the federal powers are limited to those specifically enumerated, with all other powers reserved to the states and to the people.[2] In the background, the states always retain residual law-making power in those areas in which the federal government either cannot, or does not, act. In terms of substantive law, this conception of the limited nature of the federal government's power has meant, historically, that most American law has been made by the states and, in particular, by the state courts. Under the system of "common law"

---

1. *See* Figure C, *infra.*
2. U.S. CONST. amend. X.

inherited from England, the state courts have fashioned the substantive rules of decision in such wide-ranging areas as tort, contract, property, probate, and domestic relations. Even with the vast expansion of the role of federal regulation since the New Deal, and the rise of the federal administrative state, the states have remained the predominant source of rules in these traditional areas.

More to the point, the "limited" nature of federal jurisdiction has important implications for federal judicial power as well as for federal legislative power. The federal courts' power to hear cases is strictly limited to those that are both within the constitutional grant of power and statutorily authorized. Like state courts, federal courts must show that the exercise of jurisdiction does not contravene any constitutional limitation, such as due process.[3] Unlike state courts, however, they must also show an affirmative constitutional and statutory basis in order to justify hearing a case. This requirement of a statutory basis for jurisdiction has proven extremely important in practice because Congress often has chosen not to vest the entire constitutional jurisdiction in the federal courts, but only portions of it.

The strict limits on federal judicial powers also affect the procedures by which objections to federal court jurisdiction may be made. The parties to a state court lawsuit can waive objections to the jurisdiction of the court, either by agreeing to the forum in advance of litigation or by failing to object to jurisdiction after litigation commences. Personal jurisdiction can be founded on "consent," because it is concerned with the parties' due process rights. By contrast, objections to the subject matter jurisdiction of a federal court can be raised at any time until final judgment in the highest court of appeal, and a court must dismiss a case whenever such jurisdiction is lacking.[4] Moreover, federal jurisdiction cannot be founded either on explicit consent in advance or on a failure to object at trial.[5] Because limitations on federal jurisdiction are not based on fairness to the parties, party willingness to litigate in federal court is simply not relevant. Much has been said, both pro[6] and

---

3. As discussed earlier in the context of state-court jurisdiction, due process requires that before a court exercise power over a party, it establish the existence of personal jurisdiction over that party and provide notice to the party that it intends to adjudicate its rights. In the federal judicial system, Rule 4 of the Federal Rules of Civil Procedure governs service of process, which fulfills the notice requirement and implicitly incorporates the constitutional requirement of personal jurisdiction as well. *See* 4 C. WRIGHT & A. MILLER, FEDERAL PRACTICE AND PROCEDURE § 1064 (1969 & Supp. 1985).

4. *See* Insurance Corp. of Ireland v. Compagnie de Bauxites de Guinee, 456 U.S. 694, 702 (1982); Fed. R. Civ. P. 12(h)(3).

5. *See, e.g.,* Mitchell v. Maurer, 293 U.S. 237, 244 (1934).

6. *See, e.g.,* C. WRIGHT, LAW OF FEDERAL COURTS § 7 (4th ed. 1983).

7. *See, e.g.,* Dobbs, *The Decline of Jurisdiction by Consent,* 40 N.C. L. REV. 49 (1961) (demonstrating that broad rule of no subject matter jurisdiction by consent dates only

con,[7] of this different treatment in the federal context of jurisdiction by consent. At a minimum it underscores the greater seriousness with which the limits on the powers of the federal courts are treated.

I. Constitutional Framework of the Federal Courts

It has been explained that the jurisdiction of the federal courts is a product both of the text of article III of the Constitution, which establishes their outermost potential authority, and of the jurisdictional statutes adopted by Congress to implement that authority, which dictate the actual contours of that power. However, article III actually serves two functions: not only does it dictate the categories of cases the federal courts may hear, but it also establishes the structure of the federal court hierarchy.

In terms of the federal judicial hierarchy, article III provides that the judicial power of the United States shall be vested in "one Supreme Court, and in such inferior Courts as the Congress may from time to time ordain and establish." Only the Supreme Court was constitutionally mandated, and the establishment of the lower federal courts was left entirely to the discretion of Congress. Immediately after the ratification of the Constitution, Congress exercised its option to create a system of inferior federal courts through the Judiciary Act of 1789.[8] The present federal court structure, which dates to that Act, consists of three levels of courts: a trial level of federal district courts; an intermediate appellate level of circuit courts; and a single Supreme Court, with final appellate authority over cases from within the federal system and from the highest court in each state system.

---

to mid-nineteenth century); *see also* Dobbs, *Beyond Bootstrap: Foreclosing the Issue of Subject-Matter Jurisdiction Before Final Judgment,* 51 MINN. L. REV. 491 (1967) (criticizing rule that subject matter jurisdictional objections may be raised at any point in the litigation).

8. Act of Sept. 24, 1789, ch. 20, 1 Stat. 73.

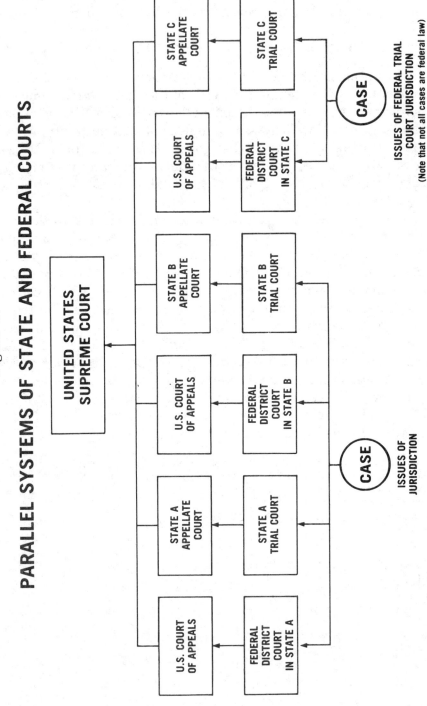

Figure C.

PARALLEL SYSTEMS OF STATE AND FEDERAL COURTS

Although these courts were established as tribunals completely independent from the state court systems, many aspects of their organization are closely related to the underlying systems of state law. For example, the jurisdiction of each federal district court is defined not solely in terms of the population served, but also in terms of state territorial boundaries: the jurisdiction of only one federal district court crosses state boundaries,[9] while every state has at least one federal district court. Similarly, the jurisdiction of the courts of appeal is generally defined not in terms of a special area of expertise, nor as a national jurisdiction, but as an area of exclusive appellate jurisdiction over cases from the federal district courts in a specified set of states, which are usually geographically contiguous. This is neither a necessary method of organization, nor, at times, an efficient one. The wide variation in the caseloads of circuit courts in different areas of the country has perennially created problems, and recently led to the congressional split of the old Fifth Circuit into two circuits, the Fifth and Eleventh.[10]

In addition to using the states' territorial boundaries, Congress also relied upon the pre-existing state court systems to supply important rules of procedure. Under the statutes that applied until the Federal Rules of Civil Procedure were adopted in 1938, federal courts typically borrowed the procedural rules of the states in which they sat.[11] Even now, federal courts use certain state procedural rules, such as long-arm jurisdictional statutes.[12]

The more important function of article III, however, was not simply to dictate questions of structure but also questions of power, defining the types of cases that federal courts may hear. The description in article III of the judicial power vested in the federal courts, which is only slightly more specific than that of the judicial hierarchy, contains five main headings of federal jurisdiction:

---

9. The federal judicial district for Wyoming encompasses the entire state and those portions of Yellowstone National Park situated in Montana and Idaho. 28 U.S.C. § 131 (1982).

10. *See* Fifth Circuit Court of Appeals Reorganization Act of 1980, § 2, 28 U.S.C. § 41 (1982).

11. *See* 4 C. WRIGHT & A. MILLER, *supra* note 3, at § 1002 (discussing history of federal procedure; C. WRIGHT, *supra* note 6, at § 61 (discussing pre-1938 federal procedure).

12. For example, under Federal Rule of Civil Procedure 4(e), the federal court is authorized to make service upon parties outside the state where the same would be allowed under state law, i.e. under a state long-arm statute. *See generally* 4 C. WRIGHT & A. MILLER, FEDERAL PRACTICE AND PROCEDURE §§ 1064-1069, 1075 (1969 & 1985 Supp.) (discussing personal jurisdiction); *see also* Fed. R. Civ. P. 4(c)(2)(C)(i) (authorizing service of process pursuant to method prescribed by state law).

(1) so-called "federal question" jurisdiction, which is defined as "all cases, in Law and Equity, arising under this Constitution, the Laws of the United States, and Treaties;"

(2) a small category of cases "affecting ambassadors, other public Ministers and Consuls;"

(3) admiralty jurisdiction;

(4) cases involving the United States as a party; and

(5) the related categories of "diversity jurisdiction," defined as "controversies between a State and Citizens of another State [or] between citizens of different States," and "alienage jurisdiction," defined as Controversies "between a State, or the citizens thereof, and foreign States, Citizens, or Subjects."

Article III also allocates these cases to some degree between the Supreme Court and other courts, both state and federal, by specifying that the Supreme Court shall have original (i.e. trial court) jurisdiction over "all Cases affecting Ambassadors, other public Ministers and Consuls, and those in which a State shall be Party," and appellate jurisdiction in "all the other cases."

Article III vests Congress with great discretion to shape the scope of federal court jurisdiction, as much was left for Congress to fill in within the interstices of these constitutional provisions. In addition, two particular provisions of article III suggest that congressional power to implement this jurisdiction is very broad indeed. First, Congress was given the choice not to establish lower federal courts in the first place, in which event no cases on the article III list would have been heard in lower federal courts at all. From this it follows that Congress has the power to create lower federal courts with jurisdiction over only certain cases.[13] Second, since Congress was authorized by article III to regulate and create exceptions to the Supreme Court's appellate jurisdiction, it has been argued that the Supreme Court's jurisdiction can be similarly curtailed. A large and subtle literature exists discussing the extent of congressional power under these provisions.[14] None of the statutory provisions actually adopted to define federal jurisdiction are particularly controversial, however.

---

13. See Lockerty v. Phillips, 319 U.S. 182, 187 (1943).

14. See, e.g., Brilmayer & Underhill, Congressional Obligation to Provide a Forum for Constitutional Claims: Discriminatory Jurisdictional Rules and the Conflict of Laws, 69 Va. L. Rev. 819 (1983); Eisenberg, Congressional Authority to Restrict Lower Federal Court Jurisdiction, 83 Yale L.J. 498 (1974); McGowan, Federal Jurisdiction: Legislative and Judicial Change, 28 Case W. Res. L. Rev. 517 (1978); Redish, Constitutional Limitations on Congressional Power to Control Federal Jurisdiction: A Reaction to Professor Sager, 77 Nw. U. L. Rev. 143 (1982); Sager, The Supreme Court 1980 Term — Foreword: Constitutional Limitations on Congress' Authority to Regulate the Jurisdiction of the Federal Courts, 95 Harv. L. Rev. 17 (1981); Van Alstyne, A Critical Guide to Ex Parte McCardle, 15 Ariz. L. Rev. 229 (1973); Wechsler, The Courts and the Constitution, 65 Colum. L. Rev. 1001 (1965).

We have already observed that federal jurisdiction as established is different from state jurisdiction in that the limitations on federal jurisdiction are treated with greater seriousness. In one respect, however, the five headings of federal jurisdiction bear an interesting resemblance to the bases for personal jurisdiction in state court. In either context, there are two ways of establishing jurisdiction. The first is based on some characteristics of the parties to the dispute. For instance, long-arm jurisdiction can be established by showing that the defendant is either domiciled (if a person) or incorporated (if a corporation) in the state. Similarly, federal jurisdiction exists if the parties are diverse or if one is an ambassador or the United States itself. The result in both cases is "general jurisdiction," meaning jurisdiction over any sort of issue between those parties, without regard to whether the court has a particular interest in the content of the dispute.

On the other hand, at times it is the content of the dispute that triggers jurisdiction, in which case the identity of the parties is irrelevant. For instance, a state might have an interest in a dispute because some of the relevant events occurred there or because the controversy concerned land that was located there. Similarly, there might be a federal interest in a dispute because the dispute involved federal rights or remedies. In either case, the identity of the claimants would be immaterial. Federal question jurisdiction and admiralty jurisdiction are based on such federal substantive interests. Finally, some cases implicate both federal rights and federally protected parties, for instance where a suit between states is also governed by federal law.

Although our discussion chiefly concerns article III courts, it should be noted that other types of federal courts also exist. Under its article I legislative powers, Congress may create courts that carry out certain of the same functions as do article III courts. The best known examples are the territorial courts and those of the District of Columbia.[15] The limitations on the scope of federal-court jurisdiction, described above, do not apply to these so-called article I, or legislative, courts.[16] Similarly, other article III limitations such as life tenure and salary protec-

---

15. Although federal courts in the U.S. territories exercised a jurisdiction commensurate with that of the regular federal courts, their authority derived from Congress's power to legislate over the territories rather than the territories' status as a branch of the federal government. *See* Glidden Co. v. Zdanok, 370 U.S. 530, 544-45 (1962) (plurality opinion). Similarly, Congress's special responsibility for legislating for the District of Columbia was held to give it authority to establish article I courts, *see* Palmore v. United States, 411 U.S. 389, 397 (1973), which it did. *See* 11 D.C. Code Ann. tit. 11 (1981).

16. *Glidden,* 370 U.S. at 545.

tion for judges do not apply. The precise limitations that do exist in article I courts are somewhat unclear,[17] and although interesting in theory, they will not be addressed in this text. Instead, we turn to the jurisdictional restrictions pertinent to different courts in the article III hierarchy.

II. Jurisdiction of the Lower Federal Courts

One noticeable feature of the jurisdiction of the lower federal courts is the divergence between the broad class of cases that could potentially be vested in the federal courts under article III, and the far narrower class of cases in which federal-court jurisdiction has actually been vested. Two factors have combined to produce this result: the restrictive jurisdictional statutes that Congress has enacted; and the often even narrower Supreme Court interpretation of those statutes. The resulting limitations on federal-court jurisdiction often reveal the areas of greatest tension in federal-state relations. Nowhere is this more true than in the two major categories of civil cases heard by the federal courts, federal question and diversity cases, both of which state and federal courts are concurrently empowered to hear.

A. FEDERAL QUESTION JURISDICTION

The historical evolution of "federal question" jurisdiction, constitutionally defined as cases "arising under" federal law, points out strikingly the divergence between constitutional and statutory grants of judicial power. Despite the fact that these cases might be considered the quintessential federal cases, only in 1875 did Congress pass a statute conferring general federal question jurisdiction on the federal district courts, and until as recently as 1980, that jurisdiction was still partially subject to a requirement that there be a minimum amount in controversy.[18] Moreover, even though the jurisdictional statute uses the language "arising under," a direct parallel to the constitutional text, the statute has been construed far more narrowly.

---

17. *See, e.g.,* Northern Pipeline Constr. Co. v. Marathon Pipe Line Co., 458 U.S. 50 (1982) (broad jurisdictional grant to article I bankruptcy courts violates Constitution); *see generally* 13 C. WRIGHT, A. MILLER & E. COOPER, FEDERAL PRACTICE AND PROCEDURE § 3528 (2d ed. 1984) (discussing history and current status of "legislative" courts).

18. Act of March 3, 1875, ch. 137, § 1, 18 Stat. 470 (giving federal courts jurisdiction over all civil suits arising under Constitution or federal law); Act of Dec. 1, 1980, Pub. L. No. 96-486, 94 Stat. 2369 (repealing minimum amount in controversy requirement of $10,000 for federal question jurisdiction).

1. "Arising Under"

Definition of the term "arising under" is the first important issue that is presented under federal question jurisdiction. The Supreme Court interpreted the constitutional language in *Osborn v. Bank of the United States*,[19] in which the challenged statute authorized federal adjudication of cases involving national banks. *Osborn* held that article III allows Congress to vest federal jurisdiction over any case in which federal law potentially "forms an original ingredient."[20] This broad definition would include a vast number of cases within the federal question jurisdiction, because it would include cases in which the federal issue was either a claim or a defense, in which it was a peripheral part, and in which it simply had the potential to be raised. One scholar has described this class of cases as virtually limitless.[21]

However, *Osborn* was an interpretation of the constitutional phrase. The comparable statutory phrase "arising under" has not been interpreted so expansively. The federal question jurisdictional provision, § 1331, provides that the district courts shall have "original jurisdiction of all civil actions arising under the Constitution, laws, or treaties of the United States." The Court has held that despite the jurisdictional statute's use of identical language, it does not confer the whole constitutional federal question jurisdiction.[22] Just what cases do "arise under" federal law, however, has not been clearly defined, although a number of alternative formulations have been offered.

The most familiar definition is the one formulated by Justice Holmes, which states that a "suit arises under the law that creates the cause of action."[23] In practice, however, this definition has not proved useful as an exclusionary principle, and the Supreme Court has rejected it in recent cases.[24] Judge Friendly's version, offered in *T.B. Harms v. Eliscu*,[25] would define a case that "arises under" federal law as one in which "the complaint discloses a need for determining the meaning or application of such a law."[26] Commentators similarly have suggested that a case should be deemed to "arise under" federal law "if in order for the plaintiff to secure the relief sought he will be obliged to

---

19. 22 U.S. (9 Wheat.) 738 (1824).

20. *Id.* at 824.

21. *See* C. WRIGHT, *supra* note 6, § 17 at 92.

22. *See, e.g.,* Verlinden B.V. v. Central Bank of Nigeria, 461 U.S. 480, 494-95 (1983).

23. American Well Works Co. v. Layne & Bowler Co., 241 U.S. 257, 260 (1916).

24. *See, e.g.,* Franchise Tax Bd. v. Construction Laborers Vacation Trust, 463 U.S. 1, 9 (1983).

25. 339 F.2d 823 (2d Cir. 1964), *cert. denied,* 381 U.S. 915 (1965).

26. *Id.* at 827.

establish both the correctness and the applicability to his case of a proposition of federal law."[27] The Supreme Court has cited each of these definitions, without, however, designating any one as authoritative.[28]

The rationale behind the federal question doctrine is the provision of a federal forum to vindicate federal substantive interests. This raises an interesting theoretical issue posed, but not answered, by *Textile Workers Union of America v. Lincoln Mills of Alabama.*[29] *Lincoln Mills* concerned a federal statute that purported to vest federal court jurisdiction over labor disputes.[30] The statute did not give any substantive guidance, however, on resolving the merits of the disputes. A majority of the Court held that Congress wished to authorize the federal courts to fashion federal rules of decision. They did not need to address, for this reason, the theoretical question of whether Congress might create federal question jurisdiction simply by passing a jurisdictional statute with no substantive content, and if it did so whether the controversy could properly "arise under" the federal jurisdictional statute. The dissent argued that it could not do so.[31]

This problem highlights what we often take for granted: the way that jurisdiction arises as a byproduct of substantive interests. Congress does not typically address the jurisdictional issue directly, but instead defines substantive interests that create jurisdiction indirectly. In certain respects this process resembles the creation of long-arm jurisdiction. Specific jurisdiction exists because of a substantive interest in certain events, such as those occurring within the forum territory. This substantive interest recognizes those events as related to the cause of action, and indirectly creates jurisdiction. Specific jurisdiction is a product of state law, although it is a product of state substantive law, and not of the long-arm statute. Whether a case "arises under" federal law in federal jurisdiction, or "arises out of" events in state court jurisdiction, jurisdiction is a byproduct of the subject matter of the dispute.

---

27. P. Bator, P. Mishkin, D. Shapiro & H. Wechsler, Hart & Wechsler's The Federal Courts and the Federal System 889 (2d ed. 1973) [hereinafter cited as Hart & Wechsler].

28. *Franchise Tax Bd.*, 463 U.S. at 8-9.

29. 353 U.S. 448 (1957).

30. Labor Management Relations Act of 1947, § 301, 29 U.S.C. § 185 (1982).

31. 353 U.S. at 460 (Frankfurter, J., dissenting).

2. The Well-Pleaded Complaint Rule and Declaratory Judgments

The Supreme Court has adopted another important limitation on federal question jurisdiction: the "well-pleaded complaint rule." A classic formulation in *Gully v. First National Bank*[32] states that the federal issue "must be an element, and an essential one, of the plaintiff's cause of action." This rule adds two crucial requirements for the invocation of federal question jurisdiction: the federal issue must appear in the complaint; and it must be a substantial issue.

First, the existence of such jurisdiction is to be determined from the plaintiff's pleadings alone, "unaided by anything alleged in anticipation of avoidance of defense which it is thought the defendant may interpose." [33] Thus a federal *defense* is not considered to constitute a "federal question" that will support federal jurisdiction under § 1331, although under the *Osborn* interpretation of the constitutional language this is solely a statutory and not a constitutional matter.

Although the practical importance of this rule cannot be overstated, its rationale is not entirely clear. As the Supreme Court has recently characterized it, the rule avoids "more-or-less automatically a number of potentially serious federal-state conflicts."[34] For example, it eliminates from federal jurisdiction many cases involving federal constitutional challenges to the enforcement of state laws, thereby allowing the state courts to pass on the constitutionality of their own laws in the first instance, and also, perhaps, obviating the need for a constitutional ruling at all, should the state court reread the state statutory language. It has this effect because such constitutional cases typically involve only federal defenses to state-law causes of action.[35]

---

32. 299 U.S. 109, 112 (1936).

33. Taylor v. Anderson, 234 U.S. 74, 75-76 (1914); *see also* Louisville & N.R.R. v. Mottley, 211 U.S. 149, 152 (1908).

34. Franchise Tax Bd. v. Construction Laborers Vacation Trust, 463 U.S. 1, 10 (1983).

35. As noted in the text, a federal constitutional challenge to a state statute often will arise as a defense to a state action seeking to enforce that statute, and thus would not fall within the federal question jurisdiction under the well-pleaded complaint rule, and could not be removed to federal court nor initiated there. One way to get around this is to seek a federal injunction against such a state prosecution, alleging the deprivation of a federal right. Under evolving Supreme Court doctrine, however, the availability of such injunctions is more and more limited, and injunctions will only issue where it can be proved that the state action is a concrete threat, but has not yet been filed. *See infra* ch. 2, sec. IVD and ch. 4, sec. II. The combination of the well-pleaded complaint rule and the restrictive injunctive remedy doctrine thus keeps most such cases, which often involve heightened federal-state tension, out of the federal district courts. This result is also supported by the Court's restrictive interpretation of the Federal Declaratory Judgments Act, discussed *infra,* which similarly refuses to allow such cases to be commenced as declaratory actions.

While a reduction in the number of constitutional challenges heard in federal courts may reduce federal-state friction, it is always necessary to ask whether any given group of cases is the appropriate one to remove from the docket. In particular, if federal courts exist in part to enforce federal rights, some portion of the docket will inevitably produce friction. Why should cases involving federal defenses, rather than federal causes of action, be singled out for elimination? One possible explanation is that it is purely hypothetical whether the federal defense will ever be raised. Jurisdiction must be decided definitively at the outset of the case, on the basis of the initial pleadings. Further, it might be argued, allowing the plaintiff to allege the defendant's federal rights in order to manufacture jurisdiction is anamolous. In this respect, the well-pleaded complaint rule is similar to the requirement that a party only has standing to raise his or her own claims.

This explanation, although apparently plausible, breaks down for several reasons. First, if federal jurisdiction is sought by the defendant in an attempt to remove the case from state to federal court then the federal claim is in no sense hypothetical. It has already been raised, because removal occurs only after the defendant has had the opportunity to answer on the merits. Moreover, in such a case, the defendant is raising his or her *own* rights as a basis for federal jurisdiction.

Second, the rule causes distorted results in the context of actions for declaratory judgment. A declaratory judgment is a procedure by which a defendant may take the initiative to request an adjudication of his or her legal rights. Declaratory judgments are allowed under the federal Declaratory Judgment Act.[36] In such cases, a federal right that would ordinarily constitute a federal defense under traditional rules of pleading will be affirmatively pleaded by the moving party as part of his or her complaint for a declaratory judgment. The Supreme Court faced the problem of whether such a cause of action should be deemed to present a federal question in *Skelly Oil Co. v. Phillips Petroleum Co.*[37] It first noted that the Declaratory Judgment Act was intended to have procedural effect only, and not to expand the federal jurisdiction. Based on this reading, it held that such cases do not "arise under" federal law if, but for the availability of the declaratory judgment procedure, the federal claim would arise only as a defense to a state created action. This holding was recently extended in *Franchise Tax Board v. Construction Laborers Vacation Trust*[38] to cover cases brought under state declaratory judgment acts. This convoluted result, in which a plainly federal cause of action may be found not to "arise under" federal law,

---

36. 28 U.S.C. §§ 2201-2202 (1982).
37. 339 U.S. 667 (1950).
38. 463 U.S. 1 (1983).

results from tying the definition of jurisdiction to antiquated pleading rules, thereby creating conflicts as the rules are modernized. The well-pleaded complaint rule has often been criticized on this basis.[39] Furthermore, federal procedure in declaratory judgment cases specifically requires that the moving party anticipate the opponent's federal claim, because the complaint must allege a cause of action from which he or she seeks protection. This federal procedure thus is precisely contrary to the policies underlying the well-pleaded complaint rule in the first place.

On the other side of these restrictive federal question doctrines, it should be noted, is an expansive view of the scope of jurisdiction over cases legitimately within § 1331. Under the doctrine of ancillary jurisdiction, the jurisdiction of a federal court extends to an entire case, including state and federal issues, even when the state-law issues could not have been heard as an original matter. Similarly, jurisdiction is determined at the time of filing, and even if the federal issue is ultimately declared unmeritorious, the court usually retains jurisdiction over the remaining state issues, whether or not they would independently support federal jurisdiction.[40] Thus the federal question jurisdiction has been interpreted as a narrow grant, but one which covers the practical necessities of litigating an entire case at once. This practical rule encourages consolidation of state and federal claims in a single case and aims for a high degree of jurisdictional certainty.

3. Substantiality and the Relationship to the Merits

In order to support federal jurisdiction, the federal question in the case not only must be part of the well-pleaded complaint, but also must be substantial.[41] This requirement prevents a plaintiff from simply manufacturing a totally frivolous federal argument and using it to gain access to federal court for what is in reality a state-law claim. To show substantiality, the plaintiff need not, of course, demonstrate a certainty of prevailing on the merits, but only some probability.

This requirement highlights the close relationship between jurisdiction and the merits. To some extent, in deciding the existence of a federal question a court is anticipating the merits of the dispute. The

---

39. *See, e.g.,* 13B C. WRIGHT, A. MILLER & E. COOPER, FEDERAL PRACTICE AND PROCEDURE § 3566 at 89-90 (2d ed. 1984) (criticizing well-pleaded complaint rule as applied to declaratory judgment actions).

40. *See* United Mine Workers of Am. v. Gibbs, 383 U.S. 715, 725-27 (1966) (discussing when federal court should exercise pendent jurisdiction over state claims); *see generally* C. WRIGHT, A. MILLER & E. COOPER, FEDERAL PRACTICE AND PROCEDURE § 3567.1 (discussing application of *Gibbs* standard of pendent jurisdiction).

41. *See, e.g.,* Hagans v. Lavine, 415 U.S. 528, 536-38 (1974).

same can be said in any circumstance in which jurisdiction is based on a substantive interest in enforcement, as opposed to the parties involved. For instance, if long-arm jurisdiction is predicated upon the occurrence of an automobile accident in the state, it requires that the defendant have caused that automobile accident. This determination forms part of the merits of the dispute; and the defendant would be responding to both jurisdiction and the merits if he asserted no involvement and alleged a case of mistaken identity.

This overlap between jurisdiction and the merits is a consequence of the desirable goal of using jurisdiction to further substantive interests. It does not mean that the two issues are identical, because jurisdiction only requires some probability of prevailing. Neither does it mean that jurisdiction never existed if the plaintiff loses the case. Jurisdiction exists as long as there is a colorable claim of right. To vacate a judgment on jurisdictional grounds simply because the defendant prevailed would leave the plaintiff free to institute a second round of litigation on the same claim, because there would be no adverse judgment on the merits.

B. DIVERSITY JURISDICTION

Unlike federal question jurisdiction, which is defined by reference to the substantive law of the case, diversity jurisdiction is defined exclusively by the nature of the parties. Although this fact may make it somewhat misleading to call this heading of jurisdiction a "subject matter" requirement, it is separate and additional to the requirement of personal jurisdiction over the parties. The Constitution defines diversity jurisdiction as extending to cases between citizens of different states, and between a state and citizens of another state, and defines the related category of alienage jurisdiction as extending to cases between a state or its citizens and a foreign state or its citizens. The diversity jurisdiction was vested in the federal district courts as early as the first Judiciary Act of 1789, but it has always been subject to certain limitations, including a minimum amount in controversy, now set at $10,000.[42] This rule has led to a complex body of case law determining how the amount in controversy should be judged, at what point in time, when claims can be aggregated to meet the minimum, and so on. As noted above, these decisions anticipate the merits to some degree; however, only a probability of recovery is required.

Diversity jurisdiction is currently contained in the jurisdictional grant of 28 U.S.C. § 1332, which parallels almost exactly the constitu-

---

42. 28 U.S.C. § 1332 (1982).

tional text. This language, again, has left much room for judicial interpretation and limitation. One important limitation is the rule established in *Strawbridge v. Curtiss*,[43] in which the Supreme Court interpreted the jurisdictional grant of § 1332 to require "complete" diversity i.e. *all* plaintiffs must be diverse from all defendants. The Constitution in fact requires only "minimal" diversity — i.e. that at least *one* plaintiff be diverse from at least *one* defendant. This has been made clear by the Supreme Court's approval of a federal statute that establishes only a requirement of minimal diversity for federal jurisdiction for certain limited sorts of cases.[44] Nevertheless, the complete diversity rule of *Strawbridge* has had far-reaching effects. It has spawned an entire body of extremely complex rules as to how the citizenship (or more precisely, domicile)[45] of different types of parties is established. The rule varies depending on whether the party is an individual, a corporation, a partnership, the representative in a class action, the administrator of a will, a guardian, and so on. The *Strawbridge* rule greatly complicates the calculus, because if a corporation were held to have the citizenship of every one of its shareholders it would be highly unlikely that the opponent would have the requisite diversity with each.

More important, the *Strawbridge* rule has created great pressure for parties seeking to establish federal diversity jurisdiction to manufacture new domiciles, or to realign the parties, so as to create complete diversity. The corresponding vigilance courts must use to police such tactics is great, and has been only slightly aided by the enactment of 28 U.S.C. § 1359, which bans collusive joinder. Moreover, the rule has implications for many related rules, such as the joinder of indispensable, necessary, and proper parties, and for permissible intervention and intervention of right. In all these instances, the fact that a slight change in the procedural posture of the case can destroy jurisdiction creates an often contradictory and technical body of rules highly subject to manipulation.[46] The *Strawbridge* rule has thus been heavily criticized.[47]

---

43. 7 U.S. (3 Cranch) 267 (1806).

44. *See* State Farm Fire & Casualty Co. v. Tashire, 386 U.S. 523, 530-31 (1967) (upholding federal interpleader statute, 28 U.S.C. § 1335).

45. *See* Gilbert v. David, 235 U.S. 561, 569 (1915) (plaintiff's domicile at time lawsuit filed determines his citizenship for diversity purposes).

46. *See generally,* 13B C. WRIGHT, A. MILLER & E. COOPER, *supra* note 6, § 3605 (discussing diversity rules in suits with multiple parties); *see, e.g.,* Butchert Singer, Inc. v. Kellam, 623 F. Supp. 418 (D. Del. 1985) (court's realignment of parties following intervention of indispensable plaintiff destroys diversity and requires dismissal of case).

47. *See, e.g.,* Currie, *The Federal Courts and the American Law Institute,* 36 U. CHI. L. REV. 1, 18-34 (1968) (discussing problems of *Strawbridge* rule).

More fundamentally, diversity jurisdiction is itself a highly controversial heading of federal jurisdiction. The criticism of diversity jurisdiction is closely related to the fact that the law applied in such cases is almost entirely state law. The only federal issues are those, such as defenses, which would not suffice for federal question jurisdiction. This gives rise to the protest that "state cases belong in state courts," which has formed one set of arguments in the continuing debate of whether diversity should be abolished, retained, or limited.

Those who support the retention of diversity jurisdiction cite first what is generally agreed to be its original rationale: the need to protect out-of-state litigants from the bias of state courts. Such bias, they argue, still continues. Several empirical studies have tested this thesis, although with inconclusive results.[48] Other supporters of diversity stress its continuing, present benefits, which include contributing to the ease of the flow of capital and increasing business confidence;[49] engendering a creative dialogue between the state and federal court systems (along with closely related arguments about the higher quality of federal justice);[50] and relieving the burden on overcrowded state court dockets.[51]

Those who seek to abolish diversity jurisdiction cite the converse burden on *federal* court dockets. They object to having federal judges, under *Erie,* function as "mouthpieces" for state courts, a role which robs judges of their creativity, deprives judicial decisionmaking of its power to make precedent, and leaves it as solely a dispute resolver in the instant case.[52] They also cite the procedural problems[53] noted

48. *Compare* Summers, *Analysis of Factors That Influence Choice of Forum in Diversity Cases,* 47 IOWA L. REV. 933, 937-38 (1962) (finding fear of prejudice to be a factor in attorney's choice of federal forum in only 4.3% of federal cases surveyed) *with* Note, *The Choice Between State and Federal Court in Diversity Cases in Virginia,* 51 VA. L. REV. 178, 179 (1965) (survey finding that 60.3% of responding attorneys indicated local prejudice as a reason for preferring a federal forum for out-of-state plaintiffs).

49. *See, e.g.,* Marbury, *Why Should We Limit Federal Diversity Jurisdiction?,* 46 A.B.A. J. 379, 380 (1960); Moore & Weckstein, *Diversity Jurisdiction: Past, Present and Future,* 43 TEX. L. REV. 1, 16-17 (1964); Taft, *Possible and Needed Reforms in Administration of Justice in Federal Courts,* 8 A.B.A. J. 601, 604 (1922).

50. *See, e.g.,* Frank, *For Maintaining Diversity Jurisdiction,* 73 YALE L.J. 7, 11-12 (1963); Wright, *The Federal Courts and the Nature and Quality of State Law,* 13 WAYNE L. REV. 317, 327 (1967).

51. *See, e.g.,* American Law Institute, Study of the Division of Jurisdiction Between State and Federal Courts 108 (1969).

52. *Cf.* Wright, *supra* note 50, at 326 (federal courts in diversity must follow, rather than lead, state courts); Richardson v. Commissioner, 126 F.2d 562, 567 (2d Cir. 1942) (because federal applies, court need not play role of "ventriloquist's dummy" to state court).

53. *See, e.g.,* Rowe, *Abolishing Diversity Jurisdiction: Positive Side Effects and Potential For Further Reforms,* 92 HARV. L. REV. 963, 984-999 (1979) (discussing various procedural problems).

above, which are, to be sure, often more a result of the *Strawbridge* rule than of diversity jurisdiction itself.

Finally, other critics cite a combination of these reasons to urge further limitations on diversity jurisdiction. If prejudice against out-of-staters is the problem, for example, then there is no reason why a party should be allowed to choose federal court over state court in his or her own state. Similarly, to solve other problems, a rule of minimal diversity could be statutorily imposed in place of the *Strawbridge* rule. These and other proposals were contained in the highly controversial American Law Institute report[54] on the division of jurisdiction between state and federal courts, as well as in the many subsequent legislative initiatives on the issue.[55] For now, at least, however, there are no signs that Congress will move to abolish the diversity jurisdiction. It therefore remains an important area of concurrent federal and state adjudicative jurisdiction.

C. Removal, Exclusive and Habeas Jurisdiction

Another basis for federal trial court jurisdiction is removal from state court. The general removal provisions under § 1441 afford the defendant a right to remove a case from state to federal court only where that case could have been brought in federal court initially, thereby tying the principles of removal to original jurisdiction. As noted earlier, however, this requirement produces anamolous results in federal question jurisdiction, because removal is not permitted even after a legitimate federal defense has been pleaded. This result has been heavily criticized, and amendments to the removal statute have been proposed.[56]

Another removal provision, 28 U.S.C. § 1443, allows for removal to federal court of state criminal prosecutions where a civil rights violation is alleged. This provision has been construed so narrowly as to make it almost ineffectual,[57] emphasizing the integrity of the state criminal system. It does present, however, the prospect of a state criminal prosecution proceeding in federal court, in order to protect the federal interests involved. It is unclear what procedural rules would

---

54. American Law Institute, *supra* note 51.

55. *See, e.g.,* Rowe, *supra* note 53, at 963 n.1 (citing statutory reform efforts in 95th Congress).

56. *See, e.g.,* American Law Institute, *supra* note 51, at 25-27 (proposed revised statute on federal removal jurisdiction).

57. *See* City of Greenwood v. Peacock, 384 U.S. 808, 828 (1966) (removal possible only where denial of civil rights is "inevitable").

apply, and the cases in which removal has been allowed have been extremely rare.[58]

There are also areas of exclusive federal jurisdiction: federal criminal law, antitrust, patent and copyright cases, bankruptcy cases, cases in which the United States is a party, and admiralty, to name the major categories.[59] The test for whether a substantive area is exclusively an issue for federal determination is whether Congress intended to make the issue a matter for exclusive federal jurisdiction, either expressly or by fair implication.[60] In such cases, the state courts are robbed of any power to adjudicate or to apply federal law.

A final important area of jurisdiction is the power of federal courts to review habeas corpus petitions, which are considered to be civil actions. In such cases, a prisoner in state (or federal) prison claims that he or she is being unconstitutionally deprived of his or her liberty because of some constitutional flaw in the process of conviction, and asks that the sentence be set aside by the federal court. Under the federal habeas statute, the federal court first must ensure that the petitioner has exhausted his or her state remedies, was deprived of a full and fair hearing on the issue sought to be presented, and is pressing a meritorious constitutional claim, before the sentence will be overturned.[61] Habeas petitions are the only significant exception to the general rule that district courts sit in a trial, not appellate, capacity. Moreover, they are the only type of case in which a federal district court sits in essence to review the judgment of the highest court of the state.

Habeas cases are also an exception to the general policies of finality of judgments. As a highly controversial aspect of federal jurisdiction, such cases challenge the assumption behind the federal system that cases proceed through either the state or federal courts, but not through both. At the same time, the habeas jurisdiction of district courts reveals the conflict between the desirability of allowing states to conduct criminal trials without interference and the reality that federal constitutional challenges frequently are raised in state criminal cases. By allowing the entire case to be heard by the state system in the first instance, critical federalism values are served; by allowing some federal review of the constitutional claim, federal interests are

---

58. *E.g.,* Georgia v. Rachel, 384 U.S. 780 (1966); *see also* C. WRIGHT, *supra* note 6, § 38, at 213 and n.26 (collecting cases).

59. *See generally* C. WRIGHT, *supra* note 6, LAW OF FEDERAL COURTS, § 10 at 35-36 (listing significant areas of exclusive federal jurisdiction).

60. *See* Claflin v. Houseman, 93 U.S. 130, 136-37 (1876); Note, *Exclusive Jurisdiction of the Federal Courts in Private Civil Actions,* 70 HARV. L. REV. 509 (1957) (discussing factors which indicate federal court jurisdiction should be exclusive).

61. 28 U.S.C. § 2254 (1982).

protected as well. Much controversy currently rages over the proper scope of federal scrutiny of state decisionmaking through habeas corpus.[62]

III. Jurisdiction of the Supreme Court

The Supreme Court's jurisdiction falls into three categories. First conceptually, but probably least important as a practical matter, is the Supreme Court's original jurisdiction. This encompasses cases that must be brought as an initial matter in the Supreme Court rather than coming to the Court through ordinary appellate processes. Second is the Supreme Court's appellate jurisdiction over cases initially filed in the lower federal courts. The third is appellate jurisdiction over cases initially litigated in the lower state courts. Each of these three types of jurisdiction is regulated by statutory and constitutional provisions.

In contrast to the jurisdiction of the lower federal courts described above, the Supreme Court's jurisdiction is characterized by its essentially discretionary nature. Although Supreme Court review can be sought through two theoretically distinct methods — the Court's discretionary certiorari jurisdiction and its "mandatory" appeals jurisdiction — in fact the trend in both areas has been toward giving the Court control over its docket. Thus the Court's jurisdiction differs significantly from that of the district courts, where a general presumption operates that once jurisdiction is established, the court is obligated to decide the case. Although a district court may, in some cases, effectively decline to decide by using doctrines such as standing, political questions, mootness, and abstention to avoid addressing the central substantive issue, such resolutions are considered decisions on the merits, which will both bar a subsequent suit based on the same wrong and create a precedent on the jurisdictional issue itself.[63]

Similarly, the jurisdiction of the courts of appeals — which is generally uncontroversial and need not be discussed at any length — is not discretionary in the sense as the jurisdiction of the Supreme Court. The appellate court must decide whether a decision coming from a district court is a "final decision" and thus within its appellate jurisdiction under § 1291, or is one of the few interlocutory decisions of the district court which may be immediately appealed under § 1292, or is within the Court's jurisdiction under a specific statute allowing for appeals from administrative agencies. However, it does not have the same latitude to decline jurisdiction without explanation.

---

62. *See generally* C. WRIGHT, *supra* note 6, § 53 at 344-46. *See infra* ch. 5, sec. IIIB.

63. For examples of precedents on these issues, see discussion on case or controversy, sec. IV *infra*.

The discretionary character of Supreme Court jurisdiction is the necessary result of a system that consists of several hundred district courts and twelve circuit courts (with a total of over 700 judges among them)[64] but only one final arbiter with nine Justices. As the caseload of the federal bench has increased over the years, additional judgeships have been added to alleviate the pressure at the trial and appeals levels. Although there have been persistent proposals to create another level of federal courts to screen the Supreme Court's caseload, such controversial measures have never actually been adopted. The need to have one body with final word over the whole system, therefore, has meant that the Supreme Court's scarce judicial resources have been allocated through its own choice amongst the cases on its docket. Its claim to do so rests first, on the congressional redefinition of its jurisdiction over the years to increase the court's discretion to decline jurisdiction, and, second, on the Court's own decisions to treat previously mandatory jurisdiction as essentially discretionary.

Although the legitimacy of the Court's assumption of discretionary power is open to question, especially with regard to its supposedly mandatory jurisdiction, its practical necessity is not. This trend toward increasing the Court's discretion can be seen in all three areas of the Supreme Court's jurisdiction set out above. As we examine the different types of Supreme Court jurisdiction there are two questions to ask. First, to what cases and issues does that jurisdiction extend? And second, to what extent has the Supreme Court exercised the jurisdiction that it has been granted?

A. ORIGINAL JURISDICTION OF THE SUPREME COURT

Although most research and criticism concerning the Supreme Court focuses on its role as an appellate court, one should not forget that the Constitution vests the Court with original jurisdiction over certain matters:

> In all Cases affecting Ambassadors, other public Ministers and Consuls, and those in which a State shall be a Party, the supreme Court shall have original Jurisdiction.[65]

Since the ratification of the Constitution it has been understood that this provision is self-executing, that it requires no enabling legislation,

---

64. *The Washington Spectator*, Mar. 1, 1986 at 3.
65. U.S. CONST. art. III, § 2.

and that Congress may neither increase nor diminish the jurisdiction granted.[66] Since the Judiciary Act of 1789, however, the Court's original jurisdiction has been described more clearly by statute. In its present form, the Judiciary Act restates the kinds of cases that may be brought pursuant to this clause:

> (a) The Supreme Court shall have original and exclusive jurisdiction of all controversies between two or more States.
> (b) The Supreme Court shall have original but not exclusive jurisdiction of:
> (1) All actions or proceedings to which ambassadors, other public ministers, consuls, or vice consuls of foreign states are parties;
> (2) All Controversies between the United States and a State;
> (3) All actions or proceedings by a State against the citizens of another State or against aliens.[67]

The primary ambiguity in the constitutional provision is whether the Court's original and appellate jurisdictions are mutually exclusive. In other words, is the Supreme Court's original jurisdiction limited only to those categories of cases named or, rather, does it include at least those listed? Furthermore, can the Court's appellate jurisdiction be extended to those cases which are enumerated as falling under the original jurisdiction? In *Marbury v. Madison,* Chief Justice Marshall argued that the Court's jurisdiction, where original, is exclusive: "If congress remains at liberty to give this court appellate jurisdiction, where the constitution has declared their jurisdiction shall be original; and original jurisdiction where the constitution has declared it shall be appellate; the distribution of jurisdiction, made in the constitution, is form without substance."[68] But Marshall's view has not prevailed. It is well-settled that the lower federal courts have concurrent jurisdiction with the Supreme Court in some cases over which the latter has original jurisdiction. In such cases, the Court has appellate as well as original jurisdiction. Indeed, the structure of § 1251 indicates a division between exclusive and non-exclusive original jurisdiction.

Invocation of the Court's original jurisdiction is rare. In the first 170 years since the ratification of the Constitution, the Court decided only 123 original jurisdiction cases.[69] During the next ten years another

---

66. Marbury v. Madison, 5 U.S. (1 Cranch) 137, 173 (1803); Wisconsin v. Pelican Ins. Co., 127 U.S. 265, 300 (1888); *see generally* 12 J. MOORE, H. BENDIX & B. RINGLE, MOORE'S FEDERAL PRACTICE ¶ 350.01[2] at 3-5 to 3-6 (2d ed. 1982) [hereinafter cited as J. MOORE].

67. 28 U.S.C. § 1251 (1982).

68. 5 U.S. (1 Cranch) 137, 174 (1803).

69. Note, *The Original Jurisdiction of the United States Supreme Court,* 11 STAN. L. REV. 665, 665 (1959).

thirty-three cases were docketed,[70] but no official court statistics have been kept since 1970. The bulk of these cases fall under § 1251(a), which concerns suits between states.

1. Suits Between States

This is the sole category where, by statute, the original jurisdiction is exclusive. The need for the Supreme Court to adjudicate controversies between states is obvious. If states were independent sovereigns bearing the same relation to each other as do different nations, disputes impossible to solve through negotiation might be resolved by war. But members of a federal system are not allowed to wage civil wars. States are therefore deemed to have consented to adjudication by a neutral body, the Supreme Court, in order to preserve domestic peace.[71] Because of this hypothetical assent, the eleventh amendment ban against federal court suits against states is inapplicable to original Supreme Court jurisdiction.[72] The eleventh amendment prohibition against federal court suits against states is discussed in Chapter 3.

Cases concerning conflicts over state boundaries and the use of interstate rivers and lakes constitute most of the disputes in this category.[73] But other types of cases include: suits by one state to enforce the financial obligations assumed by another state;[74] suits to enjoin the enforcement of another state's law, which allegedly injures interstate commerce and the public welfare of the first state;[75] suits to determine the domicile of a decedent and thus the right to estate taxes.[76]

Two important limitations on this category of suits must be noted. First, when a state brings an action against a municipality (or some

---

70. Annual Report, Director of the Administrative Office of the U.S. Courts, 204 (1970).

71. C. WRIGHT, *supra* note 6, § 109 at 766.

72. *See* Rhode Island v. Massachusetts, 37 U.S. (12 Pet.) 657, 631 (1838); United States v. Texas, 143 U.S. 621, 646 (1892).

73. *See* Note, *The Original Jurisdiction of the United States Supreme Court,* 11 STAN. L. REV. 665, 708-18 (listing all cases between states in which the Supreme Court wrote an opinion).

74. *See* South Dakota v. North Carolina, 192 U.S. 286, 312 (1904) (Court has jurisdiction over suit between states to determine status of a bond).

75. Pennsylvania v. West Virginia, 262 U.S. 544 (1923) (Pennsylvania may enjoin West Virginia from withdrawing natural gas from an established current of commerce between the states).

76. *See* Texas v. Florida, 306 U.S. 398 (1939) (dispute between states over domicile is justiciable even though the estate's funds were not exhausted). *Cf.* California v. Texas II, 457 U.S. 164, 170 (1982) (Powell, J., joined by Marshall, Rehnquist & Stevens, J.J., dissenting) ("[t]he mere possibility of inconsistent state determinations of domicile, resulting in a still more remote possibility of the estate's being insufficient to satisfy the competing claims, simply does not give rise to a case or controversy in the Constitutional sense"); *see also* ch. 13, sec. IIB for a discussion of this problem.

other political subdivision) of another state, the suit is not part of the Supreme Court's exclusive jurisdiction, but of its jurisdiction concurrent with the lower federal courts under § 1251(b)(3). For the purposes of the statute, this is no longer a suit between states, because the municipality is treated as if it were a citizen of the state.[77] Second, a state may bring an action only when it, as a sovereign entity, is the real party in interest. A state may not use its name to bring a suit if the intended beneficiaries are private interests or individual citizens, nor to collude with its citizens to circumvent the eleventh amendment.[78]

2. Suits Between the United States and a State

Section 1251(b) grants original but not exclusive jurisdiction to the Supreme Court over actions by the United States against a state and actions by the United States where the United States has waived its immunity from suit. As with suits between states, the eleventh amendment does not protect the state from suit even though it has not explicitly given its consent. Consent is assumed to flow from participation in the federal system.[79] More surprisingly, perhaps, this is so even when the suit is brought in a district court pursuant to a congressional grant of concurrent jurisdiction.[80] Indeed, most actions of this type originate in the district courts because of the Supreme Court's tendency to use its original jurisdiction sparingly, especially when the plaintiff has an alternate forum.[81]

3. Suits by a State Against Citizens of Another or Against Aliens

Here, too, by statute the Supreme Court's jurisdiction, although original,[82] is not exclusive. If Congress has conferred jurisdiction on the lower federal courts or if an action is subject to federal common law, suits of this category may be brought in the district courts.[83] As a general proposition it is in the interest of convenience, efficiency, and

---

77. See Illinois v. City of Milwaukee, 406 U.S. 91 (1972) (Illinois cannot invoke Court's original jurisdiction to sue subdivision of another state).

78. See New Hampshire v. Louisiana, 108 U.S. 76 (1883) (state cannot create controversy with another state by assuming prosecution of debts owed by second state to citizens of first state).

79. See, e.g., Monaco v. Mississippi, 292 U.S. 313, 329 (1934).

80. See, e.g., United States v. California, 297 U.S. 175, 187 (1936).

81. See Illinois v. City of Milwaukee, 406 U.S. 91, 93-94 (1972) (Court will use original jurisdiction sparingly so its appellate work will not suffer).

82. Chisholm v. Georgia, 2 U.S. (2 Dall.) 419 (1793) (Supreme Court possesses original jurisdiction over a diversity action brought against one state by a citizen of another).

83. See 12 J. MOORE, supra note 66, ¶ 356.01 at 3-62 — 3-63 (suit based on federal common law).

justice that the Supreme Court withhold its exercise of original jurisdiction and rely upon federal and state trial courts which are accustomed to, and equipped for, lengthy trials of factual issues.

For example, in *Ohio v. Wyandotte Chemicals Corp.*,[84] the Supreme
Court declined to hear a case over which it admittedly possessed jurisdiction because it thought the complex environmental issues could be
better addressed in a district court. In large measure, the Court's refusal to take jurisdiction when there is another adequate forum is
predicated upon the belief that its time and resources are better used to
address appeals:

> We seek to exercise our jurisdiction sparingly and are particu-
> larly reluctant to take jurisdiction of a suit where the plaintiff has
> another adequate forum in which to settle his claim.[85]

Other judicially crafted limitations on the Court's exercise of its
original jurisdiction have developed to deal with cases in this category.
For example, the Court has held that its original jurisdiction applies
only to civil suits and thus does not extend to the enforcement of a
state's penal laws.[86] Moreover, just as there generally must be complete
diversity of the parties for federal district court jurisdiction to exist,[87] if
a citizen of the plaintiff state is joined as an indispensable defendant
with a citizen of another state original jurisdiction is defeated.[88]

The Supreme Court has occasionally allowed states to sue as parens
patriae to protect the economic and natural resources of the state as a
whole. Such suits may be between states,[89] or between one state and
citizens of other states.[90] Parens patriae suits do not extend to actions
against the United States because it is presumed that the federal government stands in the parens patriae relationship to all its citizens.
Nonetheless, this limitation has not been observed in at least two cases
in which U.S. attorney generals have been treated as though they were
citizens of another state so as to allow for original hearing in the
Supreme Court of challenges to federal voting rights statutes.[91]

---

84. 401 U.S. 493 (1971).

85. United States v. Nevada, 412 U.S. 534, 538 (1973).

86. *See, e.g.,* Oklahoma ex rel. West v. Gulf, C. & S.F., 220 U.S. 290 (1911).

87. Strawbridge v. Curtiss, 7 U.S. 267 (1806).

88. *See, e.g.,* Georgia v. Pennsylvania R.R., 324 U.S. 439, 463 (1945) (because defendants alleged to be citizens of plaintiff state are not indispensable, Court does not lose
jurisdiction).

89. *See, e.g.,* Missouri v. Illinois, 180 U.S. 208 (1901) (Missouri is proper party to
represent its citizens in suit to prevent Illinois from discharging sewage into Mississippi River).

90. *E.g.,* Georgia v. Pennsylvania R.R., 324 U.S. 439 (1945) (state could file antitrust
action alleging that activities of defendant railroads retarded state's economic growth).

91. *See* South Carolina v. Katzenbach, 383 U.S. 301 (1966); Oregon v. Mitchell, 400
U.S. 112 (1970).

4. *Suits Affecting Ambassadors, Public Ministers and Consuls*

In the first Judiciary Act exclusive original jurisdiction was retained only for cases against ambassadors, although not for cases brought by ambassadors.[92] The statute was amended in 1978, however, so that now the Supreme Court's jurisdiction over all cases involving ambassadors, public ministers, consuls and vice consuls is non-exclusive.[93] The constitutional allocation of original jurisdiction to the Supreme Court probably reflected the concern that representatives of other nations be treated with great respect.[94] That respect is also indicated by 28 U.S.C. §§ 1351, 1364 which give the district courts, exclusive of state courts, jurisdiction of civil actions against consuls and vice consuls.

Cases have so rarely been brought under this constitutional provision that this discussion can be limited to several brief points. First, diplomatic immunity is the primary bar to bringing a suit under this section.[95] Second, while suits may be brought against the defendant as an individual, they may not be brought against him or her as an agent of his or her government.[96] And finally, this section applies only to representatives of foreign nations assigned to the United States; it is not applicable to actions against our diplomatic representatives stationed abroad.[97]

B. APPELLATE JURISDICTION

The cases which the Supreme Court hears in its capacity as an initial trial forum, under the exercise of its original jurisdiction, form only a small fraction of its caseload. The Court would in fact be ill-equipped to hear very many cases as an original matter, because juries were very early abandoned as an aspect of Supreme Court practice, and because the Justices are familiar with rules of evidence and procedure only as a secondary, piecemeal matter. Far more important, therefore, is the Court's power to review the decisions of other courts, both state and federal. As a practical matter, the Supreme Court sits almost exclusively in an appellate capacity despite the constitutional vesting of both an original and appellate jurisdiction. The Court's appellate jurisdiction can conceptually be divided into two types of appeals, review of federal cases and review of state cases. Each of these generates its own set of rules and problems.

---

92. Judiciary Act of 1789, ch. 20, § 13, 1 Stat. 73, 80. See also C. WRIGHT *supra* note 6, § 110 at 773 (in cases brought by § 8, ambassador Supreme Court had original, but not exclusive jurisdiction).

93. Diplomatic Relations Act of 1978, Pub. L. No. 95-393, 92 Stat. 808, 810.

94. *See* THE FEDERALIST No. 81, at 487 (A. Hamilton) (C. Rossiter ed. 1961).

95. *See* J. MOORE, *supra* note 66, § 353.01 at 3-49.

96. *See* Jones v. Le Tombe, 3 U.S. (3 Dall.) 384, 384-85 (1798).

97. *See* Ex parte Gruber, 269 U.S. 302, 303 (1925).

1. Review of Federal Court Decisions

Cases within the federal system normally originate in the federal district courts, from which they may be appealed to the courts of appeals, and thence to the Supreme Court. The Court's federal appellate jurisdiction thus consists predominately of cases from the courts of appeals. However, the courts of appeals have not been the only possible source of federal appeals, and although jurisdiction over their decisions is currently the most important category of federal appeals, direct jurisdiction over district court decisions must also be discussed below. One principle which governs both types of appeals is that in each area the only important source of jurisdictional rules is statutory, rather than constitutional. When cases originate from within the federal system, it may be safely assumed that constitutionally adequate federal jurisdiction has already been proven, because all cases within the original jurisdiction of the federal courts also fall within the appellate jurisdiction of the Supreme Court under article III.

a. Decisions by the Courts of Appeals

The Supreme Court's jurisdiction over decisions by the courts of appeals is governed chiefly by § 1254. Section 1254 establishes three types of review: review by writ of certiorari, review by appeal, and partial review by certification of questions.

First, under § 1254(1), the Court has certiorari jurisdiction over any civil or criminal case before a court of appeals. This is an extremely broad provision that vests a large, completely discretionary jurisdiction in the Court. The statute provides that "any party" to such a case may petition the Court for a writ of certiorari, and that the Court may grant such a writ at any time before or after a judgment is rendered by the court of appeals. The provision has been interpreted to permit the Court to deny or grant jurisdiction for whatever reasons it chooses. The Supreme Court Rules describe six factors that may induce the Court to grant certiorari, such as a split among the circuits on the particular question at issue.[98] Although it is common practice for the Court to announce in a decision on the merits the reasons underlying a grant of certiorari, it is under no obligation to explain why it refused to hear a case and it rarely does so. One exception to this norm is the practice, which has increased in recent years, of writing dissents from denials of

---

98. Sup. Ct. Rule 17.1(a).

certiorari, which may shed light on the Court's reason for declining jurisdiction.[99] As a matter of Supreme Court practice, however, petitions for certiorari are voted on in closed sessions, and require four Justices to vote to grant certiorari for a case to be placed on the Court's docket. Although the result of the vote on the petition is disclosed, the names of the Justices voting in favor of or against it are never revealed, and their reasons for voting to grant certiorari may in fact be based on widely varying factors.[100] Thus, there is often no single reason for denying certiorari, and lawyers seeking Supreme Court review under its discretionary certiorari jurisdiction have difficulty figuring out how to convince the Court to take their case. This difficulty is enhanced by the enormous number of petitions for certiorari. These number annually in the thousands, compared with the far smaller number of cases in which the Court hears argument, (about 180) or decides summarily (about 100).[101]

On the other side of the discretionary nature of the Court's certiorari jurisdiction, it should be noted, is an important balancing principle: a denial of certiorari has no precedential effect. In other words, the Court's denial of certiorari does not mean that it necessarily agrees with the merits of the lower court's decision or that it would not exercise the power to hear the identical issue in a later case. This is an important corollary to the vesting of such broad discretion to decline jurisdiction. Were such denials to be given precedental effect, the Court would effectively be forced (or allowed) to make law without ever hearing argument, having plenary consideration of the issues involved, or writing an opinion. There are a growing number of cases decided by the Court without oral argument, or with one paragraph per curiam opinions or no opinions at all, but such summary discussions have nevertheless been consciously considered by the full Court.[102] Moreover, such decisions are themselves a matter of great controversy and debate.[103]

---

99. In one case, the Supreme Court has even cited a dissent from a denial of certiorari in support of its decision, United States v. Kras, 409 U.S. 434, 442-43 (1973). The dissent was, rightly, sharply critical of this practice. *Id.* at 460-61 (Marshall, J., dissenting).

100. *See* Brown v. Allen, 344 U.S. 443, 492 (1953) (Frankfurter, J., dissenting) (discussing why Court denies certiorari).

101. *See, e.g.,* 54 U.S.L.W. 3038 (July 30, 1985) (summarizing caseload statistics for three prior Supreme Court terms).

102. *See generally* Mandel v. Bradley, 432 U.S. 173, 176 (1977) (discussing effect of Court's summary actions).

103. *See, e.g.,* Colorado Springs Amusements, Ltd. v. Rizzo, 428 U.S. 913, 917-18 (1976) (Brennan, J., dissenting from denial of certiorari) (arguing that lower federal courts should be free to disregard Court's summary decisions).

The second type of review of court of appeals decisions under § 1254 is the Court's jurisdiction under § 1254(2) for review by appeal, rather than certiorari, in a few, specified circumstances. Appeal is theoretically mandatory on the court. This aspect of the Court's jurisdiction is far more limited than review under § 1254(1), because the statute is circumscribed both by the language of the provision and by restrictive Supreme Court interpretations. Such review is available only where a state statute has been held by the court of appeals to be invalid as repugnant to federal law. A state "statute," as used in § 1254(2), has been interpreted to include municipal ordinances, state administrative agency orders, and other enactments to which the state gives the force of law.[104] The Supreme Court has recently emphasized, however, that there are limits to the availability of appeals under § 1254(2), by refusing for example to treat a collective bargaining agreement between a school district and teachers union as such a "statute."[105]

A further limitation to the review available under § 1254(2) is the statutory restriction of the scope of such review to only the federal questions presented. This is a significant restriction, because it precludes review of the complete case in any case involving issues of both state and federal law despite the extension of original federal jurisdiction to cover such state-law issues under ancillary and pendent jurisdiction, and despite the absence of any such restriction in the Court's certiorari jurisdiction. For those reasons, one practitioner recommends that attorneys in such cases seek review by certiorari rather than by appeal, assigning as one of the reasons why the Court should grant certiorari the fact that this avenue was the only method of appealing the whole case.[106] In general, the limitation advances principles of federalism by ensuring review of federal invalidation of state statutes while simultaneously proscribing repetitive federal interpretation of purely state law, and attaches a cost to discourage excessive invocation of appeal, considered mandatory on the Court, as opposed to certiorari review, which is discretionary.

Interestingly, in *City of Mesquite v. Aladdin's Castle,* the Supreme Court has recently interpreted § 1254(2) to place the courts of appeals in effectively the same position as state supreme courts. The Court there applied the constitutional doctrine of "independent and adequate state ground" developed in the context of review of state appeals

---

104. *See* J. MOORE, *supra* note 66, ¶ 435.01[1] at 6-52 n.5.

105. Perry Education Ass'n v. Perry Local Educator's Ass'n, 460 U.S. 37, 42-43 (1983).

106. C. WRIGHT, *supra* note 6, § 106 at 734.

(which will be discussed later) to federal question jurisdiction under § 1254(2).[107] Under this rule, not only is Supreme Court review limited to the federal questions presented, but if there are state grounds in the decision that would be sufficient to sustain the decision below, independently of the federal grounds, jurisdiction of the whole case including both state and federal aspects must be declined.[108] However, although such a rule may make sense in the context of state appeals, in which the need for deference to state supreme courts is clear, it is not as clear that it should be applied to bar Supreme Court review of federal interpretations of federal law, where there is no similar constitutional limitation of jurisdiction involved, and where the language of § 1254(2) does not itself compel such an interpretation. Similarly, in both situations the Court has cited as a rationale the need to avoid issuing advisory opinions,[109] but it is not clear that reviewing state-law issues decided by courts of appeals under its appeals jurisdiction is any different from such a decision under its certiorari jurisdiction which is not considered an advisory opinion. At any rate, the problem provides a clear illustration of the potential consequences that flow from opting for an appeal under § 1254(2), rather than for certiorari under § 1254(1).

It is also interesting to consider *Aladdin's Castle* in light of the Supreme Court's general willingness to treat erroneously taken appeals as petitions for certiorari despite the express provision under § 1254(2) that taking an appeal shall preclude review by writ of certiorari.[110] Although there may be a difference between establishing the *existence* of appeals jurisdiction and defining the *scope* of review under that jurisdiction, such a case could also be conceived of as possessing a jurisdictional defect as an appeal and thus eligible for certiorari jurisdiction. Clearly, there is a great potential for manipulation of these technical and complicated jurisdictional requirements to reach different results. Such manipulation becomes extremely problematic, however, if one considers another important difference between appeals and certiorari review. Denial of certiorari does not, because of its discretionary nature, set a precedent, but a dismissal of an appeal, or summary affirmance of the decision below, does.[111] Such a disposition, often for "want of a substantial federal question," is a decision on the

---

107. 455 U.S. 283 (1982).

108. *See infra* ch. 8, sec. IV.

109. *See Aladdin's Castle,* 455 U.S. at 294-95; Herb v. Pitcairn, 324 U.S. 117, 126 (1945).

110. *See* C. WRIGHT, *supra* note 6, § 106 at 733-34.

111. *See* Hicks v. Miranda, 422 U.S. 332, 344 (1975) (summary action is decision by Court on merits which lower courts must consider).

merits because appeals jurisdiction theoretically is mandatory once established. The Court's increasing practice of summarily dismissing or affirming such appeals, which has been described as its practice in most such cases,[112] has the effect of making the Court's exercise of its appeals jurisdiction as discretionary as its certiorari jurisdiction. However, given the precedential effect of the Court's dispositions of appeals, this practice is troubling.

The third avenue of Supreme Court review of decisions by courts of appeals under § 1254 is the certification process under § 1254(3). Under this provision, the courts of appeals may at any time in either a civil or criminal case certify specific questions of law to the Supreme Court for instructions. If the Supreme Court desires, it may use the occasion of certification to require the entire record of the case to be brought up for review, and § 1254(3) thus may become a channel for plenary review rather than for review of a limited question.[113] Like appeal under § 1254(2), and unlike discretionary certiorari jurisdiction, certification is considered to be theoretically obligatory on the Supreme Court.[114] Despite the long history of certification as a review mechanism, it nonetheless can be criticized on two main grounds. In theory at least, certification could allow the courts of appeals to determine the content of the Supreme Court's docket by deciding which questions deserve to be certified, and it requires the decision of important legal questions without the aid of a concrete factual record.[115] In practice, however, the Supreme Court has available to it so many technical grounds on which it may find certification to have been improper, such as that the case presents overly vague questions or mixed questions of law and fact, that the jurisdictional grant is also treated effectively as a discretionary one.[116]

Aside from review under § 1254, there is also, finally, the potential for limited Supreme Court review of decisions by courts of appeals under § 1252, which applies where "any court of the United States" has held an act of Congress unconstitutional in any civil case to which the United States is a party. This provision, however, is narrow, and in general has been more often applied where parties have sought direct Supreme Court review of a district court decision, without an intervening court of appeals decision. Such direct review forms the subject of the next section.

---

112. *See* 16 C. WRIGHT, A. MILLER & E. COOPER, FEDERAL PRACTICE AND PROCEDURE § 4003 at 501 (1977).

113. *See* 28 U.S.C. § 1254(3) (1982); Sup. Ct. R. 24.2.

114. *See generally* 12 J. MOORE, *supra* note 66, § 405.01 at 5-3 — 5-5 (discussing Court's shrinking areas of obligatory jurisdiction).

115. *See* C. WRIGHT, *supra* note 6, § 106 at 735. [1983 ed.]

116. *See generally* 12 J. MOORE, *supra* note 66, § 436.01 at 6-61 — 6-67 (discussing ways in which Court may find certification improper).

b. District Court Decisions

As an historical matter, direct Supreme Court review of district court decisions was for a time seen as highly desirable in certain cases in which the issues were thought to be of such public importance as to require prompt review, of right, by the Supreme Court.[117] Congress therefore enacted a number of jurisdictional provisions for direct appeal. Experience with such provisions, however, proved the unwisdom of the Court's deciding cases without the benefit of a court of appeals decision. Such cases clogged the Court's docket by increasing the proportion of mandatory appeals and complicating review decisions. Moreover, it was pointed out that, where necessary, prompt review could be had under existing jurisdictional provisions by writ of certiorari under § 1254(1) once a final district court decision simply was docketed in the court of appeals. Congress has acted to repeal most of the provisions for direct appeal of district court decisions, and has circumscribed the scope of the remaining provisions.[118] There are essentially three such provisions left.

First, under § 1252, decisions of district courts holding unconstitutional an act of Congress in a case involving the United States as a party may be appealed by "any party," of right, to the Supreme Court. Although the court must have invalidated the act rather than upheld it, it is enough that the act's constitutionality was raised in any manner, or that the act was found to be unconstitutional as applied rather than on its face.[119] Similarly, although the provision only applies where the government is a party, rather than in purely private litigation, the government may intervene of right at any point in a case raising the constitutionality of federal legislation.[120] The United States thus need not have been a party originally to involve the Supreme Court's jurisdiction under § 1252, but may do so by subsequent intervention. This statute has seen increasing use in recent years, but has been criticized as an "anachronism" in its provision of appeal by right.[121]

Second, under § 1253, Congress provided for direct appeal, of right, by any party from a decision by a three-judge court granting or deny-

---

117. *E.g.*, Expediting Act of 1903, ch. 544, 32 Stat. 823, 823 (direct review in antitrust case); Criminal Appeals Act of 1907, ch. 2564, 34 Stat. 1246 (direct review in certain criminal cases) (codified as amended at 18 U.S.C. § 3731 (1982)).

118. *See generally* C. WRIGHT, *supra* note 6, § 105 at 726-730.

119. International Ladies' Garment Workers' Union v. Donnelly Garment Co., 304 U.S. 243, 249 (1938) (constitutionality can be raised in any manner); United States v. American Friends Serv. Comm., 419 U.S. 7, 9 n.4 (1974) (appeal from district court decision holding statute unconstitutional as applied).

120. *See* 28 U.S.C. § 2403(a) (1982) (United States can intervene where constitutionality of federal statute "affecting the public interest" is challenged); Fleming v. Rhodes, 331 U.S. 100, 103-04 (1947).

121. C. WRIGHT, *supra* note 6.

ing an injunction in a civil case. Although § 1253 still stands, it has become essentially irrelevant because of Congress' virtual abolition in the mid-1970s of three-judge courts,[122] which had been used to decide certain potentially controversial commercial cases and cases seeking to restrain the enforcement of a federal statute.

Finally, as noted earlier, under § 1254(1) direct review of district court decisions is provided, in fact if not in name, by the provision for granting certiorari at any time before or after a court of appeals judgment, which allows the Supreme Court to review a case before the court of appeals has begun any substantial proceedings. This practice is used, however, only in exceptional cases, such as the *Nixon*[123] case or *Iranian Assets*[124] case, in which the need for an immediate Supreme Court decision is especially pressing, or the issues especially important. In fact, the Supreme Court in its rules has established a presumption that it will not grant certiorari before a final judgment of the court of appeals.[125]

2. Review of State Court Decisions

The Constitution does not expressly vest the Supreme Court with jurisdiction to decide appeals from state courts, but this power was recognized from the start as an essential element of the Court's jurisdiction. Were the Supreme Court to lack the power to review cases in which state courts interpreted federal law, the supremacy of federal law would be undermined. In fact, in the debates at the Constitutional Convention, the question was not whether review over state appeals would be vested in the Court, but rather whether a system of lower federal courts would be established at all.[126] The Court's appellate jurisdiction, constitutionally described as extending to all cases within the article III judicial power that are not already part of the Court's original jurisdiction, was understood to include review of state court decisions, and Congress included in § 25 of the first Judiciary Act a jurisdictional provision conferring such a power of review.[127]

---

122. Act of August 12, 1976, Pub. L. No. 94-381, 90 Stat. 1119, 1119 (repealing statute requiring three-judge court when injunction was sought because of alleged unconstitutionality of any federal statute).

123. United States v. Nixon, 418 U.S. 683 (1974) (President must turn over documents sought under subpoena).

124. Dames & Moore v. Regan, 453 U.S. 654 (1981) (upholding presidential orders establishing Iranian Claims Tribunal).

125. *See* Sup. Ct. R. 18 (Court will grant certiorari before judgment of court of appeals only upon showing that case is of "imperative public importance").

126. *See* HART & WECHSLER, *supra* note 27, at 11-12, 23.

127. Judiciary Act of 1789, ch. 20, § 25, 1 Stat. 73, 85-87; *see* Martin v. Hunters Lessee, 14 U.S. (1 Wheat.) 304, 347-48 (1816) (upholding Court's power to review state court decision).

This power, however, has historically been carefully circumscribed by principles of federalism. Until 1914, such review could only be had where a state court had struck down a federal act, or had upheld a state act against a claim based on federal law.[128] Even after review was broadened to include cases in which the state court had upheld as well as ruled against the federal claim, several important limitations on the jurisdiction were retained. These remain part of § 1257, the jurisdictional provision which today governs Supreme Court review of state court decisions.

3. Section 1257

Under § 1257, there is a division between appeals and certiorari jurisdiction analogous to that contained in § 1254 governing review of federal decisions. As in that area, the addition of certiorari jurisdiction reflects the historical movement toward giving the Court greater control over its own docket. In the area of state decisions, however, there are also several important limitations that apply to the review of all state decisions.

First, under § 1257, review is limited to judgments rendered by the "highest court of a State in which a decision could be had." This rule most often refers to the state supreme court, but it is not necessarily so. One of the most important cases testing this principle allowed review of a judgment of a local police court, where the fine imposed was so low that no review was available in any other state court.[129] In general, the rule requires a party to exhaust his or her appeals within the state system before seeking Supreme Court review. In that sense, it is very similar to the exhaustion requirement that applies to state prisoners' habeas corpus petitions under § 2254;[130] they must prove that they have exhausted their state remedies before they are entitled to federal review. The rationale in both cases is the same: such a rule promotes federalism by preserving the integrity of state judicial systems and allowing state courts to correct the mistakes of state officials in the first instance. In this respect, the "highest court" rule differs significantly from the Supreme Court's treatment of federal decisions. Not only is this Supreme Court review possible, if limited, for decisions both of federal trial and appellate courts, but the rationale for a presumption in favor of awaiting a final court of appeals judgment is very different from the state-federal case, relying on considerations of judicial economy rather than political deference.

---

128. *See* 12 J. MOORE, *supra* note 66, ¶ 400.06[5] at 4-63.
129. Thompson v. City of Louisville, 362 U.S. 199 (1960).
130. *See infra* ch. 5, sec. IIIB.

A second express limitation built into § 1257 is the requirement that the state decision be a "final judgment." This has been interpreted to preclude review, even where the federal issue has been decided, if "anything further remains to be determined by a State court."[131] The purpose of the rule is to avoid piecemeal review of federal issues by the Supreme Court: the argument is that where there remain further proceedings in the state system, such as a remand from the state supreme court to the trial court, it could affect the federal questions before the Court, or raise others. Thus, Supreme Court review will normally await completion of all state proceedings, unless purely ministerial. There are certain recent exceptions to this "final judgments" rule, however, recognized by *Cox Broadcasting Corp. v. Cohn.*[132] The Court will take review, even where state proceedings remain, in four situations: first, where there are further proceedings yet to occur in the state courts, but the federal issue is conclusive or the outcome of these proceedings preordained; second, where the federal issue has been decided by the highest court in the state and will require review regardless of the outcome of any further proceedings; third, where the federal issue has been finally decided and awaiting the outcome of the state proceedings on the merits will mean that review of the federal issue cannot be had; and finally, where a refusal immediately to review the state court decision might seriously erode federal policy.[133] This last exception is potentially extremely broad, but the Supreme Court recently refused to "permit the fourth exception to swallow the rule,"[134] declining to apply it to a claim of selective prosecution under a state obscenity law.[135]

A third set of limitations on all cases brought under § 1257 relates to the constitutional requirement, also reflected in the wording of the statute, that review include only the federal, and not any state, questions decided by the state courts.[136] This reflects the principle of comity, which requires that state courts be allowed to have the final word on interpretations of state law. The Supreme Court's jurisdiction is only over the federal aspects of the state decision, rather than over the whole case. This limitation parallels the restriction on Supreme Court review by appeal of federal court of appeals decisions striking down state statutes, which are limited under § 1254(2) to the federal questions presented. This means that purely state-law questions are

---

131. Flynt v. Ohio, 451 U.S. 619, 620 (1981) (quoting Radio Station WOW, Inc. v. Johnson, 326 U.S. 120, 124 (1945)).
132. 420 U.S. 469 (1975).
133. *Id.* at 479-83.
134. *Flynt,* 451 U.S. at 622.
135. *Id.*
136. Murdock v. City of Memphis, 87 U.S. (20 Wheat.) 590, 631 (1875).

rarely addressed by the Supreme Court, because review of such issues is only possible at all through certiorari review of a federal diversity case or under pendent jurisdiction. Even then, under the doctrine of *Erie Railroad*,[137] the same principles of comity require that the Supreme Court merely seek to ascertain how the highest court of the state would have decided the case. Together, these principles assure the integrity of state law, and leave the Supreme Court to concentrate on federal issues.

As far as § 1257 goes, the federal question limitation has certain important implications. It has been read by the Court to require not only that there be a federal question, but also that the federal question be a "substantial" one;[138] hence the increasing practice of dismissal of such appeals "for want of a substantial federal question" which was noted earlier.[139] Moreover, not only must the federal question be a "substantial" one, but it must also have been timely raised below, or the Court is held to lack jurisdiction.[140] The timeliness of the issue is determined by reference to the state's procedural rules. Unless these rules amount to an attempt to evade the federal question, or permit no fair opportunity to assert it, a failure to comply will bar Supreme Court review.[141] The timeliness issue is also related to another rule developed by interpretation of § 1257, which holds that the federal issue must have been "pressed or passed upon" in the state court proceedings to vest the Supreme Court with jurisdiction.[142] Both rules seek to ensure that the federal question was adequately presented in the state system, thereby serving the dual functions of creating the necessary record for review and giving the state court the chance to construe state statutes so as to avoid the federal constitutional challenge.

The Court has not always found it easy to tell if the federal question was pressed or passed upon below, because it may be difficult to tell whether an issue presented is merely an acceptable "enlargement" of the one mentioned in the initial pleadings, or represents an entirely new question, presented at Supreme Court review for the first time.

---

137. *See* ch. 6, *infra.*

138. *See* C. WRIGHT, *supra* note 6, § 107 at 743-44.

139. *See supra* sec. IIA3; *see also* Note, *The Insubstantial Federal Questions,* 62 HARV. L. REV. 488 (1949) (discussion of Court's standard for determining if federal question is "substantial").

140. New York ex rel. Bryant v. Zimmerman, 278 U.S. 63, 67 (1928).

141. Edelman v. California, 344 U.S. 357 (1953) (Court cannot consider challenges to state statutes which were not presented properly). *But see* ch. 8, sec. V (converse *Erie* and federal defenses).

142. *See* Illinois v. Gates, 462 U.S. 213, 218-220 (1983) (discussing background of "pressed or passed upon" rule).

The Supreme Court has on one recent occasion interpreted this rule extremely narrowly, in the case of *Illinois v. Gates*,[143] where the Court addressed the question of whether an exclusionary rule issue was properly "pressed or passed upon below." The State had challenged an exclusionary rule claim, although not on the grounds that the exclusionary rule ought to be modified, and the state court applied the exclusionary rule. On appeal, the Supreme Court found that it lacked jurisdiction, defining the specific issue as one of whether the exclusionary rule should be modified, and held that the state had failed to press this specific defense, and the courts below had not clearly considered it.[144] This case may be a strained interpretation of the rule explainable by reference to the specific constitutional issue involved there, which the Court described as one of "unusual significance."[145]

A final limitation that applies to all Supreme Court review of state court decisions is the "independent and adequate state ground" rule.[146] Under this rule, where a state court judgment rests on two grounds, one federal and one state, and the state ground alone would be adequate to support the judgment, independent of the federal claim, that judgment may not be reviewed by the Supreme Court, even as to the federal elements. Although the rule does not specifically appear in the language of § 1257, it has been read into the statute as an important part of the constitutional federal question limitation:[147] it means that not only must the federal question have been clearly presented to and considered by the state court under § 1257, but that court must also have clearly intended to rest its judgment squarely on that element of federal law. The rule is said to stem from the Supreme Court's obligation to avoid issuing advisory opinions.[148] Since the state court in such cases could still render the same judgment based on state law even after the Supreme Court corrected its interpretation of federal law, such review amounts to mere advice to the state court, in violation of the Court's role under article III.

Just what constitutes an "independent and adequate state ground," however, and how the Supreme Court is to ascertain whether one exists, has not always been completely clear. The adequacy requirement means that the state law ruling must have fair and substantial support in the facts, and a new rule cannot have been invented for the occasion, nor can the state rule be so strict that it interferes unduly

---

143. 462 U.S. 213 (1983).
144. *Id.* at 220-21.
145. *Id.* at 224.
146. *See* Herb v. Pitcairn, 324 U.S. 117, 125-28 (1945).
147. *See* C. WRIGHT, *supra* note 6, § 107 at 745. [1983 ed.]
148. *See Herb*, 324 U.S. at 126.

with the presentation of federal questions. At one extreme, the Court once held that a state procedural rule may not be adequate to bar review unless it serves a "legitimate state interest."[149] In general, however, evenhandedly applied state procedural rules and state substantive law claims will be found to be "adequate" state grounds without serious scrutiny of the interests that they serve.[150]

Similarly, the independence requirement serves to ensure that only judgments clearly resting on a separate state ground will bar review. Thus, where the state issue is clearly set out as an alternative basis for the holding, jurisdiction is barred. On the other hand, where a state claim could have been, but was not, relied upon as an alternative basis for the ruling, jurisdiction still exists.[151] The same is true if the state court felt compelled to construe state law in light of federal constitutional considerations, or if the state ground is so interwoven with the federal ground as not to be independent.[152]

In practice, the most difficult issue has not been that of defining "adequate" or "independent," but rather ascertaining whether such grounds exist where it is not clearly set out in the opinion below. Frequently, opinions are unclear about their real rationale. In the past, the Court has used a number of methods. At times, it has dismissed the writ of certiorari where the grounds of decision were at all unclear.[153] At others, it has remanded cases to the state court for clarification of the grounds on which the decision was meant to rest.[154] Yet another method has been that of simply reexamining the state-law issues on review to determine whether they, and not the federal ground, provided the actual basis for decision.[155] All of these have been criticized, and in *Michigan v. Long*[156] the Court sought to supply some "doctrinal consistency" to the issue, establishing a new, single approach to applying the rule. Under *Michigan v. Long,* where the state court decision "fairly appears to rest primarily on federal law, or to be interwoven with the federal law, and when the adequacy and indepen-

---

149. Henry v. Mississippi, 379 U.S. 443, 447 (1965).

150. *See generally* C. WRIGHT, *supra* note 6, § 107 at 751.

151. *See* Steele v. Louisville & N. R.R., 323 U.S. 192, 197 n.1 (1944).

152. Zacchini v. Scrippo-Howard Broadcasting Co., 433 U.S. 562, 568 (1977) (state court compelled to interpret statute in particular way); St. Martin Evangelical Lutheran Church v. South Dakota, 451 U.S. 772, 780 n.9 (1981) (state statute incorporating federal land).

153. *See, e.g.,* Lynch v. New York, 293 U.S. 52 (1934).

154. *See, e.g.,* Minnesota v. National Tea Co., 309 U.S. 551 (1940); Herb v. Pitcairn, 324 U.S. 117 (1945).

155. *See, e.g.,* Texas v. Brown, 460 U.S. 730, 733 n.1 (1983) (plurality opinion); Oregon v. Kennedy, 456 U.S. 667, 670-71 (1982).

156. 463 U.S. 1032 (1983).

dence of any possible state law ground is not clear from the face of the opinion,"[157] the Court will assume the decision was based on federal law. The decision thus establishes a presumption that cases involving both federal and state grounds were decided based on federal law, unless the state court expressly indicates otherwise in its opinion. Such a rule, in the Court's view, serves principles of federalism by providing state judges a "clearer opportunity to develop state jurisprudence unimpeded by federal interference" while also preserving the "integrity of federal law."[158] This rule serves as a message to state courts to clarify the basis of their holdings at a stage before review is sought, thereby saving time-consuming procedures and analysis.

Finally, as far as the division, under § 1257, of state cases into appeals and certiorari jurisdiction, the technical language of the statute governs. Appeals may be brought under § 1257(1) where a state court has found a federal law invalid, and under § 1257(2) where it has upheld a state law against a federal challenge. Otherwise, all state cases involving federal questions, including those that may be appealed, may be heard on a petition for a writ of certiorari under § 1257(3). All of the strategic advantages and disadvantages of seeking one type of review or another, discussed in connection with Supreme Court review of federal cases, also apply here, and the same general observation may be made of a tendency to merge the two types of jurisdiction into a single, discretionary one.[159]

IV. The Case or Controversy Requirement

As explained in the previous sections of this chapter, all federal courts are subject to jurisdictional limitations. This is true in the context of separation of powers at the federal level, as well as in the regulation of the federal-state relationship. Article III not only dictates that federal courts are limited in the kinds of substantive questions they may decide, but also in the types of disputes appropriate for federal judicial resolution.

Federal courts are empowered to decide only actual "cases" and "controversies." Article III provides that the national judiciary may decide "all cases, in Law and Equity" that involve federal questions, ambassadors and admiralty; and "controversies" involving the United States as a party, or two or more states or citizens of different states, or property claimed under conflicting grants from two states, or American citizens and foreign states or foreign citizens. Often referred to as the doctrine

---

157. *Id.* at 1040-41.
158. *Id.* at 1041.
159. *See* C. WRIGHT, *supra* note 6, § 107 at 753.

of justiciability, this requirement of a "case or controversy" for litigants in article III courts has produced a complex web of jurisprudence — some might even call it a formless morass — elaborating and refining the definition of cases for article III purposes.

Chief Justice Warren once said that the case or controversy limitation, while superficially succinct and straightforward, involves

> complexities which go to the very heart of our constitutional form of government . . . [limiting] the business of federal courts to questions presented in an adversary context and in a form historically viewed as capable of resolution through the judicial process. And in part those words define the role assigned to the judiciary in a tripartite allocation of power to assure that the federal courts will not intrude into areas committed to the other branches of government.[160]

The examination of the constitutional limits of justiciability, therefore, is bound up with fundamental questions concerning the proper role of the judiciary in the United States. Over time, the development of the law of justiciability has produced several branches of article III jurisprudence.

This section will describe the case or controversy requirement, focusing first on the definition of a case for constitutional purposes, and then on the long-standing prohibition of advisory opinions. We will then consider the federal law of standing to sue and the related notions of mootness and ripeness, and will conclude with an analysis of the political question doctrine.

A. The Definition of a Case or Controversy

The terms "case" and "controversy" have been interpreted by the Supreme Court as virtually synonymous, although "case" actually designates a wider class of disputes — including both criminal and civil cases — whereas "controversy" only includes civil suits.[161] The content of the requirement of an actual case has been described as involving a "justiciable" controversy, appropriate for submission to a court for resolution:

> A justiciable controversy is thus distinguished from a difference or dispute of a hypothetical or abstract character; from one that is academic or moot. The controversy must be definite and concrete, touching the legal relations of parties having adverse legal interests. It must be a real and substantial controversy admitting of specific relief through a decree of a conclusive character, as distin-

---

160. Flast v. Cohen, 392 U.S. 83, 94-95 (1968), quoted in C. WRIGHT, *supra* note 6, 53-4 (4th ed. 1983).

161. Aetna Life Ins. Co. v. Haworth, 300 U.S. 227, 239 (1937).

guished from an opinion advising what the law would be upon a hypothetical set of facts.[162]

A case or controversy, according to this pronouncement, has four main attributes. First, the dispute must not be hypothetical or abstract. Second, it must be live — that is, the controversy must not lie in the uncertain future nor can it be already resolved by events. Third, it must be tied to real parties who have actual interests at stake in the litigation. Finally, a case must be capable of conclusive resolution by the courts — a dispute is not a case if a judicial decision would not affect the actual legal position of the parties. In short, a justiciable case consists of the real circumstances that give meaning and content to a court's decisions. By contrast, a dispute that does not meet the definition of a case or controversy divorces judicial action from the living forum that gives decisions their judicial character.

Although it limits federal courts to questions arising in an appropriate manner, this notion of a concrete dispute for which there is a legal remedy[163] provides a powerful justification for judicial review of the actions of other branches of government. In *Marbury v. Madison*,[164] Chief Justice Marshall wrote that the authority to construe the law rests on the constitutional extension of the judicial power to decide "cases" and "controversies." In order to adjudicate disputes properly before the Court, *Marbury* determined, the judiciary must necessarily construe the applicable law, including the constitutionality of legislation or executive action where necessary. In this view, judicial review is the inevitable counterpart of the case-or-controversy provision: the only way to determine the merits of a case is to construe the relevant law.[165]

B. THE PROHIBITION OF ADVISORY OPINIONS

The earliest product of judicial interpretation of the case-or-controversy requirement is the rule against advisory opinions. In 1793, then Secretary of State Thomas Jefferson requested the advice of the Su-

---

162. *Id.* at 240-1 (citations omitted).

163. The rule in Hayburn's Case, 2 U.S. (2 Dall.) 409 (1792), a precursor to the fuller treatment of the case-or-controversy requirement in Marbury v. Madison, 5 U.S. (1 Cranch) 137 (1803), dictates that a case must be finally resolved through adjudication. In that case, circuit courts were required by statute to certify disabled veterans for pensions to the Secretary of War, who would then enter the names on the pension list unless he suspected fraud or mistake. The Court refused to entertain such certification petitions, holding that because the resulting judicial decisions would be subject to executive and legislative review, they were not "properly judicial, and to be performed in a judicial manner." 2 U.S. (2 Dall.) at 410.

164. 5 U.S. (1 Cranch) 137 (1803).

165. *See* Bickel, *The Supreme Court 1960 Term: Foreword: The Passive Virtues,* 75 HARV. L. REV. 40, 42 (1961).

preme Court on twenty-nine questions of international law. In reply, the Court declined to decide questions outside the case-or-controversy context, emphasizing that "the lines of separation drawn by the Constitution between the three departments of the government . . . . afford strong arguments against the propriety of our extra-judicially deciding the questions . . . ."[166]

Several policy considerations have traditionally justified this refusal to decide undisputed questions: concern for the full development of facts and argument before the courts; the separation of powers; and the legitimacy of the judicial enterprise. First, courts called upon to decide what should be done in future situations are asked to foresee future events — an uncertain enterprise, at best. As the Court has often noted, concrete cases produce an essential "clash of adversary argument exploring every aspect of a multifaceted situation embracing conflicting and demanding interests."[167] As Professor Bickel argued, there may also be a positive value in assuring that "the flesh-and-blood facts of an actual case" form the basis on which judicial review is built. The ability to "observe and describe in being what the legislature may or may not have foreseen as probable — this opportunity as much as, or more than, anything else enables the Court to appeal to the nation's second thought."[168]

Second, the doctrine of separation of powers dictates that judicial review examine only those questions that have arisen through the test of time. According to *Marbury v. Madison,* the interpretation of the law is only valid when conducted as part of the adjudication of an actual case. This institutional separation allows courts to remain as interpreters rather than initiators of action. Professor Bickel viewed this division as fundamental to the continued survival of the federal courts. The prohibition of advisory opinions, he argued, allows the federal courts to avoid the worst of the political fallout generated by judicial review of the actions of the other branches of national government.[169]

Third, adjudicating only "flesh and blood" cases protects the legitimacy of courts, because it ensures the representation in court of those who have an interest in vindicating their rights. This argument against advisory opinions emphasizes that legislatures do not always adequately take unpopular and minority viewpoints into account. A

---

166. 3 H. JOHNSTON, CORRESPONDENCE AND PUBLIC PAPERS OF JOHN JAY 486-9 (1891), quoted in HART & WECHSLER, *supra* note 27, at 65 (1973).

167. Flast v. Cohen, 392 U.S. 83, 97 (1968), quoting United States v. Fruehauf, 365 U.S. 146, 157 (1961).

168. A. BICKEL, THE LEAST DANGEROUS BRANCH: THE SUPREME COURT AT THE BAR OF POLITICS 116 (1962).

169. *Id.*

live case, on the other hand, allows those aggrieved by a particular action to participate in judicial review — a process designed to avoid the pitfalls of majoritarian decisionmaking. "This guarantee [of judicial review through actual cases] should be seen as a minimal element of the legitimacy of a legal system which imposes legal burdens upon its members."[170]

While the prohibition of advisory opinions is considered fundamental to the proper functioning of the federal courts, not all states have followed the federal lead. In Massachusetts, for example, the Supreme Judicial Court is required by the state constitution to give advisory opinions upon questions presented by the governor or the state legislature.[171] Congress also has some control over what constitutes a justiciable case, although not the power that the Massachusetts legislature has to request a true advisory opinion. Where it chooses to expand the remedies available to litigants, this may extend the opportunities for the federal courts to adjudicate their claims.

For example, the prohibition against advisory judgments has been held not to preclude actions brought under declaratory judgment statutes.[172] Because no immediate relief is afforded in such a judgment, it could technically be argued that a decision in such a case is nothing more than an expression of opinion. Indeed, in the early part of this century the Supreme Court implied that a suit for declaratory relief is not justiciable, since without an executable judgment the litigants merely receive judicial prediction about the validity of statutes or legal claims, rather than an actual decision.[173]

---

170. Brilmayer, *The Jurisprudence of Article III: Perspectives on the "Case or Controversy" Requirement*, 93 HARV. L. REV. 297, 310 (1979).

171. MASS. CONST. Part II, ch. 3, art. II provides:

> Each branch of the legislature, as well as the governor or the council, shall have authority to require the opinions of the justices of the supreme judicial court, upon important questions of law, and upon solemn occasions.

See, e.g., Opinion of the Justices of the Senate, 390 Mass. 1201, 458 N.E.2d 1192 (1984) (advisory opinion determining use of words "sexual preference" in legislation not unconstitutionally vague); Opinion of the Justices, 386 Mass. 1201, 436 N.E.2d 935 (1982) (advisory opinion only appropriate where judicial determination of issues would enable other branches to carry out duties imminently confronting them).

172. BLACK'S LAW DICTIONARY 368 (5th ed. 1979) defines a declaratory judgment as:

> Statutory remedy for the determination of a justiciable controversy where the plaintiff is in doubt as to his legal rights. A binding adjudication of the rights and status of litigants even though no consequential relief is awarded. Such judgment is conclusive in a subsequent action between the parties as to the matters declared and, in accordance with the usual rules of issue preclusion, as to any issues actually litigated and determined (citations omitted).

173. Muskrat v. United States, 219 U.S. 346 (1911) (Indians denied standing to challenge modification of allotment statute because no legal judgment available). *See also* Willing v. Chicago Auditorium Ass'n, 277 U.S. 274, 289 (1928) (dictum) ("To grant [declaratory] relief is beyond the power conferred upon the federal judiciary.").

In the 1930s, however, the Court retreated from its former disapproval of declaratory judgments, first granting review of an action brought under a state declaratory judgment statute[174] and then upholding a federal statute.[175] "The judiciary clause of the Constitution defined and limited judicial power," the Court held, "not the particular method by which that power might be invoked."[176] Declaratory relief, the Court emphasized, is "procedural only,"[177] and does not alter the justiciability of an otherwise cognizable case by expanding the remedial powers of the courts. When there is a well-defined controversy between real parties in interest, the declaratory nature of the relief does not preclude adjudication. Although there may be some lingering judicial reluctance to adjudicate important constitutional issues in declaratory suits,[178] actions for declaratory relief are commonplace throughout the federal courts.

C. STANDING TO SUE IN THE FEDERAL COURTS

The case or controversy requirement dictates that federal courts dismiss a suit for lack of standing unless the "controversy [is] definite and concrete, touching the legal relations of parties having adverse legal interests."[179] This emphasis on concreteness and adversity is a fundamental element of justiciability.

The aim of the law of standing is to ensure that judicial review remains the by-product of decisions in cases, rather than becoming itself the focus of litigation, with plaintiffs reduced to mere vestigial remnants. Maintaining a system that respects the almost imperceptible line between a case in the constitutional sense and a nonjusticiable dispute is a delicate and complicated task that has produced a specialized body of standing law. The Supreme Court has acknowledged that the judicial doctrine resulting from interpretation of this actual-case principle is complex and opaque. As Justice O'Connor recently noted, "standing doctrine incorporates concepts concededly not susceptible of precise definition."[180]

---

174. Nashville, C. & St. L. Ry. v. Wallace, 288 U.S. 249 (1933) (case or controversy for constitutional purposes met in declaratory judgment setting).

175. Aetna Life Ins. Co. v. Haworth, 300 U.S. 227 (1937) (federal Declaratory Judgment Act of 1934 constitutional).

176. 288 U.S. at 264.

177. 300 U.S. at 240.

178. *See* C. WRIGHT, *supra* note 6, at 59 n.35, for a discussion of cases denying judicial review of significant challenges to the constitutionality of state and federal actions where the challenge is mounted through declaratory judgment statutes.

179. Aetna Life Ins. Co. v. Haworth, 300 U.S. 227, 240-1 (1937).

180. Allen v. Wright, 104 S. Ct. 3315, 3325 (1984). *See also* Valley Forge Christian College v. Americans United for Separation of Church & State, Inc., 454 U.S. 464, 475

With due regard for the dangers of attempting to impose order on an area in which disorder has been the norm, this section will outline the parameters of standing law, as well as the policies that animate it. Standing doctrine may generally be divided into two categories — constitutional limitations and prudential considerations. While both are intrinsically tied to the separation of the judicial function from those of the other branches of government, constitutional principles are of course first in importance and in consistency of judicial application.

1. Constitutional Elements of Standing Law

A litigant seeking federal adjudication must satisfy the court that the dispute involves: (1) an injury in fact, that has been (2) caused by the defendant's conduct, and that will be (3) redressed by granting the requested relief.[181] These requirements are the product of the gradual evolution of caselaw, rather than of any settled and constant approach, although a certain consistency has emerged over the last decade in the Court's more restrictive approach to standing.[182]

a. Injury-in-Fact

"[T]he gist of the question of standing," said the Supreme Court in an oft-quoted opinion, "is a personal stake in the outcome of the litigation . . . ."[183] This emphasis on injury-in-fact — also referred to by the Court as "distinct and palpable injury"[184] — is designed to assure the level of concreteness and specificity necessary for a court to render an

---

(1982) ("[T]he concept of 'Art. III standing' has not been defined with complete consistency [;] . . . this very fact is probably proof that the concept cannot be reduced to a one-sentence or one-paragraph definition.").

181. As Justice Rehnquist announced in Valley Forge Christian College v. Americans United for Separation of Church and State, Inc., 454 U.S. 464, 472 (1982):

> [A]t an irreducible minimum, Art. III requires the party who invokes the court's authority to "show that he personally has suffered some actual or threatened injury as a result of the putatively illegal conduct of the defendant," and that the injury "fairly can be traced to the challenged action" and "is likely to be redressed by a favorable decision." (citations omitted).

182. See, e.g., Allen v. Wright, 104 S. Ct. 3315, 3341 (1984) (Brennan, J., dissenting) (stricter standing requirements deny litigants proper judicial form); Chayes, Foreword: Public Law Litigation and the Burger Court, 96 Harv. L. Rev. 1, 14 (1982) (recent standing decisions invalidly attempt to limit public law litigation); Brilmayer, supra note 170, at 298 (commentators have misunderstood standing restrictions as denying public law litigants access to courts); Tushnet, The New Law of Standing: A Plea for Abandonment, 62 Cornell L.Q. 663 (1977) (modern limitations on standing are thinly-veiled attempts to avoid difficult cases).

183. Baker v. Carr, 369 U.S. 186, 204 (1962).

184. Warth v. Seldin, 422 U.S. 490, 501 (1975).

informed judgment. The injury, therefore, may not be "abstract," "speculative" or "generalized," but must be "direct" and "palpable." For example, in *Sierra Club v. Morton*,[185] the Court held that the Sierra Club did not have standing to challenge plans for the development of an area of striking natural beauty, despite the group's undoubtedly sincere interest in the protection of natural resources and wildlife. Because the Club did not allege that its members would actually be damaged in any way — economic or aesthetic[186] — by the proposed development, it had not met the requirement of an injury-in-fact, but had only demonstrated an abstract interest.

Generalized grievances, such as the interest of any citizen in seeing that government follows the dictates of the Constitution, also fail to meet the injury-in-fact requirement. Thus in *Schlesinger v. Reservists Committee To Stop the War*[187] and *United States v. Richardson*[188] the Court held that neither as citizens nor as taxpayers may litigants invoke the jurisdiction of federal courts on the basis of nothing more than the "abstract injury [sustained by all citizens] in nonobservance [by government officials] of the Constitution . . . ."[189]

The area of federal taxpayer standing has produced the most exhaustive — but often impenetrable — analysis of constitutional standing. If a claimant is permitted to base a challenge to federal actions on the fact that the action cost money and his or her taxes are part of the federal fisc, citizens will clearly have a way to challenge almost any federal action in the courts. Consequently, such claims were strictly prohibited until the late 1960s.

When faced for the first time with an irate taxpayer's challenge to the validity of a federal statute in 1923, the Supreme Court had held in *Frothingham v. Mellon*[190] that the plaintiff did not have standing to sue. Distinguishing earlier cases in which the Court had recognized suits by municipal taxpayers, *Frothingham* held that the interest of any one federal taxpayer in the national fisc is too "remote, fluctuating and uncertain"[191] to meet the injury-in-fact requirement. As Professor

---

185. 405 U.S. 727 (1972).
186. *See, e.g.,* Duke Power Co. v. Carolina Envtl. Study Group, Inc., 438 U.S. 59, 73-74 (1978) ("environmental and aesthetic consequences" sufficient to confer standing); United States v. SCRAP, 412 U.S. 669 (1973) (hikers and other users of wilderness area have standing to challenge proposed development).
187. 418 U.S. 208 (1974).
188. 418 U.S. 166 (1974).
189. 418 U.S. at 223 n.13.
190. 262 U.S. 447 (1923).
191. *Id.* at 487.

Wright has noted, *Frothingham* virtually precluded challenges to the federal spending power, and found little favor with legal scholars.[192]

A major modification in taxpayer standing came in 1968 with *Flast v. Cohen*.[193] That decision upheld a federal taxpayer's standing to challenge the constitutionality of a federal statute providing aid to parochial schools. Unlike the plaintiff in *Frothingham*, who had claimed that a national maternity program violated the powers reserved to the states in the tenth amendment, the *Flast* plaintiffs relied on the establishment clause. The Court held that if a taxpayer can show that a challenged action is part of the taxing and spending power of Congress, and in addition that the action allegedly infringes a constitutional provision limiting the taxing and spending power, the litigant will show the requisite "taxpayer's stake in the outcome of the controversy."[194] Thus a taxpayer plaintiff must be able to claim both that a particular expenditure was made pursuant to the taxing and spending power of art. I, § 8, and that a specific constitutional provision, such as the establishment clause, applies as a limit on that power.

The reasoning of the *Flast* majority was attacked by the dissent as reaching a level of "formidable obscurity,"[195] and two concurrences read the exception to *Frothingham* as applying only in establishment clause cases.[196] Justice Douglas would have done away with *Frothingham* altogether, rather than trying artificially to reconcile it with *Flast*.[197] Some critics argued that *Flast* went too far;[198] others, that it did not go far enough.[199]

The debate over the reach of *Flast* raged until 1982, when the Court held that an establishment clause claim does not lighten a plaintiff's burden to show injury-in-fact. In *Valley Forge Christian College v. Americans United for Separation of Church and State, Inc.*,[200] Justice Rehnquist, writing for a 5-4 majority, held that a separatist group did not have standing to challenge HEW's transfer of surplus federal property to a sectarian college. Americans United, the Court noted, failed

---

192. C. WRIGHT, *supra* note 6, at 61-62.
193. 392 U.S. 83 (1968).
194. *Id.* at 103.
195. *Id.* at 124 (Harlan, J., dissenting).
196. *Id.* at 114 (Stewart, J., concurring); *id.* at 115 (Fortas, J., concurring).
197. *Id.* at 107 (Douglas, J., concurring).
198. *Id.* at 130 (Harlan, J., dissenting); Bittker, *The Case of the Fictitious Taxpayer: The Federal Taxpayer's Suit Twenty Years After* Flast v. Cohen, 36 U. CHI. L. REV. 364 (1969).
199. Davis, *The Case of the Real Taxpayer: A Reply to Professor Bittker,* 36 U. CHI. L. REV. 375 (1969); Davis, *Standing: Taxpayers and Others,* 35 U. CHI. L. REV. 601 (1968); Jaffe, *The Citizen as Litigant in Public Actions: the Non-Hohfeldian or Ideological Plaintiff,* 116 U. PA. L. REV. 1033 (1968).
200. 454 U.S. 464 (1982).

the first prong of the *Flast* taxpayer nexus by challenging an executive decision, rather than an exercise of congressional power under art. I, § 8.[201] The Court stressed that the sweep of the *Flast* exception had already been clearly limited to claims brought under the taxing and spending power in *United States v. Richardson*[202] and *Schlesinger v. Reservists Committee to Stop the War*.[203] Those decisions had denied standing to taxpayers challenging legislation allowing the CIA to withhold information about its expenditures, and to taxpayers claiming that membership by congressmen in the armed forces reserve was unconstitutional. Neither of those taxpayer actions was directly tied to the plaintiffs' status as taxpayers, the Court held, and the *Valley Forge* plaintiffs failed the *Flast* test for the same reason — they attempted to challenge as taxpayers an executive action not directly related to the congressional taxing power.[204]

In dissent, Justice Brennan would have allowed an establishment clause exception to standing requirements, emphasizing that "[t]he taxpayer was the direct and intended beneficiary of the prohibition on financial aid to religion."[205]

In short, the Supreme Court, although it has often considered the standard for an injury-in-fact, is manifestly divided over exactly where to draw the line between an acceptably "palpable" injury, and one too "abstract," "generalized" or remote to warrant federal jurisdiction.

b. Causation

A plaintiff must not only demonstrate an actual injury, but must also show that the appropriate defendant has been haled into court. In short, a litigant must sue the person or entity that caused the injury. This second part of the constitutional standing limitation is of more recent vintage than the requirement of injury-in-fact. First articulated in 1973, the emphasis on causation limits standing to those actions based on the conduct of the defendant, so that if the plaintiff cannot show that the defendant is the proximate cause of the injuries, he or she will not have standing to litigate the claim. Thus in *Linda R.S. v. Richard D.*[206] the Court denied a private litigant standing to force the state of Texas to enforce a criminal statute that set a mandatory prison

---

201. *Id.* at 479-80.
202. 418 U.S. 166 (1974).
203. 418 U.S. 208 (1974).
204. 454 U.S. at 480.
205. 454 U.S. at 504 (Brennan, J., dissenting) (emphasis omitted). *See also id.* at 515 (Stevens, J., dissenting) ("[T]he essential holding of [*Flast*] attaches special importance to the Establishment Clause.").
206. 410 U.S. 614 (1973).

term for delinquency in child-support payments. The plaintiff claimed that criminal prosecution of the defendant would force him to make the overdue payments he owed her. Her standing was defective, according to the majority, because she could not show that the failure to pay child-support payments was attributable to the state.[207] Justice White rejected this reasoning, arguing in dissent that it is assumed that penal statutes are designed to discourage certain kinds of behavior, and that it is reasonable to presume that a criminal penalty for non-compliance will encourage prompt child-support payments.[208]

Since *Linda R.S.,* the Court has consistently stressed that a litigant must show a causal connection between the injury and the defendant's conduct, stating that the injury must be "fairly traceable" to the challenged actions.[209] For example, in *Simon v. Eastern Kentucky Welfare Rights Organization*[210] the Court dismissed a challenge to tax regulations that allow hospitals to qualify as charities for income-tax purposes even when they don't furnish non-emergency medical services to indigents. The connection between charitable status for hospitals and failure to care for the poor, the Court stated, was "purely speculative," since only four percent of hospital revenues come from individual donations.[211]

Most recently, *Allen v. Wright*[212] dismissed under the causality requirement a claim that IRS grants of tax exemptions to racially discriminatory schools denies children in desegregating school districts an opportunity to receive an integrated education. Justice O'Connor, writing for a 5-3 majority, first conceded that a child's "diminished ability to receive an education in a racially integrated school [is] . . . one of the most serious injuries recognized in our legal system."[213] As

---

207. *Id.* at 617-18.

208. *Id.* at 621 (White, J., dissenting).

209. Duke Power Co. v. Carolina Envtl. Study Group, Inc., 438 U.S. 59, 77-8 (1978) (environmental group had standing to challenge federal statute encouraging development of nuclear power plants, since "but for" passage of statute, power companies would not construct nuclear plants).

210. 426 U.S. 26 (1976).

211. *Id.* at 42-43. *See also* Warth v. Seldin, 422 U.S. 490 (1975). In that case, the Court held that a group of city taxpayers did not have standing to challenge the zoning laws of an affluent suburb. The taxpayers claimed that the suburb's refusal to allow construction of low- and moderate-income housing forced the city to bear a higher tax burden to support low-income residents' housing needs. "Apart from the conjectural nature of the asserted injury," Justice Powell wrote for the majority, "the line of causation between [the suburb's] actions and such injury is not apparent from the complaint . . . . [T]he injury complained of — increases in taxation — results only from decisions made by the appropriate [city] authorities, who are not parties to this case." *Id.* at 509.

212. 104 S. Ct. 3315 (1984).

213. *Id.* at 3328.

in *Simon,* however, the injury was not caused by the defendant — here, the IRS — but rather by the independent conduct of a third party not before the court — here, racially discriminatory private schools.[214] For the injury to be "fairly traceable" to the unlawful grant of tax exemptions, the plaintiffs would have to show that "there were enough racially discriminatory private schools receiving tax exemptions in [plaintiffs'] communities for withdrawal of those exemptions to make an appreciable difference in public-school integration."[215]

In dissent, Justice Stevens attacked the majority's application of the causality requirement, arguing that it had ignored principles of "elementary economics"[216] — the more expensive a thing (such as a private education) becomes, the less consumers will buy.[217] Justice Brennan, also in dissent, implied that the causation component in recent standing decisions is "no more than a poor disguise for the Court's view of the merits of the underlying claims."[218] Although the application of the causality requirement has thus caused heated debate among the Justices in several cases, and despite Justice Brennan's criticism that it is a ploy for deciding against the plaintiff on the merits, it seems to have become a permanent part of constitutional standing doctrine.

c. Redressability

Closely tied to the injury-in-fact and causation analyses is the third and final component of constitutional standing — the requirement that the plaintiff's injury be substantially redressable by a favorable decision. A litigant's dispute must be capable of judicial resolution.

In *Simon,* for example, Justice Powell stressed that, in addition to failing the causation analysis, the plaintiffs had not shown that a decision granting the requested relief would alleviate their injury: "It is . . . speculative whether the desired exercise of the court's remedial powers in this suit would result in the availability of [non-emergency medical] services [for indigents]."[219] The decision by hospitals not to provide medical services to the poor, according to this analysis, may well be entirely unconnected to anticipated tax consequences.[220] And in

---

214. *Id.*
215. *Id.*
216. *Id.* at 3344-45 (Stevens, J., dissenting).
217. Thus Justice Stevens, like Justice White dissenting in *Simon,* agreed that a causality analysis should be applied in determining standing, but disagreed with the majority's conclusion in both cases that a statute designed to regulate conduct cannot be used to confer standing to challenge or enforce the conduct by a third party.
218. 104 S. Ct. at 3341 (Brennan, J., dissenting).
219. Simon v. Eastern Ky. Welfare Rights Org., 426 U.S. 26, 43 (1976).
220. *Id.*

Allen, the Court held that judicial review of IRS enforcement procedures to ensure that racially-discriminatory schools are not granted
charitable status is inappropriate where the correction of unlawful
charitable gains is not substantially likely to increase the plaintiffs'
access to an integrated public-school education.[221]

Obviously, the connection between the defendants' causation of the
plaintiff's injury and the redressability of the injury by a favorable
decision is a strong one. To date, all cases that have failed to meet the
causation requirement have also been judged incapable of redress in
the courts. The Court presumably believes these two aspects of standing law to be independent, or it would not have stated them as two
separate standards. Yet it is hard to envision a plaintiff who has suffered a palpable injury caused by the defendant that would not also be
able to demonstrate a substantial likelihood of redress from a favorable
decision.

2. *Prudential Considerations*

Above and beyond the constitutional limitations on standing to sue
in federal courts, the judiciary has imposed on itself a set of prudential
barriers to standing. These "counsels of prudence,"[222] while not mandatory like the constitutional rules of standing, are also based on the
policies behind art. III — ensuring a factual setting for adverse litigation of claims, respecting the autonomy of those most likely to be
affected by adjudication and generally preserving the separate spheres
of the three branches of government.

In recent cases, the Supreme Court has emphasized three prudential
principles as complementary to the constitutional components of standing. These principles hold that: (1) each party must assert his or her
own legal rights rather than raising the claims of third parties, (2) the
plaintiff must not ask the court to adjudicate widely-shared,
generalized grievances that are more appropriately addressed in the
representative branches, and (3) the complaint must fall within the
zone of interests regulated or protected by the statute or constitutional
right invoked.[223]

---

221. Allen v. Wright, 104 S. Ct. 3315, 3328-9 (1984).

222. Valley Forge Christian College v. Americans United for Separation of Church
& State, Inc., 454 U.S. 464, 475 (1982).

223. *See generally* 454 U.S. at 474-75; Allen v. Wright, 104 S. Ct. 3315, 3324-5
(1984) (listing prudential considerations).

a. Jus Tertii

The first of these prudential considerations — that a plaintiff may not raise the legal claims of others — is often referred to as the "jus tertii" rule.[224] The goal is to limit access to the courts to those whose interests are most likely to be affected by a judicial decision.[225] This rule has not been uniformly applied,[226] and commentators have observed that the rule "has been markedly relaxed in recent years."[227] Nonetheless, the Supreme Court has continued to find the principle relevant to standing decisions, and has used it to deny standing in a significant number of cases.

In *Tileston v. Ullman*[228] for example, a physician was not allowed in an action for a declaratory judgment to raise his patients' interests in order to challenge a statute forbidding doctors to give their patients advice about birth control.[229] Similarly, in *Laird v. Tatum*[230] Chief Justice Burger's majority opinion denied standing to the plaintiffs' first amendment challenge to army surveillance of peaceful anti-Vietnam War demonstrations. Even assuming that the complaint presented a justiciable controversy, the Court observed, the plaintiffs had not claimed that they themselves had been adversely affected by the army's "data-gathering system." Because the plaintiffs sought to raise the rights of those "'millions' whom they believe are so chilled [in their exercise of first amendment rights], respondents clearly lack that 'personal stake in the outcome of the controversy' essential to standing."[231]

On the other hand, litigants have been allowed to raise third-party claims where "it would be difficult if not impossible for the persons whose rights are asserted to present their grievance before any court."[232] Thus the Court allowed a white defendant in an action for

---

224. Literally, jus tertii means "the right of the third party." BLACK'S LAW DICTIONARY 777 (5th ed. 1979).

225. In this sense, the rule provides for "representation" in the legal process of those who will be required to bear the burden of an unfavorable decision, or who will benefit from a favorable one. Further, the rule allows those most directly interested in an issue to decide whether or not they wish to litigate — thus allowing for "self-determination." Brilmayer, *supra* note 170 at 306-15.

226. As the Court noted in *Flast*, "this rule has not been imposed uniformly as a firm constitutional restriction on federal court jurisdiction." 392 U.S. at 99 n.20.

227. C. WRIGHT, *supra* note 6, at 72. *See also* G. GUNTHER, CASES AND MATERIALS ON CONSTITUTIONAL LAW 1648-50 (10th ed. 1980).

228. 318 U.S. 44 (1943) (per curiam).

229. Some twenty years later a physician from the same state was allowed to raise the constitutional rights of his patients in the context of a criminal prosecution. The Court distinguished *Tileston v. Ullma* because the plaintiff there did not risk criminal prosecution. Griswold v. Connecticut, 381 U.S. 479, 481 (1965).

230. 408 U.S. 1 (1972).

231. *Id.* at 14 n.7.

232. Barrows v. Jackson, 346 U.S. 249, 257 (1953).

damages for breach of a racially restrictive covenant to raise the equal protection rights of the black purchaser.[233] And a physician was permitted to raise the claims of his patients as well as his own when challenging a statute limiting the availability of abortions.[234] Vendors have also been allowed to assert the rights of their customers.[235]

It is, in short, always uncertain whether a federal court will choose to apply the rule against jus tertii to deny standing to particular litigants. But because the rule remains first in the Court's list of prudential considerations, it is wise to bear in mind the rule's existence.

b. Generalized Grievances

Just as a litigant may not raise claims properly belonging to others, she may not base her claim on any injury that belongs to the people as a whole. Both rules are a gloss on the injury-in-fact requirement. Unlike the rule against jus tertii, however, the prudential doctrine that federal courts will not decide cases in which the claimed injury is a generalized grievance retains considerable vitality. Even where a litigant has met the minimum constitutional requirement of an injury-in-fact, the court may refuse to decide the case when "the asserted harm is a 'generalized grievance' shared in substantially equal measure by all or a large class of citizens."[236]

The classic case dealing with the justiciability of a widely-shared grievance was *Schlesinger v. Reservists to Stop the War*,[237] in which an association of Reservists challenged the constitutionality of permitting members of Congress to belong to the Reserves. The incompatibility clause — art. I, § 6, cl. 2 — provides that "no Person holding any Office under the United States, shall be a member of either House during his Continuance in Office." Simultaneous membership in Congress and the Reserves, the plaintiffs claimed, created "inconsistent obligations" for congressmen, and subjected all citizens to the possibility that their elected representatives were subject to "undue influence by the Executive Branch."[238]

---

233. 346 U.S. 249 (1953).

234. Singleton v. Wulff, 428 U.S. 106 (1976).

235. *See, e.g.,* Carey v. Population Servs. Int'l, 431 U.S. 678 (1977) (mail-order seller of contraceptives has standing to raise privacy objections to statute restricting distribution and advertising of contraceptives); Craig v. Boren, 429 U.S. 190 (1976) (seller of 3.2% beer has standing to challenge sex discrimination in statute prohibiting sale of beer to men 18-20 but allowing purchase to women of same age).

236. Warth v. Seldin, 422 U.S. 490, 499 (1975).

237. 418 U.S. 208 (1974).

238. *Id.* at 212.

Writing for the majority, Chief Justice Burger held that the vindication of "the generalized interest of all citizens in constitutional governance"[239] is not a sufficient basis for federal jurisdiction. The majority showed little sympathy for the argument that if the plaintiffs didn't have standing, no one else would either.[240] As Justice Rehnquist observed in a later case, "this view [if accepted] would convert standing into a requirement that must be observed only when satisfied."[241]

c. Zone of Interests

The third and final prudential component of standing doctrine is the requirement that the alleged injury be "within the zone of interests to be protected or regulated by the statute or constitutional guarantee in question."[242] If the sweep of a particular statute or constitutional provision can reasonably be said to include the plaintiff, he or she will have satisfied the "zone of interests" rule.

For example, in *Association of Data Processing Service Organizations, Inc. v. Camp*,[243] sellers of information processing services had standing to challenge an executive agency ruling that allowed national banks to provide the same kind of service. Although the information processors were not directly regulated by the ruling, they clearly were materially affected by the decision to allow banks to provide such services to their customers. In a companion case, *Barlow v. Collins*,[244] the Court held that tenant farmers had standing to challenge a regulation issued by the Secretary of Agriculture that allowed them to assign a portion of benefits received under the upland cotton program to their landlords. Because the legislative history and the provisions of the Food and Agriculture Act both imply that the goal of the Act is to protect the interests of tenant farmers, they were within the "zone of interests" of the regulation.[245]

Concurring in the results of both cases, Justice Brennan argued that the constitutional requirement of an injury-in-fact should end the inquiry into standing. The prudential analysis of the relevant zone of interests protected by a statute or constitutional provision, he maintained, constitutes an invalid determination of the merits of the claim

---

239. *Id.* at 217.

240. "The assumption that if [plaintiffs] have no standing to sue, no one would have standing, is not a reason to find standing." *Id.* at 227.

241. Valley Forge Christian College v. Americans United for Separation of Church and State, Inc., 454 U.S. 464, 489 (1982).

242. Association of Data Processing Serv. Orgs. v. Camp, 397 U.S. 150, 153 (1970).

243. 397 U.S. 150 (1970).

244. *Id.* at 159.

245. *Id.* at 164.

at a stage when the inquiry should be limited to whether there is an injury.[246] Thus, not all members of the Court have accepted the notion that prudential considerations should limit the jurisdiction of federal courts. Scholars, too, have debated the propriety and even the constitutionality of superimposing prudential restraints on a constitutional framework.

In his classic work *The Least Dangerous Branch*, Alexander Bickel points out that a "strict constructionist" of article III must argue that prudential restraints are unconstitutional.[247] Bickel urged, however, that, as a practical matter, prudential limitations on federal jurisdiction are essential to the survival of the judiciary. Courts should never, he continued, decide cases for which there is no clear constitutional principle available as a decisional tool. Given the counter-majoritarian nature of the judicial branch, according to Bickel's analysis, self-imposed restraint is the key to national acceptance of such an anti-democratic yet powerful institution.[248]

Another conception of legitimacy emphasizes respect for the individuality and autonomy of plaintiffs, rather than the brute survival of courts. Prudential doctrines such as the rule against jus tertii help to guarantee that federal courts decide only those cases that have been litigated by parties who properly represent those most affected by state action.[249] The goals of judicial continuity, representative parties, and self-determination for those affected are all served by rules that prevent premature or overly-broad decisions.[250]

Notwithstanding the seemingly unimpeachable impulse of self-restraint, scholars on the other side have argued that prudential limitations artificially close the federal courts to those who most deserve to have their claims adjudicated. Professor Wechsler, for example, has argued that article III dictates adjudication in all cases that meet the case-or-controversy requirement.[251] The provision that the "Judicial Power shall extend to all Cases,"[252] he maintains, means that the judiciary may not avoid deciding cases on prudential grounds.[253]

---

246. *Id.* at 168-69 (Brennan, J., concurring and dissenting).
247. A. BICKEL, *supra* note 168, at 118.
248. *Id.* at 16-23.
249. Brilmayer, *supra* note 170, at 306-10.
250. *Id.* at 314-15. "[T]he factors involved in standing are [indistinguishable] from the issue of paternalism. If I have a personal interest in the dispute, a tangible stake, then I seem to have both a moral and a legal right to involve myself. It does not count as sufficient reason for either legal or moral action that I believe the action will help some person who does not want the 'benefit'."
251. Wechsler, *Toward Neutral Principles of Constitutional Law,* 73 HARV. L. REV. 1, 1-6 (1959).
252. U.S. CONST. art. III, § 2.
253. Wechshler, *supra* note 251 at 4-5.

Professor Gunther, responding to Bickel's "passive virtues" thesis,[254] has pointed out that Bickel, in his adherence to principle in constitutional decisionmaking, has mistakenly asserted "an amorphous authority to withhold adjudication altogether."[255] The judicial restraint advocated by Bickel, Gunther argues, is actually "a virulent variety of free-wheeling interventionism,"[256] since it impermissibly extends judicial discretion whether to decide beyond the acceptable limits of narrowly-decided cases and certiorari jurisdiction.[257]

Finally, responding to the defense of judicial restraint devices as means of protecting the individuality of litigants, Professor Tushnet claims that adherence to traditional rules requiring injured plaintiffs is unnecessary: strategy impels public interest lawyers, for example, to search out actual plaintiffs with real injuries.[258] As a practical matter, Tushnet argues, flesh-and-blood plaintiffs make for successful lawsuits,[259] and only minimal standing requirements are necessary to ensure a complete, concrete record.[260]

It is plain, then, that both judges and scholars disagree about the validity of prudential standing rules. The debate involves fundamental issues of article III interpretation, that will undoubtedly continue to be hotly contested. At present, however, the three prudential components of standing law appear entrenched in Supreme Court jurisprudence.

D. RIPENESS AND MOOTNESS

Thus far, our consideration of justiciability has asked whether a certain plaintiff or his claimed interest in litigating gives him the right to invoke the jurisdiction of the federal courts, or whether a certain kind of question is appropriate for federal adjudication. Determining the justiciability of a particular dispute, however, entails an additional line of inquiry. The doctrines of ripeness[261] and mootness[262] assure that

---

254. Gunther, *The Subtle Vices of the "Passive Virtues" — A Comment on Principle and Expediency in Judicial Review,* 64 COLUM. L. REV. 1 (1964).

255. *Id.* at 10.

256. *Id.* at 25.

257. *Id.*

258. Tushnet, *The Sociology of Article III: A Response to Professor Brilmayer,* 93 HARV. L. REV. 1698, 1713 (1980).

259. *Id.* at 1713-14.

260. *Id.* at 1706-07.

261. The inquiry into ripeness, as Professor Gunther says, concerns whether "a dispute [is] sufficiently real, well developed, and specific [enough] to elicit adjudication." G. GUNTHER, CASES AND MATERIALS ON CONSTITUTIONAL LAW 1655 (10th ed. 1980).

262. "A case is moot when a determination is sought on a matter which, when rendered, cannot have any practical effect on the existing controversy." BLACK'S LAW DICTIONARY 909 (5th ed. 1979).

a dispute is not litigated before it has matured into an actual case, or after it has been resolved by a change in the facts or the law.

The inquiries into ripeness and mootness, then, are designed not to determine whether the plaintiff is a proper litigant or the dispute is appropriate for judicial determination, but whether the case has been fully defined or, alternatively, is already over. A simple example of the three possible stages in the career of a dispute — premature, ripe, moot — illustrates the relationship of the maturity of a dispute to the art. III case-or-controversy requirement. Suppose the city of Gotham passed a law prohibiting citizens from carrying handguns. If a Gothamite wished to challenge the law, she could not claim merely that she might someday want to arm herself — her claimed injury would be speculative, and the case would not be "ripe." If, on the other hand, she presently owned a handgun and would be forced to stop carrying it, her dispute with Gotham would be ripe. But if during the course of his lawsuit Gotham repealed the law, the suit would then be moot.

In the first instance, when the plaintiff had not yet been adversely affected by the city ordinance but was worried he might be in the future, allowing her to litigate the claim would eventually undermine the rules of standing imposed by art. III limitations on federal courts.[263] The injury must be real rather than speculative. In the final stage of the example, when Gotham repealed its handgun statute during the pendency of the suit, continuing the litigation would also involve a court in deciding a case in which the injury was not real. In both cases, the plaintiff has asked the court to step outside the bounds of a concrete dispute. A judicial decision in either case would amount to an advisory opinion — judicial prediction without an actual, live case to tie the decision to reality.

1. Ripeness

As the Supreme Court stated in the classic case *United Public Workers v. Mitchell*[264] in 1947:

> The power of the courts, and ultimately of this Court to pass upon the constitutionality of acts of Congress arises only when the interests of the litigants require the use of this judicial authority for their protection against actual interference. A hypothetical threat is not enough.[265]

Any deviation from this rule, the Court noted, would require the adjudication of disputes that properly belong in the political realm, and

---

263. See discussion of constitutional limitations on standing in sec. C1, *supra*.
264. 330 U.S. 75 (1947).
265. *Id.* at 89-90.

would deserve both "rebuke and restriction from [the] other branches [of government]."[266]

Thus the doctrine of ripeness, like the injury-in-fact requirement, is designed to preserve the legitimacy of the federal courts by preventing unnecessary and anticipatory decisions in disputes before they have reached the stage of "concreteness." As in the standing area, the finer points of the Supreme Court's ripeness analysis are not always clear; the recurring theme, however, is unwillingness to invoke the powerful tool of judicial review except when an actual, mature case provides the framework within which the courts may validly adjudicate. Although the ripeness doctrine is firmly entrenched, it is not clear whether its strictures are discretionary or constitutionally-compelled. As one scholar has noted, "a dispute may be sufficiently concrete to meet the minimum requirements of art. III but nevertheless sufficiently contingent to warrant dismissal on ripeness grounds in the exercise of judicial discretion as to the federal declaratory judgments remedy."[267]

In *United Public Workers,* for example, the Court declined to decide a case in which government employees sought a declaratory judgment of the constitutionality of a statute that restricted the political activities of public employees. Because they had failed to show that they intended to engage in specifically prohibited political activities, the Court held that they had not demonstrated that they faced an actual threat of reprisal other than the threat posed "by the existence of the law and the regulations."[268] Later, in *Poe v. Ullman,*[269] another in the series of cases challenging Connecticut's birth-control statute, the Court held that the plaintiffs must show not only that they wish to break a particular provision of an allegedly unconstitutional regulation; but also that they are likely to be punished for their transgression. In *Poe,* past prosecution under the birth-control statute had been virtually non-existent, and the Court concluded that the necessary "danger of sustaining some direct injury as a result of [the] enforcement"[270] of Connecticut's statute was lacking.[271]

---

266. *Id.* at 91.

267. G. GUNTHER, *supra* note 254, at 1661. *See also* HART & WECHSLER, *supra* note 27, at 145-6 (ripeness doctrine in federal courts contain elements of both case-or-controversy analysis and judicial discretion inherent in equity and declaratory judgment jurisdiction).

268. 330 U.S. at 91.

269. 367 U.S. 497 (1961).

270. *Id.* at 505. The phrase comes from Massachusetts v. Mellon, 262 U.S. 447, 488 (1923).

271. 367 U.S. 507-09. Professor Bickel argued that *Poe* is not a ripeness case at all, but rather an extremely rare application of the civil law doctrine of desuetude. A. BICKEL, *supra* note 164, at 154-56.

These cases have been criticized as requiring litigants to break the law and face punishment before their claims will be heard.[272] While this is probably an exaggeration, plaintiffs under *United Public Works* and *Poe* are required to show both that they have an actual intention to violate a law and that the violation will have adverse consequences for them.[273] Thus in *Abbott Laboratories v. Gardner*,[274] the Court held that a drug manufacturer's pre-enforcement challenge to a federal drug labeling requirement was justifiable, since the company had specific objections to the regulations and faced severe penalties for noncompliance. In contrast, in *Roe v. Wade*,[275] a case that will be more fully discussed in connection with mootness, the Court dismissed a claim by a nonpregnant couple who had argued that they might violate anti-abortion statutes should the wife become pregnant. The *Roe* majority held that such a claim was entirely too speculative to be ripe for judicial review.[276]

Most recently, the Supreme Court declined to adjudicate a claim by a Los Angeles resident that the city police should be enjoined from using dangerous chokeholds when making routine arrests. In *Los Angeles v. Lyons*[277] the plaintiff alleged that during a standard arrest, without provocation, the defendant officers had applied a chokehold causing him to lose consciousness. Lyons further claimed that the procedure was standard police practice and sought to prevent future chokeholds by claiming that he faced an undue risk of irreparable harm should he be stopped by the police. The Court held that a litigant could not validly base a claim of an imminent threat on the possibility of a future arrest.[278] From one perspective, the Court was denying the plaintiff the

---

272. *See, e.g.,* D. CURRIE, FEDERAL JURISDICTION IN A NUTSHELL 23 (2d ed. 1981) ("the only way a person could test the validity of a statute . . . was to violate it first and incur the risk of punishment"); E. BORCHARD, DECLARATORY JUDGMENTS 278 (1934) (Court's ripeness decisions effectively tell litigants that "the only way to determine whether the suspect is a mushroom or a toadstool is to eat it").

273. These requirements are not always strictly enforced. For example, in *Adler v. Board of Educ.,* 342 U.S. 485 (1952) a teacher was permitted to challenge a law that required dismissal of teachers who advocated the violent overthrow of the government, despite the fact that he did not claim an intention to advocate such an overthrow. The majority did not address the issue of the ripeness of such a claim, but Justice Frankfurter in dissent would have dismissed the suit, or at the very least investigated the content of the teacher's claim to determine whether he could validly claim to have violated the statute before reaching a decision on the merits. 342 U.S. 504-08 (Frankfurter, J., dissenting).

274. 387 U.S. 136, 148-54 (1967).

275. 410 U.S. 113, 127-29 (1973).

276. *Id.* at 128. "But we are not prepared to say that the bare allegation of so indirect an injury is sufficient to present an actual case or controversy."

277. 461 U.S. 95 (1982).

278. *Id.* at 107-08.

right to claim a threat of prejudicial interference when he had not met the first requirement of the ripeness doctrine — an immediate intention to act in such a way as to produce the challenged chokehold. A strong dissent by Justice Marshall argued that the grave danger posed by routine use of such chokeholds should trigger judicial review, and that a plaintiff need not show that he was certain to be stopped by the city police in the near future.[279]

The doctrine of ripeness, then, is designed to preserve the Court's constitutional decisionmaking power for those cases in which judicial review can take place in the context of a well-defined dispute. The doctrine of mootness, while closely related to the prohibition on deciding premature cases, does not turn on whether the litigants present a concrete case, but on whether the decision will actually determine the outcome of the dispute.

2. Mootness

If the law or facts giving rise to a dispute have changed since the case was filed, the suit may be moot. When a judicial decision would not affect the position of the parties to a dispute because the underlying facts or law have changed in a way that decides the issue, the case must be dismissed and any decisions below vacated.

It is easy to see that there is no case or controversy once a dispute has been mooted, but, as one commentator has noted, the content of the term "mootness" has undergone considerable change in recent years.[280] Traditionally, a criminal case was treated as moot once the defendant had served his sentence. In two cases decided in 1968,[281] however, the Court recognized that a criminal conviction entails adverse legal consequences beyond those of incarceration or financial penalties: a criminal case in which the penalty has been paid is no longer doomed to end "ignominiously in the limbo of mootness."[282] But the consequences must be legal ones if they are to save a case from dismissal for mootness[283] — a litigant's emotional stake in vindicating her conduct

---

279. *Id.* at 128-31 (Marshall, J., dissenting).

280. C. WRIGHT, *supra* note 6, at 55 (noting that in recent cases, the Court has had difficulty deciding mootness issues).

281. Carafas v. La Vallee, 391 U.S. 234 (1968) (a prisoner's writ of habeas corpus held not to be moot merely because sentence has been served); Sibron v. New York, 392 U.S. 40 (1968) ("[A] criminal case is moot only if it is shown that there is no possibility that any collateral legal consequence will be imposed on the basis of the challenged conviction.") *Id.* at 57.

282. *Sibron,* 392 U.S. at 55 citing Parker v. Ellis, 362 U.S. 574, 577 (1960) (dissenting opinion).

283. *See* Lane v. Williams, 455 U.S. 624 (1982) in which the majority held that the collateral consequences of a criminal conviction must be statutory to save the case

is not enough.[284] Furthermore, an agreement between the parties that the case is not moot will not save it.[285]

An exception to the traditional rule of mootness once the facts have made the dispute obsolete is the concept of an issue that is "capable of repetition, yet evading review."[286] Justice Blackmun's majority opinion in *Roe v. Wade*,[287] holding that a woman has a privacy right to abortion in her first trimester of pregnancy, offers the most famous application of this exception. As one might expect, the named plaintiff was no longer pregnant by the time her appeal reached the Supreme Court. Because the usual pace of litigation combined with what the majority called "the normal 266-day human gestation period,"[288] means that no plaintiff would ever be able fully to litigate her challenge to statutes prohibiting abortion, the Court held that the dispute was justiciable.

E. Political Questions

The "political question" doctrine embodies the notion that courts are not empowered to decide questions of a political nature. Like the other rules of adjudication discussed above, this doctrine has both constitutional and prudential aspects, both of which are controversial and confused.[289]

---

from mootness. A claim of continued harm based on possible prejudicial inferences in a future criminal proceeding against the plaintiff, or difficulties in finding employment because of a criminal record do not meet the collateral legal consequences requirement. Justice Marshall's dissent argued first, that collateral consequences should be presumed to flow from criminal convictions and secondly, that collateral consequences in fact existed in this case.

284. *See, e.g.,* Ashcroft v. Mattis, 431 U.S. 171 (1977) (father lacks standing to challenge fatal shooting of son by police officer, since good faith defense prevents any relief other than emotional satisfaction for grieved parent).

285. *See* Murphy v. Hunt, 455 U.S. 478 (1982) (felons claim to pretrial bail is moot after conviction despite state's and defendant's arguments to the contrary); DeFunis v. Odegaard, 416 U.S. 312 (1977) (per curiam) (challenge to law school admissions policy was moot, despite both parties' claims that case was still justiciable, because plaintiff had virtually completed law school at time of oral argument).

286. Roe v. Wade, 410 U.S. 113, 124-5 (1973); Southern Pac. Terminal Co. v. ICC, 219 U.S. 498, 515 (1911) (because orders of the Interstate Commerce Commission are usually continuing they are "capable of repetition, yet evading review" and the case is not moot).

287. 410 U.S. 113 (1973).

288. *Id.* at 125.

289. *See, e.g.,* C. Wright, *supra* note 6, at 74 ("No branch of the law of justiciability is in such disarray as the doctrine of the 'political question.'"); McGowan, *Congressmen in Court: The New Plaintiffs,* 15 Ga. L. Rev. 241, 256 (1981) ("The use of standing doctrine to address the separation-of-powers concerns arising when federal legislators sue the executive branch in federal court is fraught with difficulties both in theory and in application").

In simple terms, a political question is nonjusticiable because adjudication would require a court improperly to invade the realm of coordinate branches of federal government. The various aspects of political question doctrine all aim to preserve the separation of powers.[290] Respect for the autonomy of the legislative and executive branches precludes judicial determination of disputes when they turn on questions that are properly answered by other branches, or when prudential considerations counsel against judicial involvement in areas that require nonjudicial expertise.

Unlike the doctrines of ripeness, mootness, standing and advisory opinions, the political question notion has little to do with the position or interests of the parties. When the Court determines that a dispute presents a political question, the issue itself is foreclosed from adjudication, rather than merely held in abeyance until properly placed parties raise the issue again. As Justice Brennan stated, "the doctrine of which we treat is one of 'political questions,' not one of 'political cases.'"[291] The refusal to adjudicate political questions, then, is an explicitly substantive stance rather than a procedural restraint.

Justice Powell, concurring in the judgment of a recent case, divided the political question doctrine into three categories.[292] First, according to Powell, courts examine the Constitution to determine whether it presents "'a textually demonstrable constitutional commitment of the issue to a coordinate political department.'"[293] If such a commitment is uncovered, the question is a political one, and the dispute is clearly not justiciable.

Second, courts inquire into whether resolution of the question before them requires nonjudicial expertise. This aspect of political question doctrine focuses on the judicial function, dictating that when a judge is faced with a dispute that requires him or her to step outside "judicially discoverable and manageable standards for resolving [cases],"[294] the case itself presents a political question. A case that requires a judge to make a policy determination that is clearly not a matter for judicial discretion should be dismissed for failure to state a justiciable claim.

Third, if judicial determination would embarrass the government by undermining respect for the coordinate branches or by failing to recog-

---

290. Baker v. Carr, 369 U.S. 186, 210 (1962). ("The nonjusticiability of a political question is primarily a function of the separation of powers").

291. *Id.* at 217. *See also* Scharpf, *Judicial Review and the Political Question: A Functional Analysis,* 75 YALE L.J. 517, 537 (1966) (political question is unique in justiciability law because it turns on issue presented rather than specific constellation of parties in a case).

292. Goldwater v. Carter, 444 U.S. 996, 998 (1979) (Powell, J., concurring).

293. *Id.* quoting Baker v. Carr, 369 U.S. at 217.

294. *Id.* at 999 quoting Baker v. Carr, 369 U.S. at 217.

nize that special circumstances might require judicial restraint, the federal courts will declare the dispute to be a political one.[295] This final area of the political question analysis emphasizes that under extraordinary circumstances extraordinary measures may be necessary and the courts should not embarrass coordinate branches of government. In contrast to the second component of political question doctrine, which is designed to ensure the integrity of the judicial function, the third aspect centers on the need for cohesion among the three branches, either in recognition of an emergency situation or for avoidance of unnecessary friction.

The very existence of the second, and especially the third aspects of political question jurisprudence is controversial, however. Scholars debate the validity of using "prudential considerations" to deny adjudication of what are otherwise justiciable cases.[296]

1. Textually Demonstrable Commitment to a Coordinate Branch

All commentators agree that if the Constitution expressly places the determination of an issue in another branch of government, the issue is not justiciable. This threshold determination, as Professor Wechsler has pointed out, involves constitutional interpretation.[297] If, upon examination of the relevant constitutional provision, it is apparent that the final decision rests outside the judiciary, a case will be dismissed on political question grounds.

For example, in *Colegrove v. Green*[298] Justice Frankfurter's 4-3 majority opinion held that a challenge to an Illinois congressional districting scheme was not justiciable:

> [T]his controversy concerns matters that bring courts into immediate and active relations with party contests. From the determination of such issues this Court has traditionally remained aloof. It is hostile to a democratic system to involve the judiciary in the politics of the people . . . . [D]ue regard for the Constitution as a viable system precludes judicial correction. Authority for dealing with such problems resides [in Art. I, § 4]. The short of it is that the Constitution has conferred upon Congress exclusive authority to secure fair representation in [Congress].[299]

---

295. *Id.* at 1000.

296. *See infra* text accompanying notes 247-257.

297. Wechsler, *supra* note 251, at 7-8.

298. 328 U.S. 549 (1946).

299. *Id.* at 553-54, Justice Rutledge, concurring in result, thought that the case was justiciable, but that the Court should nonetheless dismiss the complaint because of the extreme delicacy of the issue. *Id.* at 564 (Rutledge, J., concurring).

Article IV, § 4, known as the guarantee clause, provides that "The United States shall guarantee to every State in this Union a Republican Form of Government." It was invoked in 1849 by a citizen of Rhode Island, who challenged the legitimacy of the recognized state government. *Luther v. Borden*[300] "arose out of the unfortunate political differences which agitated the people of Rhode Island in 1841 and 1842."[301] Chief Justice Taney held in *Luther* that, given the language of the guarantee clause, the judiciary was not empowered to decide the controversy.[302]

In the most important political question decision of modern times, *Baker v. Carr*,[303] the Court held that while enforcement of the guarantee clause presents a political question,[304] a challenge to a malapportionment of state congressional districts on equal protection grounds states a justiciable claim.[305] An equal protection case, Justice Brennan wrote for the majority, invokes a political right that has been explicitly committed to the judicial branch. The fact that the rights involved are political, the Court held, does not defeat justiciability; "political questions" are not synonymous with "political cases."[306]

The Court further elaborated upon the clear textual commitment aspect of political question doctrine in *Powell v. McCormack*.[307] That case held that article I, § 5, which provides that "Each House shall be the Judge of the . . . Qualifications of its own members," does not give the House of Representatives the power to exclude an elected representative who meets the constitutionally-mandated qualifications of age, citizenship and residency.[308] The House had voted to exclude Rep. Adam Clayton Powell because of alleged misuse of House funds while Powell was chairperson of the Committee on Education and Labor. In his opinion for the majority, Chief Justice Warren held that art. I, § 5 does not confer discretion to exclude members by majority vote for

---

300. 48 U.S. (7 How.) 1 (1849) (issue was which of two governments of Rhode Island was the legitimate one).

301. *Id.* at 34.

302. *Id.* at 42-45.

303. 369 U.S. 186 (1962).

304. *Id.* at 210.

305. *Id.* at 226-27. This reasoning has also been held to apply to national congressional apportionment. Wesberry v. Sanders, 376 U.S. 1 (1964).

306. *Id.* at 217.

307. 395 U.S. 486 (1969).

308. U.S. CONST. art. I, § 2 cl. 2 provides:

No Person shall be a Representative who shall not have attained the Age of twenty five Years, and been seven Years a Citizen of the United States, and who shall not, when elected, be an Inhabitant of that State in which he shall be chosen.

misbehavior. Because the Constitution clearly provides for expulsion by a two-thirds vote,[309] and because the records of the Constitutional Convention reveal a strong disapproval of exclusion of duly-elected representatives,[310] the Court held that there was no "textual commitment" sufficient to bar adjudication on political question grounds.[311]

The most recent political question decision, *Goldwater v. Carter*,[312] involved a challenge by Senator Goldwater to President Carter's abrogation of a defense treaty with Taiwan upon executive recognition of the Peking Government. The Court vacated the District of Columbia Circuit's judgment upholding the President's action. In a statement joined by three other Justices, Justice Rehnquist stated that the case presented a political question "because it involves the authority of the President in the conduct of our country's foreign relations and the extent to which the Senate or the Congress is authorized to negate the action of the President."[313]

2. The Judicial Function

The second aspect of political question jurisprudence focuses on the limits of judicial expertise. As Justice Brennan stated in *Baker v. Carr,* federal courts will not decide a case that involves "a lack of judicially discoverable and manageable standards for resolving it; or the impossibility of deciding without an initial policy determination of a kind clearly for nonjudicial discretion."[314] In the area of foreign relations, for example, courts have often held that the recognition of a particular government as the sovereign of a nation is a political, not a judicial, function.[315]

In *Goldwater v. Carter*,[316] Justice Rehnquist's concurring opinion acknowledged that the Constitution is silent as to the proper manner of abrogating a treaty.[317] Because of this silence, Justice Rehnquist stated, it is possible that a variety of abrogation procedures are appro-

---

309. Art. I, § 5, cl. 2.

310. 395 U.S. at 532-541.

311. 395 U.S. at 547-48. "In short, both the intention of the Framers, to the extent it can be determined, and an examination of the basic principles of our democratic system persuade us that the Constitution does not vest in the Congress a discretionary power to deny membership by a majority vote."

312. 444 U.S. 996 (1979).

313. *Id.* at 1002.

314. 369 U.S. 186, 217 (1962).

315. *See, e.g.,* Oetjen v. Central Leather Co., 246 U.S. 297 (1918) (Court will defer to executive recognition of proper government of Mexico during civil war); Jones v. United States, 137 U.S. 202 (1890) (both British and American courts defer to legislative and executive recognition of foreign governments).

316. 444 U.S. 996 (1979).

317. *Id.* at 1003 (Rehnquist, J., concurring).

priate for different treaties. In such a situation; the case "must surely be controlled by political [rather than judicial] standards."[318] Justice Powell disagreed, stating that the decision of a case involving a dispute about who has power to abrogate treaties "may not be easy, but it only requires us to apply normal principles of interpretation to the constitutional provisions at issue."[319]

In addition, the power to declare the dates of duration of hostilities — to decide when a war officially has ended as well as to declare war — has been held to be a political question. Because the power to declare war is explicitly legislative, the ability to determine the date and the manner of cessation is exclusively legislative: thus if Congress declared a war over on a certain date, yet had extended legislation enacted during wartime beyond the end of the war, the legislation was still valid, since the decision as to when the consequent effects of hostilities should cease is political.[320]

Judicial restraint in the areas of the conduct of foreign affairs and the conduct of war is essentially a recognition that adjudication would require a court to step outside its traditional judicial function into the realm of politics. One legal scholar has argued that political question doctrine can be explained by a kind of functional approach to judicial decisionmaking. The international political arena and questions of war, Professor Scharpf maintains, is not susceptible to Article III judicial review because the political nature of the dispute makes it unlikely that the court will have all the information it needs to make a final decision on the merits.[321] The information-producing goal of the case-or-controversy requirement is therefore not satisfied in cases where courts do not have access to the data used by political decisionmakers.

3. Prudential Factors

This functional theory does not, however, explain the third component of political question doctrine. In contrast to the first two areas, the final, purely prudential element of political question jurisprudence is

---

318. *Id.* (citing Dyer v. Blair, 390 F. Supp. 1291, 1302 (N.D. Ill. 1975) (three-judge court)).

319. *Id.* at 999 (Powell, J., concurring).

320. Commercial Trust Co. v. Miller, 262 U.S. 51, 57 (1923) (upholding application of Trading With Enemy Act beyond date of legislation declaring WWI to have ended): "A court cannot estimate the effects of a great war and pronounce their termination at a particular moment of time, and that its consequences are so far swallowed up that legislation addressed to its emergency had ceased to have purpose or operation with the cessation of conflicts in the field."

321. Scharpf, *supra* note 291, at 567-73.

not based on the commands of the Constitution or on the traditional limits of judicial decisionmaking. Rather, as Justice Brennan stated in *Baker v. Carr,* the prudential aspect of the political question doctrine bars judicial review if a case cannot be decided without "expressing lack of the respect due coordinate branches of government; or [transgressing] an unusual need for unquestioning adherence to a political decision already made; or [creating] the potentiality of embarrassment from nullifarious pronouncements by various departments on one question."[322] In other words, the concept of judicial caution permits a court to use its discretion to sidestep an especially hot political issue.

The sources of this discretion are, to say the least, obscure. In his opinion in *Baker,* Justice Brennan did not cite any cases that were decided on the basis of these prudential considerations;[323] and subsequent cases, such as *Powell v. McCormack*[324] and *Goldwater v. Carter,*[325] have cited only *Baker* for the proposition that such prudential factors are part of political question doctrine. Not all commentators, moreover, accept this premise. Indeed, the *Baker v. Carr* brand of judicial restraint has been challenged as an assault on the very concept of judicial review.

The opinion of Chief Justice Marshall in *Marbury v. Madison*[326] established that the power of judicial review arises out of the courts' obligation to determine the law applicable to cases. This principle, as was noted by the Chief Justice himself in a later case,[327] seems to require adjudication of all disputes that meet the case-or-controversy requirement:

> It is most true that this Court will not take jurisdiction if it should not, but it is equally true, that it must take jurisdiction if it should. The judiciary cannot, as the legislature may, avoid a measure because it approaches the confines of the constitution. We cannot pass it by because it is doubtful. With whatever doubts, with whatever difficulties, a case may be attended, we must decide it, if it be brought before us. We have no more right to decline the exercise of jurisdiction which is given, than to usurp that which is not given. The one or the other would be treason to the constitution.[328]

As Justice Marshall would have it, courts have no discretion to apply prudential considerations when determining justiciability. Many legal scholars share this view.

---

322. 369 U.S. at 217.
323. *Id.*
324. 395 U.S. 486, 548-9 (1969).
325. 444 U.S. 996, 1000 (1979).
326. 5 U.S. (1 Cranch) 137, 177-8 (1803).
327. Cohens v. Virginia, 19 U.S. (6 Wheat.) 264 (1821).
328. *Id.* at 404.

Professor Wechsler, for example, argues that: "all the [political question] doctrine can defensibly imply is that the courts are called upon to judge whether the Constitution has committed to another agency of government the autonomous interpretation of the issue raised, a finding that itself requires an interpretation."[329] Justice Douglas apparently agreed with Wechsler when he stated that: "Where the Constitution assigns a particular function wholly and indivisibly to another department, the federal judiciary does not intervene."[330] Such a statement implies that where the Constitution does not assign a function completely to another department, any action taken in connection with that function should be subject to judicial review.

Notwithstanding these scruples, scholars have developed a range of explanations to justify the application of prudential self-restraint in political cases. One of the earliest commentators argued that the term political question "applies to all those matters of which the court, at a given time, will be of the opinion that it is impolitic or inexpedient to take jurisdiction."[331] This analysis of the political question doctrine would not foreclose future litigation of an issue, and thus more closely resembles traditional justiciability rules. This theory does not, however, explain why the Court often chooses to deal directly with difficult and controversial problems — it would seem to argue for avoidance of a decision on the merits in every case that involves political controversy.[332]

In a dissenting opinion in a political question case, Justice Frankfurter emphasized that federal courts should only decide cases that are capable of resolution by recognized judicial standards.[333] One commentator has called this approach a "cognitive" theory, since it attempts to

---

329. Wechsler, *supra* note 251 at 7-8.

330. Baker v. Carr, 369 U.S. 186, 246 (1962) (Douglas, J., concurring) (many of the "so-called 'political question' cases" were wrongly decided).

331. Finkelstein, *Judicial Self-Limitation,* 37 HARV. L. REV. 338, 344 (1924).

332. Professor Scharpf, *Judicial Review and the Political Question, supra* note 291, at 555, points out that a desire to avoid "impolitic" or "inexpedient" questions need not lead to a total avoidance of adjudication. "As long as the Court is not ready to abandon its responsibility for the formulation and vindication of principle, it will usually find ways to sidestep, postpone, limit, or in some other way make manageable potential clashes with the political institutions and with public opinion without having to resort to complete abdication."

333. Baker v. Carr, 369 U.S. 186, 322-23 (1962) (Frankfurter, J., dissenting) (malapportionment is political issue because there is no "standard by which the place of equality as a factor in apportionment can be measured"). *See also* Field, *The Doctrine of Political Questions in the Federal Courts,* 8 MINN. L. REV. 485, 512 (1924) (political questions involve issues for which there are no available legal principles to use in reaching a decision).

explain all political question cases in terms of a lack of available craft or knowledge for decisionmaking.[334] This explanation, like the theory that rests on inexpediency, is underinclusive — it does not account for cases in which legal standards are clearly available but where adjudication would be embarrassing or impolitic.

Professor Bickel, consistent with his defense of the prudential components of standing law, would allow a court to avoid as a matter of prudence any case that does not present a substantive question that can be decided consistent with principle.[335] If no clear principle is available to the courts, they should defer to the majoritarian interest in expediency, taking jurisdiction only when a judgment on the merits would be securely based on enduring, constitutional principle. This viewpoint, like that of Professor Scharpf, stresses the function of federal courts as interpreters of the Constitution only where they have access to sufficient means of decision.[336] Professor Scharpf, however, would explain the existence of prudential political question notions as efforts to avoid deciding cases in which a decision will be factually uninformed, such as in international law and foreign relations, or in domestic areas that are predominantly determined by political rather than legal factors.[337]

All of these theories of prudential political question doctrine, while they explain more or less completely the reality — perhaps even the desirability — of such prudential considerations, fail to provide constitutional justifications for declining jurisdiction in a case that otherwise presents a valid case or controversy. And because the determination that a dispute is nonjusticiable on political question grounds effectively bars future litigation of the issue through the principle of stare decisis, such prudential considerations are potentially more damaging to the constitutional rights of litigants than the prudential aspects of standing law, because a denial of standing only operates against a given plaintiff or class rather than withdrawing an issue altogether.

Conclusions

As this chapter suggests, the limitations and powers of the federal courts are qualitatively different from those of the state courts. We hinted in the introduction at some reasons why this might be so. The more restrictive definition of federal judicial power stems, first, from the limited nature of centralized government in a federal system. Thus the fact that the federal courts are *federal* is one source of the limita-

---

334. Scharpf, *supra* note 291, at 555-8.
335. A. BICKEL, *supra* note 168, at 183-98.
336. Scharpf, *supra* note 291, at 534.
337. *Id.* at 596-7.

tions. The second is that the federal courts are *courts.* Thus they are limited by the modest traditional notions of the judicial function. This is particularly true where they wield the constitutional power of judicial review, which is sufficiently potent as to require balancing by restrictions on its exercise.

In the next chapter, we see another source of limitations on judicial power. This time it is a limit that applies to state and federal courts alike; the doctrine of sovereign immunity. Again, the limitations prove most stringent when federal courts exercise the power of judicial review; in that case, the constraints on federal court action reflect deference towards the states and the elected branches of government. We turn now to that doctrine, its historical antecedents and current usage.

Chapter 3

SOVEREIGN IMMUNITY

I. Theoretical Foundations

Sovereign immunity, the concept that the government cannot be sued without its consent, is a very old notion, dating back at least to the early English common-law rule that "the King can do no wrong." Historians have now determined that this English common-law rule had a double source: the practical reality that there was no sovereign power above the King who could review the validity of his actions, and the theoretical principle that the King was not privileged to do wrong.[1] Over the centuries, this doctrine evolved such that Blackstone described sovereign immunity as arising from the King's inability to do wrong: "the King, moreover, is not only incapable of doing wrong, but of thinking wrong: he can never mean to do an improper thing."[2]

Despite the Founding Father's resounding rejection of the monarchy and its attendant royal trappings, the doctrine of sovereign immunity took root in America. Although the exact origin of the rule in the United States is unclear, there is ample evidence that American courts have espoused the doctrine since the earliest days of the republic.[3] What are the theoretical and practical justifications for such a doctrine? Over the years, courts and commentators have mentioned at least four.

The first justification is found in the concept of sovereignty itself. Since the sovereign can choose not to create a cause of action, the reasoning goes, then it follows logically that the sovereign can choose to create a cause of action that is not applicable to itself. We can recognize this as an example of the oft-stated maxim that the greater power entails the lesser. In the strong words of Hamilton, writing in *The Federalist,* "[i]t is inherent in the nature of sovereignty not to be amenable to the suit of an individual *without its consent.* This is the general sense, and the general practice of mankind . . . ."[4] Therefore, without clear consent by the sovereign, it must be presumed that no one may sue the sovereign.

---

1. Note, *Rethinking Sovereign Immunity After* Bivens, 57 N.Y.U. L. REV. 597, 604-06 (1982).

2. 1 W. BLACKSTONE, COMMENTARIES 367, § 346(a) (corrective for royal mistakes) (1976 ed. Claitor's Publishing Division).

3. *See, e.g.,* the dictum of Chief Justice Marshall in Cohens v. Virginia, 19 U.S. (6 Wheat.) 264, 411-12 (1821): "The universally received opinion is, that no suit can be commenced or prosecuted against the United States; that the judiciary act does not authorize such suits."

4. THE FEDERALIST No. 81, at 487 (C. Rossiter ed. 1961).

Justice Holmes advanced a second "justification" when he noted the "logical and practical ground that there can be no legal right as against the authority that makes the law on which the right depends."[5] This Holmesian justification rests on the positivist model of law as the command of the sovereign.[6] According to that view, it is senseless to speak of rights against the sovereign since the sovereign itself creates all legal rights and can at any time abolish or modify those rights. Scholars and courts have questioned the validity of this statement, and in recent years it has been dismissed as unpersuasive and outdated.[7] Rather than being a separate justification, this statement by Holmes seems little more than a restatement of the first justification already advanced. It is worth noting, however, that the Supreme Court recently repeated this rationale in *Nevada v. Hall* as an explanation for why "no sovereign may be sued in its courts without its consent."[8]

The third justification for the doctrine of sovereign immunity is more pragmatic, stemming from the inability of courts to enforce judgments without assistance from the executive. It is argued that the court, as essentially a declaratory branch of government, is without the power to enforce judgments against either the executive or legislative branches on whom the judiciary relies. Note, however, that this justification, advanced by Chief Justice Jay in *Chisholm v. Georgia*,[9] seems at least arguably inconsistent with the very notion of judicial review and limited government. It is not clear that telling the legislature that it cannot enforce a law which the court has determined to be unconstitutional is very different from telling the commissioner of transportation that his or her department was negligent in not adequately maintaining the highways.

In the modern era there appears to be general agreement that the major justification for sovereign immunity is social policy. The core concern, modern courts and commentators state, is the prevention of

---

5. Kawananakoa v. Polyblank, 205 U.S. 349, 353 (1907).

6. C. JACOBS, THE ELEVENTH AMENDMENT AND SOVEREIGN IMMUNITY 155 (1972). The quintessential positivist model is found in J. AUSTIN, LECTURES ON JURISPRUDENCE; OR, THE PHILOSOPHY OF POSITIVE LAW (1861).

7. *See, e.g.,* Byse, *Proposed Reforms in Nonstatutory Judicial Review: Sovereign Immunity, Indispensable Parties, Mandamus,* 75 HARV. L. REV. 1479 (1962); Jaffe, *Suits Against Governments and Officers: Sovereign Immunity,* 77 HARV. L. REV. 1, 4 (1963); Block, *Suits Against Government Officers and the Sovereign Immunity Doctrine,* 59 HARV. L. REV. 1060 (1946).

8. 440 U.S. 410, 416 (1979).

9. Chisholm v. Georgia, 2 U.S. (2 Dall.) 419, 478 (1793):

[I]n all cases of actions against States or individual citizens, the National Courts are supported in all their legal and Constitutional proceedings and judgments, by the arm of the Executive power of the United States; but in cases of actions against the United States, there is no power which the courts can call to their aid.

114

undue judicial interference in the everyday functioning of the state. According to Chief Justice Vinson, "The interference of the Courts with the performance of the ordinary duties of the executive departments of the government, would be productive of nothing but mischief . . . ."[10] This focus on interference encompasses both a concern with decisionmaking and administration of governmental programs (autonomy), and a particular reluctance to curtail the discretion of the legislature and the executive to control government funds (fiscal control). Although these concerns with autonomy and fiscal control are the ones most often advanced by courts today, it is important to keep in mind the other, more theoretical justifications which underlie the original concept of sovereign immunity.

II. General Principles

Under the general principle of sovereign immunity, the sovereign cannot be sued without its consent. The paradigmatic case involves a suit brought by a citizen of the sovereign, against the sovereign, in one of the sovereign's own courts. However, as we know, the American system of federalism, with its fifty-one sovereigns and multitude of courts, is likely to pose special problems for such a general principle. Rather than a single box which contains a suit against Nation *A*, in Nation *A*'s court, where Nation *A*'s law will apply, we have a matrix with three variables — the sovereign (state or federal), the court (state or federal) and the law (state or federal). The different problems represented by the different cells in the matrix are discussed in different sections of this chapter.

	state A court	state B court	federal court
state A as defendant	section IIA	section IIIA	section IV
federal gov't as defendant	section IIIB		section IIB

In subsequent sections, we will discuss the special problems that arise due to the federal system, but for now, let us look at how the doctrine operates in the simple case of a suit brought by a citizen of State *A* in a State *A* court.

---

10. Larson v. Domestic & Foreign Commerce Corp., 337 U.S. 682, 704 (1949), quoting from Decatur v. Paulding, 39 U.S. (14 Pet.) 497, 516 (1840).

A. State Immunity in State Court

With a strict application of the doctrine of sovereign immunity, it would be impossible for anyone to sue the state or to sue anyone who was a state officer without the state's consent. Out of concern that such absolute sovereign immunity would allow the government to trample on the legal rights of citizens, the state courts have created a variety of techniques by which suits may be brought.

The primary device for getting around the blanket prohibition on suits against the state has been the "officer's suit." Rather than naming the state itself as defendant — which would bar the suit[11] — the plaintiff was required to name the state officer as an individual defendant who had, by his action or inaction, interfered with the plaintiff's rights. Then, unless the defendant could persuade the court that he was acting in accordance with a valid state law, the suit would be allowed. By this legal sleight of hand, the officer was stripped of his official character and treated as a private citizen who would be responsible for his tortious acts. In other words, the state official was said to be acting *ultra vires,* and therefore was no longer entitled to the protective mantle of sovereign immunity. As we will see later in this chapter, the Supreme Court used this same legal fiction in *Ex parte Young,* where the Court held that a challenge to the constitutionality of a state official's action was not a suit against the state, and thus not barred by the eleventh amendment.[12] Note, however, that the mere fact of tortious action by a state official does not in and of itself make the action ultra vires, if the action is within the officer's general authority.[13]

The case of *Litchfield v. Bond* is typical of such an officer's suit.[14] Plaintiff had brought suit in a New York trial court against defendant, the New York state engineer, for cutting down trees within plaintiff's land while defendant was making boundary surveys pursuant to legislative authority. The New York Court of Appeals held that plaintiff could sue defendant because

> The trespasses committed upon the plaintiff's land were not the acts of the state, but the unauthorized and unlawful wrongs of the defendants, who, although the agents of the state within their sphere of duty, were naked usurpers in assuming to do that which the state could neither do nor authorize to be done . . . .
> [D]efendants, though professing to act as officers of the state, are threatening a violation of the personal or property rights of the

---

11. *Cf.* Osborn v. Bank of United States, 22 U.S. (9 Wheat.) 738 (1824).
12. 209 U.S. 123, 159-60 (1908).
13. *Larson,* 337 U.S. at 689.
14. 186 N.Y. 66, 78 N.E. 719 (N.Y. 1906).

complainant, for which they are personally and individually liable.[15]

Thus that which is done contrary to state law or the Constitution is not an act of the sovereign, and the putative agent of the state is not entitled to claim immunity based on such "lawless" acts. Such logic clearly stems from the notion that the sovereign can do no wrong — illegal or improper acts done in the name of the sovereign are not truly acts of the sovereign and the evil-doers cannot cloak themselves in the protective mantle of the state's sovereign immunity.

A successful plaintiff in an officer's suit would then be entitled to the same remedies he would have if the defendant were a private citizen. In essence, the suit is transformed from one between a private citizen and the sovereign into one between two private parties. One of the most important consequences flowing from the use of this ultra vires rationale is that the court is limited to the use of common-law remedies, particularly injunction and mandamus. If the defendant owed a legal duty to the plaintiff that the defendant had failed to perform, the plaintiff might seek an order to force the defendant to perform that duty.[16] Similarly, as in the case of *Litchfield v. Bond* above, the plaintiff might seek an injunction to prevent the putative state agent from treading on the plaintiff's rights. Although such remedies may be adequate in some circumstances, it is easy to see how they might be inadequate in others.

Take the example of a suit arising out of the destruction of property during an illegal police search. The plaintiff is likely to ask for an injunction against further warrantless searches, and for money damages. Although the court would most certainly provide injunctive relief, if the police officer is judgment-proof, as is often the case, the plaintiff is out of luck in his damage claim. The court could not order the state to pay damages, since by definition the police officer was not acting in his official capacity at the time. As we will see below, despite substantial relaxation of the doctrine of sovereign immunity by congressional acts the recovery of money damages is still problematic. This doubtless relates back to our discussion of the justifications for sovereign immunity, including the reluctance of the courts to hand down judgments that would require the state to dip into the state treasury.

Some state courts have avoided an absolute bar on suits against the state by dividing activities into two categories — "governmental" activities, which generally receive the protection of immunity, and "pro-

---

15. *Id.*, at 725-26.
16. Byse, *supra* note 7, at 1499-1502.

prietary" activities which are not entitled to protection. The essence of the distinction is this: governmental activities are those in which the state is acting *as sovereign,* e.g., providing police and fire protection. Proprietary functions, on the other hand, are those activities in which the state is acting like an ordinary, private party, such as providing electric service or renting out the state's fair grounds. Often the distinction turns on whether the governmental entity is acting "solely for the public benefit."[17] For example, Michigan has retained the governmental-proprietary distinction in its statutes, defining proprietary activities as "any activity which is conducted primarily for the purpose of producing a pecuniary profit for the state, excluding however, any activity normally supported by taxes or fees."[18]

In theory, this distinction serves to limit invocation of immunity to those instances where the state is acting as sovereign. Presumably, when the state is not acting in its sovereign capacity, there is no justification for the state to be protected from liability. Although the rationale for the distinction is somewhat tautological, its function is clear. The governmental-proprietary distinction has served to limit the doctrine of sovereign immunity by "draw[ing] a line between situations where the state interest in immunity should prevail and those where the individual's interest in a remedy is the more compelling."[19] While one can see the validity of the distinction in some cases, it is not hard to imagine the difficult line-drawing problems occasioned by such a rule. As the Supreme Court itself recognized, "[t]he basis of the distinction is difficult to state, and there is no established rule for the determination of what belongs to the one or the other class."[20] One sees current analogues to the governmental-proprietary distinction in the discretionary-ministerial acts test[21] and the traditional or essential function test.[22]

The third exception to the sovereign immunity bar is waiver or consent by the sovereign. In many states, the doctrine of sovereign immunity has been prospectively abrogated by the courts.[23] Those state

---

17. Austin v. City of Baltimore, 286 Md. 51, 65, 405 A.2d 255, 262 (1979).

18. Mich. Comp. Laws Ann. § 691.1413 (West 1968).

19. Wells & Hellerstein, *The Governmental-Proprietary Distinction in Constitutional Law,* 66 Va. L. Rev. 1073, 1090 (1980).

20. City of Trenton v. New Jersey, 262 U.S. 182, 191-92 (1923).

21. Costa v. Josey, 83 N.J. 49, 60, 415 A.2d 337, 343 (1980) (holding that statute immunizing a public entity from liability for injury resulting from exercise of judgment or discretion protects only basic policy determinations and not simple operational decisions).

22. Idaho Potato Comm'n v. Washington Potato Comm'n, 410 F. Supp. 171, 175 (D. Idaho 1975).

23. *See, e.g.,* Evans v. Board of County Comm'rs, 174 Colo. 97 (1971); Pruett v. City of Rosedale, 421 So. 2d 1046 (Miss. 1982); Board of Comm'rs of the Port of New Orleans

courts that have abolished sovereign immunity in some contexts have usually done so under the theory that sovereign immunity is itself a court-made doctrine that is therefore within the authority of the court to modify or eliminate.[24] In other words, as the voice of the sovereign that articulated the need for protection of the sovereign from suit, the court is authorized to voice the sovereign's intention not to be so protected.

In other instances, states have expressly waived their sovereign immunity by statute, as in the case of California.[25] As with any state statute, the interpretation of a statute that purports to waive the state's sovereign immunity is itself a matter of state law.[26] Courts have also traditionally construed such statutory waivers rather strictly, presuming that no waiver is intended unless there is an explicit legislative statement to the contrary.

A final method for avoiding the state immunity doctrine is to sue some governmental entity other than the state itself, such as a municipality or state agency. Early cases relied solely on the pleadings of the parties to determine whether the suit was "against the state." However, it soon became apparent that such a rule was subject to manipulation by the plaintiff who merely had to name some state officer as the defendant in order to escape the sovereign immunity bar. The difficulty with identifying when a suit is a suit against the sovereign is especially acute in the case of suits against administrative agencies. Is a suit naming the state department of transportation a "suit against the state"? What about a suit against the head of the state welfare commission, or a suit naming the chief of police of the state's largest city? One can imagine that there are nearly limitless variations possible, making bright-line rules almost impossible. As we will see below in the discussion of other immunity problems, this issue is one of continuing controversy that admits of no easy solution. For instance, it also arises when the federal government is sued in federal court, a problem which we next address.

---

v. Splendour Shipping & Enters. Co., 273 So. 2d 19 (La. 1973); Lorence v. Hospital Bd. of Morgan County, 322 So. 2d 631 (Ala. 1975); Hargrove v. Town of Cocoa Beach, 96 So. 2d 130 (Fla. 1957); Hicks v. State, 544 P.2d 1153 (N.M. 1975); Molitor v. Kaneland Community Unit District No. 302, 163 N.E.2d 89 (Ill. 1959); Jones v. State Highway Comm'n, 557 S.W.2d 225 (Mo. 1977); Mayle v. Pennsylvania Dep't of Highways, 388 A.2d 709 (Pa. 1978); Long v. City of Weirton, 214 S.E.2d 832 (W. Va. 1975); Brown v. Wichita State Univ., 540 P.2d 66 (Kan. 1975).

24. *E.g.,* Pruett v. City of Rosedale, 421 So. 2d at 1046.

25. CAL. CONST. art. III, § 5 (West 1983) and Tort Claims Act, Cal. Gov. Code § 900 et seq. (West 1980). It is worth noting that such an express waiver by a state, while controlling in its own courts, does not automatically subject the state to suit in federal court. *See* Kennecott Copper Corp. v. State Tax Comm'n, 326 U.S. 573 (1946).

26. Smith v. Reeves, 178 U.S. 436, 441 (1900).

B. Federal Immunity in Federal Court

The rationale concerning suits against the federal government in federal courts has been rather similar to that found in cases against the state brought in state court. Although there is no explicit constitutional provision discussing the sovereign immunity of the United States, the Court has long held that absent its consent, the federal government is immune from suit in federal court.[27] The United States government, as the supreme sovereign in our federal system, is given extensive leeway to determine for itself just when and how it will allow itself to be sued. Acting as the voice of the sovereign, Congress may waive that immunity by statute. As in the case of state sovereign immunity, statutory waivers of federal sovereign immunity have been strictly construed.[28] In recent years the Court has been less hostile to suits against the United States, and has accordingly viewed waivers of sovereign immunity more liberally.[29]

Congress has seen fit to waive immunity in a variety of cases. The earliest example of such consent to be sued is the United States Court of Claims, created in 1855 with jurisdiction to assess money damages against the federal government based on Acts of Congress, regulations by executive agencies, or contracts (express or implied) with the government.[30] This consent was expanded in 1887 with the passage of the Tucker Act, which grants jurisdiction to the Court of Claims or to the federal district courts (to the latter only if the amount in controversy is less than $10,000) in suits based on the Constitution and in civil and admiralty damage actions, exclusive of tort suits.[31] The Tucker Act did not, however, create any substantive rights against the federal government — its reach is purely jurisdictional.[32]

The Federal Tort Claims Act of 1946 is the third important congressional waiver of federal immunity.[33] The principle behind the statute is that the federal government should be liable for the negligence of its employees to the same extent as would a private individual in similar circumstances. The FTCA provides for jurisdiction exclusively in the federal district courts. The substantive coverage of the FTCA is, however, qualified by a multitude of exceptions, leaving much misconduct without remedy.

---

27. Kansas v. United States, 204 U.S. 331, 342-43 (1907).
28. *See, e.g.,* United States v. Sherwood, 312 U.S. 584, 590 (1941) and Schillinger v. United States, 155 U.S. 163, 166 (1894).
29. *See, e.g.,* United States v. Yellow Cab Co., 340 U.S. 543, 550 (1951).
30. Act of Feb. 24, 1855, 10 Stat. 612, now codified at 28 U.S.C. § 1491 (1982).
31. Act of Mar. 3, 1887, 24 Stat. 505, now codified at 28 U.S.C. §§ 1346(a)(2), 1491 (1982).
32. United States v. Mitchell, 449 U.S. 535 (1980), *reh. den.,* 446 U.S. 992.
33. Act of Aug. 2, 1946, Title IV, 60 Stat. 812, 842 (1946).

In addition to the Court of Claims, the Tucker Act, and the FTCA, there are a number of other statutes in which Congress has explicitly consented to suit, including suits to recover taxes,[34] suits on contracts,[35] actions in which the United States is a joint tenant or tenant in common,[36] suits in admiralty,[37] suits based on the Social Security Act,[38] and actions concerning the rights to Indian lands.[39]

One of the most problematic areas of federal sovereign immunity concerns the ability of citizens to sue federal officials and administrative agencies. As the federal government has taken on a much more active role in the provision of social welfare, the lack of a general statute granting jurisdiction over such suits has become more serious. For many years the only way for a plaintiff to obtain relief was to convince the court that the federal official named as defendant had been acting ultra vires, either by exceeding his statutory authority, or by acting under statutory powers that were themselves unconstitutional.[40] These ultra vires arguments were rarely available and left many aggrieved plaintiffs without recourse.[41]

Congress's first response to the problem was to give district courts original jurisdiction over mandamus actions to compel federal officers or agencies to perform a duty owed to the plaintiff.[42] In 1976 Congress again addressed the problem of sovereign-immunity bars to suits against federal officials by amending the Administrative Procedures Act and removing the amount in controversy requirement under 28 U.S.C. § 1331 as to suits brought against the United States or any federal officer or agency. The amendment to the A.P.A. provided that an action

> seeking relief other than money damages and stating a claim that an agency or officer or employee thereof acted or failed to act in an official capacity or under color of legal authority shall not be dismissed nor relief therein be denied on the ground that it is against

---

34. 28 U.S.C. § 1346(a)(1) (1982).

35. 41 U.S.C. § 113(b) (1982).

36. 28 U.S.C. §§ 1347, 2409 (1982).

37. 46 U.S.C. §§ 741 et seq. (1982).

38. 42 U.S.C. § 405(c)(5)(g) (1982).

39. 28 U.S.C. § 1353 (1982).

40. *See, e.g.,* United States v. Lee, 106 U.S. 196, 220-21 (1882); Yearsley v. Ross Constr. Co., 309 U.S. 18, 21 (1940).

41. *E.g.,* Larson v. Domestic & Foreign Commerce Corp., 337 U.S. 682, 695 (1949) (injunctive and declaratory suit against federal officer to prevent sale of coal under contract to plaintiff was one against the United States and was therefore barred, even if such actions by the governmental officers were tortious and therefore illegal under general law).

42. Act of Oct. 5, 1962, Pub. L. 87-748, § 1(a), 76 Stat. 744, codified at 28 U.S.C. § 1361 (1982).

the United States or that the United States is an indispensable party.[43]

It is noteworthy that this waiver of sovereign immunity does not apply to suits for money damages.

C. Sovereign Immunity in the International Context

As shown above, the concept of sovereign immunity typically refers to the inability of citizens to sue the sovereign in its own courts. The paradigmatic suit involves a claim brought by a citizen of State *A* against State *A* in a State *A* court. Despite ancient notions that sovereign immunity is absolute, the recent trend has been to provide some remedy for claims against a government in its own courts. However, each state (and the federal government) has been given quite a free hand to decide for itself what the contours of its sovereign immunity will be, *in its own courts.*

The treatment of sovereign immunity in the international context helps to highlight some of the subject's fundamental principles. For most of the United States' history, foreign governments have been given absolute immunity from suit in U.S. courts and have also been protected by the so-called "act of state" doctrine.[44] According to the federal common-law doctrine of act of state, as enunciated in *Banco Nacional de Cuba v. Sabbatino,* federal courts are prevented from inquiring into the legality of public acts undertaken by sovereigns on their own soil.[45] Despite earlier loose language, the Supreme Court has clarified that the act of state doctrine is not a requirement of international law, but that it is a matter of the internal law of each country.[46] In the United States, the application of the act of state doctrine is treated as a federal question, not to be resolved by reference to state laws.[47]

The act of state doctrine, like most doctrines of sovereign immunity, is grounded in both practical and theoretical concerns. The classic statement of the doctrine is found in the 1897 case of *Underhill v. Hernandez.*[48] Underhill, a United States citizen, had brought suit in a federal court in New York to recover damages from Hernandez, commander of the revolutionary army of Venezuela, for acts taken by

---

43. 5 U.S.C. § 702 (1982).
44. The Schooner Exchange v. M'Faddon, 11 U.S. (7 Cranch) 116, 136-37 (1812); Banco Nacional de Cuba v. Sabbatino, 376 U.S. 398 (1963).
45. 376 U.S. 398, 400-01 (1964).
46. *Id.* at 421-27.
47. *Id.* at 425. *See also* Restatement (Second) Foreign Relations Law of the United States § 41 (1965).
48. 168 U.S. 250 (1897).

Hernandez when both were in Venezuela. The Supreme Court refused to inquire into the validity of the actions of Hernandez, whom the Court viewed as a leader of the legitimate Venezuelan government. (The State Department had recognized Hernandez' revolutionary forces as the legitimate government of Venezuela.) In words oft-quoted in later opinions, the Court declared:

> Every sovereign State is bound to respect the independence of every other sovereign State, and the courts of one country will not sit in judgment on the acts of the government of another done within its own territory. Redress of grievances by reason of such acts must be obtained through the means open to be availed of by sovereign powers as between themselves.[49]

This statement illustrates the three fundamental justifications for absolute foreign sovereign immunity. First, the rule of absolute sovereign immunity can be seen as homage to the notion that no one may question the acts of the sovereign within its own territory. It is up to the acting sovereign and the acting sovereign alone to determine whether and when it will allow its actions to be questioned in a judicial proceeding. Second, it can be seen as relying on principles of comity within the international system. If the United States were to allow anyone to sue another country in U.S. courts, it would not take long for other countries to retaliate by subjecting the U.S. to suit in *their* foreign courts. As a matter of comity, therefore, the federal sovereign respects the sovereign rights of all other "equal" sovereigns (nation states), at least as to actions taken by foreign nations within their own territorial boundaries. This reasoning mirrors the considerations of comity that we have seen the courts refer to in both the federal and state contexts.

Absolute international immunity can also be understood as a function of separation of powers. Although the Court has held that the Constitution does not require the act of state doctrine, the Court has said that the doctrine has "constitutional underpinnings" arising from the judiciary's strong sense that its involvement in determining the validity of foreign acts of state would be more likely to impede rather than advance the United States' goals.[50]

This is not the first time that we have seen the system of separation of powers and concerns with institutional competence as justifications for sovereign immunity. One of the primary justifications for the doctrine in the state and federal contexts has always been the desire to prevent undue judicial interference in the activities of the executive and legislative branches. This concern with avoiding undue interfer-

---

49. *Id.* at 252.
50. Banco Nacional de Cuba v. Sabbatino, 376 U.S. at 423.

ence is all the more heightened in the international sphere where the courts have long recognized the executive as the premier body authorized to deal with matters of foreign policy.[51] For example, as the Court stated in *Oetjen v. Central Leather Co.,* the determination of who is the sovereign of a foreign territory is a political, not a judicial decision.[52]

In recent years there has been growing pressure for limitations on the principle of absolute immunity for foreign sovereigns, similar to the pressure we have seen in both the state and the federal contexts. In 1976 Congress responded to that pressure by passing the Foreign Sovereign Immunities Act which, although placing some limits on foreign sovereign immunity, nevertheless demonstrates acceptance of its general principles.[53] In essence, the FSIA seeks to restrict foreign sovereign immunity to cases where the foreign government is engaged in a governmental as opposed to a commercial activity.[54] The FSIA can thus be seen as a congressional expression of the negative implication of the act of state doctrine: namely, when a foreign government is not acting in its sovereign capacity, it should not be entitled to immunity. However, the number of provisions in the FSIA devoted to defining when an action will be considered the act of a foreign sovereign demonstrates the persistence of practical and theoretical difficulties in identifying when the sovereign has acted as a sovereign. These difficulties parallel those encountered in the state sovereign-immunity context where courts have struggled to fashion a workable governmental-proprietary function test.

III. Special Problems of Federalism

With fifty co-equal state sovereigns, and one supreme federal sovereign, the American system poses special difficulties for the application of sovereign immunity. Because the notion of sovereign immunity is so clearly about the power of the sovereign itself, this doctrine highlights many of the most intractable disagreements about the appropriate spheres not only for the states versus the federal government, but also for the states versus the federal courts, and the states versus one another.

In specific, we will address three special problems of sovereign immunity in the federal system. First, we consider the problems that

---

51. United States v. Belmont, 301 U.S. 324, 330 (1937); United States v. Pink, 315 U.S. 203, 229 (1942).

52. 246 U.S. 297, 302 (1918), citing Jones v. United States, 137 U.S. 202, 212 (1890).

53. Pub. L. No. 94-583, 90 Stat. 2891 (1976), esp. as codified at 28 U.S.C. §§ 1602-1611 (1982).

54. Texas Trading Milling Corp. v. Federal Republic of Nigeria, 647 F.2d 300, 308 (2d Cir. 1981), *cert. denied,* 454 U.S. 1148 (1982).

arise from suits brought in state courts naming other states as defendants. Second, we will briefly examine the case of federal immunity in state courts. Finally, we will discuss the complicated and varied problems of suits against the state or against state officers brought in federal court. This section will detail the history of the eleventh amendment and the long line of cases discussing the extent of state immunity in a federal forum.

A. Sovereign Immunity in Sister State Courts

One of the first difficult problems of federalism arises when a plaintiff brings suit in State *A*'s court naming State *B* as a defendant. Ever since the passage of the eleventh amendment, there has been little doubt that states are largely immune from suit in federal court, with exceptions to be discussed below. And each state has been left to determine as a matter of state law whether and when it will allow itself to be sued in its own courts. What happens, however, when suit is brought in State A's court against State B?

For many years courts assumed that the Constitution implicitly prohibited such suits.[55] It is not difficult to understand their rationale. If the federal courts, which are a branch of the admittedly supreme government, are not allowed to hear suits in which a state is a defendant because to do so would be to violate the state's sovereignty, how much more clear it is that a suit in State *A* against State *B* should not be permitted? Another state seems particularly poorly suited to entertain such sister-state suits for several reasons. First, there are problems of discrimination. Most often such suits are brought by a local plaintiff to whom the state court is likely to be favorably disposed. The defendant is, by definition, an outsider. Other than the fear of retaliation, there is little to prevent the local forum from helping out the local plaintiff at the direct expense of the other state. Second, when State *B* is actually a party to an action in State *A,* the affront to State *B*'s sovereignty is particularly egregious. Although State *B* is arguably always concerned when one of its citizens is haled into a State *A* court and forced to pay damages to a citizen of State *A,* the concern is increased a hundredfold when the state itself is the defendant.

---

55. *See, e.g.,* Florida State Hosp. v. Durham Iron Co., 194 Ga. 350 (1942) (Georgia court grants defendant's motion to quash attachment and levy on land in Georgia owned by state of Florida); Paulus v. South Dakota, 58 N.D. 643, 649 (1929) ("Should the judicial branch of the government of one state undertake to define the legal obligations of a nonconsenting sister state, it would, in effect, be denying the sovereign of the latter. A state cannot remain the supreme master of its own affairs if it must yield to external conceptions in matters of justice and right.").

Under the constitutional system, furthermore, the states are co-equal sovereigns. How, then, does one such partner have the right to judge the actions of another? To allow such a suit in State *A* would seem to lead to the kind of interstate rivalries and warfare which led to the downfall of the Articles of Confederation and the creation of the Constitution. In fact, even prior to the Constitutional Convention, the Pennsylvania Court of Common Pleas held that Virginia was immune from a suit brought by a Pennsylvania resident in Pennsylvania court.[56]

The courts and commentators have also pointed to the full faith and credit clause as evidence that sovereign immunity should apply in state courts.[57] Although no clause in the Constitution specifically regulates the extent to which states must recognize each other's sovereign immunity, the full faith and credit clause requires each state to recognize the laws and judgments of all other states. Arguably, then, it should require each state to respect every other state's rule of sovereign immunity. If sovereign immunity is viewed as a jurisdiction-limiting law, it would seem that full faith and credit requires State *A* to respect State *B*'s sovereign immunity in the same way that it would have to respect a substantive law.

However, when the Supreme Court finally considered whether the Constitution requires state courts to recognize the immunity claims of sister states, it held that there was no such constitutional requirement. *Nevada v. Hall,*[58] decided in 1979, dealt with the issue of whether California could disregard the sovereign immunity claims of the defendant state (Nevada), whose instrumentality had injured two Californians in California. In holding that the California plaintiffs could sue Nevada, the Court concluded that neither article III nor the eleventh amendment denied California the power to exercise jurisdiction over other states. As to the full faith and credit defense raised by Nevada, the Supreme Court noted that in some circumstances full faith and credit might require the courts of one state to apply the statutory laws of another state (including, by implication, the other state's law of sovereign immunity), but stated that this was not such a case.[59]

How can one explain this decision, which would seem to threaten the integrity of the federal system by allowing state courts to disregard the sovereignty of sister states? There are two specific facts of this case which help to place it within traditional notions of limitations on sov-

---

56. Nathan v. Virginia, 1 U.S. (1 Dall.) 77 (1781).
57. U.S. Const. art. IV, § 1: "Full Faith and Credit shall be given in each State to the public Acts, Records and Judicial Proceedings of every other State. . . ."
58. 440 U.S. 410 (1979).
59. *Id.* at 421-24.

ereign immunity. First, Nevada was acting outside of its territorial borders when the incident occurred that gave rise to the cause of action. Under some traditional notions of sovereignty, an agent of the sovereign who acts outside of the territory governed by the sovereign cannot claim to be acting as a sovereign. In essence, the state is sovereign only within its own borders.[60]

Second, California supplied the applicable law. Had the plaintiffs brought suit in Nevada under Nevada law, there is no doubt that the result would have been different. Nevada courts would have been certain to honor Nevada's claim of sovereign immunity as a matter of state law. However, since California had abolished its own sovereign immunity in such cases, it seemed perfectly reasonable for the California court to hold that Nevada could not claim sovereign immunity. There are two respects in which the applicable law was California law: on the sovereign immunity issue and on the substantive liability issue. First, the California court could argue that it was not treating Nevada any differently than it would treat itself; i.e. it applied California sovereign immunity law to all who came before it. In essence, this argument postulates that the sovereign can apply to all other sovereigns whatever local sovereign immunity law it applies to itself. Second, California could claim that as the creator of the applicable substantive law, it was entitled to decide whether any sovereign would be immune from that substantive law. This is recognizable as a restatement of the traditional view espoused by Holmes: the sovereign that creates the cause of action is entitled to exclude sovereigns as defendants.[61]

It is worth noting that these varied explanations could lead to different results if the fact pattern were altered slightly. For instance, if California were to entertain a suit based on a Nevada cause of action, the rule of applying local sovereign immunity law would lead to California refusing to recognize any immunity of Nevada, whereas the Holmesian "law of the sovereign that created the cause of action" rule would result in California according Nevada the sovereign immunity provided for under Nevada law. Furthermore, both of these rationales which rely upon the applicability of California law differ from the rationale which relies upon the location of the injury in California. Under that rationale, Nevada would automatically be protected if the accident occurred there.

Recent cases such as *Ehrlich-Bober & Co. v. University of Houston*,[62] illustrate the unanswered questions implicit in *Nevada v. Hall.*

---

60. *Id.* at 428 (Blackmun, J., dissenting), citing Hall v. University of Nevada, 74 Cal. App. 3d 280, 284 (1977), quoting Hall v. University of Nevada, 8 Cal. 3d 522, 525, 503 P.2d 1363, 1365 (1972), *cert. denied,* 414 U.S. 820 (1973).

61. Kawananakoa v. Polyblank, 205 U.S. 349, 353 (1907).

62. 49 N.Y.2d 574 (1980).

Ehrich-Bober involved a suit by a New York municipal securities dealer against the University of Houston for breach of contract (which allegedly arose out of telephone calls from plaintiff's New York office). The New York Court of Appeals held that under *Nevada v. Hall,* the Constitution did not require the New York court to apply a Texas statute limiting jurisdiction over suits against the University to certain Texas courts. What is noteworthy, and disturbing, about the case is that the New York Court of Appeals made this holding despite the fact that under New York law, suits against the State University of New York are subject to similar forum restrictions. This result seems fairly clearly to violate even the minimal standards of comity observed in *Nevada v. Hall,* amounting to discrimination against another state. Whether such results will be tolerated by the Supreme Court remains to be seen.

The recognition of sovereign immunity in sister state courts is but one example of the general question of what constitutional limits there are on choice of law in the state/state context. The extraterritorial effect of a state's sovereign immunity is, after all, a matter of state choice of law. Given the Court's unwillingness to place anything but the most minimal due process limits on a forum state's ability to apply forum law, it should not be surprising that the Court would be similarly deferential to the forum state's decision not to apply another state's law of sovereign immunity. We discuss this larger issue, generally, in Chapter 9.

B. Suits Against the Federal Government in State Court

Just as the case of a suit against the state brought in federal court raises issues of federalism, so, too, does the prospect of suits brought in state court naming the federal government as defendant. Although the structure and the ethos of the federal system mitigates against a state court overtly discriminating against the federal government in such a case, it is easy to imagine that the state court might often be tempted to favor the local plaintiff at the expense of legitimate sovereign immunity claims by the federal official. Aware of the temptation to discriminate, and concerned with possible interference with the smooth functioning of the federal government, Congress provided for removal of suits against federal officers from state to federal court.[63] As a practical matter, such suits were and are removed to federal court even when the cause of action is based entirely on state law.

---

63. Currently codified at 28 U.S.C. § 1442 (1982).

However, since substantive common-law developments and the amending of the Administrative Procedure Act to permit suits against federal administrative officials,[64] most suits brought against the federal government and its officers are brought under federal law. Such suits can be brought in federal court initially, and even if brought in state court, they are removable to federal court. Therefore, as a practical matter, there is not a significant category of cases involving suits against the federal government being heard in state court. One of the prerogatives of supreme sovereignty is the power to have cases involving the misconduct of its agents be heard in its own courts.

IV. States' Immunity in Federal Court

Principles of sovereign immunity limit adjudicative jurisdiction by circumscribing not only the power of courts to decide cases brought against their own sovereign, but also the power of the federal courts to hear cases involving states as defendants. In this area, a complex and at times contradictory body of rules has emerged to govern both what cases may be heard, and the available remedies. The seeming technicality of these rules, however, should not mask the serious debates about federalism that often lie just below the surface. The prospect of allowing the federal courts, armed with the power to issue far-reaching injunctive decrees, to oversee the day-to-day operations of state governmental institutions is one that raises delicate issues of federal-state relations. Suits against states typically involve challenges to activities that the state considers its fundamental sovereign responsibilities — prison administration, public education, and welfare benefits are typical examples — but in which there is also a keen federal constitutional interest.

The jurisdictional debates surrounding states' sovereign immunity to suits in federal court often reveal basic disagreements about both the existence and contours of the substantive rights involved, and the appropriate role of the federal and state governments. In many ways, these disputes are at the heart of the problems raised by our federal system. In addition, the debates are further complicated by the fact that, unlike principles of sovereign immunity in either a single state system or in that of the federal government, which derive from the common law, the states' sovereign immunity in the federal context has been codified in the eleventh amendment. Its constitutional status greatly increases the importance of state immunity as a jurisdictional bar.

---

64. Currently codified at 5 U.S.C. § 702 (1982). Federal courts have recognized common-law remedies for violations of the Constitution by federal officers since Bivens v. Six Unknown Named Agents of the Federal Bureau of Narcotics, 403 U.S. 388 (1971); *see also* Davis v. Passman, 442 U.S. 228 (1979).

A. The Eleventh Amendment

Article III of the United States Constitution specifically includes within the federal jurisdiction cases "between a State and Citizens of another State."[65] Acting under this provision, the Supreme Court early in its history took jurisdiction over *Chisholm v. Georgia*,[66] a suit brought by a citizen of South Carolina against the state of Georgia to recover on bonds that the state had confiscated. A majority of the Court ruled against the state, with Justice Wilson emphasizing that the constitutional prohibition against laws impairing the obligation of contracts would mean little if a state could avoid paying its debts by simply invoking sovereign immunity.[67] Public reaction to the decision, however, was "such a shock of surprise"[68] at the Court's having assumed jurisdiction, that the eleventh amendment was quickly proposed and adopted in 1798. The amendment explicitly overrules the decision — a rare occurrence in our constitutional history. Addressed specifically to the facts in *Chisholm*, the amendment reads:

> The Judicial power of the United States shall not be construed to extend to any suit in law or equity, commenced or prosecuted against one of the United States by Citizens of another State, or by Citizens or Subjects of any Foreign State.[69]

Thus, it includes within its language only suits against a state by citizens of another state or of a foreign nation, and does not mention suits against a state by its own citizens. The amendment has, however, been interpreted both more broadly and more narrowly than the language might suggest.

One possible reading of the amendment would have been to interpret it simply as a limitation on diversity jurisdiction. That is, the amendment might imply that diversity is not a sufficient basis for suits by a citizen of one state against another state, although other bases such as diversity jurisdiction not involving a state as a defendant, or involving a federal question would survive. This was Chief Justice Marshall's position.[70] Similarly, the amendment could have been read in light of its historical context, solely to bar contract actions against the state, or other suits related to the states' debts.

---

65. U.S. Const. art. III, § 2, cl. 1.
66. 2 U.S. (2 Dall.) 419 (1793).
67. *Id.* at 465.
68. Monaco v. Mississippi, 292 U.S. 313, 325 (1934).
69. U.S. Const. amend. XI.
70. *See* Cohens v. Virginia, 19 U.S. (6 Wheat.) 264, 348-49 (1821); Employees v. Missouri Pub. Health Dep't, 411 U.S. 279, 311-313 (1973) (Brennan, J., dissenting).

Both of these restrictive readings, however, were rejected early, and a far more expansive approach to the limitation on federal jurisdiction was taken instead. In *Hans v. Louisiana*,[71] decided in 1890, the Court applied the amendment to a suit brought by a citizen against his own state, a result that the language of the amendment clearly does not require. The majority found that the constitutional debates on the scope of article III revealed that the Framers never contemplated federal jurisdiction over suits against unconsenting states.[72] This conclusion was later reiterated in *Monaco v. Mississippi*.[73] The *Monaco* Court characterized *Hans* as having held that the eleventh amendment "exemplified the broader and more ancient doctrine of sovereign immunity,"[74] an essential postulate which the Court in *Monaco* found to lie behind both article III and the eleventh amendment itself.[75]

The disagreement over the proper scope of the eleventh amendment persists; Justice Brennan has suggested that *Hans* imposes a constitutional bar to jurisdiction only for suits that fall within the amendment's literal language and a nonconstitutional immunity for suits against a state by its own citizens.[76] Nevertheless, the eleventh amendment has been read expansively as a constitutional limitation on the federal judicial power, thereby implicitly barring all suits against the state.[77] Thus the amendment's application is broader than might be surmised from an initial reading.

At the same time, however, its potentially broad implications for federal jurisdiction has been narrowed significantly by the Supreme Court in other ways. For example, the Court has consistently interpreted the amendment's omission of the United States or other states among the parties commencing suit to mean that states have no immunity from suits initiated by such parties.[78] More significantly, however, the amendment's reach has been narrowed by a set of rules that limit the group of cases deemed to be against the state.

---

71. 134 U.S. 1 (1890).

72. *Id.* at 12-15.

73. 292 U.S. 313 (1934).

74. Pennhurst State School & Hosp. v. Halderman, 104 S. Ct. 900, 930 & n.18 (1984) (Stevens, J., dissenting) (describing holding in *Monaco*).

75. *Monaco*, 292 U.S. at 322-23.

76. *Pennhurst*, 104 S. Ct. at 921-22 (Brennan, J., dissenting).

77. *See id.*, at 906-07.

78. *See, e.g.*, United States v. Mississippi, 380 U.S. 128 (1965) (Supreme Court has jurisdiction to adjudicate suit by United States against a state).

B. Suits Not Lying Against the State

Determining whether a particular suit should be deemed "against one of the United States"[79] has been one of the most difficult problems plaguing eleventh amendment analysis. The Supreme Court soon recognized that if the amendment's limitation on federal jurisdiction was interpreted expansively, every case against a state department or official would be barred.[80] The federal courts would then be unable to hear the vast majority of claims against state governments — including cases seeking to vindicate constitutional provisions specifically drawn to provide protection *against* the state. Thus such cases would be relegated to the state courts in the very state against which the claim was brought, where state-law principles of sovereign immunity presumably would govern whether the case could proceed at all. Such a system clearly would be ill-equipped to guarantee enforcement of basic federal rights.

Three principles have evolved that allow adjudication of certain cases in the federal courts, notwithstanding the eleventh amendment. First, not all governmental subunits are considered states for purposes of the eleventh amendment. Second, under the doctrine of *Ex parte Young,* the federal courts may hear cases against a state official that allege acts that are either unconstitutional or lack *any* authority under state law. And third, the federal courts can hear cases in which the state has "waived" its immunity to federal suit.

1. Separate Governmental Units

Where the defendant is a state-affiliated governmental body, such as an agency, board, or public institution, a federal court will first ask whether the suit is against an arm of the state, and therefore really against the state itself, or whether it can more accurately be characterized as a suit against a separate governmental unit. In general, suits against the state, its agencies, or departments are deemed to fall into the former category, where the eleventh amendment proscribes jurisdiction unless subject to one of the other exceptions.[81] At the other extreme, counties and cities usually are not considered arms of the

---

79. U.S. Const. amend. XI.

80. *See* discussion in sec. IVB2 *infra.*

81. *See, e.g.,* Employees v. Missouri Pub. Health Dep't, 411 U.S. 279 (1973) (state agency is immune from suit for overtime pay brought by employees).

state, at least for eleventh amendment purposes, and can be sued in federal court.[82]

In between, however, fall a wide range of governmental bodies that the court must independently examine for qualification for constitutional immunity. The result depends upon a number of factors, including the state law creating the body; the body's status under state sovereign immunity law; and its powers to contract, sue on behalf of, and raise and expend funds in the name of the state.[83] Particularly if the latter powers are present, a court is highly likely to find the defendant to be an arm of the state.[84]

While state law and immunities are taken into account in determining whether a state governmental body should be immune in federal court, whether a state defendant is an arm of the state is ultimately a federal question.[85] A state cannot, for example, insulate a school district from suit in federal court by statutorily labelling it as a state entity.[86] In most cases, the key question is whether recovery from the defendant eventually would come from the state treasury.[87]

This rule, which is a sensible reading of the immunity that the eleventh amendment was designed to incorporate, allows federal suits to proceed against separate governmental units such as cities, school boards, and counties.

2. Ex Parte Young

The question whether the defendant is an arm of the state is only the beginning of the inquiry, since such cases often involve defendants who are amenable to the limited jurisdiction permissible under *Ex parte Young* and its progeny. Decided in 1908, the "watershed"[88] case *Ex parte Young*[89] created a major exception to the general rule barring challenges to state action, by holding that a suit challenging the constitutionality of a state official's action is not a suit against the state. This improbable result was accomplished by adopting the fiction that

---

82. *See* Mount Healthy Bd. of Educ. v. Doyle, 429 U.S. 274, 280 (1977); *see also* Owen v. City of Independence, 445 U.S. 622 (1980); Monell v. Department of Social Servs., 436 U.S. 658 (1978). Conversely, however, counties and cities *are* considered arms of the state for the purpose of substantive liability under the fourteenth amendment; this paradox is discussed in sec. IVB2 *infra*.

83. *See* 13 C. WRIGHT, A. MILLER, & E. COOPER, FEDERAL PRACTICE AND PROCEDURE § 3524 at 134-36 (1984) [hereinafter cited as WRIGHT, MILLER & COOPER].

84. *Id.* at 136.

85. *Id.* at 137-39.

86. *Cf. Mount Healthy*, 429 U.S. at 280-81.

87. *See* Dugan v. Rank, 372 U.S. 609, 620 (1963); Ford Motor Co. v. Department of Treasury, 323 U.S. 459, 464 (1945).

88. *See, e.g.,* Edelman v. Jordan, 415 U.S. 651, 664 (1974).

89. 209 U.S. 123 (1908).

since an unconstitutional state statute cannot be given the authority of state law, a state official attempting to enforce such a statute is "stripped of his official or representative character" and becomes subject to liability.[90] Such a case is simply not considered one against the state, and thus falls outside of the eleventh amendment's protection.

The problems created by such a fiction are apparent. Any remedy necessarily must run against the official not only in her personal but also in her official capacity, involving as it does enforcement of a state law. Furthermore, the very behavior that is not attributed to the state for eleventh amendment immunity purposes may at the same time be viewed as "state action" for the purpose of substantive liability under the fourteenth amendment; this has been described by the Supreme Court itself as a "well-recognized irony."[91] More than simply an irony, however, the tension reflects the fact that the two amendments are in contradiction at a fundamental level. The fourteenth amendment is designed to subject state officials to federal liability for their unconstitutional acts. The eleventh amendment, on the other hand, protects states from suit in federal court. The two are necessarily at odds.

Ex parte Young represents an accommodation of these conflicting interests. Unless some suits are allowed to proceed against state officials in federal courts, important federal constitutional guarantees — specifically those embodied in the fourteenth amendment — can never be fully implemented, and allowed "to serve as a sword, rather than merely as a shield" from unconstitutional state conduct.[92] Otherwise, such claims could only be raised as defenses in state prosecutions, or as initial claims in the state courts — a forum that was, at the time of the passage of the fourteenth amendment at least, not perceived as fair and unbiased. Thus a federal forum must be provided in at least some cases against the state government to ensure the supremacy of federal law.

On the other hand, given the context of the adoption of the amendment, protection of state treasuries lies at the heart of its protection.[93] Generally, recovery from the state treasury means that the suit is against the state. But the notion that state officials who act unlawfully cannot be considered to represent the state has produced a jurisdictional aberration — the jurisdiction to hear a whole case, yet provide

---

90. *Id.* at 159-60.

91. *Pennhurst,* 104 S. Ct. at 910, quoting Florida Dep't of State v. Treasure Salvors, Inc., 458 U.S. 670, 685 (1982) (Stevens, J., plurality opinion).

92. Edelman v. Jordan, 415 U.S. at 664.

93. *See Pennhurst,* 104 S. Ct. at 935 (Stevens, J., dissenting) ("There is general agreement that the Amendment was passed because the States were fearful that federal courts would force them to pay their Revolutionary War debts, leading to their financial ruin.").

only partial relief. The permissible scope of the liability established under *Young,* and the cases that have followed it, is carefully limited. *Young* itself involved an injunction, and soon it was established that the exception extended only to equitable relief, and did not include awards of damages against the state.[94] Under the *Young* doctrine the key is the difference between permissible, prospective relief and impermissible, retroactive monetary relief.[95]

This principle is illustrated in several modern cases applying the *Young* doctrine. In *Edelman v. Jordan,*[96] the Supreme Court faced a decree under which, in the name of "equitable restitution," the trial court had ordered the state to pay retroactive welfare benefits wrongfully withheld, as well as prospectively to change illegal state welfare procedures.[97] The Court held that the award of retroactive benefits was "in practical effect indistinguishable in many aspects from an award of damages against the State," and therefore outside the scope of federal jurisdiction.[98] In the same case on remand, *Quern v. Jordan,*[99] the court below revoked its order of retroactive benefits, and substituted instead a requirement that the state send a notice to welfare recipients informing them that state administrative procedures were available to seek back benefits. The Supreme Court upheld this relief, since it found that the notice did not determine the state's liability retroactively, but merely formed a part of the prospective, injunctive relief in the case.

While the state may be required to expend some funds, at times even a significant amount of funds, to comply with a judicial decision, such expenses must be "ancillary" to the injunctive relief.[100] For instance, *Milliken v. Bradley*[101] upheld prospective elimination of the *continuing* conditions of inequality created by the prior maintenance of a segregated school system. Similarly, the Supreme Court has found that awards of attorneys fees for bad faith conduct are in aid of the court's jurisdiction and thus within the court's power to enforce an injunctive decree.[102] Since questions about whether the relief is prospective or retroactive in nature, or in aid of the court's jurisdiction or not, do not

---

94. *See* Ford Motor Co. v. Department of Treasury, 323 U.S. 459, 464 (1945) ("When the action is in essence one for the recovery of money from the state, the state . . . is entitled to invoke its sovereign immunity even though individual officials are nominal defendants.").
95. For a discussion of the intricacies of distinguishing between permissible and impermissible relief, see WRIGHT, MILLER & COOPER *supra* note 83, § 3524 at 190-212.
96. 415 U.S. 651 (1973).
97. *Id.* at 665.
98. *Id.* at 668.
99. 440 U.S. 332 (1979).
100. *Edelman,* 415 U.S. at 668.
101. 433 U.S. 267 (1977).
102. Hutto v. Finney, 437 U.S. 678 (1978).

effect the extent of the impact on the state treasury, such distinctions often seem artificial. The Court itself has admitted that the difference between permissible and impermissible relief "will not in many instances be that between day and night."[103]

However, as a theoretical matter at least, prospective relief does give the state the option to bring its behavior into compliance voluntarily. In addition, the distinction has also been cited as avoiding federal interference in the fiscal problems of states.[104]

3. Suits Alleging Violations of State Law

All of these cases involved suits against state officials in federal court based on alleged violations of federal law. *Young* involved a challenge to a state statute as invalid under the federal Constitution, while *Edelman* involved federal statutory violations. However, cases have also arisen, albeit less frequently, in which the state is sued in federal court based on a violation of *state* law. In such cases, the Supreme Court has at times been willing to allow a *Young* injunction to issue, but only where the state official acted without any statutory authority whatsoever. The plaintiff must show that the suit is not one against the state because there is simply *no* authority under state law for the official's action. That is, when the state official stepped *outside* his duty, it is possible to maintain a suit consistent with the eleventh amendment not because the state *cannot* authorize such behavior, but because it *hasn't*. Thus, in *Florida Department of State v. Treasure Salvors, Inc.*[105] the Court held that because state officials' actions in holding artifacts seized from a treasure hunt was without any statutory authority, a case against those officials was not a suit against the state and thus fell within the federal jurisdiction.

The opposite result follows when there is some statutory basis for authority. For instance, the Court in *Cory v. White*[106] affirmed the immunity of the states to a declaratory judgment suit brought against California and Texas under federal interpleader rules to determine the domicile of Howard Hughes for the purpose of probating his will and assessing estate taxes. Since the state officials in that case had both acted according to state law, and the case raised no federal questions, the suit was barred by the eleventh amendment.

The Court recently strengthened this principle in *Pennhurst State School & Hospital v. Halderman*,[107] where it found a case against state

---

103. *Edelman*, 415 U.S. at 667.
104. Great Northern Life Ins. Co. v. Read, 322 U.S. 47, 54 (1944).
105. 458 U.S. 670, 696 (1982) (plurality opinion).
106. 457 U.S. 85 (1982).
107. 104 S. Ct. 900 (1984).

officials based solely on state law barred by the eleventh amendment as a suit against the state itself. The Court noted that the officials were "clearly acting within the scope of their authority," apparently relying on the fact they were vested with great discretion in administering the state mental hospital.[108] The dissent argued that the officials no longer represented the state because of proven state-law violations.[109] In *Pennhurst,* unlike *Cory,* it was not altogether clear that the state officials were simply carrying out their duty, since their conduct was ultimately found to be illegal under state law. By relying on the "broad discretion" vested in those officials under state law,[110] the Court in *Pennhurst* thus carried the statutory authority analogy significantly farther than it had previously been extended.

4. Federalism Concerns

The majority decision in *Pennhurst* points up many of the problems with the *Young* doctrine. In finding that the case "so plainly [runs] against the State," the Court relied on the fact that "reality" showed that the clear effect of the relief — an injunction against state officials — was to operate against the state.[111] Since all of the relief ordered was "institutional and official in character," and the hospital so heavily funded by the state,[112] the Court felt it was misleading to reach any other conclusion. Yet, as the dissent pointed out, exactly the same arguments could be made against any injunction under *Young.*[113] The effect of the relief cannot therefore really be the answer, nor can the issue turn on whether the suit is really one against the state.

The explanation must lie in differing views of federalism, a consideration central to the *Pennhurst* analysis of *Young* and *Edelman.* The unseemliness of a federal court administering a far-reaching injunctive decree against a state institution, founded solely on state law, was the real controversy in the case. While the dissent argued that such enforcement served the state's interests by respecting its law, the majority determined that such an intrusion violated basic principles of federalism and state integrity. Focusing so closely on the literal language of the amendment, the whole "state authority" requirement is misleading. The real concern underlying the debate is the proper relation of the federal government to states as sovereigns. The same is true of another important issue in this area, the issue of the state's waiver of immunity or "consent."

---

108. *Id.* at 908-09 n.11.
109. *Id.* at 939 (Stevens, J., dissenting).
110. *Id.* at 913-14.
111. *Id.* at 911-12 & n.17.
112. *Id.* at 912, 920-21 n.34.
113. *Id.* at 935 (Stevens, J., dissenting).

C. State Consent to Suit

So far, the discussion has assumed that the state, or its agencies or officials, is seeking to invoke immunity under the eleventh amendment. It is also possible, however, for a state to waive its constitutional immunity, just as it can waive its common-law sovereign immunity in the state system, and "consent" to suit. As a jurisdictional matter, this creates the anomoly of federal jurisdiction by consent, allowing the parties to override limitations expressly built into the constitution.[114] On the other hand, sovereign immunity could also be regarded as analogous to questions of personal jurisdiction, which is always susceptible to establishment by consent.[115] Sovereign immunity, like immunity to personal jurisdiction, is arguably a constitutional right held by the state, which it can waive as it pleases.[116] In any case, the fact remains that the state may waive its eleventh amendment rights, and thereby consent to suit in federal court, and can do so in several ways.

First, where Congress clearly states its intention to do so, it may abrogate the state's eleventh amendment immunity. For example, in *Fitzpatrick v. Bitzer*[117] the 1972 amendments to the Civil Rights Act of 1964 specifically authorize damage awards against the states, and the Court upheld this as a legitimate exercise of Congress's power under section 5 of the fourteenth amendment. Such a congressional waiver, however, must be explicit.[118] This point was reiterated in *Hutto v. Finney*,[119] which found a clear congressional intent to abrogate state immunity in the Civil Rights Attorneys Fees Act of 1976.

It is unclear whether section 1983 of the Civil Rights Act abrogates the state's eleventh amendment immunity, and thus subjects the state to the whole panoply of remedies under the statute, including damages. In *Fitzpatrick*, the Court held that statutes enacted pursuant to section 5 of the fourteenth amendment *could* do so.[120] Later, however, in dicta in *Quern v. Jordan*,[121] the Court seemingly reversed its position, stating its view that section 1983 did not "explicitly and by clear language indicate on its face an intent to sweep away the immunity of the States."[122] In dissent, Justice Brennan disagreed, stating that sec-

---

114. *See, e.g.,* Wright, Miller & Cooper *supra* note 83, § 3524 at 159-166.
115. *See* ch. 1, sec. IB (discussion of minimum contacts).
116. *Cf. Edelman,* 415 U.S. at 673 ("Constructive consent is [inapplicable because] not a doctrine commonly associated with the surrender of constitutional rights, and we see no place for it here.").
117. 427 U.S. 445 (1976).
118. *See Edelman,* 415 U.S. at 673; *Fitzpatrick,* 427 U.S. at 456.
119. 437 U.S. 678, 693-94 (1978).
120. 427 U.S. at 456.
121. 440 U.S. 332 (1979).
122. *Id.* at 345.

tion 1983 should be read to override the state's eleventh amendment immunity.[123]

While it may seem unfair to characterize this sort of congressional action as a waiver by the *state* of its constitutional immunity, the theory is that since all the states are represented in Congress, the state's interests in maintaining immunity are adequately protected. Admittedly, this is not entirely realistic. Perhaps *Fitzpatrick* really represents Court's realization that the eleventh amendment is in tension with the fourteenth amendment, and must sometimes give way to allow effective enforcement of constitutional rights.

A more plausible waiver theory holds that states may be required by Congress to waive eleventh amendment rights as a condition for receiving federal funds in a congressional spending program. Here, the element of state "consent" is more realistic, since the state can decide whether or not to participate in a federal program, with all the conditions attached. In some of the early cases, however, the Court made the "consent" requirement less than rigorous, by finding mere participation by the state in a funding program constituted "implied waiver" of immunity. In *Parden v. Terminal Railway of the Alabama State Docks Department*,[124] for example, the Court held that by operating a railroad after the enactment of the Federal Employers Liability Act, which conditions the right to operate interstate railroads on amenability to suit, the state necessarily accepted this condition, and consented to suit. Thus the continuance of an activity after federal regulation was sufficient to constitute a waiver.

More recently, however, the Court has required a clearer indication of consent. *Employees of the Department of Public Health and Welfare v. Department of Public Health and Welfare*[125] held that congressional silence on the state immunity issue preserved the states' immunity under the Fair Labor Standards Act, despite the congressional extension of that Act specifically to cover state employees.[126] Similarly, in *Edelman v. Jordan*,[127] the Court found that the state had not implicitly waived its immunity to suit simply by participating in a federal funding program under the Social Security Act. The fact that there was no explicit congressional authorization of suit against "a class of defen-

---

123. *Id.* at 365.
124. 377 U.S. 184 (1964).
125. 411 U.S. 279 (1973).
126. *Id.* at 285.
127. 415 U.S. 651 (1974).

dants which literally includes States" was determinative of the constructive consent issue.[128] In *Florida Department of Health and Rehabilitative Services v. Florida Nursing Home Association*[129] participation in the Medicaid program was not found to abrogate eleventh amendment immunity, despite the state's waiver of sovereign immunity in its own courts.

Florida Nursing Home Association also illustrates an interesting aspect of the difference between general doctrines of sovereign immunity and eleventh amendment immunity; a state can consent to suit only in state and not federal court. This is often explained by the fact that the state's interest is not only in "*whether* it may be sued, but *where* it may be sued."[130] It also reflects the fact that waiver of a common-law right does not imply the waiver of a constitutional right. The latter may be retained even if the former is foregone.[131] On the other hand, the state's common-law sovereign immunity may at times be retained when its eleventh amendment immunity is abrogated. Thus a federal court may apply *state* immunity law to dismiss a diversity case against a state that would not otherwise be barred under the eleventh amendment.[132]

V. Conclusion

The issue of sovereign immunity raises many important and difficult problems of federalism. It also raises many of the most difficult questions of political theory. What does it mean to be a sovereign? Can the sovereign ever act not as the sovereign? Fundamentally, it forces us to address the question of whether the sovereign can violate the law which it, itself, has created.

As we have seen, one of the persistent themes of this chapter is that when the sovereign or its agent acts ultra vires, sovereign immunity does not apply. To say that the government is stripped of its protective mantle of immunity when it acts outside of its lawful sphere of authority is to say that there are limits on governmental authority. Thus, the notion that the sovereign can act ultra vires is fundamentally based on the theory that our government is one of limited powers. When a governmental actor transgresses those boundaries, be they statutory, constitutional, or (as is implied in *Nevada v. Hall* and in the foreign sovereign immunity context) territorial, the sovereign ceases being the sovereign. If we can intelligibly speak of the sovereign violating its

---

128. *Id.* at 672.
129. 450 U.S. 147 (1981).
130. *See, e.g., Pennhurst,* 104 S. Ct. at 907.
131. *See id.,* at n.9.
132. *See* WRIGHT, MILLER & COOPER *supra* note 83, § 3524 at 160-61 n.74.

own laws, then we still must ask if the judiciary, as a branch of the sovereign, can judge whether such a violation has occurred. And, if the judiciary can make such an inquiry, may it do so without the express consent of the sovereign to the judicial inquiry?

With the rise of the modern welfare state, these questions have taken on an important practical as well as a theoretical significance. We have seen that although the presumption has long been that the sovereign is immune from suit, that presumption has been curtailed by a variety of judicial doctrines and legislative acts. As the federal, state, and local governments have taken active roles in a variety of fields far removed from the "core" functions of the sovereign, the need for relaxation of the doctrine of absolute sovereign immunity has increased. However, most of the relaxation that has occurred has come in the most traditional form — that of consent by the sovereign itself in the guise of legislative acts permitting suits. Despite express waivers of immunity by the legislature, the courts will continue to face the difficult task of determining when the sovereign has acted. Nevertheless, curtailment of sovereign immunity by consent is arguably the governmental response which most appropriately balances the need to respond to the misfeasances of the government and its agents, while simultaneously preserving the integrity and legitimacy of the sovereign.

Chapter 4

THE REFUSAL TO ASSERT JURISDICTION

I. Deference and Discrimination

To this point, we have been concerned primarily with the outer limits to which courts may go in asserting jurisdiction. We have assumed, in other words, that courts prefer to exercise their jurisdiction to the fullest. There have been minor exceptions. For example, we saw in Chapter 1 that states sometimes adopt modest long-arm statutes that voluntarily limit their jurisdiction to less than what the due process "minimum contacts" standard would permit.[1] We also saw in Chapter 2 that, when Congress passes jurisdictional statutes, it does not always vest the federal courts with the fullest jurisdiction that article III would allow.[2] These are examples of a more general phenomenon: the refusal to assert jurisdiction based upon awareness that another court system may be better situated to adjudicate a case.

In this section we explore the "refusal to assert jurisdiction" by courts and legislatures. In doing so we must face one of the fundamental issues in jurisdiction: how much freedom should plaintiffs be allowed in determining where they bring suit? As we have seen, the Supreme Court has permitted the states to extend the jurisdictional reach of their long-arm statutes as a means of adjusting to the nationwide, even international, scope of business activities.[3] In response, as we shall see below, some state courts and legislatures have sought devices to reject cases involving foreign elements as a means of controlling forum-shopping by plaintiffs. Similarly, federal-court jurisdiction has been vastly enlarged by the tremendous growth of federal substantive law, which gives rise to "federal question" jurisdiction. In response, the federal courts have sought devices to reject cases that they believe should more properly be brought in a state forum. In both of these examples, the solution to the problem posed by plaintiffs' greater freedom to choose their forum — and to impose burdens upon both defendants and forum courts — is to turn away cases even though a plaintiff has satisfied the statutory jurisdictional requirements: to refuse to assert jurisdiction which is given.

Defendants, therefore, have two levels of protection against being dragged into an inhospitable forum: (1) externally imposed limits on what the forum may do; and (2) the willingness of the courts themselves to refuse to assert jurisdiction in cases where the externally-mandated jurisdictional standards are met.

---

1. *See* ch. 1, sec. IB.
2. *See* ch. 2, sec. IIA.
3. *See* ch. 1, sec. IIA.

In the context of state-court jurisdiction, the best known device in the arsenal of courts' refusals to assert jurisdiction is the doctrine of forum non conveniens. Discussed in greater detail below, this doctrine allows a state court, on defendant's motion, to dismiss a case to a more convenient state forum after balancing a variety of factors. Other devices used to dismiss cases include public policy, localizing statutes, and various statutory provisions modeled on forum non conveniens.

Comparable problems exist in the context of federal court systems. States have on occasion declined to adjudicate cases involving federal causes of action. Conversely, federal courts have declined to exercise jurisdiction where the court determined that a case would better be brought in state court because of substantial state-law elements in the case. These are the so-called "abstention" doctrines. Finally, there have been proposals for congressional legislation that would take away federal-court jurisdiction over certain predominately constitutional causes of action, leaving these federal constitutional claims to be brought in state court.[4] All of these devices would route litigation to an alternative forum.

While less obvious than the constitutional limits on a forum's attempts to overreach, there are also some limits on a court's power to decline to hear a case. Certain types of refusals, such as enactment of a modest long-arm jurisdictional statute, seem virtually beyond serious constitutional scrutiny. The Supreme Court has said that a state need not supply a forum if it prefers not to do so.[5] Other types of refusals nonetheless have been invalidated under the full faith and credit or supremacy clauses.[6] While the different treatment is unexplained in the cases, and seems puzzling at first, the key issue in analyzing such cases is whether the refusal to assert jurisdiction is motivated by deference to the other forum or discrimination against it.

In section A we recount the development and application of the widely-used doctrine of forum non conveniens and of other legitimate transfer devices. Section B explores instances of the refusal to assert jurisdiction which have been treated as constitutionally suspect. Section C discusses why some dismissal devices are constitutionally permissible and others are not, and illustrates the problem with certain federal court devices used to dismiss causes of action as better brought

---

4. *See generally* Brilmayer & Underhill, *Congressional Obligation to Provide a Forum for Constitutional Claims: Discriminatory Rules and the Conflict of Laws,* 69 VA. L. REV. 819, 819-21 (1983) (discussing court-stripping proposals and constitutional basis for them).

5. Perkins v. Benguet Consolidated Mining Co., 342 U.S. 437, 440 (1952) ("The suggestion that federal due process *compels* the State to open its courts to . . . a case has no substance.").

6. *See infra* sec. IB (discussion of *Hughes, Testa*).

in state court. And Part II, which follows these sections, describes the use of abstention as a device to refuse to assert jurisdiction.

A. FORUM NON CONVENIENS

1. The Doctrine

Forum non conveniens (FNC) permits a court to dismiss a case that otherwise meets its venue and jurisdictional requirements; it can then be brought in another, more convenient, forum where the case also could have been brought in the first instance. The court, in considering defendant's motion to dismiss for FNC, is attempting to control two potential problems: (1) the harassment of the defendant by a plaintiff suing in a seriously inconvenient forum; and (2) the improper imposition on the court's jurisdiction, and the resulting time and expense involved, where the dispute and the parties have no more than a tenuous connection to the forum. As we will see, the doctrine of FNC has been codified as it applies to transfers within the federal court system. As a common-law doctrine, it continues to have a healthy life both as applied among the states and in the international context.

2. History and Background

The very words forum non conveniens have the ring of an ancient and venerable doctrine, perhaps dating from the Justinian Code. Actually, however, 19th century Scottish courts first consciously developed and articulated the doctrine.[7] Before FNC, these courts recognized that for some matters they were "forum non competens" — that they did not have jurisdiction over the parties or subject matter and thus could not act. Later, these courts began to distinguish "forum non competens" from the case where, although possessing jurisdiction, the Scottish courts were not the best or most convenient forum for adjudicating this dispute. In these cases the courts dismissed the case and allowed the plaintiff to bring suit in that other, more convenient, forum. The courts provided a number of examples of the sorts of inconveniences that would qualify for FNC dismissal. These included the foreign location of the contract, tort, or will in dispute; the distant location and unavailability of the necessary witnesses; and the expense and inconvenience associated with requiring the defendant to respond in the Scottish courts, compared to the inconvenience that plaintiff would suffer if forced to bring suit in the alternative forum. A prerequisite to the application of FNC and the dismissal of the case was the availability of

---

7. *See, e.g.,* M'Morine v. Cowie, 7 Dunlop 270 (1845); Tulloch v. William, 8 Dunlop 657 (1846); Clements v. Macaulay, 4 Macph. 583 (1866); Macadam v. Macadam, 11 Macph. 860 (1873).

an alternative forum. This requirement survives to the present; courts frequently dismiss a case conditionally upon the defendant consenting to personal jurisdiction in the alternative forum and waiving any statute of limitations objections.[8]

The doctrine gradually began to appear in American common law. In the United States, FNC was applied in a number of state courts unwittingly, "without benefit of the Latin phrase." As Paxton Blair put it in his seminal article on forum non conveniens, "the courts of this country have been for years applying the doctrine with such little consciousness of what they were doing as to remind one of Moliere's M. Jourdain, who found he had been speaking prose all his life without knowing it."[9] In some of these cases courts acted on an ad hoc basis, dismissing cases on grounds of public policy or inconvenience without settled standards. These cases often were concerned with the fact that witnesses were unavailable or that cases with only minimal contacts with the forum were an improper imposition which increased administrative expenses and delayed justice. However, FNC was not judicially recognized as a formal common-law doctrine for dismissing cases until Blair's 1929 Columbia Law Review article gave it academic credibility. From that point, it was only eighteen years before FNC became a "well settled doctrine" in a major Supreme Court case, *Gulf Oil Corp. v. Gilbert.*[10]

A third source in the development of the doctrine was admiralty law cases, some dating to the beginning of the 19th century. In the United States, courts of admiralty were empowered with broad jurisdiction, which was interpreted to include the "high seas." Admiralty courts thereby were relieved of the usual venue requirements applicable to suits *terra firma.* In admiralty, jurisdiction was typically satisfied in rem by attaching a vessel in the forum in which it could be found.[11] Courts were often confronted with cases involving disputes solely between foreign parties — for example seamen's wage cases and maritime collisions. At first there was some question whether U.S. courts were competent to hear cases involving only foreign parties, facts, and laws.[12] Eventually, though, the courts developed the device of the *dis-*

---

8. *See* R. Weintraub, Commentary on the Conflict of Laws 207 (2d ed. 1980) citing Vargas v. A.H. Bull S.S. Co., 44 N.J. Super. 536, 131 A.2d 39 (1957). *Cf.* Air Prods. & Chem., Inc. v. Lummus Co., 252 A.2d 543 (Del. 1969).

9. Blair, *The Doctrine of Forum Non Conveniens in Anglo-American Law,* 29 Colum. L. Rev. 1, 21-22 (1929).

10. 330 U.S. 501 (1947).

11. *See* G. Gilmore & C. Black, The Law of Admiralty 35-37 (2d ed. 1975).

12. *See, e.g.,* Mason v. The Blaireau, 6 U.S. (2 Cranch) 240, 263 (1804) (rejecting argument that Court has no jurisdiction over case where all parties are foreign); The Belgenland, 114 U.S. 355, 363-64 (1885) (discussing circumstances in which Court may decide to take jurisdiction of controversy between foreign parties).

cretionary dismissal to dispose of cases which they determined to be better suited to adjudication in another "home" forum, when one existed.

3. Modern Developments

a. The *Gilbert* Decision

All of these developments, along with English doctrinal developments growing out of the Scottish cases,[13] figured in the development of the doctrine leading to the Supreme Court's first comprehensive attempt to survey and apply the law in this area. In *Gulf Oil Corp. v. Gilbert,*[14] decided in 1947, the Supreme Court addressed the question of when and how a federal district court hearing a case in diversity could dismiss the case to be brought in a more convenient forum. The case involved a diversity suit in New York brought by a Virginia resident against a Pennsylvania corporation qualified to do business in Virginia and New York. The suit sought damages for an allegedly negligent delivery of gasoline which resulted in the destruction of plaintiff's warehouse in Lynchburg, Virginia. Justice Jackson's majority opinion, relying in part on earlier factors discussed by the Scottish and English courts, set out the considerations applicable to a decision on dismissal. They were grouped into two major headings: "private interest factors" and "public interest factors." Though not an exclusive list, those factors that Justice Jackson described have shaped to a large degree the later discussion of the subject and bear quoting at length here.

> The doctrine leaves much to the discretion of the court to which plaintiff resorts, and experience has not shown a judicial tendency to renounce one's own jurisdiction so strong as to result in many abuses.
>   . . . [One] interest to be considered, and the one likely to be most pressed, is the private interest of the litigant. Important considerations are the relative ease of access of unwilling, and the cost of obtaining attendance of willing witnesses; possibility of view of premises, if view would be appropriate to the action; and all other practical problems that make trial of a case easy, expeditious and inexpensive. There may also be questions as to the enforceability of a judgment if one is obtained. . . . It is often said that the plaintiff may not, by choice of an inconvenient forum, "vex," "harass," or "oppress" the defendant by inflicting upon him expense or trouble not necessary to his own right to pursue his remedy. But unless the balance is strongly in favor of the defendant, the plaintiff's choice of forum should rarely be disturbed.

---

13. *See* Logan v. Bank of Scotland [1904-07] All E.R. Rep. 438, 443 (proceeding stayed where vexatious to defendants and there was another, more convenient tribunal).

14. 330 U.S. 501 (1947).

Factors of public interest also have place in applying the doctrine. Administrative difficulties follow for courts when litigation is piled up in congested centers instead of being handled at its origin. Jury duty is a burden that ought not to be imposed upon the people of a community which has no relation to the litigation. In cases which touch the affairs of many persons, there is reason for holding the trial in their view and reach rather than in remote parts of the country where they can learn of it by report only. There is a local interest in having localized controversies decided at home. There is an appropriateness, too, in having the trial of a diversity case in a forum that is at home with the state law that must govern the case, rather than having a court in some other forum untangle problems in conflict of laws, and in law foreign to itself.[15]

The most striking feature of this rather inclusive list of factors is the enormous latitude judges have in determining the proper weight to be applied to each of these concerns and the method by which to balance them. In *Gilbert* and the subsequent case law, the courts have placed greater and greater emphasis on the "discretion" of the district court, the need to retain flexibility, and the fact that decisions will be reviewed only under an "abuse of discretion" standard — a standard that is rarely transgressed.[16] One particularly vague discretionary factor raised by *Gilbert* is the balance a court must strike between the strong presumption in favor of plaintiff's choice of forum and the "public interest factors" relating to court congestion, administrative difficulties, and the burdens imposed on local courts and taxpayers by "foreign" cases.[17] Different judges will weigh these factors differently, often resulting in highly inconsistent decisions.

In *Piper Aircraft v. Reyno*,[18] decided thirty-four years later, the Supreme Court could have clarified some of the problems that had developed in the circuits regarding the manner in which the *Gilbert* factors should apply. Unfortunately, the rather narrow ruling in that case disappointed hopes that the Supreme Court would clarify some troublesome issues. In *Reyno*, the Court merely held that a FNC dismissal would not be automatically barred because the law to be applied in the alternative forum would be less favorable.

Reyno involved the crash of an airplane in Scotland in which the six passengers, all Scottish residents, were killed. The airplane had been manufactured by a Pennsylvania corporation and the propellers by an

---

15. *Id.* at 508-09.

16. *See* Friendly, *Indiscretion About Discretion*, 31 EMORY L.J. 747, 748-54 (1982) (discussing Supreme Court decisions requiring nearly complete deference to district court ruling on forum non conveniens).

17. 330 U.S. 508-09.

18. 454 U.S. 235 (1981).

Ohio corporation. All other factors, including the domicile of next of kin, pointed to Scotland as forum. A California state court appointed Gaynell Reyno administratrix of the estates of the passengers, and wrongful death suits against the U.S. corporations were brought there. The case was removed to federal court and transferred to a Pennsylvania federal district court where Piper Aircraft moved for dismissal pursuant to FNC. Part of the motivation was undoubtedly that strict liability rules and contingent fee awards are not available in Scotland.

The district court granted the motions after applying the *Gilbert* FNC factors to the facts of the case; the court of appeals reversed, holding that the district court had abused its discretion. The court of appeals stated that dismissal is not appropriate where the law of the alternative forum is less favorable to the plaintiff. The Supreme Court reversed. Only seven Justices participated in the decision, and five Justices agreed that an otherwise valid FNC motion would not fail automatically if plaintiff showed that the substantive law of the alternative forum would be less favorable to him than that of the chosen forum.

The Court's holding — that the possibility of an unfavorable change in law should not, by itself, bar dismissal — is perhaps more interesting for the issues it could *not* settle. The opinion's discussions of two significant issues were endorsed by only four Justices. First, the opinion suggested that a plaintiff's choice of its home forum was presumed to be convenient and therefore warranted greater deference. Second, it argued vigorously that the district court's FNC analysis should be accorded great deference and should be reversed only when there has been a "clear abuse of discretion." *Reyno* also left unresolved the question whether forum non conveniens as applied in federal district court was governed by federal standards or state-law standards.[19]

Finally, despite the lack of a clear holding on some issues, the tenor of the opinion in *Reyno* seems to encourage district courts to exercise even wider discretion in applying FNC. Some scholars fear that this discretion is being exercised too freely, without standards which would add a measure of predictability to the process.[20] *Reyno* seems to provide lower courts with a rationale for paying greater attention to the "public interest factors" while tipping the scales towards dismissal and slighting the supposedly strong presumption in favor of plaintiff's choice of forum.

b. The Federal Transfer Statute, 28 U.S.C. § 1404(a)

The decision in *Gilbert* prompted an addition to the Judicial Code codifying FNC in the transfer of cases between federal district courts:

---

19. 454 U.S. 248 n.13.
20. *See* Friendly, *supra* note 16.

"for the convenience of parties and witnesses, in the interests of justice, a district court may transfer any civil action to any other district or division where it might have been brought," 28 U.S.C. § 1404(a). Actual dismissal of a case, as in FNC, is not required. Section 1404(a) is widely used today to transfer cases among the federal district courts. The standards guiding transfer under § 1404(a) are more easily satisfied than those for a traditional FNC dismissal.[21]

There are important differences between FNC and transfer under § 1404(a). Most obviously, § 1404(a) is only available between two federal courts. Where the alternative forum is in a foreign nation, or where either the original forum or the alternative forum is a state court, transfer is impossible and forum non conveniens dismissal provides the only solution. A second important difference is that, under § 1404(a), the transferee court must apply the same law as the transferor court would have. In *Van Dusen v. Barrack*[22] the Supreme Court held that a § 1404(a) transfer amounts to a change in courthouse, but not a change in law. For example, in the *Reyno* case, the dispute originally had been transferred from a California federal court to a Pennsylvania federal court under § 1404(a), and it was in Pennsylvania that the forum non conveniens motion was made. Had the case been litigated in Pennsylvania, that district court would have applied California choice-of-law rules instead of Pennsylvania choice-of-law rules. Contrast this with the consequences of a forum non conveniens dismissal. If the case were reinstated in Scotland, Scottish choice-of-law rules would apply. Thus § 1404(a) preserves for the plaintiff much more of the advantage of the initially chosen forum than does forum non conveniens.

c. State Law Codifications of Forum Non Conveniens

While many states have adopted forum non conveniens as a matter of common law, a few have codified the doctrine in statutes. Some examples of these can be found in California, Florida and Massachusetts.[23] As applied in these states, FNC is almost identical to the doctrine that Justice Jackson described and analyzed in *Gilbert,* although some states have modified it in minor details. The California statute, for example, includes an option to stay the case, rather than dismiss it,

---

21. *See* Norwood v. Kirkpatrick, 349 U.S. 29, 31-32 (1955) (§ 1404(a) was intended to permit transfers upon a lesser showing of inconvenience).

22. 376 U.S. 612, 639 (1964).

23. *See* Cal. Civ. Proc. § 410.30 (West 1973); Fla. Stat. Ann. § 47.122 (West Supp. 1985); Mass. Gen. Laws Ann. ch. 223A, § 5 (West 1985).

in the event that suit in the alternative forum should prove impossible.[24]

Elements of FNC have also been incorporated in other statutes, such as the Uniform Child Custody Jurisdiction Act.[25] The UCCJA was designed to remove any incentive for "forum shopping" to obtain favorable revisions of child custody orders. Previously, the availability of forum shopping had encouraged parental "kidnapping" of children from the state in which the original child custody order was rendered to a more favorable forum in another state. Because since child custody orders were subject to modification in the rendering state, a second forum also could revise the decree without technically violating "full faith and credit."[26]

The UCCJA established restrictions on the power of any court other than the rendering court to modify the child custody decree, effectively removing any incentive for forum shopping. Under the statute, any other court is forum non conveniens for purposes of modifying the child custody decree and must dismiss the case on that basis.

d. Matters of Purely Local Interest

The state and federal court systems generally view some matters as being of purely local concern and thus appropriately adjudicated only in the local forum. These local matters include marriage, real property, taxation, worker's compensation, criminal law, and probate.[27] Federal courts typically decline to adjudicate domestic relations disputes even when an adequate basis for jurisdiction, such as diversity, exists.[28] Taxation, domestic law, and criminal law are discussed in subsequent chapters.[29]

B. THE PROHIBITION AGAINST DISCRIMINATORY DISMISSALS

1. State Refusal to Adjudicate Causes of Action Arising in Other States

State courts sometimes refuse to entertain actions with predominantly foreign elements because entertaining the action would require

---

24. Cal. Civ. Proc. § 410.30(a) (West 1973). This provision was applied in the celebrity divorce case of Mick and Bianca Jagger, where a stay of the California proceeding was granted pending the outcome of a concurrent English case. Jagger v. Superior Ct., 96 Cal. App. 3d 579, 158 Cal. Rptr. 163 (1979).

25. 9 U.L.A. 111-70 (1979). Section 3 is the jurisdictional provision of the act, 9 U.L.A. 122-23.

26. For a discussion of full faith and credit in child custody proceedings, see ch. 12.

27. See R. WEINTRAUB, supra note 8, at 345 n.9 (2d ed. 1980); D. LOUISELL & G. HAZARD, PLEADING AND PROCEDURE, 336-40 (4th ed. 1979) (local action rule).

28. See ch. 12, sec. I.

29. See Part III.

application of foreign law. A court may be disinclined to apply foreign law either because it is unfamiliar or because it is contrary to local public policy. Historically, the dismissal of a case based on public policy was appropriate only where the foreign law to be applied contravened important moral values of the forum, i.e. the foreign law was so "obnoxious" that the forum could not in good faith apply it. Examples of such cases, which will be discussed in a later chapter,[30] include those relating to gambling and contracts against competition.[31] This refusal is analogous to the FNC refusal based on the complexity of the foreign law or the difficulty of administering it: where the foreign law is obnoxious, the forum court cannot trust itself to adjudicate the dispute properly. However, dismissals based on public policy differ from FNC in that they rely on a single factor as a sufficient basis for dismissal, as opposed to the multitude of factors involved in FNC.

One of the most notorious examples of an attempt to dismiss a case on the grounds of public policy is *Hughes v. Fetter.*[32] Harold Hughes, a resident of Wisconsin, was killed in an automobile accident in Illinois. Suit was brought in Wisconsin, the location of the defendant driver and his insurance company. Since the accident occurred in Illinois, however, the Illinois wrongful death statute formed the basis of the suit. The trial court held that the Wisconsin statute, which created a right of action only for deaths caused in Wisconsin, established a local public policy against having Wisconsin entertain suits brought under wrongful death acts of other states. The Wisconsin Supreme Court affirmed.

In reversing this decision, the U.S. Supreme Court conceded that full faith and credit did not compel a forum state to subordinate its important local policy to a conflicting public act of another state. The Court noted, however, that the situation in *Hughes* did not reflect conflicting public policies. The dismissal was not motivated by hostility to wrongful death actions per se, but merely by hostility to *foreign* wrongful death actions. Wisconsin courts freely could entertain suits brought under the state's own wrongful death statute. In this case the Wisconsin court and statute provided no reasonable basis for the forum to close its courts' doors to the foreign cause of action, and thus the state's "door closing" statute was unconstitutional. In other words, the full faith and credit clause prohibited dismissals that discriminated against causes of action merely because they arose out of state.

---

30. Ch. 7, sec. II3C.

31. *See* Ciampittiello v. Ciampittiello, 134 Conn. 51, 54 A.2d 669 (1947) (gambling contract made in Rhode Island was unenforceable in Connecticut as against public policy); C. & D. Farms, Inc. v. Cerniglia, 189 So. 2d 384 (Fla. Dist. Ct. App. 1966) (contract against competition allegedly governed by Georgia law was unenforceable in Florida as against public policy), *aff'd,* 203 So. 2d 1 (Fla. 1967).

32. 341 U.S. 609 (1951).

The converse principle, that a forum which provides even-handed treatment to foreign causes of action does not violate the full faith and credit clause, is illustrated by a case involving conflicting statutes of limitation. In *Wells v. Simonds Abrasive Co.,*[33] a wrongful death action was brought in federal district court in Pennsylvania based on the Alabama wrongful death statute. The Alabama statute had a two-year statute of limitation, and Pennsylvania had only a one-year statute of limitation. The district court applied Pennsylvania's shorter statute and dismissed the case. The U.S. Supreme Court upheld the application of the forum's statute of limitation as not violating full faith and credit. It distinguished *Hughes* as a case where the forum "laid an uneven hand on causes of action arising within and without the forum state."[34] Pennsylvania's rule was valid because the one-year statute of limitation was applied to *all* wrongful death actions, wherever they arose.

In some respects, the contrasting treatment given the dismissal in *Hughes* and other types of dismissal and transfer devices is puzzling. The dismissal in *Hughes* seems somewhat analogous to forum non conveniens dismissals, which the Supreme Court has clearly approved. The *Hughes* court distinguished forum non conveniens on the grounds that the doctrine was unavailable because all of the parties were from Wisconsin, the forum state. The usual FNC factors relating to convenience to the parties thus could not explain the dismissal. Any alleged difficulty in applying Illinois' Wrongful Death Act also could not have been a valid basis to dismiss, because that statute was not very different from Wisconsin's wrongful death statute. The only explanation for the dismissal was discrimination against foreign causes of action.

One wonders, however, whether the dismissal would have been upheld if the trial court, in its discretion, had alluded to the out-of-state location of evidence and witnesses, to congestion in local courts, or to other traditional factors in the forum non conveniens calculus. Perhaps a more troubling question is the relationship between *Hughes* and many modern long-arm statutes. Many states have long-arm statutes that differentiate between causes of action that arise in the state and those that arise in other states.[35] Presumably a state can decline to assert long-arm jurisdiction over foreign causes of action.[36] But does this run counter to the *Hughes* prohibition on discriminating against foreign causes of action?

---

33. 345 U.S. 514 (1953).

34. *Id.* at 518.

35. *See, e.g.,* Illinois Ann. Stat. ch. 10, § 2-209 (Smith-Hurd 1982) and Delaware Code Ann. tit. 10, § 3104(c) (1975) (1980 Supp.).

36. *See* Perkins v. Benquet Consol. Mining Co., *supra* note 5.

Just as *Hughes* is puzzling when contrasted with these obviously constitutional long-arm statutes, so *Wells v. Simonds Abrasive* is puzzling when compared to cases upholding "borrowing statutes." Borrowing statutes are statutes which "borrow" the statute of limitations of the state where the cause of action arose. For instance, if Pennsylvania had a two-year statute of limitations and Alabama had a one-year statute, Pennsylvania might choose to apply the shorter limitations period of Alabama to cases that were governed by Alabama substantive law. The ordinary rule that the forum always applies its own statute of limitations, which we shall see in a later chapter,[37] motivates plaintiffs to shop among the fifty states for one where the statutory limitations period has not run. To prevent such forum shopping, many states borrow the limitations period of the place where the cause of action occurred, if it is shorter. This policy obviously results in laying "an uneven hand" on causes of action that arose outside the state, to use the phrase employed by *Wells v. Simonds Abrasive.* Yet the practice has been approved[38] despite its "discrimination," a point to which we shall return shortly.

2. State Refusal to Adjudicate Federal Causes of Action

States have on occasion attempted to close their doors to federal causes of action. But the supremacy clause requires that state courts hear federal causes of action if the courts are otherwise competent to hear such cases. For example, the Supreme Court has held that a state court may not decline jurisdiction in a Federal Employers Liability Act (FELA) action where the court's ordinary jurisdiction, as prescribed by local laws, is adequate to the occasion.[39] Similarly, a state court may not decline to hear an FELA action based on out-of-state events where the state would entertain a similar foreign tort case with no FELA claim.[40] The Court explicitly rejected the arguments that unfamiliarity with federal law counseled dismissal, and that federal law might be contrary to local public policy. When Congress legislates, said the Court, it creates local policy for the states under the supremacy clause.

In *Testa v. Katt*,[41] the plaintiff brought an action in a Rhode Island state court seeking treble damages under the Federal Emergency Price

---

37. *See* chs. 12 & 13.
38. *See* Canadian N.R.R. v. Eggen, 252 U.S. 553 (1920) (borrowing statute constitutional despite favoring resident plaintiffs) and Watkins v. Conway, 385 U.S. 188 (1966) (per curiam) (borrowing statute regarding statute of limitation for enforcing judgment valid despite fact it applies unevenly to residents and nonresidents).
39. Second Employers' Liability Cases, 223 U.S. 1, 55-59 (1912).
40. McKnett v. St. Louis & S.F. R.R., 292 U.S. 230 (1934).
41. 330 U.S. 386 (1947).

Control Act. The Rhode Island Supreme Court dismissed the case by characterizing the federal act as a "penal statute" which it was not required to enforce under state law. The U.S. Supreme Court reversed, holding that Rhode Island had to entertain the suit and could not dismiss on these grounds. Quite simply, the supremacy clause invalidated any contrary state law in this instance. Looking to the facts of the case, the Rhode Island courts clearly would have entertained this case if it were based on Rhode Island law. To deny access to the Rhode Island courts merely because the case is based on federal law was inexcusable.

One could say that *Testa v. Katt* is the *"Hughes v. Fetter"* of the federal context. As in *Hughes,* courts which were established to hear cases of a certain type cannot refuse to hear an equivalent foreign case merely because of its "foreignness." This does not mean that there are no instances in which such cases can be refused, but simply that such refusals must be based on principles *uniformly applied.* Ordinarily, if the state has a jurisdictional rule which it applies to local and foreign causes of action alike, that rule will be upheld. Only discriminatory rules that single out other sovereigns' causes of action are suspect under *Hughes* and *Testa.*

An interesting question, for which there is not yet a definitive answer, concerns whether Congress ever can preempt a nondiscriminatory state rule. *Testa* invalidated a discriminatory rule, but did not clearly hold that all nondiscriminatory door-closing rules were automatically valid. In *Brown v. Gerdes,* Justice Frankfurter took the position that neutral door-closing rules should be automatically upheld. Federal causes of action, he said, must "take the state courts as they find them".[42] States have the power, under this view, to structure their court systems as they wish, without interference by the federal government except where they attempt to discriminate. Because Congress has not clearly attempted to override neutral state jurisdictional rules, the issue has never been squarely presented, although one recent case, *Federal Energy Regulatory Comm'n (F.E.R.C.) v. Mississippi,*[43] suggests that minor federal intervention may be permissible.

F.E.R.C. involved Mississippi's challenge to provisions of the Public Utility Regulatory Policies Act (PURPA) requiring state utility regulatory commissions to review and consider adopting certain proposed federal standards and ratemaking procedures, to implement certain other federal rules, and to adjudicate any resulting disputes. Mississippi claimed that these provisions of PURPA interfered with state sovereignty in violation of the tenth amendment. The Supreme Court,

42. 321 U.S. 178, 190 (1944) (Frankfurter, J., concurring).
43. 456 U.S. 742 (1982).

in upholding these provisions, held that the act was not an unconstitutional interference because such "dispute resolution was the very type of activity in which the Mississippi Public Service Commission customarily engaged.[44] Refusing to adjudicate these disputes merely because they arose from a federal statute improperly discriminated against federal law in the same manner which *Testa v. Katt* had earlier rejected.

There is some additional support for the view that Congress may specifically preempt neutral state jurisdictional rules when it creates a federal cause of action. As will be discussed at greater length in a later chapter, Congress may provide subsidiary procedural rules when it creates a federal cause of action.[45] These rules, such as rules concerning burden of proof, will apply even in state court. As a result, although the state usually is free to apply any nondiscriminatory state procedural rules when it hears federal claims, Congress may preempt some neutral rules in the process of defining the contours of the federal cause of action. It is not clear, however, whether Congress is as free to preempt state jurisdictional rules as it is to preempt state procedural rules that have implications for the case's substantive contours.

A brief review of congressional action and the Supreme Court's response in two other contexts, antitrust and FELA, provides some additional guidance on Congress' power to alter otherwise valid jurisdictional rules.

In *United States v. National City Lines,*[46] the Supreme Court held that the Clayton Act's broad venue provision, allowing an antitrust suit to be brought where a corporation is an inhabitant, is found, or transacts business, constituted sufficient evidence of congressional intent, along with the act's legislative history and context, to deprive a court of any power to refuse jurisdiction and dismiss under FNC. This decision was tempered shortly thereafter, though, when the Court held that federal courts could *transfer* such cases under § 1404(a).[47]

The Supreme Court acknowledged the right of state courts to refuse FELA cases under certain circumstances as early as 1928 in *Douglas v. New York, N.H. & H.R. Co.*[48] That case allowed New York to refuse jurisdiction because the plaintiff was a nonresident, as long as it applied its statute in a nondiscriminatory manner. Other cases held that

---

44. *Id.* at 760.
45. Ch. 8, sec. IV ("converse Erie" doctrine).
46. 334 U.S. 573 (1948).
47. United States v. National City Lines, 337 U.S. 78 (1949).
48. 279 U.S. 377 (1929).

such dismissals were *not* valid when motivated by discriminatory and hostile attitudes toward the federal statute.[49] The Supreme Court in *Baltimore & O.R. R. v. Kepner*[50] held that an Ohio court could not enjoin a FELA action in New York even though the cause of action arose in Ohio, because the "privilege of venue" contained in FELA cannot be frustrated for FNC-related reasons of convenience or expense. After passage of § 1404(a) the Supreme Court held that FELA actions could be transferred from one federal district court to another.[51] Finally, *Missouri ex rel. Southern Ry. v. Mayfield*[52] held that *neutral* FNC rules were applicable to FELA cases, reaffirming the *Douglas* case of 1928.

What emerges from these cases is that a neutral jurisdictional rule (such as FNC), applied in a nondiscriminatory manner, is valid, except where Congress has addressed the choice of venue issue clearly and unambiguously and intended that plaintiff's choice of forum be binding. This leaves open the possibility that the forum's discretion under FNC will be abused by applying the dismissal standard, with its trappings of neutrality, in a discriminatory way. Such discriminatory application probably would be difficult to demonstrate.

C. DISCRIMINATION AND DEFERENCE

Refusals to adjudicate that are constitutionally suspect share one key feature: they are characterized as discriminatory. The fatal flaw of the jurisdictional rules in both *Hughes* and *Testa* was that they laid an uneven hand upon local and externally created causes of action. But what does discrimination mean? Most obviously, discrimination involves a difference in treatment because a foreign cause of action is involved. If that were the entire meaning of discrimination, however, then other valid kinds of dismissals, such as forum non conveniens, also would be discriminatory. Yet forum non conveniens and long-arm statutes that differentiate between local and foreign causes of action have never been invalidated. Furthermore, as a matter of common sense it does not seem reasonable to characterize them as discriminatory.

Discrimination requires more than a difference in treatment. The structure of the federal system *requires* certain sorts of difference in treatment because of the presence of foreign elements in the dispute. For example, under the minimum contacts standard for personal juris-

---

49. Second Employers' Liability Cases, 223 U.S. 1, 58 (1912); McKnett v. St. Louis & S.F. Ry., 292 U.S. 230 (1934).

50. 314 U.S. 44, 54 (1941).

51. Ex parte Collett, 337 U.S. 55 (1948).

52. 340 U.S. 1 (1950).

diction, an assertion of jurisdiction over a foreign cause of action is more tenuous than an assertion of jurisdiction over a local cause of action, other things being equal. States have to differentiate between local and foreign disputes for certain purposes; a mere difference in treatment cannot be automatically invalid. A difference in treatment instead may be an appropriate response to the fact that a case is properly within another court system's jurisdiction. The different treatment is not invidious when it amounts to recognition of another state's interests in adjudicating the case, given its foreign elements. This is preferential treatment, not discrimination.

The same action, dismissing a case because of foreign elements, can be either deferential treatment or discrimination, depending on the circumstances. The policy behind the dismissal may be either a belief in the superiority of some alternative forum or a selfish aversion and lack of local interest in adjudicating the dispute. *Hughes v. Fetter* displays the latter policy but not the former. The sole reason for the dismissal was local antipathy to foreign wrongful death claims; as the Court pointed out, there was no pretense that another forum would be more convenient to the parties. Contrast with *Hughes* a typical application of forum non conveniens. The convenience of parties and witnesses is a significant factor there, and the existence of an alternative forum is required. Although congestion of local dockets is one consideration, the greater interest of the alternative forum in vindicating locally-created rights is also important. Forum non conveniens involves deference to an alternative forum and not discrimination against its local causes of action.

Other door-closing rules that are valid even though they treat foreign causes of action differently are similar in these respects to forum non conveniens. Earlier we mentioned the Uniform Child Custody Jurisdiction Act, which deprives a court of jurisdiction to consider foreign child custody cases. The rationale clearly is deference to a superior forum; the purpose of the Act was to reduce forum shopping through child kidnapping. The consequences of failure to entertain the foreign case were a greater respect for the other court's judgment and protection of the party who initially prevailed from repeated and inconvenient litigation. Another example mentioned earlier was borrowing statutes, which require application of the shorter statute of limitations of the state where the cause of action accrued. *Wells v. Simonds Abrasive* condemns "laying an uneven hand on causes of action arising out of state," but it does so only when the uneven treatment is discriminatory.

The same principle applies in the federal/state arena. No one would claim that the dismissal was anything other than discriminatory in cases such as *Testa v. Katt,* where states refused to hear federal claims. Convenience to the parties was not offered as an explanation. The dismissal would have been deferential had it been based upon congressional desire that federal courts have exclusive jurisdiction over such actions. In such situations, refusal to assert jurisdiction is clearly constitutional. But in the FELA cases and *Testa v. Katt,* state and federal jurisdiction were concurrent, not exclusive to the federal courts. The state court in *Testa* dismissed the case simply because the state preferred not to entertain the penal claims of other sovereigns. In the FELA cases, courts relied on local public policy, as well as the likelihood of confusion in applying unfamiliar law. These explanations were inadequate given that Congress establishes public policy for the states, under the supremacy clause.

A final instance of refusal to adjudicate provides a detailed example of how dismissal of a cause of action can be based upon deference to an alternative forum. We have already examined state refusals to entertain other states' causes of action and state refusal to entertain federal causes of action. There are also, however, federal refusals to adjudicate cases where an adequate basis for federal jurisdiction exists under both article III and the jurisdictional statutes. This federal refusal to adjudicate is analyzed under the rubric of "abstention."

II. Abstention

Many critics view the various doctrines of federal abstention, which dictate either dismissal of an action or at least a delay in federal jurisdiction, to be of questionable legitimacy. The federal courts, although they clearly have jurisdiction to hear a particular case, will decline to do so — or "abstain" — if the circumstances or procedural posture of the case falls into any of the categories in which the Supreme Court has determined abstention is appropriate. The Court has determined that the substantial interest in avoiding friction and inconvenience in the interaction between state and federal legal systems may dictate restraint on the part of the federal judiciary, even though the case actually falls within federal jurisdictional boundaries.

Notwithstanding an ongoing dispute over the wisdom and legality of such jurisdictional maneuvering, abstention doctrines are firmly established in Supreme Court jurisprudence. This section will outline the various doctrines of abstention before examining the arguments of scholars on each side of the debate. Beginning with the first abstention case, *Railroad Commission of Texas v. Pullman Co.,*[53] the Court has

---

53. 312 U.S. 496 (1941).

created at least four distinct strands of abstention doctrine and has justified each on grounds of furthering the amicable relations between state and federal governments which it finds an important element of "our federalism."

The validity of such deference to the interests of other sovereigns in a particular case varies with the circumstances, of course, and critics have accused the Supreme Court of discriminating against certain causes of action and hiding this discrimination behind the language of deference to a foreign sovereign. The final section of this chapter will investigate the theoretical arguments for abstention and against it.

A. *PULLMAN* ABSTENTION: AMBIGUOUS STATE LAW

In 1941, Pullman porters challenged a Texas Railway Commission regulation that effectively ensured that no black Pullman porter would be put in charge of a sleeping car within the state of Texas. The plaintiffs based their complaint on due process, equal protection and commerce clause objections to the regulation. In *Railroad Commission of Texas v. Pullman Co.,*[54] Justice Frankfurter's opinion for the Court stated that the federal courts should abstain from deciding the constitutional issues raised by the plaintiffs because it was unclear under Texas law whether the Railroad Commission in fact had the authority to issue such a regulation. If the Commission actually were violating state law, the constitutional issue would not have to be addressed, and the federal court would not be required to spend precious constitutional capital.[55] But since the Texas courts had not yet decided a case involving the regulations, they had had no opportunity to determine whether the Commission's actions violated Texas law. The state should have the chance to resolve the ambiguity of the Commission's actions under state law, the Court held, before a federal court properly could decide the constitutional issues.

"In *Pullman,* abstention holds that a federal court must decline jurisdiction when an ambiguous state law is challenged on constitutional grounds. In this situation a federal court . . . is asked to decide an

---

54. *Id.*

55. "If there was no warrant in state law for the Commission's assumption of authority there is an end of the litigation; the constitutional issue does not arise." *Id.* at 501. In his famous concurring opinion in Ashwander v. TVA, 297 U.S. 288, 347 (1936), Justice Brandeis laid down the cardinal rule of federal jurisprudence that "if a case can be decided on either of two grounds, one involving a constitutional question, the other a question of statutory construction or general law, the Court will decide only the latter." In *Pullman,* the Court did not have a definitive construction of state law, which might have provided an alternative ground for decision, and would have allowed the Court to avoid an unnecessary constitutional ruling.

issue by making a tentative answer which may be displaced tomorrow by a state adjudication."[56] This policy helps further "the harmonious relation between state and federal authority without the need of rigorous restriction of [the federal judiciary's equitable] powers."[57] Deference to the sovereign interest of states in construing their own law before it is subjected to federal scrutiny, under this viewpoint, requires federal courts at least to delay their consideration of constitutional challenges. *Pullman* and its progeny[58] imply that our federal system would be marked by strife and ill will without this kind of respect for the multiplicity of sovereigns existing within our national boundaries. The litigants, however, may have the federal court retain jurisdiction to decide any constitutional issues remaining after a definitive construction of local law by the state courts.[59]

Whether the states perceive *Pullman*-type abstention as an accommodation of their inherent sovereignty, federal plaintiffs have been inconvenienced mightily by the *Pullman* line of cases. Although the Court has emphasized that abstention does not "involve the abdication of federal jurisdiction, but only the postponement of its exercise,"[60] the substantial cost of drawn-out litigation undoubtedly has discouraged more than one litigant. The protracted delays in final adjudication also must be factored into any assessments of the price of litigation after *Pullman* abstention.[61] Justice Douglas once termed the *Pullman* doctrine "a legal research luxury."[62]

---

56. 312 U.S. at 500. There is also a constitutional interest in having a federal decision be the final adjudication of the merits of a case. One of the oldest jurisdictional rulings of the Supreme Court, Hayburn's Case, 2 U.S. (2 Dall.) 409 (1796), involved the refusal of the federal judiciary to entertain petitions for veterans' benefits, when the decisions were reviewable by the Secretary of War. The prohibition of advisory opinions militates against any decision that may subsequently be mooted by the action of another body. *See generally* ch. 2, sec. IV *supra*.

57. 312 U.S. at 501.

58. *See, e.g.,* Government & Civic Employees Organizing Comm. v. Windsor, 353 U.S. 364 (1957); Clay v. Sun Ins. Office, 363 U.S. 207 (1960).

59. England v. Louisiana State Bd. of Med. Examiners, 375 U.S. 411 (1964) (plaintiff may expressly or impliedly reserve right to federal adjudication of merits after state courts have construed local law).

60. Harrison v. NAACP, 360 U.S. 167, 177 (1959).

61. *See, e.g.,* Clark, *Federal Procedural Reform and States' Rights: To A More Perfect Union,* 40 TEX. L. REV. 211, 221 (1961) (abstention has "shuffled [litigants] back and forth between state and federal courts, and cases have been dragged out over eight- and ten-year periods); Wright, *The Abstention Doctrine Reconsidered,* 37 TEX. L. REV. 815, 817-18 (1959) (describing *Government & Civic Employees Organizing Comm. v. Windsor,* involving state employees who wanted to join labor unions: after two trips to Supreme Court and two to highest state court over a five-year period, the plaintiffs still had no adjudication on the merits of their claim).

62. England v. Louisiana State Bd. of Medical Examiners, 375 U.S. 411, 425 (1964) (Douglas, J., concurring).

The attendant costs to litigants have been exacerbated by the fact that, if the federal court retains jurisdiction of the constitutional question,[63] the relevant state court may be prevented from deciding the local-law question by state prohibitions of advisory opinions.[64] In a proposal designed to cure this problem of justiciability, the American Law Institute has suggested that the federal courts generally should not retain jurisdiction in *Pullman*-type abstention cases. The U.S. Supreme Court would provide adequate review of any state decisions on federal constitutional issues under this proposal.[65]

Despite the cost and delay to litigants, *Pullman* abstention is both commonly ordered by the Supreme Court, and rarely questioned by the member Justices.[66] The federal courts must abstain when a state law is "fairly subject to an interpretation which will render unnecessary or substantially modify the federal constitutional question."[67] Considered the jurisdictional price of a functioning federalism, *Pullman* abstention is settled law and unlikely to be abandoned.

B. *YOUNGER* ABSTENTION: ONGOING STATE CRIMINAL PROCEEDINGS

The second major form of abstention, first articulated only fifteen years ago in *Younger v. Harris*,[68] has been attacked by scholars as an unacceptably drastic abdication of federal jurisdiction in the name of federalism. *Younger* involved a prosecution under California's Criminal Syndicalism Act. The defendants in the criminal proceeding, together with a college professor who claimed the prosecution made him uncertain about the ability of the state to punish him for his teaching and reading practices, challenged the California statute in federal court, seeking an injunction against the prosecution.

---

63. Retention of jurisdiction pending state interpretation of the ambiguous state law is the usual practice in *Pullman* abstention cases. *See* American Trial Lawyers Ass'n v. New Jersey Supreme Court, 409 U.S. 467, 469 (1973) (retention of federal jurisdiction is "proper course" in *Pullman* abstention).

64. *See, e.g.,* United Servs. Life Ins. Co. v. Delaney, 396 S.W.2d 855 (Tex. 1965); In re Richards, 223 A.2d 827 (Me. 1966). *But see* Leiter Minerals, Inc. v. California Co., 241 La. 915, 132 So. 2d 845, 850 (1961) (giving construction of state law out of respect for U.S. Supreme Court, despite Louisiana law prohibiting advisory opinions). As discussed in ch. 3, however, some state courts, such as those in Massachusetts, are permitted to give advisory opinions. *See generally* 40 TEX. L. REV. 1041 (1962) (case note discussing justiciability problems in state court caused by *Pullman* abstention).

65. *See* C. WRIGHT, THE LAW OF FEDERAL COURTS 307 & n.26 (4th ed. 1984) (discussing American Law Institute Study, § 1371(c), (d)).

66. *See* C. WRIGHT, *supra* note 65, at 304.

67. Babbitt v. United Farm Workers Nat'l Union, 442 U.S. 289, 306 (1979), quoting Harman v. Forssenius, 380 U.S. 528, 535 (1965).

68. 401 U.S. 37 (1971).

Justice Black's majority opinion held that the federal courts do not have jurisdiction to enjoin ongoing state criminal proceedings, absent a showing of bad faith on the part of state authorities.[69] *Younger* involves a more sweeping form of judicial abstention than *Pullman,* since a federal court abstaining under *Younger* does not retain jurisdiction pending the outcome of the state proceeding, but dismisses the action all together.

The Court refers to three general policy justifications for this federal deference to the states' judicial processes in the *Younger* opinion. First, traditional doctrines regarding equitable remedies such as injunctions dictate that "courts of equity should not act . . . when the moving party has an adequate remedy at law and will not suffer irreparable injury if denied equitable relief."[70] Mounting a defense to a single criminal prosecution, the Court held, cannot be called an "irreparable injury." Further, the defendants' opportunity to litigate his or her federal defense to the prosecution in state court constitutes an adequate legal remedy, so that equitable intervention is unnecessary.

Second, the general interest in judicial economy would be undermined if state defendants automatically could enjoin criminal proceedings while litigating a federal defense in a different forum. Overlapping jurisdiction would make for needless "duplication of legal proceedings and legal sanctions where a single suit would be adequate to protect the rights asserted."[71] Tied to this interest in economy also may be an interest in preserving the role of the jury in criminal proceedings, because traditionally no jury is available when a court sits in equity.[72]

Most importantly, the notion of federal "comity" — respect for the judicial processes of separate sovereigns within the federal system —

---

69. The majority thus distinguished Dombrowski v. Pfister, 380 U.S. 479 (1965), in which the state was found to have prosecuted the plaintiff in bad faith. Under *Dombrowski,* a defendant in a state criminal proceeding will be able to seek federal injunction of the prosecution to protect her right not to be prosecuted without reasonable cause. Further, an injunction is also available when a criminal defendant can demonstrate bias against her in the state tribunal, see Gibson v. Berryhill, 411 U.S. 564 (1973), or when the defendant has been unconstitutionally incarcerated prior to trial. *See* Gerstein v. Pugh, 420 U.S. 103 (1975).

70. 401 U.S. at 43-44.

71. *Id.* at 44.

72. Subsequent decisions and commentators have overlooked this justification for abstention in *Younger.* In his majority opinion, however, Justice Black stressed that, although the doctrine of equitable restraint "may originally have grown out of circumstances peculiar to the English judicial system and not applicable in this country, . . . its fundamental purpose of restraining equity jurisdiction within narrow limits is equally important under our Constitution, in order to prevent erosion of the role of the jury . . . ." 401 U.S. at 44.

dictates that "[s]tates and their institutions [should be] left free to perform their separate functions in their separate ways."[73] Our federalism mandates respect for the legitimate activities of the states, which produces a fundamental policy against interference in state criminal prosecution, except in cases of immediate, irreparable injury to federal rights.[74]

In lone dissent, Justice Douglas argued that "[w]hatever the balance of the pressures of localism and nationalism prior to the Civil War, they were fundamentally altered by the war. . . . [Section] 5 of the Fourteenth Amendment cemented the change in American federalism brought on by the war. . . ."[75] Indeed, the jurisdictional statute involved, 28 U.S.C. § 1343,[76] does not speak of any exceptions to jurisdiction in the interests of federalism. As Justice Douglas pointed out, mistrust of state procedures for the vindication of federal rights motivated the post-Civil War amendments and their expansive jurisdictional counterparts.

Despite Justice Douglas' misgivings, the Court has applied *Younger* abstention to declaratory judgment proceedings as well as suits seeking injunctive relief.[77] In addition, abstention is proper when a federal plaintiff seeks an injunction collateral to the state prosecution. In *Perez v. Ledesma,*[78] a suit to enforce exclusion of illegally obtained evidence, the Court applied the *Younger* principle against interference with ongoing state proceedings and held that abstention was required.

The applicability of *Younger* abstention to civil cases is uncertain. In his concurrence in *Younger,* Justice Stewart stressed that "since [this case] involve[s] state criminal proceedings, we do not deal with the considerations that should govern a federal court when it is asked to intervene in state civil proceedings, where . . . the balance might be struck differently."[79] In *Huffman v. Pursue, Ltd.,*[80] however, *Younger* abstention was applied in a civil setting, although the Court found a

---

73. *Id.*

74. The *Younger* Court cited Ex parte Young, 209 U.S. 123 (1908) (enjoining actions of state officer on ground that he exceeded valid statutory authority), as support for the doctrine that injunctions against ongoing state proceedings are available only when "absolutely necessary." *Id.* at 45.

75. 401 U.S. at 61 (Douglas, J., dissenting).

76. 28 U.S.C. § 1343 (1982).

77. *See* Samuels v. Mackell, 401 U.S. 66 (1971) (declaratory relief improper when prosecution involving challenged statute is pending in state court before federal suit is initiated).

78. 401 U.S. 82 (1971).

79. 401 U.S. at 55 (Stewart, J., concurring).

80. 420 U.S. 592 (1975).

suit to enforce nuisance laws to be a civil proceeding "in aid of and closely related to criminal statutes."[81] Justice Brennan's dissent in *Huffman* argued for a different standard, since outside the criminal setting, a defendant has no recourse to habeas corpus as a means of avoiding res judicata.[82]

The similarity of *Younger* abstention to a federal statutory basis for refusing to interfere with ongoing state proceedings — the Anti-Injunction Act, 28 U.S.C. § 2283 — complicates its conceptual status. This act allows federal courts to enjoin state court actions in only three limited circumstances.[83] This statute might seem a solid basis for the *Younger* doctrine, were it not for the Court's decision in *Mitchum v. Foster.*[84] The Court held there that civil rights actions constitute an exception to the Anti-Injunction Act. In so doing, the Court undercut perhaps its only possible statutory rationale for *Younger v. Harris.* *Younger* abstention must rest on federalism concerns that the Court itself divines in the Constitution, and not upon any legislative instructions.

Subsequent cases have further emphasized the federalism concerns underlying *Younger* abstention. In *Steffel v. Thompson,*[85] for example, the majority stressed "the principle that state courts have the solemn responsibility, equally with the federal courts 'to guard, enforce, and protect every right granted or secured by the Constitution . . . .'"[86] A federal court's assumption of jurisdiction suggests that state courts will not fulfill that responsibility. In *Steffel,* the *Younger* doctrine was held not to apply, however, since there was no pending state-court prosecution. *Younger* abstention requires dismissal of the federal action only if the state prosecution already had commenced before the federal court began "any proceedings of substance on the merits."[87]

The practical upshot of the *Younger* abstention doctrine is that a federal plaintiff must be sure to reach the steps of the federal courthouse before the state prosecutor reaches the steps of the state courthouse. Not only must the federal plaintiff file first, he or she must also ensure that the pace of the federal litigation moves swiftly enough to

---

81. *Id.* at 604.

82. *Id.* at 615.

83. These circumstances are where an exception has been "expressly authorized by Act of Congress"; "where necessary in aid of [federal] jurisdiction," and where necessary "to protect or effectuate [federal] judgments." 28 U.S.C. § 2283.

84. 407 U.S. 225 (1972).

85. 415 U.S. 452 (1974).

86. *Id.* at 460-61 (quoting Robb v. Connolly, 111 U.S. 624, 637 (1884)).

87. Hicks v. Miranda, 422 U.S. 332, 349 (1975) (complaint should have been dismissed because state court proceeding began before any proceedings of substance on the merits had taken place in the federal court).

reach the merits of the claim before state prosecutors file their case. This race to the courthouse may impose some inconvenience on litigants — or, more accurately, on their lawyers — but this, the Court has held, is one of the costs of "our federalism."

C. BURFORD ABSTENTION: COMPLEX STATE ADMINISTRATIVE SCHEMES

In *Burford v. Sun Oil Co.,*[88] a sharply divided Supreme Court expanded abstention doctrine beyond the limits of constitutional and criminal law. Even where no constitutional issue is presented and no interference with an ongoing state criminal proceeding is threatened, lower federal courts must abstain from interfering with complex state administrative schemes. A federal decision in such a situation would involve an intrusion into a state's management of its own affairs.

The justification for *Burford* abstention is based on notions of federalism which by now must be familiar to the reader. Respect for "the rightful independence of state governments in carrying out their domestic policy"[89] dictates that federal courts should abstain from exercising jurisdiction to avoid federal-state friction over the state's conduct of its own affairs.

In *Burford* abstention, it should be noted, the proper course is dismissal of the action, rather than retention of federal jurisdiction pending state resolution of ambiguous law. In a subsequent *Burford* abstention case, the Court held that "intervention of a federal court is not necessary for the protection of federal rights" where review of a state administrative order is available in state courts.[90] Review in the Supreme Court provides an adequate safeguard against infringement of federal rights.

In dissent, Justice Frankfurter attacked the plurality decision in *Burford* as a violation of the congressional grant of diversity jurisdiction.[91] He argued that courts may not decline jurisdiction on federalism grounds when Congress has expressly determined that the very harm to be avoided through diversity jurisdiction is adjudication of state-law claims in which one of the parties is not a citizen of the state.

The plurality's determination that complex state administrative schemes may not be included in the federal diversity jurisdiction seems directly contrary to the holding in *Meredith v. Winter Haven.*[92] Handed down only six months after *Burford, Meredith* held that:

---

88. 319 U.S. 315 (1943).
89. *Id.* at 318 (quoting Pennsylvania v. Williams, 294 U.S. 176, 185 (1935)).
90. Alabama Pub. Serv. Comm'n v. Southern Ry., 341 U.S. 341, 349 (1951).
91. 319 U.S. at 344-45 (Frankfurter, J., dissenting).
92. 320 U.S. 228 (1943).

[T]he difficulties of ascertaining what the state courts may hereafter determine the state law to be do not in themselves afford a sufficient ground for a federal court to decline to exercise its jurisdiction to decide a case which is properly brought to it for decision.[93]

The Court distinguished *Burford* on the ground that no complex system of state regulation would be disturbed by federal adjudication of the dispute, which involved non-payment of deferred-interest coupons attached to bonds issued by the city of Winter Haven. Although state law on the question apparently was unsettled, the Court held that no special federalism interests were present to justify the decision to abstain.[94]

Even if *Meredith* can be distinguished from *Burford* on the ground that it involved no complex state system of administration and review, it is nevertheless difficult to see how *Meredith* can be reconciled with the next category of abstention to be discussed, which turns solely on the fact of unsettled state law. Although it is sometimes treated as a separate abstention doctrine,[95] the form of abstention upheld in *Louisiana Power & Light Co. v. Thibodaux*[96] is so closely related to *Burford* that it may make more sense to treat it as a subset. *Thibodaux* involved a state eminent domain proceeding, which had been removed to federal court by the utility company, a Florida corporation. The district judge, faced with a city condemnation proceeding that apparently violated state law,[97] had stayed the federal action to allow Louisiana courts to interpret the applicable state law. Justice Frankfurter's 6-3 majority opinion held that the decision to abstain was a proper exercise of the district judge's discretion.

Despite the fact that no constitutional issue was involved in the case, so that the principle against deciding constitutional questions unnecessarily was inapplicable, the Court held that the interests of federalism and the unique nature of an eminent domain proceeding justified abstention. Although presumably not required, abstention from inter-

---

93. *Id.* at 234.

94. "Decision here does not require the federal court to determine or shape state policy governing administrative agencies. It entails no interference with such agencies or with the state courts. No litigation is pending in the state courts in which the questions here presented could be decided." *Id.* at 237.

95. 360 U.S. 25 (1959).

96. Professor Wright argues that *Thibodaux* could validly be considered a distinct form of abstention. If not a separate strand of abstention doctrine, he maintains, *Thibodaux* belongs in the *Burford* line of abstention cases. C. WRIGHT, *supra* note 65, at 308-09.

97. An opinion of the Louisiana Attorney General had concluded in a similar case that a city did not have power to condemn property; whereas a Louisiana statute apparently authorized such proceedings. 360 U.S. at 30.

ference with an ongoing eminent domain action — a "special and peculiar" proceeding implicating the state's "sovereign prerogative"[98] — was a proper use of judicial discretion.

The Court found that two of the three elements of *Pullman* abstention were present. The first was the traditional limitations on equitable relief. An eminent domain proceeding, although not traditionally understood as equitable, is so unique that it also cannot strictly be said to be an action at common law. Equitable discretion to defer to an alternate forum, then, should not be foreclosed in such a suit.

More important, *Pullman* abstention "reflect[s] a deeper policy derived from our federalism."[99] Similar policy considerations apply in an eminent domain setting and in the administrative scheme involved in *Burford:* "The considerations that prevailed in conventional equity suits for avoiding the hazards of serious disruption by federal courts of state government or needless friction between state and federal authorities are similarly appropriate in a state eminent domain proceeding brought in, or removed to, a federal court."[100]

In a blistering dissent, Justice Brennan attacked the majority decision as a violation of the congressionally imposed diversity jurisdiction.[101] The only valid exceptions to the federal courts' obligation to adjudicate cases in which the litigants meet all jurisdictional requirements are the principles against deciding constitutional questions prematurely and of avoiding unsettling a particularly delicate relationship between the federal government and the states. Clearly no constitutional issue was involved, so that one of the elements of *Pullman* abstention was obviously missing. Furthermore, the dissent emphasized, "this case does not involve the slightest hazard of friction with a State . . . ."[102] And because an eminent domain proceeding is not an equitable proceeding, any reliance on the traditional discretion of courts sitting in equity was misplaced.[103]

The Court declined to apply *Thibodaux* abstention in a similar case decided within days of *Thibodaux*. In *County of Allegheny v. Frank Mashuda Co.*,[104] the Court, with Justice Brennan writing for the majority, reversed a federal court's dismissal of an eminent domain action. The only difference between the two cases was that the state law in-

---

98. *Id.* at 28.
99. *Id.*
100. *Id.*
101. 360 U.S. at 32 (Brennan, J., dissenting).
102. *Id.* at 34.
103. *Id.* at 34-35.
104. 360 U.S. 185 (1959).

volved in the second case was clear, while the law in *Thibodaux* was unsettled.

D. *Colorado River* Abstention: Parallel State Court Proceedings

The Supreme Court decision in *Colorado River Water Conservation District v. United States*[105] is widely regarded as establishing a fourth form of abstention, despite the Court's explicit statement that abstention was not involved.[106] Although the Court affirmed the principle that a federal court may not decline jurisdiction because the litigants are parties to a parallel or concurrent state judicial proceeding,[107] it held that in exceptional circumstances deference to state proceedings is appropriate in the interest of "wise judicial administration."[108]

In his majority opinion, Justice Brennan found that several factors present in *Colorado River* combined to create such an exceptional circumstance. The case involved water rights in the dry southwestern states. A federal statute by which the United States consented to state jurisdiction for adjudication of federal water rights[109] provided evidence that the federal wanted to avoid piecemeal litigation of such claims.[110] The Court also found relevant the facts that no proceedings on the substance had taken place in the federal court, that the federal court was 300 miles away from the local state court, and that some 1000 state defendants were named in the federal complaint.[111]

---

105. 424 U.S. 800, 813 (1976) ("the dismissal [by the district court out of deference to state court proceedings] cannot be supported under [abstention] doctrine in any of its forms").

106. *See* C. Wright, *supra* note 65, at 317; Redish, *Abstention, Separation of Powers, and the Limits of the Judicial Function*, 94 Yale L.J. 71, 96 (1984).

107. *See* McClellan v. Carland, 217 U.S. 268, 282 (1910) ("the pendency of an action in the state court is no bar to proceedings concerning the same matter in the Federal court having jurisdiction"); Kline v. Burke Constr. Co., 260 U.S. 226 (1922).

108. 424 U.S. at 818.

109. Known as the McCarran Amendment, 43 U.S.C. § 666 (1982) provides for joinder of the United States as a defendant in suits involving water rights.

110. "The clear federal policy evinced by that legislation is the avoidance of piecemeal adjudication of water rights in a river system. This policy is akin to that underlying the rule requiring that jurisdiction be yielded to the court first acquiring control of property, for the concern in such instances is with avoiding the generation of additional litigation through permitting inconsistent dispositions of property." 424 U.S. at 819.

111. *Id.* at 820.

The circumstances in *Colorado River* were so unique that some commentators,[112] and even Justice Brennan himself,[113] anticipated that the "exceptional circumstances" requirement rarely would be met. In a case decided only two years after *Colorado River,* however, the Court greatly expanded the scope of abstention in deference to parallel state proceedings. In *Will v. Calvert Fire Insurance Co.,*[114] the plurality of the Court held that a stay was proper even when the sole issue involved in the federal court was a question of federal law.[115] Because the same underlying facts already were being litigated in state court, the district judge granted the defendant's motion to defer the federal proceedings. Reviewing the grant of mandamus by the court of appeals directing the trial judge to try the federal claim, the Supreme Court held that such deference was within the discretion of the district court.[116]

In his dissent, Justice Brennan — the author of the *Colorado River* majority opinion — argued that the plurality had misapplied the strict standards required for abstention in *Colorado River.*[117] In fact, the Court may have retreated from an expansive view of abstention in deference to parallel state court proceedings in a 1983 decision.[118] Although the case involved contract law, and thus not a federal question, the Court held that the federal court had no authority to defer to a parallel state proceeding. It distinguished *Calvert* on the ground that that case involved review of the extraordinary writ of mandamus.[119]

---

112. *See, e.g.,* C. WRIGHT, *supra* note 65, at 317 (*Colorado River* actually argues against use of such abstention in routine cases because of its unusual fact situation and Court's heavy emphasis that only "exceptional" circumstances permit dismissal of this sort).

113. *See* 424 U.S. at 818.

114. 437 U.S. 655 (1978).

115. At issue in *Will v. Calvert Fire Insurance* was a dispute about whether a reinsurance fund could be guilty of a 10b-5 violation of the Securities Exchange Act of 1934. The federal courts have exclusive jurisdiction over any suits brought under the act. 15 U.S.C. § 78aa (1982).

116. Justice Rehnquist's plurality opinion stated that:

No one can seriously contend that a busy federal trial judge, confronted both with competing demands on his time for matters properly within his jurisdiction and with inevitable scheduling difficulties because of the unavailability of lawyers, parties and witnesses, is not entrusted with a wide latitude in setting his own calendar.

437 U.S. at 665.

117. *Id.* at 674 (Brennan, J., dissenting) (accusing plurality of "ignoring wholesale the analytic framework set forth in *Colorado River*").

118. Moses H. Cone Memorial Hosp. v. Mercury Constr. Corp., 460 U.S. 1 (1983).

119. *Id.* at 18.

E. Traditional Abstention in Domestic Relations and Probate Cases

Although not based on concepts of federalism, the constitutionality of federal deference to state proceedings in domestic relations and probate matters rarely has been questioned.[120] Federal court abstention in these areas instead resulted from the deference which the English common law accorded to yet another kind of sovereign — ecclesiastical courts.[121] Because traditionally both probate and domestic relations disputes were adjudicable only in ecclesiastical courts, the argument runs, they are not "legal" or "equitable" cases and were not included in the grant of diversity jurisdiction.[122] Federal courts thus have stated that they have no jurisdiction to grant a divorce,[123] or to probate a will.[124]

This rationale based on deference to ecclesiastical courts has long since been discredited as a ground for abstention, but the actual practice of abstaining in such cases has survived. One scholar has speculated that this form of abstention may reflect "a conviction that such matters are of peculiarly local concern."[125] The decision to abstain in domestic and estate matters, which will be touched upon again in a later chapter, may reflect a disinclination on the part of federal courts to become embroiled in family squabbles.[126]

F. Abstention, Federalism and Separation of Powers Doctrine

The various doctrines of abstention have provoked both criticism and support in the legal literature. Supporters have praised the deference

---

120. *But see* Dragan v. Miller, 679 F.2d 712, 713 (7th Cir. 1982) (criticizing deference of federal courts in probate matters and improper application of English procedures to American courts).

121. C. Wright, *supra* note 65, at 143-44. "These two exceptions were developed at a time when the diversity statute granted jurisdiction of 'suits of a civil nature in law or in equity' and it was thought that the domestic relations and probate cases, being matters that would have been heard in the ecclesiastical courts, did not fit this description."

122. *See* C. Wright, *supra* note 65, at 143-44. In domestic cases involving disputes between husband and wife, federal courts generally declined jurisdiction on the traditional legal fiction that a wife's residence was always the same as her husband's. This justification for refusing to adjudicate domestic cases has long since been abandoned. *See* Note, *Application of the Federal Abstention Doctrines to the Domestic Relations Exception to Federal Diversity Jurisdiction,* 1983 Duke L.J. 1095, 1098.

123. Barber v. Barber, 62 U.S. (21 How.) 582 (1859) (federal court cannot grant divorce, but it can grant equity relief to wife pursuant to a valid alimony argument from a state court).

124. Markhan v. Allen, 326 U.S. 490, 494 (1946) (dictum) (federal court has no jurisdiction to probate a will but it may entertain suits to establish claims to the state as long as this does not interfere with the probate proceeding).

125. D. Currie, Federal Jurisdiction in a Nutshell 195 (1981).

126. *See* ch. 12.

to state sovereignty inherent in all abstention doctrines, while critics have claimed that the language of deference masks an underlying discrimination against certain types of cases. Perhaps the best-known scholars on either side of the debate are Professors Paul Bator and Martin Redish.

Professor Bator has argued that abstention is a proper exercise of judicial power.[127] Even in the area of constitutional rights, Bator maintains, "neither the federal courts nor the state courts are to be given a monopoly. Both must and will continue to be partners in the task of defining and enforcing federal constitutional principles. The question remains as to where to draw the lines; but line-drawing is the correct enterprise."[128] Despite the fact that jurisdictional statutes such as §§ 1331 and 1343 seem to leave no room for judicial narrowing of their absolute grants of jurisdiction, such statutes must not be "woodenly and anachronistically read," according to Bator.[129] The federal courts must harmonize the post-Civil War jurisdictional statutes with pre-existing jurisdictional doctrines and laws.[130] Another commentator argues, in a similar vein, that the expansion of federal jurisdiction was largely judicial in the first instance, so that contraction of power poses no separation of powers problems.[131]

Given this essential judicial duty to interpret statutes in light of the entire legal universe, the various abstention doctrines should be evaluated in terms of the policies of cooperative federalism that they are designed to promote. In the interests of avoiding duplication of judicial decisionmaking[132] and of allowing questions of state law and fact to be adjudicated in state courts,[133] Bator argues, abstention is both wise federal policy and correct interpretation of jurisdictional statutes.

Most important, abstention may be an essential method of preserving federal constitutional rights.[134] Because the supremacy clause re-

---

127. Bator, *The State Courts and Federal Constitutional Litigation*, 22 Wm. & Mary L. Rev. 605 (1981).

128. *Id.* at 622.

129. *Id.* at 622 n.49.

130. "[T]hese statutes were . . . passed against the background of a large body of standing law . . . . As is true of all legislation, it is a major problem of *interpretation* how to fit the new enactment into this preexisting texture. No statute recreates the entire legal universe. The fact that a given remedial doctrine is not explicitly mentioned therefore does not automatically mean that the statute was intended wholly to supersede it." *Id.* (emphasis in original).

131. Wells, *Why Professor Redish Is Wrong About Abstention*, 19 Ga. L. Rev. 1097 (1985).

132. *Id.* at 618.

133. *Id.* at 619.

134. Judicial review, the notion that the Supreme Court has the authority to review the constitutionality of state court decisions, formed the basis of Justice Marshall's decision in the landmark case Marbury v. Madison, 5 U.S. (1 Cranch) 137 (1803).

quires state courts to consider and apply the Constitution as part of state law, state courts are as fully bound by constitutional principles as are federal courts. Because Congress could abolish the jurisdiction of the lower federal courts, the state courts possibly could become the only protection against infringement of constitutional rights. "We must never forget that under our constitutional structure it is the state, and not the lower federal, courts that constitute our ultimate guarantee that a usurping legislature and executive cannot strip us of our constitutional rights."[135]

In light of the possibility that Congress either could abolish the lower federal courts or severely limit their jurisdiction, Bator maintains that it is in the interest of those wishing to protect litigants against "tyrannous government"[136] to treat state courts as partners in adjudication rather than as inferior and hostile rivals of federal courts. Such an attitude of superiority not only ignores the real vulnerability of lower federal courts, but also runs the risk of creating the very hostility it seeks to escape through federal adjudication. "If we want state judges to feel institutional responsibility for vindicating federal rights, it is counterproductive to be grudging in giving them the opportunity to do so."[137]

On the other side of the debate, Martin Redish argues that abstention not only fails to serve the implicit principles of federalism it purports to uphold, but also may violate essential rules governing the separation of powers at the federal level.[138] Instead of focusing only on the federal/state relationship, courts also should realize that a decision to abstain where Congress has explicitly granted jurisdiction to adjudicate implicates questions about the proper role of courts in a tripartite system of government.

Redish concludes that the various forms of abstention all transgress fundamental separation-of-powers principles "as a matter of legal process and separation of powers, wholly apart from [their] advisability."[139] Federal courts simply do not have the power to ignore a legislative directive for any reason other than the unconstitutionality of the

---

Although there was some resistance in state courts even after *Marbury v. Madison*, the notion of judicial review was widely accepted long before. *But see* C. BLACK, STRUCTURE AND RELATIONSHIP 73 (1969) ("There simply is no problem about the fundamental legitimacy of judicial review of the actions of the states for federal constitutionality.").

135. Bator, *supra* note 127, at 627.

136. *Id.* at 629.

137. *Id.* at 625.

138. Redish, *Abstention, Separation of Powers, and the Limits of the Judicial Function*, 94 YALE L.J. 71 (1984).

139. *Id.* at 74.

directive. The federal judiciary may not overturn legislation that it considers unwise.[140] In essence, Redish argues that the abstention doctrines, which the courts justify in terms of restraint and deference, are in fact striking examples of judicial activism and discrimination.

In light of this separation-of-powers analysis, only compelling federalism arguments could override the interest in enforcing valid jurisdictional directives. None of the abstention doctrines pass muster under this analysis, according to Redish. *Pullman* abstention, even though involving only a postponement of federal jurisdiction while issues of ambiguous state law are resolved, violates clear statutory language.[141] Furthermore, it causes as much harm through delay in enforcing federal rights as it avoids through showing deference to state interests.[142]

Younger abstention also fails the separation-of-powers test, Redish argues. The drafters of § 1983 and its jurisdictional counterpart were especially concerned that state criminal prosecutions would not be conducted in good faith, and therefore they provided for federal jurisdiction in all cases claiming a violation of constitutional rights. The majority decision in *Younger* is an egregious violation of the congressional determination that plaintiffs alleging deprivation of constitutional rights are entitled to a federal forum, because that case requires, rather than merely allows, abstention. "*Younger* represents considerably more than judicial discretion to restrike the balance in individual cases. Qualified only by a narrow set of rarely-used exceptions, *Younger* abstention is all but total."[143] Redish further claims that the social policy justifications behind *Younger,* such as disruption of state proceedings and avoidance of federal/state friction, probably will not result if federal courts assume jurisdiction. Because a state criminal prosecution itself only rarely will be considered a violation of constitutional rights — the primary exception being in the first amendment area[144] — federal courts are unlikely to enjoin them.

Burford and *Thibodaux* receive short shrift from Redish, who calls them "by far the least justifiable forms of abstention."[145] Despite the desirability and even the wisdom of giving states the exclusive administration of complex regulatory schemes and eminent domain suits,

---

140. *Id.* at 72.

141. *Id.* at 85.

142. *Id.* at 95.

143. *Id.* at 88.

144. "If one accepts the 'chilling effect' concept (and it has a venerable heritage in the law of the First Amendment), then under the unique circumstances of a First Amendment violation, the very existence of the prosecution constitutes a deprivation of liberty. As such, it constitutes a violation of section 1983." *Id.* at 93.

145. *Id.* at 98.

separation-of-powers analysis dictates that Congress should make the decision that such policy considerations outweigh a valid jurisdictional statute.[146] *Colorado River* abstention, Redish maintains, is nothing more than a judicial prohibition of a valid litigation strategy — initiating a parallel proceeding in order to take the offensive. Although such strategies may be unfair at times, they do not justify the avoidance of federal jurisdiction to rectify the balance.[147]

III. Conclusion

The question of refusal to exercise jurisdiction is not so simple as might appear. It might seem that the greater power includes the lesser; that the power to assert jurisdiction includes the power to decline jurisdiction. But as demonstrated by the discussion above, declining to assert jurisdiction is often controversial and sometimes actually unconstitutional.

Assessing the legitimacy of a refusal is no different from examining any other assertion of a lesser included power. Even where power is acknowledged, the line drawing function must be performed in a legitimate way. Thus states may not discriminate against other states and the legal rights they create, nor against the federal governments and federal rights. There is no mechanical method, however, for determining whether a difference in treatment is deferential or discriminatory, as the abstention controversy demonstrates. A comparable controversy, too subtle for proper treatment here, concerns the routing of certain federal constitutional claims away from federal into state courts.[148] The analytical difficulties are far from solved. To frame the problem in terms of the tension between deference and discrimination, however, should at least help clarify the basis underlying issues.

---

146. *Id.*
147. *Id.* at 97.
148. *See* Brilmayer & Underhill, *supra* note 4.

Chapter 5

JUDGMENTS IN THE INTER-JURISDICTIONAL SETTING

The fact that a litigant has won a favorable judicial decision does not necessarily mean that the legal battle is over. In fact, the judgment of the court could be the starting point for a whole new set of legal squabbles. The victorious party often has problems finding assets adequate to satisfy the judgment and may have to take the judgment elsewhere to get it enforced. Or one of the parties may instigate further litigation that is related, but not identical, to the first lawsuit. To what degree should the parties in the new lawsuit be allowed to use the first judgment as either a "sword" or a "shield"?

Although these problems can arise within the confines of a single legal system, they take on added complexity when a litigant takes a judgment across the border between two legal systems. In our federal system, this "border crossing" involves the systems of either two states or the federal system and a state. This gives litigants a second opportunity, even once the process of direct appeal is exhausted, to attack the decision. This second opportunity is referred to as collateral, in contrast to direct, attack.[1] It raises issues about the deference the second forum should accord the decision of the first forum, and whether it may ever treat a judgment with less respect simply because it is foreign. This question has close ties to issues of adjudicative jurisdiction, because lack of adjudicative jurisdiction is frequently urged as a rationale for non-enforcement. These jurisdictional problems are, in fact, the primary focus here.

This chapter addresses the topic of judgments in this inter-jurisdictional context. It begins by discussing briefly the rationale for rules giving preclusive effect to judgments and the terminology used in the area. The following section examines various ways a judgment rendered in Forum A can be attacked by a litigant in Forum B. The final section discusses certain situations in state-state and state-federal relations where the usual rules governing treatment of judgments may not apply.

I. Basic Concepts and Terminology

The fundamental motivation for rules governing the effects of judgments is the "[p]ublic policy [which] dictates that there be an end of litigation."[2] This "policy of preclusion" seeks to protect interests which

---

1. A collateral attack on a judgment is an attack made by or in an action or proceeding that has an independent purpose other than impeaching or overturning the judgment. BLACK'S LAW DICTIONARY 237 (5th ed. 1979).
2. Baldwin v. Iowa State Traveling Men's Ass'n, 283 U.S. 522, 525 (1931).

have vested as a result of previous litigation, to prevent harassment of litigants, and to minimize the burden on courts from repetitious litigation.[3]

State policies on judgments derive from a number of common-law doctrines, which bear brief explanation. The concept of res judicata means that a decision by a competent court on the merits of a claim is conclusive as to the rights of the parties and forms a barrier to any subsequent action on the same claim. In modern parlance, this is called "claim preclusion." Through res judicata, the plaintiff's cause of action is merged into the judgment (merger), and the defendant may set the judgment up as a bar against a new suit by the plaintiff based on grounds which could have been raised in the original action (bar). Collateral estoppel, or "issue preclusion" in modern terms, gives a prior judgment preclusive effect in a subsequent action between the same or different parties as to those particular issues decided in the first action which were necessary to the decision. Under the doctrine of mutuality, a judgment could have preclusive effect only between the parties or those in privity with them, and could not be used against third parties or by them. These policies operate not only where a second action challenging the first decision is brought in the same forum, but also where the action challenging the judgment is brought in another judicial system. In a federal system such as the United States, such a policy is necessary to ensure cooperation and unity among the states making up the system.

The Constitution requires that each state give "Full Faith and Credit . . . to the . . . Judicial Proceedings of every other State."[4] The statute implementing this provision, 28 U.S.C. § 1738, states that the "Acts, records and judicial proceedings" of any state "shall have the same full faith and credit in every court within the United States . . . as they have by law or usage in the courts of such State, . . . from which they are taken."[5] The requirement of full faith and credit not only extends to relations between courts in sister states, but also requires both federal[6] and state[7] courts to give full faith and credit to the other's proceedings.

---

3. E. SCOLES & P. HAY, CONFLICT OF LAWS 916 (1982). In *Ferrer's Case* Lord Coke stated that the goal of all law is "rest and quietness," 77 Eng. Rep. 263 (K.B. 1599).

4. U.S. CONST. art. IV, § 1.

5. 28 U.S.C. § 1738 (1982).

6. *See generally* Degnan, *Federalized Res Judicata,* 85 YALE L.J. 741 (1976).

7. *See* Stoll v. Gottlieb, 305 U.S. 165, 177 (1938) (federal courts decision in bankruptcy case has res judicata effect in later state-court proceeding); Degnan, *supra* note 6, at 744-45 (although it is a clearly established rule that state courts must give full faith and credit to federal court decisions, no explicit constitutional or legislative authority mandates this result).

The full faith and credit requirement makes state policies about the effect of judgments a matter of federal concern.[8] Specific rules of res judicata are not constitutionally compelled.[9] A state might choose to have a very limited notion of judgment finality as a domestic matter. But given that states have such rules, the Supreme Court polices enforcement of judgments in two ways. It ensures, first, that states treat foreign judgments with appropriate deference and second, that the rules do not violate the due process rights of parties.[10]

II. Ways to Attack a Judgment

In general, full faith and credit requires that one legal system defer to the judgments of another — either in a state-state or a state-federal context. Even where a court has made a patently erroneous determination as to important matters in the litigation, its judgment must be accorded full faith and credit by courts in other states. According to the literal language of § 1738, the second forum apparently should apply the res judicata rules of the forum rendering the judgment to determine how much "faith" and "credit" are due. However, a judgment is subject to collateral attack on a number of grounds, outlined below.

A. FINALITY

A judgment which is not a final determination under the law of the forum which rendered it need not be recognized in other states.[11] Sister states are obliged to recognize a foreign judgment only to the extent it is recognized in its home state. A non-final judgment would not have preclusive effect in the rendering state, and therefore, sister states have no obligation to give it preclusive effect.[12]

B. LAST IN TIME

A court in State A, where enforcement of a State B judgment is sought, could be confronted by a claim that the State B judgment should not be enforced because the situation actually is governed by another judgment rendered in State C. In this case, the State A court

---

8. *See* Brilmayer, *Credit Due Judgments and Credit Due Laws: The Respective Roles of Due Process and Full Faith and Credit in the Interstate Context,* 70 IOWA L. REV. 95, 99-100 (1984).

9. *See id.* at 99.

10. *Id.* & n.30.

11. *See* Maner v. Maner, 412 F.2d 449 (5th Cir. 1969) (divorce decree is sufficiently final to enforce in Alabama because Florida courts which rendered it would enforce it); RESTATEMENT (SECOND) OF CONFLICT OF LAWS § 107 (1971) [hereinafter cited as RESTATEMENT].

12. RESTATEMENT, *supra* note 11, at § 107, comment b.

should enforce the judgment rendered last in time, if it is otherwise valid.[13] This result seems anomalous, given that the court which rendered the later judgment evidently failed to accord preclusive effect to the original judgment and entered a second inconsistent judgment. However, the policy of preclusion overrides this problem. Whether or not enforcement is owing is rarely an open and shut question, and like all issues, some forum must decide this question. Good-faith errors are possible but the loser under the second judgment had the opportunity to raise the preclusion issue in the state of rendition and either failed to do so or did not do so persuasively. For this reason, even an erroneous determination that enforcement was unnecessary is entitled to preclusive effect in this proceeding, as a unanimous Supreme Court has recently emphasized.[14]

C. LACK OF JURISDICTION

The second forum is generally free to examine whether the rendering court had personal jurisdiction over the parties. It is also sometimes said that it may examine whether there was subject matter jurisdiction over the controversy,[15] although this is more debatable. The requirements of personal and subject matter jurisdiction have different origins and problems regarding the two generally arise in different contexts. The problem of lack of personal jurisdiction typically arises in the state/state context — that is, in a situation where enforcement of a judgment from one state is sought in another state.[16] The lack of subject matter jurisdiction usually becomes an issue when the federal courts are involved — usually with regard to a state-court decision in an area of more-or-less exclusive federal jurisdiction.[17] These differences lead to a difference in the way collateral challenges to lack of jurisdiction are treated.

---

13. *See* Treinies v. Sunshine Mining Co., 308 U.S. 66, 76-78 (1939); RESTATEMENT, *supra* note 11, at § 114.

14. *See* Parsons Steel, Inc. v. First Ala. Bank, 54 U.S.L.W. 4144 (1-28-86); *see also* Treinies v. Sunshine Mining Co., 308 U.S. 66 (1939) (Idaho determination that Washington court did not have jurisdiction should be given preclusive effect in an interpleader action for enforcement).

15. *See* Thompson v. Whitman, 85 U.S. 457, 464 (1873) (subject matter jurisdiction of the rendering court legitimate basis for collateral attack).

16. Of course, this includes federal courts exercising their diversity jurisdiction.

17. *See* Kalb v. Feuerstein, 308 U.S. 433, 440 (1939) (federal law deprived state court of jurisdiction over a bankruptcy case); *cf.* Durfee v. Duke, 375 U.S. 106 (1963) (court in one state attempted to adjudicate title to land which may have been situated in another state, showing that subject-matter jurisdiction problems also can arise in the state-state context).

The requirement that a court have personal jurisdiction is an individual right that stems from the due process clause. A court's personal jurisdiction can be established by consent and a defense of lack of personal jurisdiction is waived if not raised in timely fashion.[18] States have established a device of limited appearance whereby a party appears in court solely for the purpose of challenging the court's jurisdiction over him. If the party's challenge of such jurisdiction is unsuccessful, however, this is viewed as a conclusive decision on the question of jurisdiction and the issue is res judicata if challenged in a later enforcement action. The Supreme Court has approved this device as it provides the defendant with a full opportunity to contest the jurisdictional question.[19]

On the other hand, in a situation where the defendant never appeared in State A to challenge jurisdiction and a default judgment was entered, it only seems fair to afford the defendant an opportunity to contest jurisdiction. Therefore, in cases where the defendant never appeared to contest jurisdiction in State A, State B may examine the question of the jurisdiction of State A in rendering the original judgment.[20] If State A indeed did not have personal jurisdiction over the defendant, State B rightfully can refuse to enforce the original judgment. Indeed, if the rendering court lacked jurisdiction, its judgment cannot lawfully be enforced even within the rendering state.[21] If State B finds that State A had jurisdiction, it will enforce the judgment, cutting off any opportunity the defendant would have had to defend on the merits.

Subject matter jurisdiction has a different nature. In the federal context, subject matter jurisdiction is limited to what the Constitution and Congress grant to the federal courts.[22] Subject matter jurisdiction cannot be established by consent of the parties and its absence is grounds for dismissal at any stage of the litigation.[23] However, if the question of subject matter jurisdiction was or could have been fully litigated in the original forum, the issue typically cannot be re-examined in a second action.[24]

---

18. *See* Insurance Corp. of Ireland, Ltd. v. Compagnie des Bauxites de Guinee, 456 U.S. 694, 703 (1982).

19. Baldwin v. Iowa State Traveling Men's Ass'n, 283 U.S. 522, 524-527 (1931).

20. *Id.* at 523.

21. Pennoyer v. Neff, 95 U.S. 714 (1877) ("The authority of every tribunal is necessarily restricted by the territorial limits of the state in which it is established. Any attempt to exercise authority beyond those limits would be deemed in every other forum . . . an illegitimate assumption of power and be resisted as mere abuse.").

22. *See* U.S. Const. art. III, § 2 cl. 1; Insurance Corp. v. CBG, 456 U.S. at 701-02.

23. *Id.* at 702.

24. *See, e.g.,* Durfee v. Duke, 375 U.S. 106 (1963); Trienies v. Sunshine, 308 U.S. 66 (1939); Stoll v. Gottlieb, 305 U.S. 165 (1938).

This result seems odd, given the seemingly "inflexible" requirement that a federal court decline to act when it lacks jurisdiction.[25] The situation, however, can be viewed as analogous to the limited appearance device in personal jurisdiction: the court has the authority to determine whether it has subject matter jurisdiction and its decision in this regard is binding. This grant of preliminary jurisdiction allows a court to "bootstrap" itself into jurisdiction and to have its determination accorded full faith and credit so long as the defendant was present to litigate the issue.[26]

Since full faith and credit is defined by statute, Congress can make exceptions to these general principles. In several instances, therefore, the Supreme Court has refused to accord full faith and credit to prior judgments where important federal policies were involved. For example, in *Brown v. Felsen*,[27] the Court held that a prior state-court proceeding relating to the discharge of debt was not res judicata in a later federal court proceeding on the same issue. These exceptions are difficult to explain, especially when compared to other cases where the Court did apply full faith and credit to cases which seemingly involved equally important federal policies.[28]

In *Marrese v. American Academy of Orthopedic Surgeons*,[29] the Supreme Court held that the decision whether a state-court proceeding bars a federal antitrust case was first a question for state law. Only if the rendering state's law would bar the claim would the court be forced to decide whether an exception should be made to § 1738. The Court went on to state, however, that in considering whether such an exception should be made, the determining factor would be the intent of Congress in drafting the antitrust laws. Thus, it is as yet unclear whether an exception to § 1738 will be made for the antitrust laws.

---

25. *See* Mansfield, Coldwater & Lake Michigan Ry. v. Swan, 111 U.S. 379, 382 (1884).

26. *See* Dobbs, *The Validation of Void Judgments: The Bootstrap Principle* (Pts. 1 & 2), 53 VA. L. REV. 1003, 1009-1014, 1241 (1967).

27. 442 U.S. 127 (1979); *see also* United States v. Fidelity & Guar. Co., 309 U.S. 506, 512 (1940) (judgment against United States rendered when government failed to assert its immunity could be attacked in later proceeding); Kalb v. Feuerstein, 308 U.S. 433 (1940) (state-court judgment of foreclosure rendered during pendency of federal bankruptcy petition held void in later action).

28. *See* Chicot City Drainage Dist. v. Baxter State Bank, 308 U.S. 371, 376-78 (1940) (judgment rendered under jurisdictional statute later held unconstitutional could not be attacked in second lawsuit by same parties).

29. 105 S. Ct. 1327, 1332-35 (1985) (remanded for a determination whether state law would preclude the action).

Commentators have attempted to explain the distinction, but no clear pattern on the part of the Court is apparent.[30] The best explanation, however, seems to be some notion of congressional intent.[31] This topic will receive further treatment in the discussion in Part III of the effect of state judgments in areas of exclusive federal jurisdiction.

D. Public Policy

Historically, a state had no full faith and credit obligation to enforce tax and penal judgments for reasons of territorial sovereignty and public policy.[32] The area where nonrecognition is allowable has shrunk with time, however. In the tax area, the Supreme Court has held that "a judgment is not to be denied full faith and credit merely because it is for taxes."[33] There is thus no question that a liquidated tax claim must be enforced and most state courts also enforce unadjudicated interstate tax claims.[34]

The Supreme Court has also limited the type of penal claim to which full faith and credit does not apply.[35] In *Huntington v. Atril*,[36] the Court held that unless a judgment is based upon a penal claim, as defined by the Supreme Court, it must be enforced. Although there is no precedent specifically on point, subsequent Supreme Court decisions may have so limited the penalty exception that a claim of *any* sort reduced to judgment should be given under full faith and credit.[37]

Similar questions arise in the situation in which a state seeks to close its courts to foreign judgments based on causes of action which could not have been initially brought in the enforcing forum. An early

---

30. For instance, in Brown v. Felsen, 442 U.S. 127 (1979), the latest Supreme Court decision dealing with the preclusive effect of state-court judgments in bankruptcy, the Court did not mention Stoll v. Gottlieb, 305 U.S. 165 (1938), an earlier decision dealing with preclusion and bankruptcy.

31. *See* Marrese v. American Academy of Orthopaedic Surgeons, 105 S. Ct. at 1335; *see also* Dobbs, *supra* note 26, at 1247-58 (Court will not accord full faith and credit to state-court judgment where preclusion would thwart legislative intent or go against public policy); Smith, *Full Faith and Credit and Section 1983: A Reappraisal,* 63 N.C. L. Rev. 59, 81-101 (1984) (Court will not give preclusive effect to state-court judgment if doing so would be contrary to congressional intent).

32. *See* Wisconsin v. Pelican Ins. Co., 127 U.S. 265, 291 (1888) (common-law rule that states will not enforce the penalties of another is not affected by full faith and credit clause); E. Scoles & P. Hay, *supra* note 3, at 948.

33. Milwaukee County v. M.E. White Co., 296 U.S. 268, 279 (1935).

34. E. Scoles & P. Hay, *supra* note 3, at 948-49.

35. *Id.*

36. 146 U.S. 657 (1892) (question of whether statute is "penal," for the purposes of interstate enforcement, depends on whether its purpose is to punish for a public offense or to provide a remedy to a private person injured by the wrongful act).

37. *See* E. Scoles & P. Hay, *supra* note 3, at 950; Milwaukee County v. M. E. White Co., 296 U.S. 268 (1935) citing Fauntleroy v. Lum, 210 U.S. 230 (1908).

Supreme Court case upheld a New York court's dismissal of a claim based on a foreign judgment under a statute that denied foreign corporations the right to sue on foreign causes of action.[38] The Court held, in effect, that the Constitution does not require the state to provide a competent court.[39] Subsequent decisions have narrowed this ruling, so that the exception may operate only where the statute withdrawing the court's jurisdiction is one which involves limitations upon parties, rather than causes of action.[40]

Although a judgment validating activity which is illegal in the state where enforcement is sought might offend that state's public policy, a court may not refuse to enforce it on that ground.[41] Similarly, a judgment which is based on an error of fact or law must be enforced by the court in the second forum even if it discovers the error.[42] The party resisting enforcement presumably could have appealed the erroneous decision in the original jurisdiction and thus is not allowed a second route of appeal through collateral attack.[43]

E. Substance vs. Procedure

Full faith and credit does not mean that all states must accord judgments the exact same effect, although a literal reading of § 1738 might suggest as much. In internal disputes, different states have made different choices as to who is bound by a judgment and who can take advantage of a prior adjudication.[44] The full faith and credit requirement to accord the judgment the same effect as it would have in the state of rendition should arguably not hold true as to the procedural or remedial effects of a judgment.[45] The general rule that a state applies its own procedural rules is discussed in Chapter 8.

---

38. Anglo-American Provision Co. v. Davis Provision Co., 191 U.S. 373, 394 (1903) ("If the plaintiff can find a court into which it has a right to come, then the effect of the judgment is fixed by the Constitution and the act in pursuance of it which Congress has passed . . . . But the Constitution does not require the state to provide such a court.").

39. *Id.* at 374.

40. E. Scoles & P. Hay, *supra* note 3, at 946-48 citing G. Stumberg, Conflicts of Laws 119-20 (3d ed. 1963).

41. *See* Milliken v. Meyer, 311 U.S. 457, 462 (1940); Fauntleroy v. Lum, 210 U.S. 230, 237 (1908); *but see* Restatement (Second) of Conflict of Laws § 103 (1971) (exception to rule of interstate recognition exists where important interests of sister state involved).

42. *See* Milliken v. Meyer, 311 U.S. 457, 462 (1940); Fauntleroy v. Lum, 210 U.S. 230, 237 (1908).

43. *See* Restatement, *supra* note 11, at § 106 comment a (1971).

44. *See* Brilmayer, *supra* note 8, at 99-100 & n.28.

45. *See* Restatement, *supra* note 11, at § 99; Averill, *Choice-of-Law Problems Raised by Sister-State Judgments and the Full-Faith-and-Credit Mandate,* 64 Nw. U.L. Rev. 686 (1969).

The treatment of statutes of limitations illustrates how some rules might be viewed as "procedural," so that the rules of the first forum need not be followed in the second. State B cannot refuse to enforce a State A judgment on the grounds that the State B statute of limitations for bringing the action originally has expired.[46] However, if the State B statute of limitations for enforcement of judgments has expired at the time enforcement of the State A judgment is sought, State B is not required to give the judgment full faith and credit.[47] State B is merely prohibited from discriminating between local and foreign judgments as to the length of the statute of limitations.[48] Furthermore, revival of the judgment in State A should mean that it is entitled to full faith and credit in State B.[49]

III. Special Substantive Problems in Full Faith and Credit

Beyond the general principles discussed above, certain sorts of substantive causes of action present special cases of full faith and credit recognition of foreign judgments. The issues which have generated the most interest include land, workers' compensation, and domestic relations judgments where enforcement is sought in a second state, the effect of state judgments on matters within exclusive federal jurisdiction, and certain types of civil rights disputes.

A. STATE-STATE RELATIONS

Certain types of litigation have traditionally been treated differently for purposes of full faith and credit. Two such situations — land and workers' compensation — will be discussed here. Domestic relations, a particularly thorny and important example, will be discussed in Chapter 12.

1. Land

If a plot of land is located in State A, courts in State B have no jurisdiction to enter a judgment that purports directly to affect title to the land, and State A does not have to honor such a decree.[50] This is because courts in the state where the land is located are considered to

---

46. See Roche v. McDonald, 275 U.S. 449 (1928); RESTATEMENT, supra note 11, at § 118(1).
47. See Watkins v. Conway, 385 U.S. 188 (1966); RESTATEMENT, supra note 11, at § 118(2).
48. Watkins v. Conway, 385 U.S. 188, 189-91; RESTATEMENT, supra note 11, § 118(2); Brilmayer, supra note 8, at 102.
49. Watkins v. Conway, 385 U.S. 188 (1966); E. SCOLES & P. HAY, supra note 3, at 959-61; Brilmayer, supra note 8, at 102.
50. Fall v. Eastin, 215 U.S. 1, 11-12 (1909).

have exclusive subject matter jurisdiction over the land. While an early rationale for this rule was that the court in another state can never have jurisdiction over the *res* — the land itself — and can therefore never enter a judgment which operates as source of title to that land,[51] a more modern explanation relies on the situs state's interest in the integrity of the local title recording system and the protection of local residents who rely on that system.[52]

As the rule now stands, courts in State B do have the jurisdiction to enter judgments which have an *indirect* effect on land located in State A, such as a judgment ordering the conveyance of title between two litigants who both appear in State B's court. The power to enter such judgments derives from State B's *in personam* jurisdiction over the litigants, which allows it to determine the rights and liabilities between those parties.[53] Such a conveyance may even be required to be enforced by State A's courts.[54] It is only effective, however, as to the parties which appeared in State B's courts, and not as to all claims to that land.[55] The law of State A, and not the State B judgment, governs a State A suit to determine the rights of third parties.[56]

An interesting case is presented when there is a dispute as to whether the land is located in State A or in State B. In this situation, the Supreme Court has essentially compromised. It has required State A to give preclusive effect to State B's determination that the land is in State B rather than State A but has declared that judgment to be binding only between the actual parties to State B's proceeding — *in personam* treatment.[57] The general rule which requires deference to jurisdictional issues which were actually litigated in the State B courts is not thought to override State A's interest in independently determining whether it has jurisdiction over the land when other parties or the state itself becomes enmeshed in later litigation.

2. Worker's Compensation

The Supreme Court has charted an uncertain course regarding the question whether State B is barred by the full faith and credit clause

---

51. *Id.* at 11. A state may for similar considerations of the *situs* of the property transferred have exclusive subject matter jurisdiction in relation to probating the estate of a deceased resident. *See* Tilt v. Kelsey, 207 U.S. 43, 59-60 (1907).

52. *See* E. Scoles & P. Hay, *supra* note 3, at 931 n.2.

53. Fall v. Eastin, 215 U.S. at 8-10.

54. E. Scoles & P. Hay, *supra* note 3, at 932.

55. Durfee v. Duke, 375 U.S. 106, 115 (1963).

56. *See Fall,* 215 U.S. at 14-15 (Holmes, J., concurring); E. Scoles & P. Hay, *supra* note 3, at 932.

57. *See* Durfee v. Duke, 375 U.S. 106 (1963).

from giving a supplemental award to a worker who has already received a workers compensation award in State A. Full faith and credit would seem to bar a subsequent award where the award in the first state was intended to determine the full liability of the employer as to that injury. The Court's first decision in the area held that the first award must be given preclusive effect, so that the second state could not supplement it.[58] Four years later, however, the Court allowed the second state to make a supplemental award so long as the worker's compensation statute in the rendering state did not contain "unmistakable language" precluding such an award.[59] This willingness to allow modification reflects in part the fact that a worker's compensation award can usually be readily modified in the state of rendition. Where the award is, in effect, not "final," the second state should have no duty to give it full faith and credit. In practice, courts rarely found state statutes to contain such unmistakable language, so that the result of these decisions was that such supplemental awards were freely given.

The Supreme Court returned to the question again in 1980 in *Thomas v. Washington Gas Light Co.*[60] In *Thomas,* a divided Court gave two reasons why full faith and credit permitted the District of Columbia to give a worker a supplemental award although he had already received an award under the Virginia statute. First, a majority of the Justices agreed that the Virginia statute did not contain the "unmistakable language" which would preclude an award by another state.[61] Second, a four-Justice plurality questioned the logic of the existing rule. Examining the different state interests at stake in the conflict between the laws of the two states, they concluded that one state has "no legitimate interest within the context of our federal system in preventing another State from granting a supplemental compensation award when that second State would have had the power to apply its workmen's compensation law in the first instance."[62] Because an employer should know that his liability could be as great as that of the most generous state whose laws apply, an interest in preventing the more generous award cannot justify the "unmistakable language" rule. Nor, more fundamentally, would an administrative agency in one state have the jurisdiction that a court of general jurisdiction would have to determine the worker's rights under another state's law. The

---

58. Magnolia Petroleum Co. v. Hunt, 320 U.S. 430, 441 (1943).

59. Industrial Comm'n of Wis. v. McCartin, 330 U.S. 622, 628 (1947).

60. 448 U.S. 261 (1980). There was no majority opinion in *Thomas.* Three justices joined in an opinion written by Justice Stevens. Two justices joined in an opinion concurring in the judgment written by Justice White. Justice Marshall joined in Justice Rehnquist's dissenting opinion.

61. 448 U.S. at 269 (plurality opinion), 289-90 (White, J., concurring).

62. *Id.* at 286.

agency's determination cannot preclude a claim that it never would have had the power to consider. The state's interest in upholding the agency's determination cannot extend to an interest in barring other state's awards.

The reasons which convinced the plurality would, however, effectively provide no protection to such judgments at all. Although ostensibly limited to the workers compensation area, the reasoning in *Thomas* could affect the application of full faith and credit to other sorts of disputes.[63] If there is no preclusive effect to judgments rendered simply because a state tribunal is statutorily required to apply its own laws, then why should there be such an effect where the state court is bound by choice-of-law rules to do so? The *Thomas* opinion thus seems to undercut the policy of finality underlying full faith and credit and hinders the ability of the clause to act as a "nationally unifying force."[64]

B. STATE-FEDERAL RELATIONS

Congress has granted exclusive jurisdiction over certain areas of law to the federal courts.[65] In integrating cases within their own jurisdiction, however, state courts at times consider questions which may be relevant to the decision of a later case exclusively within federal jurisdiction. To what extent should the state decision be given preclusive effect? Similarly, Congress has enacted statutes which allow challenges to the propriety of official state activity.[66] If a state court already has entered a judgment validating this activity in some way, to what extent should a federal court be bound by this judgment when deciding a claim brought under the federal statute? Supreme Court doctrine in the area is somewhat inconsistent, but the current trend is to accord preclusive effect to state court determinations.

---

63. *See id.* at 286-88 (White, J., concurring).

64. *Id.* at 289.

65. *See, e.g.,* 28 U.S.C. § 1334 (1982) (giving district courts exclusive jurisdiction over bankruptcy matters); 28 U.S.C. § 1338 (1982) (giving district courts exclusive jurisdiction over patent matters); General Inv. Co. v. Lake Shore & M.S.R. Co., 260 U.S. 261, 286-88 (1922) (interpreting 28 U.S.C. § 1337's grant to district courts of original jurisdiction over antitrust law claims as a grant of exclusive jurisdiction).

66. *See* 28 U.S.C. §§ 2241-2254 (1982) (habeas corpus procedure); 42 U.S.C. § 1983 (1982) (giving cause of action to any person injured under color of state law).

1. Exclusive Federal Jurisdiction

The need for uniform national policy has led Congress to enact statutes which give federal courts exclusive jurisdiction over such areas as bankruptcy, patent validity, and federal antitrust violations.[67] State courts, however, may be called upon to decide questions relevant to the federal claim as part of an action properly in state court, as for example in a breach of contract case which relates to patent infringement. One could argue that normal preclusion principles should be sacrificed in such circumstances, allowing the federal court to ignore any previous state proceeding, because of the important federal policies reflected in the grant of exclusive jurisdiction.[68] The Supreme Court has not adopted this approach, however.

In a recent decision on Sherman Antitrust Act claims, containing language indicating its applicability to all claims within exclusive federal jurisdiction, the Court outlined how a federal court should determine the proper preclusive effect to be given a related state court judgment.[69] A court must look first to state preclusion law to determine what preclusive effect, if any, the state would give the judgment.[70] If state law would bar relitigation of the issue despite the state court's lack of jurisdictional competence to decide the federal claim itself, then the court must examine whether the exclusive federal statutory scheme involved express or implied repeal of full faith and credit requirements. In the case of claim preclusion, the court also should consider whether subject-matter jurisdiction limitations on the state court prevented the plaintiff from using a certain legal theory or seeking a certain remedy.[71] If such limitations exist, the state-court judgment will not have preclusive effect. The federal court is not allowed to give the state-court judgment greater preclusive effect than the state court would give it.[72] The Court recently applied similar reasoning to a claim under Title VII, although it is not an area where federal courts have exercised exclusive jurisdiction.[73]

---

67. *See supra* note 65.
68. *See* Smith, *supra* note 31, at 95.
69. Marrese v. American Academy of Orthopaedic Surgeons, 105 S. Ct. 1327 (1985).
70. *Id.* at 1332.
71. *Id.* at 1333 (quoting RESTATEMENT (SECOND) OF JUDGMENTS § 26(1)(c) (1982)).
72. *Id.* at 1334.
73. Kremer v. Chemical Constr. Co., 456 U.S. 461 (1982). The Court in *Kremer* expressly declined to consider whether Title VII claims could be brought exclusively in the federal courts.

The bankruptcy area has received less consistent treatment from the Court. Claim and issue preclusion are generally applicable to bankruptcy proceedings.[74] However, in two cases the Court has allowed a federal court to ignore an earlier state-court judgment relating to the bankruptcy.[75] These exceptions are difficult to explain but seem based on the extent to which granting preclusive effect to the state judgment would undercut congressional policies giving federal courts exclusive jurisdiction in the field.[76]

2. Section 1983

Much of the doctrine developed in the preceding section regarding areas of exclusive federal jurisdiction has application to civil rights suits under § 1983. Although such lawsuits are not exclusively within the jurisdiction of the federal courts,[77] some courts and commentators had argued that the special nature and history of § 1983 actions require exemptions from the usual principles of res judicata.[78] These authorities point to the legislative history of the statute — one of the post-Civil War civil rights acts — which shows that congressional concern about the deficiencies of state-court enforcement of federally-created rights was a primary motive for its passage.[79] Such concern would obviously be greatest where a state court is evaluating the actions of a state official. To give preclusive effect to a decision of one of these tribunals would undermine the important purpose of § 1983, namely to protect the constitutional rights of individuals. These authorities also argued that, although the Congress which enacted § 1983 in 1871 might have intended that the statute be subject to the narrow res judicata rules in use at that time, it could not have intended that the more expansive preclusion rules used today would apply to § 1983.[80]

---

74. *See* Smith, *supra* note 31, at 96.

75. *See* Brown v. Felsen, 442 U.S. 127 (1979); Kalb v. Feuerstein, 308 U.S. 433 (1940).

76. Smith, *supra* note 31, at 97-98.

77. *See, e.g.,* Long v. District of Columbia, 469 F.2d 927 (D.C. Cir. 1972); Espinoza v. O'Dell, 633 P.2d 455 (Colo. 1981).

78. *See, e.g.,* Lombard v. Board of Educ., 502 F.2d 631, 635 (2d Cir. 1974), *cert. denied,* 420 U.S. 976 (1975); Ney v. California, 439 F.2d 1285, 1288 (9th Cir. 1971); *Developments in the Law — Section 1983 and Federalism,* 90 HARV. L. REV. 1133, 1335-43 (1977); Theis, *Res Judicata in Civil Rights Act Cases: An Introduction to the Problem,* 70 Nw. U.L. Rev. 859 (1976); Averitt, *Federal Section 1983 Actions After State Court Judgment,* 44 U. COLO. L. REV. 191 (1972).

79. The congressional debate surrounding the adoption of § 1983 is discussed extensively in Mitchum v. Foster, 407 U.S. 225, 240-42 (1972).

80. *See* Currie, *Res Judicata: The Neglected Defense,* 45 U. CHI. L. REV. 317, 329 (1978).

The Supreme Court addressed these contentions in *Allen v. McCurry*[81] and rejected them. *Allen* involved a state criminal defendant who had unsuccessfully attempted to suppress evidence seized by the police. After a jury convicted him, he brought suit in federal court under § 1983, seeking damages from the police officers who conducted the allegedly illegal search. The officers argued that the suit should be dismissed because the illegal search issue had already been decided in the state criminal proceedings.[82] The Supreme Court acknowledged the special role which Congress intended § 1983 and the federal courts to play in vindicating individual rights, but found only "the most equivocal support" for the argument that Congress intended to override the full faith and credit statute and common-law res judicata doctrine.[83] The Court rejected as totally without support the apparent holding of the court of appeals that every person asserting a federal right was entitled to one clear opportunity to litigate that right in federal district court, regardless of the legal posture in which the federal claim arose.[84]

The Supreme Court did, however, recognize two situations where a prior state-court judgment need not be given preclusive effect. As a general rule applicable to any type of proceeding, preclusion does not apply where the party against whom the prior decision is asserted did not have a full and fair opportunity to litigate the issue in the prior case.[85] The second situation, peculiar to § 1983 actions, is based upon an understanding of the role of § 1983 in the legal system. Preclusion principles are inapplicable "where state law did not provide fair procedures for the litigation of constitutional claims, or where a state court failed to even acknowledge the existence of the constitutional principle on which a litigant based his claim."[86] The scope of this exception is not entirely clear, but the Court indicated that it was similar to the "full and fair opportunity to litigate" exception.[87] A state-court decision which happens merely to be erroneous does not fall within the exception.[88]

---

81. 449 U.S. 90 (1980).

82. McCurry could not present his claims through federal habeas corpus because of the effect of the Supreme Court decision in Stone v. Powell, 428 U.S. 465 (1976). The § 1983 action apparently was McCurry's only route to present his federal claim in a federal court.

83. 449 U.S. at 99.

84. *Id.* at 103-04.

85. *Id.* at 101.

86. *Id.*

87. *Id.* Smith, *supra* note 31, at 108-10, provides an extensive analysis of how to determine whether the "understanding-of-Section-1983 exception" should apply.

88. 449 U.S. at 101.

Allen involved issue preclusion, but the Supreme Court in *Migra v. Warren City School District*[89] extended its doctrine to the claim preclusion. Claim preclusion occurs where a litigant could have raised a federal issue in the earlier state-court proceeding but failed to do so. The Court saw no reason why the policy behind § 1983 would require distinguishing between the issue-preclusive and claim-preclusive effects of state-court judgments.[90] A system which gave issue-preclusive effect to state-court judgments, but not claim-preclusive effect, would allow state courts to apply their expertise to state claims while leaving federal courts free to apply their own expertise to federal claims. However, the Court rejected such a system as out of line with the policy behind full faith and credit:

> That statute [§ 1738] embodies the view that it is more important to give full faith and credit to state-court judgments than to ensure separate forums for federal and state claims. This reflects a variety of concerns, including notions of comity, the need to prevent vexatious litigation, and a desire to conserve judicial resources.[91]

Therefore, in general, the federal court must first look to the law of the state which rendered the prior judgment to determine what preclusive effect the state would give the judgment. The federal court should not give the state judgment greater preclusive effect than it would have under state law; it must give the state judgment the same preclusive effect.[92]

Determining that preclusive effect is no easy task. Many § 1983 actions are brought by convicted criminal defendants. Even as a matter of state law, the question of the degree to which the state conviction should preclude a subsequent federal civil rights action raises difficult questions.[93] Traditionally, a criminal judgment was given no preclusive effect in a subsequent civil action.[94] This policy resulted from the doctrine of strict mutuality of parties to which courts adhered, from the narrow definitions of "cause of action" and "issue" employed at the time, and from the difference in the burden of proof between civil and criminal proceedings. The underpinnings of the traditional rule have eroded, as for instance many courts have abandoned mutuality requirements.[95] In addition, the difference in proof levels may not be

---

89. 465 U.S. 75 (1984).

90. *Id.* at 84.

91. *Id.*

92. *See Marrese,* 105 S. Ct. at 1334 (discussing *Migra*).

93. It is also one of the few areas where courts have given consideration to the differences and similarities of civil and criminal actions, a topic discussed in ch. 11.

94. *See* A. VESTAL, RES JUDICATA/PRECLUSION 373 (1969).

95. *See, e.g.,* Blonder-Tongue Labs., Inc. v. University of Ill. Found., 402 U.S. 313 (1971) (eliminating mutuality requirement in federal court suits).

significant. The fact that a criminal defendant is acquitted, under the beyond-a-reasonable-doubt standard, does not mean that he necessarily would be found blameless under the civil preponderance-of-the-evidence standard. Some commentators have argued that a criminal defendant has had "every opportunity and incentive"[96] to litigate the issue of his guilt, such that it would be fair to give the conviction preclusive weight because the "full and fair opportunity to litigate" requirement had been met.[97] Given these modern trends in preclusion law, it may not be anamolous that nothing in the Court's reasoning suggested that its treatment of the preclusion question was affected by the fact that a criminal judgment was involved.

The dissent in *Allen,* however, focused importantly on the fact that it was a criminal defendant who raised the § 1983 claim.[98] The dissent pointed to the differences in issues and remedy at stake in a criminal trial as opposed to a § 1983 action. It also stressed that a state criminal defendant (unlike other § 1983 plaintiffs) does not "voluntarily" choose to litigate his constitutional claim in state court; rather, "[t]he risk of conviction puts pressure upon him to raise all possible defenses" in the state proceeding.[99] The dissent concluded that the majority position would put the criminal defendant with a potential § 1983 claim in the "fundamentally unfair" position of having to choose between forgoing either a potential defense or a federal forum for his constitutional claim.[100]

While not acceding to such arguments generally, the Court has shown some sensitivity to the pressures of the criminal process in a situation where the criminal defendant's initial conviction was based on a guilty plea. In *Haring v. Prosise,*[101] the Court held that a defendant who had pled guilty to state narcotics charges in Virginia was not barred from bringing a subsequent § 1983 action based on an allegedly illegal search. The Court looked first at Virginia preclusion law and found that the criminal proceeding accepting the guilty plea did not address the legality of the search and could not have done so.[102] Recognizing the myriad factors which motivate a guilty plea, the Court denied that the defendant, by pleading guilty, had either admitted the legality of the search or waived any claim challenging it. Such an argument "would be wholly contrary to one of the central concerns

---

96. *See, e.g.,* A. VESTAL, *supra* note 94, at 382.
97. *See* Currie, *supra* note 80, at 335-36.
98. Justice Blackmun, joined by Justices Brennan and Marshall, dissented in *Allen.*
99. 449 U.S. at 115 (Blackmun, J., dissenting).
100. *Id.* at 116.
101. 462 U.S. 306 (1983).
102. *Id.* at 314-17.

which motivated the enactment of 1983, namely, the 'grave congressional concern that the state courts had been deficient in protecting federal rights.'"[103] The Court pointed out that allowing a § 1983 action by a defendant who has pled guilty does not infringe on several of the interests which underlie the policy of preclusion — such as the repetitive use of judicial resources and the possibility of inconsistent decisions — because the state court simply has not adjudicated the issues that might be the foundation of a subsequent § 1983 claim.[104]

Although *Haring* held that a prior guilty plea does not preclude a subsequent § 1983 action related to the defendant's conviction, it did not consider what weight the plea should have in the subsequent civil action. The plea would probably have some effect where the gist of the § 1983 action is based on nonexistence of an important aspect of the crime or where the defendant seeks to profit from the act to which he pled guilty.[105] One commentator argues that the guilty pleas should be admissible in the subsequent civil action, with a presumption accorded to the facts necessary to sustain the plea.[106] The criminal defendant would then have to rebut this presumption by explaining the motivation for his guilty plea.[107]

3. Habeas Corpus

The writ of habeas corpus, through which a person in government custody can test the legality of his detention or imprisonment, is an explicit exception to the full faith and credit accorded judgments. Because of the subject's intricacy, we can only highlight a few important points. The Constitution requires that the writ be available, and an elaborate statutory scheme governs its operation.[108] Although the statute originally extended protection only to persons in federal custody,[109] Congress expanded its coverage after the Civil War to reach "all cases

103. *Id.* at 323 (quoting *Allen,* 449 U.S. at 98-99).

104. *Id.* at 322 n.11.

105. This would comport with statutes in certain states which prevent convicted killers (either by trial or guilty plea) from inheriting from their victims. *See, e.g.,* Ohio Rev. Code Ann. § 2105.19 (Page Supp. 1983); Colo. Rev. Stat. § 15-11-803 (1973).

106. *See* Shapiro, *Should a Guilty Plea Have Preclusive Effect?,* 70 Iowa L. Rev. 27, 49-50 (1984); *see also* RESTATEMENT, *supra* note 11, at § 85, comment b (1982) (defendant who pleads guilty may be estopped in subsequent civil litigation from contesting facts representing elements of offense).

107. Shapiro, *supra* note 106, at 50.

108. U.S. CONST. art. 1, § 9 cl. 2 ("The privilege of the Writ of Habeas Corpus shall not be suspended, unless when in Cases of Rebellion or Invasion the public Safety may require it."); *see* 28 U.S.C. §§ 2241-2254 (1982).

109. *See* Act of Sept. 24, 1789, ch. 20, § 14, 1 Stat. 73.

where any person may be restrained of his or her liberty in violation of the Constitution, or any treaty or law of the United States."[110] This gave the federal courts jurisdiction over the claims of state prisoners held in violation of the federal constitution or statutes.[111]

Federal courts have equitable discretion to issue the writ on behalf of state prisoners, but decision to do so requires balancing two competing concerns. On one hand, Congress through the habeas statute has shown its desire to provide a federal forum for the vindication of the constitutional rights of state prisoners.[112] However, the states also have an interest in the integrity of their rules and proceedings and in the finality of their criminal judgments.[113] The decision to issue the writ thus implicates the policy of comity between the states and the federal government.

The Supreme Court has struck a wavering balance between these two competing interests over the last century. The Court originally took a restrictive view of federal habeas authority.[114] The 1953 decision in *Brown v. Allen*[115] seemed to transform the writ into a vehicle allowing relitigation of *all* federal constitutional claims of state prisoners in a federal court.[116] Within the last decade, however, the Burger Court has been restricting the scope of the federal habeas remedy in a variety of ways.

For the one thing, the availability of habeas has been limited in situations when the defendant has pled guilty; he or she may attack only the guilty plea itself in the habeas proceeding.[117] The Court also recently imposed a rule of total exhaustion, which requires the district court to dismiss a habeas petition containing both claims for which the petitioner has attempted to pursue his or her state remedies and claims for which he or she has not.[118] The petitioner with both exhausted and unexhausted claims thus has the option of either postponing assertion of the exhausted claims while litigating the unexhausted claims in state court *or* deleting the unexhausted claims hoping later to resubmit them to the federal court. This latter course could, however, lead to

---

110. Act of Feb. 5, 1867, ch. 28, § 1, 14 Stat. 385.

111. *See* Ex parte Royall, 117 U.S. 241 (1886).

112. *See* Reed v. Ross, 104 S. Ct. 2901, 2907 (1984).

113. *See id.*

114. *See* Note, *A Comparison of Section 1983 and Federal Habeas Corpus in State Prisoners' Litigation,* 59 NOTRE DAME L. REV. 1315, 1320-21 (1984).

115. 344 U.S. 443 (1953).

116. *See* Peller, *In Defense of Federal Habeas Corpus Litigation,* 16 HARV. C.R.-C.L. L. REV. 579, 583 (1982).

117. Tollett v. Henderson, 411 U.S. 258 (1973).

118. Rose v. Lundy, 455 U.S. 509 (1982).

forfeiture of the deleted claims, if the district court finds that a subsequent petition raising those claims constitutes abuse of the writ.[119] The purpose of this total exhaustion requirement is to provide an incentive for state prisoners to seek state-court relief for all their claims as an initial matter.

In addition, the Court has sought to limit in various ways the types of issues that can be raised through federal habeas. For example, habeas review of fourth amendment claims is unavailable if the state courts provided a full and fair opportunity to litigate the claims.[120] The Court has also deemed certain issues to be "factual issues" so that the state court's findings on such issues are "presumed to be correct" and not subject to later review under 28 U.S.C. § 2245(d).[121] The result of these limitations is increased federal deference to state-court judgments.

The Court also has increased in another way the consequences of failure to pursue certain claims in state court. Under traditional doctrine, a defendant was foreclosed from presenting a federal habeas claim only if he had "deliberately bypassed" an opportunity to present the claim on a state level.[122] This standard has been supplanted by a test which demands strict adherence to state procedural rules. Failure to comply with such rules forms an adequate state ground for the conviction.[123] Habeas review of such issues is possible only when the defendant demonstrates cause for his failure to comply with the state procedural rule and prejudice resulting from the error which forms the basis of the petition.[124] The defendant's ignorance of the constitutional claim now raised through habeas does not generally constitute "cause" for failure to raise it.[125] Only where a constitutional claim "is so novel that its legal basis is not reasonably available to counsel" does the defendant have sufficient cause for his failure to raise the claim through relevant state procedures.[126]

This stringent standard for failure to pursue claims in state court results from concerns about comity and the accuracy and efficiency of state judicial systems.[127] The Supreme Court has indicated that the

---

119. *See id.,* at 520-21.
120. Stone v. Powell, 428 U.S. 465 (1976).
121. *See, e.g.,* Patton v. Yount, 104 S. Ct. 2885 (1984); Wainwright v. Witt, 105 S. Ct. 844 (1985).
122. Fay v. Noia, 372 U.S. 391, 438 (1963).
123. *See* Wainwright v. Sykes, 433 U.S. 72 (1977).
124. *Id.* at 87.
125. Engle v. Isaac, 456 U.S. 107 (1982).
126. Reed v. Ross, 104 S. Ct. 2901, 2910 (1984).
127. *Id.* at 2909.

states should be allowed to make a good faith attempt to uphold constitutional rights.[128] The Court's adoption of the "cause and prejudice" standard introduces concepts of claim preclusion into the habeas realm and greatly limits the availability of the writ.

C. Summary

An obvious difference appears when comparing the Supreme Court's treatment of special cases in state-state relations (primarily worker's compensation) with its treatment of special cases in state-federal relations. A court in State B faced with a worker's compensation award from State A can do almost as it likes. In sharp contrast, a federal court confronted with a state-court decision relating to one of these areas of special federal concern must bend over backwards to make sure it does not deny the state judgment its proper measure of respect.[129]

Why is the state's interest in relitigating issues so important in one context, where another state is involved, while its interest in the integrity of judgments is determinative when a federal court is the second forum? It could be that the Court has more sympathy for injured workers who make the wrong choice of forum than for prisoners or other civil rights plaintiffs.[130] Although an acceptable rationale from a legal realist's standpoint, this explanation seems too simplistic. The unique characteristics of worker's compensation law may explain the difference,[131] but similar tendencies by the Court are apparent in other areas. As will be discussed below, the Court has shown a similar willingness to give state courts greater freedom than federal courts in the area of legislative jurisdiction.[132] As this discussion of the adjudicative jurisdiction comes to a conclusion, we direct our reader's attention to that second context, legislative jurisdiction, as it applies to both state/federal and interstate relations.

---

128. *See* Engle v. Isaac, 456 U.S. at 128.

129. *See* Brilmayer & Lee, *State Sovereignty and the Two Faces of Federalism,* 60 Notre Dame Law. 833, 841 (1985).

130. *See id.,* at 843.

131. *See id.,* at 845; Thomas v. Washington Gas & Light Co., 448 U.S. 261, 289-90 (1980) (White J., concurring).

132. *See* ch. 8 (Substance and Procedure); and compare ch. 6 (The Doctrine of *Erie Railroad*) with chs. 7 and 9 (state choice of law and its constitutional limits).

PART II

LEGISLATIVE JURISDICTION

The preceding chapters have dealt primarily with the authority of courts. Even the material on judgments implicates judicial jurisdiction, since lack of adjudicative jurisdiction is one ground for refusing enforcement.

In the following chapters, we address legislative jurisdiction, or "choice of law." Many of the same themes are represented: the necessity to restrict the reach of federal law to protect the authority of the states, and the need to limit the reach of state power to protect the states from one another. Particularly regarding that latter issue, legislative jurisdiction relies on the same basic concept as adjudicative jurisdiction, namely the contact between the litigation and the state. However, the state doctrines of legislative jurisdiction are more theoretically interesting than the comparable state long-arm provisions. We therefore devote an entire chapter to their elucidation.

Finally, analysis of legislative jurisdiction necessitates special attention to the international arena. Although adjudicative jurisdiction is not altered as one moves from the interstate to the international arena, legislative jurisdiction takes a rather different turn. This is due to an idiosyncrasy of American federalism. While federal courts apply the long-arm statutes of the state in which they sit, Congress and the federal courts that interpret congressional enactments are not analogously limited by state choice of law rules. Further, states use the same long-arm statutes and choice of law rules in the international as the interstate arena. The result is that federal courts power is limited by state long-arm rules, which are the usual interstate ones. Being free to develop peculiarly federal choice of law principles for problems of international law, however, the federal courts have exercised this power to develop principles that are rather at odds with the ones developed by the states for interstate problems.

We commence the discussion with perhaps the single most important precedent in American jurisdictional jurisprudence: namely, *Erie Railroad v. Tompkins.*

Chapter 6

THE ERIE DOCTRINE

Nothing illustrates the fundamental role that jurisdiction plays in the legal scheme as well as the landmark case *Erie Railroad v. Tompkins.*[1] Although technically addressing only a specific question of the powers of federal courts, *Erie* represents a profound shift in American jurisprudence. This shift was occurring even before the case was decided, of course, and was not complete until long afterwards (if, indeed, it is complete even today). But *Erie* represents the symbolic point at which the Supreme Court officially transferred its allegiance from one school of legal philosophy to another.

The *Erie Railroad* case has many layers of meaning. At the most superficial level, it merely reinterprets a federal statute, the Rules of Decision Act,[2] to include state judicial rules as "laws" that bind federal courts when they are adjudicating state law claims. The case thus addresses the proper method of defining state-created rights in federal courts, particularly in federal diversity jurisdiction.[3] However, *Erie* also purports to interpret the federal Constitution, suggesting that this statutory interpretation is constitutionally compelled.

Beyond these questions of what *Erie* actually says, moreover, are the questions of what *Erie* stands for. The jurisprudential implications of *Erie Railroad* transcend specific issues of the law to be applied in the federal district courts. The *Erie* doctrine involves questions of the role of courts, generally. And these questions, in turn, have implications for other problems of jurisdiction. We accordingly address three topics below: what *Erie* says, what *Erie* stands for, and what *Erie* means for jurisdiction.

I. Historical Background

The precise holding of *Erie Railroad* must be understood against its historical background. The Rules of Decision Act, section 34 of the Judiciary Act of 1789, provides that "the laws of the several states, except where the Constitution, treaties, or statutes of the United

---

1. 304 U.S. 64 (1938).

2. Section 34 of the Judiciary Act of 1789 (codified as amended at 28 U.S.C. § 1625 (1982)).

3. By definition, diversity cases are in federal court because of the identities of the parties and not because they are based on federal questions. Thus they necessarily present issues of state law. But federal question cases often raise state-law questions, also, because the plaintiff appends a state-law cause of action to the federal one, or because federal law explicitly incorporates state law. *See generally* Westen & Lehman, *Is There Life for* Erie *After the Death of Diversity?* 78 MICH. L. REV. 311 (1980).

201

States shall otherwise require or provide, shall be regarded as rules of decision in civil actions in the courts of the United States, in cases where they apply."[4] This statute clearly requires the federal courts to follow state law unless that state law is preempted by federal Constitution, treaty, or statute.

The problem, however, was the meaning of the phrase "state law." Obviously, it included state legislation; almost as obviously, it included state constitutional provisions. But it was less certain whether the states' judicial decisions were "laws." From one perspective, case reports are not themselves laws; laws are specific rules that have been codified, and not the reasoning and analogies that constitute judicial decisions. From another viewpoint, those judicial decisions are part of "the law of the land." For instance, a judge applying past precedents undeniably is involved in deciding a question of "law."

Justice Story, writing in the early nineteenth century, thought that the plural term "laws" in the Rules of Decision Act had the former meaning, encompassing primarily statutes and state constitutional provisions. "In the ordinary use of language," he wrote in *Swift v. Tyson*, "it will hardly be contended, that the decisions of courts constitute laws. . . . The laws of a state are more usually understood to mean the rules and enactments promulgated by the legislative authority thereof, or long-established local customs having the force of laws."[5] Because judicial decisions did not themselves constitute laws, the Rules of Decision Act did not preclude the federal courts from consulting their independent judgment about the proper resolution of common law problems.

Swift v. Tyson involved an issue of commercial law — the consideration necessary for the enforceability of negotiable instruments. New York state courts had held that such instruments were unenforceable when the sole consideration was a pre-existing debt. According to Story, disputes about commercial law were "questions of a more general nature, not at all dependent upon local statutes or local usages."[6] The proper effect of negotiable instruments was to be found "not in the decisions of the local tribunals, but in the general principles and doctrines of commercial jurisprudence."[7] The role of federal courts was therefore identical to that of state courts, namely to consult "general reasoning and legal analogies."[8] And thus, Story concluded, "[i]t be-

---

4. 28 U.S.C. § 1625 (1982) (formerly 28 U.S.C. § 725 (1940 ed.)).
5. 41 U.S. (16 Pet.) 1, 18 (1842).
6. *Id.* at 19.
7. *Id.*
8. *Id.*

comes necessary for us . . . to express our own opinion of the true result of the commercial law upon the question now before us."[9]

In this way, Story divided legal authority into two categories, more or less conforming to the division into statutory and decisional law. The first category, positive law, included all state legislative decisions and constitutional provisions. Less obviously, positive law encompassed judicial decisions that constitute local rules. Local rules, like statutes, are products of deliberate decisions to shape the law one way or another; they represent a choice among competing approaches to a problem. Local rules are judicial decisions that might be expected to differ in different localities.[10]

Both statutes and local rules contrast with the second category, general common law. General common law supposedly contained the underlying principles of contracts, torts, commercial law, and so forth. It is produced by legal reasoning, not legal choice. On issues of general common law, it was assumed that there could be only one correct answer, and that the answer could best be discovered through logic and analogy. Thus, concluded Story, the common-law decisions of state courts were not themselves law, but only evidence of what the "true result" actually was.[11] Federal judges had a right and an obligation to consider such issues on their own, for their judgments were as accurate as the decisions of state-court judges. In the words of a later justice, "[w]e shall never immolate truth, justice, and the law, because a State tribunal has erected the altar and decreed the sacrifice."[12]

In one respect, Story's jurisprudence accords with common ways of talking about law. Particularly in the first year of law study, we become accustomed to thinking about what "the law" is. Should an acceptance become effective when it is dropped into the mailbox, or only upon its receipt by the offeror? Should the same rule apply to revocations of offers? We study the precedents from different states interchangeably, expecting them to be more or less reconcilable and to form some general law of contracts. *Swift v. Tyson* approved this view of the judicial function as merely declaratory of pre-existing rights. It lasted almost one hundred years; but signs of trouble were apparent almost from the beginning.

Most important, the problem of uncertainty in the definition of what constituted local law and what constituted general law created difficul-

---

9. *Id.*
10. For a discussion of how this distinction fared in practice, see 2 WARREN, THE SUPREME COURT IN UNITED STATES HISTORY 89 (rev. ed. 1935).
11. *Id.*
12. Gelpcke v. City of Dubuque, 68 U.S. (1 Wall.) 175, 206-07 (1863).

ties for litigants. Only with regard to this latter class of rules were federal courts authorized to exercise their independent judgment.[13] The extreme difficulty of this determination exacerbated another problem — that of predictability. One could not be sure in advance whether an issue was one of general or local law. Further, if the federal courts exercised independent judgment on such issues, then individuals could never be certain which version of the general law would be applied to their commercial dealings. The law thus became unpredictable in two ways: It was difficult to predict whether independent judgment would be exercised, and even if it was clear that independent judgment was appropriate, one could not know which brand of justice one would receive.

Ironically, Story envisioned the role of federal courts as putting an end to such uncertainty.[14] The concept of a universal general common law had much appeal to those who wanted to rationalize and unify the law of commercial transactions. All states should agree on the content of this law, and the vehicle for unification would be the federal courts, acting under one centralized supreme court. Unfortunately, the state courts declined to follow the federal tribunals' lead. Convinced that they, too, had independent insight into the dictates of truth and logic, state judges typically disregarded federal pronouncements on issues of general common law, and the gap between the state and federal courts widened over time.

Added to unpredictability was a second problem: the encouragement of forum shopping. Since different rules prevailed in state and federal courts, the choice of forum often dictated whether a party would win or lose. This choice of forum in turn depended on whether diversity jurisdiction was available. Diverse parties might obtain the federal version of general common law, either through original federal jurisdiction or through removal. Nondiverse parties were relegated to the state version.

This problem is most vividly illustrated by *Black & White Taxicab & Transfer Co. v. Brown & Yellow Taxicab & Transfer Co.*[15] There, the Court decided that the legality of a railroad's agreement to give exclusive taxicab privileges to one company was governed by general common law. The prevailing party had qualified for this general version of common law, however, by dissolving and then reincorporating in another state in order to generate diversity of citizenship. Justice Holmes dissented, in an opinion joined by Justices Brandeis and Stone:

---

13. *See, e.g.,* Baltimore & O.R.R. v. Baugh, 149 U.S. 368 (1893) (tort law issue subject to independent judgment because not "local law").

14. For a description of Story's impact on the decision, see J. GRAY, THE NATURE AND SOURCES OF THE LAW 253 (2d ed. 1921).

15. 276 U.S. 518 (1928).

Books written about any branch of the common law treat it as a unit, cite cases from this Court, from the Circuit Courts of Appeals, from the State Courts, from England and the Colonies of England indiscriminately, and criticise them as right or wrong according to the writer's notions of a single theory. It is very hard to resist the impression that there is one august corpus, to understand which clearly is the only task of any Court concerned. If there were such a transcendental body of law outside of any particular State but obligatory within it unless and until changed by statute, the Courts of the United States might be right in using their independent judgment as to what it was. But there is no such body of law. The fallacy and illusion that I think exist consist in supposing that there is this outside thing to be found. Law is a word used with different meanings, but law in the sense in which courts speak of it today does not exist without some definite authority behind it.[16]

Holmes, Brandeis and Stone were in the minority in *Black & White Taxicab.* Ten years later however, in *Erie Railroad v. Tompkins,* Brandeis spoke for the majority.

II. The Erie *Opinion*

Tompkins, a citizen of Pennsylvania, was injured on a dark night while walking along a railroad right of way. A passing freight train owned by the defendant struck him with what looked like a door projecting from one of the moving cars. Tompkins brought suit in federal district court in New York, the home state of the Erie Railroad Company, claiming that the railroad had operated the train in a negligent manner. Pennsylvania courts had earlier held that persons in Tompkins' position were trespassers, and would therefore have a cause of action only for wanton or willful injury. The district court held that general common law applied, and that trespassers on an established right of way were owed a duty of due care.

Justice Brandeis' opinion for the Court gave several reasons for reversing the lower courts' result. The opinion first relied upon the Rules of Decision Act. The railroad argued that the language "the laws of the several states . . . shall be regarded as rules of decision" included judicial decisions, so that the federal district court was obliged to follow state common law. Brandeis accepted this argument, relying upon historical scholarship that had been published after *Swift v. Tyson* was decided.[17] That research had uncovered evidence of an earlier version of the act, which had explicitly included state common law as being obligatory in the federal courts.

---

16. *Id.* at 533.

17. Warren, *New Light on the History of the Federal Judiciary Act of 1789,* 37 HARV. L. REV. 49 (1923).

The opinion also emphasized the "mischievous results" of the doctrine of *Swift v. Tyson,* including the divergence between the state and federal versions of common law, and the difficulty in differentiating between questions of local law and questions of general common law. Not only did the result vary between state and federal courts; but also, whether the federal version was available to the litigants depended upon the accident of diversity of citizenship. "Thus, the doctrine rendered impossible equal protection of the law."[18]

The Court then noted that if the problem were merely one of statutory construction, the appropriate remedy might be legislative revision. However, the rule of *Swift v. Tyson* was not merely wrong as a matter of statutory construction; it was also unconstitutional. Except where the Constitution or federal legislation addressed an issue, the law to be applied had to be the law of the state. Justice Brandeis stated that "whether the law of the State shall be declared by its Legislature in a statute or by its highest court in a decision is not a matter of federal concern. There is no federal general common law."[19] The federal Constitution, continued Brandeis' opinion, recognizes and preserves the autonomy of the states in both their legislative and judicial departments. And the opinion quoted Holmes' dissent in *Black & White Taxicab:* "the common law so far as it is enforced in a State, whether called common law or not, is not the common law generally but the law of that State existing by the authority of the State without regard to what it may have been in England or anywhere else."[20]

The *Erie* opinion is unclear in several respects. Because of the multiplicity of reasons that were given for the decision, it is difficult to interpret precisely how broadly the opinion should be read. One might take the statutory issue as conclusive of the case, and treat the constitutional discussion as mere dictum. This would certainly slight the majority's intention, however. It was undoubtedly clear to Justice Brandeis that the discussion might simply have terminated with the reinterpretation of the Rules of Decision Act; yet he also addressed the other issues.

In addition, the final point about the unconstitutionality of *Swift v. Tyson* is itself unclear. Justice Brandeis seemed to merge two arguments, one about state autonomy and one about the federal judicial function. His argument was that the states had a right to be free from federal judicial interference. But what is the relationship between state autonomy and the role of federal judges? The state autonomy argument might mean that the particular issue in question (duty of

---

18. 304 U.S. at 75.
19. *Id.* at 78.
20. *Id.*

care to a trespasser on a railroad right of way) is simply not within the scope of federal rule-making authority. Since Congress had no basis for regulating this issue, the federal courts were exceeding their jurisdictional limitations by developing a federal rule on the subject. Taken by itself, the state autonomy argument does not differentiate between legislative and judicial power; it simply puts certain substantive issues beyond the reach of any federal exercise of power.

But there must be more to *Erie* than that. In the first place, it is not clear that Congress could not regulate issues about the tort liability of railroads pursuant to its commerce clause powers; at any rate, this issue would have deserved far more discussion than Justice Brandeis gave it. Second, it does not seem that *Erie's* holding is limited to issues that Congress could not address. Rather, it seems also to apply to issues that Congress could address, but has chosen not to. For this reason, the "autonomy" interest that Brandeis relied upon is of a curious sort. It is not a simple right to be free from interference. It amounts to protection from federal judicial interference, but not necessarily from federal legislative interference. State autonomy is necessarily intertwined with the jurisprudential issue of whether courts should create law.

III. *Legal Positivism and Judicial Legitimacy After* Erie

Regardless of one's interpretation of the precise rationale underlying the opinion, its holding is clear and remains unshaken. Federal courts are obliged to follow state judicial decisions to the same extent that they adhere to state legislative decisions. In all circumstances where the state law has not been preempted by a federal rule, federal courts must apply state law. The jurisprudential implications are as profound and far-reaching as the jurisdictional holding of the case. *Erie* is a symbolic watershed in American law.

The jurisprudential issue concerns whether courts make the law, or merely find the law. Legislatures, obviously, make law. The very motivation behind legislative action is that the present state of affairs is unsatisfactory for some reason, and it is hoped that the contemplated legislation will correct the situation. In contrast, courts are not motivated by dissatisfaction with the existing law; their primary object is to apply the law and to decide particular cases. It is not clear, therefore, that it is part of the judicial role to change the law nor that judges typically set out to do so. As between making new law and applying old law, judicial decisions are ambiguous.

The so-called "Blackstonian" view of the judicial function[21] held that courts merely decided cases by applying pre-existing legal principles.

---

21. This characterization was employed by the Supreme Court in Linkletter v. Walker, 381 U.S. 618, 622-23 (1965).

Although this view, adopted into American law by Story's opinion in *Swift v. Tyson*, is generally disfavored today, it still has adherents.[22] The opposing view, associated both with the legal positivism of writers such as John Austin[23] and with legal realism,[24] holds that courts do not merely ascertain the content of pre-existing rules, but actually make choices informed by policy considerations.

The impact of the philosophical shift to legal positivism is not limited to technical questions of jurisdiction. Most important, the recognition that courts make law has important ramifications for the question of judicial legitimacy. Legislatures are elected explicitly to make laws. Judges typically are not elected: federal judges, in particular, are both appointed and protected from removal for unpopular decisions.[25] By what right do judges make law?

Most pointedly, if judges invalidate statutes (which are the product of a democratic process) are they behaving in an illegitimate fashion? The enforcement of pre-existing constitutional rights seems clearly valid, because that does not require the exercise of discretion. But if judges are making policy decisions in the same way that legislatures do, then such law-making power seems illegitimate unless supported by some form of popular approval.[26] The post-*Erie* philosophy highlights the legitimacy difficulties of the institution of judicial review, because after *Erie* it is no longer possible to mask judicial decisionmaking as merely the value-neutral discovery of pre-existing law.

The retroactivity of judicial decisions illustrates these difficulties. Retroactivity is an important question in the administration of criminal law, because incarceration is a remedy that extends over a period of time. A decision may be rendered in a later case that raises doubts of the legality of the prisoner's continued confinement. At that point, the prisoner may attempt to rely upon the later case to obtain release by bringing a federal habeas corpus action.[27]

---

22. *See*, in particular, R. DWORKIN, TAKING RIGHTS SERIOUSLY (1977) (describing decision according to pre-existing legal principles).

23. The Court termed the positivist view "Austinian" in *Linkletter*, 381 U.S. at 623-24.

24. *See, e.g.*, J. FRANK, LAW AND THE MODERN MIND (1935).

25. Article III of the United States Constitution protects judges from diminution in salary and removal.

26. The classic discussion of this objection to judicial review is A. BICKEL, THE LEAST DANGEROUS BRANCH: THE SUPREME COURT AT THE BAR OF POLITICS (1962).

27. Habeas corpus is discussed in ch. 5, sec. IIIB3, *supra*.

The retroactivity issue was directly addressed by the Supreme Court in *Linkletter v. Walker.*[28] The petitioner in that case had been convicted prior to the decision of *Mapp v. Ohio,*[29] which applied the exclusionary rule to the states. The conviction had been legal at the time that it was entered, since the state courts had no constitutional obligation to exclude illegally seized evidence. When the prisoner later challenged his conviction on the basis of *Mapp,* the Court was obliged to determine whether that holding should be applied retroactively.

In deciding that it should not, the Court addressed the same fundamental philosophical issues of judicial method that had been discussed in *Erie.* If judges merely declare pre-existing law, then *Mapp* was the proper rule all along, and the petitioner's conviction would have been invalid. If instead, judges actually make law, *Mapp* might represent a change in the law, so that the petitioner's conviction was valid when it was rendered. The Court adopted the positivist view, held that *Mapp* was merely a prospective rule, and declined on policy grounds to apply it to invalidate the petitioner's conviction.

Since the decision in *Linkletter,* it has been necessary to analyze every precedent recognizing a constitutional right of criminal defendants to determine whether it creates a new, positivist right or simply declares the pre-existing law. Pre-existing rights are always applied to earlier cases, because to recognize such a right is to admit that the earlier case constituted error. But new rights are not necessarily applied retroactively. The very resolution of the retroactivity issue, for this reason, requires the Court to sort its precedents into two categories: those pre-existing rights that "really" stem from the constitutional text and are applied to earlier cases, and those that the justices simply "created" for policy reasons, that therefore need not be applied retroactively. The retroactivity issue forces the Court repeatedly to confront its own arguable illegitimacy.

IV. Erie *as a Limitation of Federal Judicial Power*

A second difficulty arising out of the post-*Erie* philosophy concerns the differential jurisprudential status of state and federal courts. In rejecting the right of federal courts to exercise independent judgment about the "general common law," *Erie* acknowledged that courts do in fact make law. When state courts hand down judicial decisions, they are making state law, and federal courts are not entitled to disregard it. But if this is true for state courts, then it seems also true for federal courts. Like state courts, they make law when they decide cases, although since they are federal courts the law they make is federal law.

28. 381 U.S. 618 (1965).
29. 367 U.S. 643 (1961).

However, *Erie* implies that while state courts legitimately make state law, federal courts are not equally entitled to make federal law. There is a state common law entitled to recognition in the federal courts, but, after *Erie,* there is no general federal common law. State judges, therefore, arguably have more law-making power than their federal counterparts. In certain situations, this is perfectly comprehensible: there are substantive issues that simply are not subject to federal regulation, since the Constitution limits federal power to enumerated areas. But there are also many topics that are potentially federal concerns, but as to which Congress has not acted. With regard to issues not potentially subject to federal regulation, it is clear why state but not federal courts may exercise law-making power. But with regard to issues of potential federal interest, the recognition that courts, also, make law seems to open these areas to federal common-law development.

The irony of *Erie,* therefore, is that while recognizing a positivist role for state courts, it limits the federal courts to the more modest Blackstonian posture. State courts may make law; federal courts may not. One possible explanation lies in the literal wording of the Rules of Decision Act. That act states that the laws of the several states are binding in federal court as rules of decision, unless preempted by federal Constitution, treaties, or *statutes.* This wording creates an asymmetry between federal and state authority; the latter encompasses all "laws" (including judicial decisions), while the former includes only constitutional or legislative provisions. This explanation is not adequate if Justice Brandeis was correct that *Erie* was constitutionally compelled, however.

A second explanation recognizes that *Erie* is as much a case about federalism as about jurisprudence. Admittedly, *Erie* rests on the proposition that courts are sources of law, and not merely discoverers of law. The reason for limiting this proposition to state courts, however, is to limit the power of federal preemption to the Congress. Herein lies the state autonomy thread of Brandeis' opinion: although there may be few areas of state authority that are protected absolutely from all federal intrusion, state autonomy is nonetheless protected by limiting such intrusions to actions of the federal legislative branch. For one thing, elimination of one potential source of intrusion reduces the probability that federal power will be exercised.

Further, there are several reasons that legislative incursions on state authority are likely to be less extensive than judicial intrusions. The states have more power in Congress than in the federal courts, through elected representatives that owe some allegiance to state interests.[30] Additionally, a congressional decision not to intrude upon state sovereignty might be interpreted as a deliberate reservation of certain powers to the states. Finally, because of the difficulty of enacting statutes, Congress is more oriented to the status quo, and less likely to preempt state law. By contrast, courts necessarily must address the issues presented by cases, and the need to resolve those issues makes it more likely that federal law will be created in the process. It is more difficult for courts simply to decide not to decide.[31]

The importance of this federalism theme — and its primacy over the literal wording of the Rules of Decision Act as a basis for the *Erie* holding — is illustrated in the one context in which the post-*Erie* view that courts properly create law has taken hold in federal courts. On the same day that *Erie* debunked the idea of a "general common law," the Supreme Court recognized the existence of a special federal common law. In *Hinderlider v. La Plata River & Cherry Creek Ditch Co.*[32] the Court fashioned a federal common law of interstate water rights. And in other areas in which the need for uniformity was paramount and resort to state law seemed inappropriate, the Court has also sanctioned judicially created federal law.[33]

The conflict between such federal common law and the literal wording of the Rules of Decision Act is evident. The continuing existence of specialized areas of federal common law suggests that the important *Erie* concern is not the precise wording of the Rules of Decision Act, but general principles of federalism and a respectful, if not absolute, regard for state autonomy.

Restricting the power to make law to the state courts results in greater state freedom from federal intervention. But the reasons for thinking this result desirable have less to do with jurisprudence than with federalism. Jurisprudence by itself dictates a comparable role for state and federal courts; but under *Erie* the roles of federal and state courts are sharply differentiated. While *Erie* is indeed a jurispruden-

---

30. J. CHOPER, JUDICIAL REVIEW AND THE NATIONAL POLITICAL PROCESS 177-184 (1980); Wechsler, *The Political Safeguards of Federalism*, 54 COLUM. L. REV. 534 (1954).

31. We discussed in ch. 2, sec. IV and ch. 4, sec. II the "case or controversy" and abstention doctrines, which involve decisions not to decide. However, these developments are *doctrinal:* they do not authorize courts simply to exercise the power not to decide on an ad hoc or political basis. A closer analogy would be the Supreme Court's discretionary docket. Since the discretion whether to decide is limited to the Supreme Court, however, it cannot prevent lower federal courts from pre-empting state law.

32. 304 U.S. 92 (1938).

33. The classic discussion is Friendly, *In Praise of* Erie — *and of the New Federal Common Law,* 39 N.Y.U. L. REV. 383 (1964).

tial watershed, it stands for more than a repudiation of the Blackstonian legal philosophy. More important, *Erie* stands for the modest role of federal courts in a federal system committed in substantial part to decision according to state law.

V. What Erie Means for Jurisdiction

As the discussions of retroactivity and federal common law demonstrate, the impact of *Erie* extends far beyond its precise holding. Yet *Erie* has its most direct and substantial implications in the realm of jurisdiction. Both of the important underlying themes — federalism and judicial lawmaking — are important precisely because the United States is a nation of multiple sovereignties.

The relationship between these themes and the jurisdictional arrangements among multiple sovereigns is illustrated by *Erie* itself, where the linkage between federalism and jurisdiction is particularly clear. Federalism is, of course, a dominant theme in the American jurisdictional scheme because federalism is itself a commitment to a particular sort of jurisdictional arrangement. But the declaratory/creative jurisprudential dichotomy is equally a jurisdictional problem. In *Erie*, for example, the reason for the dichotomy was that two separate spheres of sovereignty were involved. If there were only one sovereign involved, there would be no possibility of a second sovereign exercising independent judgment about the correct result. Blackstonian jurisprudence cannot lead to two divergent bodies of law except in a world of two or more authoritative institutions.

Multiple sovereignties create the potential for difference of opinion, and in this way raise the problem of whether two different opinions are conflicting views of the same pre-existing rights (with one opinion necessarily incorrect) or simply two different choices, both permissible. In this sense, it is the existence of multiple jurisdictions that makes the *Erie* question important. Conversely, the positivist answer to the *Erie* question makes jurisdictional rules themselves more important. Once it is conceded that different sovereigns can adopt different approaches to the same problem, it becomes important for an individual to know precisely which sovereign's rule he or she will be subjected to.

This interplay between jurisprudence and jurisdiction transcends the precise *Erie* context. The problem involved in *Erie* was the relationship between state and federal courts. A second problem, addressed at great length in the following chapters, also involves a conflict between multiple sovereignties, although not between federal and state rule-making authority (as in *Erie*) but instead between the rule-making authority of the several states. Again, one must decide whether there exists a "superlaw" or whether each state is free to decide as it likes. This is particularly crucial with regard to choice of law rules. What is the institutional source of the choice of law rules that apportion legislative jurisdiction among the fifty states? Do courts *make* choice of law rules, or do they *find* them? Even in state/state contexts, then, jurisprudence informs one's jurisdictional approach.

Without unduly anticipating the discussion in the following chapters, it is possible to generalize about the jurisprudential overtones of the state/state choice of law issue. Early approaches to the choice of law problem assumed that choice of law rules were true in some ultimate sense.[34] The function of courts and commentators was to discover the correct approach to choice of law, and to apply that approach to particular cases. It was this aspect of the established choice of law methodology that led a prominent critic to describe it as "metaphysical."[35]

The new jurisprudence of *Erie* made such an approach to choice of law anachronistic. No longer did it seem possible to derive first principles of choice of law from abstract logic and legal reasoning. Instead, it became progressively clearer that there were only two possible sources of choice of law rules: state law, and federal law. Federal law was necessarily judge-made, since Congress had never exercised its prerogative to legislate choice of law rules.[36] This heightened awareness of institutional sources of authority, stemming from the jurisprudence underlying *Erie Railroad,* eliminated general common law as a source of rules.

The Supreme Court holding in *Klaxon Co. v. Stentor Electric Manufacturing Co.* that federal courts were obliged to adhere to state choice of law rules was a natural result of *Erie.*[37] So long as the states do not transgress the constitutional limits on choice of law,[38] they may choose a number of different solutions to a choice of law problem. After *Erie,* there could no longer be a single correct answer to choice of law problems. While there have been forcefully argued suggestions that the choice of law problem is an appropriate subject for federal common law,[39] the Court remains committed to the principle that states are free to adopt any one of a number of choice of law approaches, subject only to constitutional limitations.[40]

---

34. *See* ch. 7, sec. I, *infra.*
35. *Id.*
36. Congress has such authority under the full faith and credit clause of article IV.
37. 313 U.S. 487 (1941).
38. For a discussion of the constitutional limitations on choice of law, see ch. 9 *infra.*
39. Horowitz, *Toward a Federal Common Law of Choice of Law,* 14 U.C.L.A. L. REV. 1191 (1967); Hart, *The Relations Between State and Federal Law,* 54 COLUM. L. REV. 489 (1954); Baxter, *Choice of Law and the Federal System,* 16 STAN. L. REV. 1 (1963).
40. *See, e.g.,* Allstate Ins. Co. v. Hague, 449 U.S. 302, 307-08 (1981).

Yet ironically, the ghost of Blackstone still haunts the conflict of laws. Although denouncing metaphysics and espousing adherence to the policy decisions actually made by the various state legislatures, the proponents of new orthodoxy in choice of law are as committed to their first principles as the old orthodoxy was to its own. The conflation of the state law and constitutional reasoning into a single normative inquiry, the failure to accord respect to the choice of law decisions of other states, and the judicial second guessing of legislative preferences that do not accord with tenets of the new methodology are all evidence of this metaphysical trend.[41]

The warning should be clear enough for all to see. Even in this post-*Erie* age, the Blackstonian declaratory theory of jurisprudence has not lost its appeal. Whenever scholars or decisionmakers have independent views about which result is better (and don't they always?) there is a temptation to exercise independent judgment when given the opportunity and then to ascribe the decision to self-evident truth. But probably enough has been said already about the underlying jurisprudential issues of choice of law. We turn next to the ways in which this jurisprudential drama of choice of law has actually unfolded.

---

41. *See generally,* Brilmayer, *Governmental Interest Analysis: A House Without Foundations,* 46 Ohio St. L.J. 459, 468-69 (1985).

Chapter 7
THE CONFLICT OF LAWS

"Conflict of laws" refers to the domain of rights, duties, and disputes among persons and events in different places. More narrowly, a conflict of laws exists when a case is connected to more than one jurisdiction, and the laws of the jurisdictions differ on a point at issue. In such a situation, the forum must decide whether to apply its own law or the law of another jurisdiction as the rule of decision in the case. The potential for conflicts arises wherever separate jurisdictional units co-exist, each with its own laws. The United States, with its fifty jurisdictions and one super-jurisdiction, offers particularly fertile soil for choice of law problems. This is especially true nowadays, as residents of different states communicate and trade with each other, and move freely from place to place.

Automobile accidents are a common source of conflicts problems. A 1969 New York case, *Tooker v. Lopez*[1] is typical. Three roommates at Michigan State University decided to drive to Detroit for the weekend. They had an accident en route, which killed the driver of the car, Marcia Lopez, and one of her passengers, Catharina Tooker. The second passenger, Susan Silk, was injured. Both Marcia Lopez and Catharina Tooker were New York domiciliaries. The car belonged to Marcia's father who lived in New York, where the car was registered and insured. Catharina's father, Oliver P. Tooker, Jr., sued Myer Lopez, Marcia's father and the owner of the car, in New York state court for the wrongful death of his daughter.

Faced with the wrongful death action, the New York court had to decide whether to apply New York or Michigan law as the rule of decision in the case. Michigan had a guest statute barring recovery by a passenger for an injury caused by the negligence of the driver. New York had no such statute. The very existence of a cause of action in a New York court, therefore, depended upon whether the forum state decided to apply its own law, permitting recovery, or whether it applied the law of the place where the accident occurred, barring recovery.[2]

I. Introduction to Conflict of Laws

A. HISTORICAL BACKGROUND

While contemporary mobility has increased the potential for cases implicating several jurisdictions, the conflict of laws has long existed

---

1. 24 N.Y.2d 569, 301 N.Y.S.2d 519, 249 N.E.2d 394 (1969).

2. The court applied New York law on the ground that New York, as the state of domicile of both the plaintiff and the defendant had the only real interest in having its law applied. To understand the *Tooker* court's reasoning see the discussion of "interest analysis" in sec. III, *infra*.

as a problem and as a scholarly focus. Writing in the fourteenth century, the Italian Bartolus of Sassoferato led a group of jurists called the "statutists," who sought to define the jurisdictional reach of laws by classifying statutes as either "real" or "personal." The real statute applied only within the territory of the city-state whose law it was, whereas the personal statute followed a citizen wherever he or she might go.[3] Although this tidy dichotomy failed to account even for the legislative reality of its own day, its legacy has survived in the modern opposition between territorial and domiciliary approaches to jurisdiction.[4]

By the sixteenth century, leadership in the field of conflicts had shifted to France, where such luminaries as Charles Dumoulin, Bertrand d'Argentré, and Guy Coquille busied themselves with strategies to overcome the conflicts among France's confederation of provinces, each with its own provincial law, or coûtume.[5] The modern rubric "conflict of laws" first surfaced in the writings of the seventeenth-century Dutch jurist, Ulric Huber, who applied the theories of his Italian and French predecessors to the problems of the newly-confederated Netherlands.[6]

In the United States, the field of conflicts took shape at the hand of Harvard law professor and Supreme Court Justice Joseph Story. Story's *Commentaries on the Conflict of Laws,* published in 1834, brought together the learning of continental scholars and the principles of English and American case law, thereby furnishing the bedrock for the development of American conflicts law in this century.[7]

B. Sources of Choice of Law Rules

In the United States, choice of law rules are primarily judge-made. However, statutes dictate choice of law rules in a few specific areas; and where statutory provisions exist, they supercede common-law rules. The Constitution, in theory a rich source of choice of law principles, has in practice functioned chiefly to constrain, rather than to prescribe, positive choice of law rules.[8]

1. Statutes

The following are examples of statutory choice of law provisions.

---

3. R. Cramton, D. Currie, H. Kay, Conflict of Laws 2-3 (3d ed. 1981). *See also* Juenger, *A Page of History,* 35 Mercer L. Rev. 419 (1984).

4. See discussion of choice of law theories as they relate to territorial and domiciliary approaches to jurisdiction in secs. IIA and IIIB, *infra.*

5. J. Beale, A Treatise on the Conflict of Laws 30-38 (1916).

6. *Id.* at 42.

7. *Id.* at 50-51.

8. For a discussion of the constitutional limits of choice of law, see ch. 9.

No-Fault Insurance. — Most of the emerging automobile insurance statutes that allow compensation without proof of fault specify their territorial application, but the treatment of interstate accidents varies from statute to statute. Most plans provide compensation to insured domiciliaries injured out of state. Many plans, however, do not grant tort exemption for out-of-state accidents. Thus a local citizen can still be sued in tort for an accident that occurs elsewhere. Conversely, for in-state accidents some plans grant reparation benefits, but not tort exemption, to out-of-staters, while others extend coverage only to insured domiciliaries. The interstate provisions vary depending on the extent to which a given statute makes territorial or domiciliary factors a basis for coverage.[9]

"Borrowing" Statutes. — Many states have enacted statutes of limitations which "borrow" the limitations period of the jurisdiction in which the cause of action arose. Otherwise, plaintiffs might shop for the forum with the most generous limitations period.[10]

Uniform Commercial Code. — Section 1-105 of the UCC specifies that parties may decide contractually that the law of a given state will govern their rights and duties, as long as the transaction bears some reasonable relation to the state or nation chosen.[11]

Federal Torts Claims Act. — This statute (28 U.S.C. §§ 1346, 2671 et seq.) subjects the United States to tort liability "under circumstances where the United States, as a private person, would be liable to the claimant in accordance with the law where the act or omission occurred." The Act has been read to require the application of not just the substantive law but also the conflict of law rules of the place where the defendant's acts or omissions occurred.[12]

Other Statutes. — Many states have statutes specifying that wills executed according to the formalities required by the state of execution will be recognized, even if the formalities under forum law have not been met.[13] Likewise, many worker's compensation laws contain choice of law provisions.[14] As the number of state regulatory regimes increases, we can expect a corresponding rise in statutory choice of law directives.

9. *See* generally Kozyris, *No-Fault Automobile Insurance and the Conflict of Laws — Cutting the Gordian Knot Home-Style,* 1972 DUKE L.J. 331, *No-Fault Insurance and the Conflict of Laws — An Interim Update,* 1973 DUKE L.J. 1009.
10. *See generally* R. CRAMTON, D. CURRIE, H. KAY, *supra* note 3, at 188-96.
11. *See id.* at 183-85.
12. *See* Richards v. United States, 369 U.S. 1, 11 (1962).
13. *See, e.g.,* Cal. Prob. Code § 26 (Deering 1974).
14. *See, e.g.,* Alaska Packers Ass'n v. Industrial Accident Comm'n, 294 U.S. 532 (1935).

2. Common Law

Because neither the Constitution nor statutes have produced many positive choice of law rules, courts rely principally on the theories advanced by scholars to resolve conflicts problems. These theories do not form a coherent whole. Indeed, one commentator, writing in 1933, claimed that scholarly disputes "have produced fruits so diverse that pragmatic appraisal is impossible."[15] Apparently sharing this perception, the Supreme Court, in a 1981 case, suggested that each of the fifty American jurisdictions "applies its own set of malleable choice-of-law rules."[16] The section that follows attempts to bring order to the choice of law proposals scholars have advanced and courts have followed.

The choice of law regimes at use in the various states range from the traditional "vested rights" approach of the *First Restatement* or the "most significant relationship" approach of the *Second Restatement,* to the "center of gravity," "governmental interest," "comparative impairment," "better law," "principles of preference," "functional," or "lex fori" approaches.[17] Notwithstanding the multiplicity of rubrics, each of these theories can be traced to one of two fundamental — and contrasting — perspectives on the conflict of laws: a "vested rights," or a policy-oriented, approach.

Under a "vested rights" theory the forum court is directed to apply the law of the place in which the legal right is created. In tort, the right vests at the place of injury; in contract, it is the place in which the legal relationship is established. A court applying "interest analysis," on the other hand, asks not where a given right attaches, but rather what policies lie behind the differing laws implicated in a multijurisdiction case. The theory of interest analysis is that most multijurisdictional issues are in fact "false conflicts," in which only one of the two or more ostensibly competing jurisdictions actually has an interest in the outcome of the case. Where interest analysis uncovers a "true conflict" between interested jurisdictions, the forum court is directed to apply its own law.

II. The Vested Rights Approach

A. THEORY

The vested rights approach to conflict of laws is grounded in a vision of law as a set of rules, or norms, to govern future transactions. This

---

15. Cavers, *A Critique of the Choice-of-Law Problem,* in J. MARTIN, PERSPECTIVES ON CONFLICT OF LAWS: CHOICE OF LAW 25, 26 (1980).

16. Piper Aircraft Co. v. Reyno, 454 U.S. 235, 252, n.18 (1981).

17. Kay, *Theory Into Practice: Choice of Law in the Courts,* 34 MERCER L. REV. 521, 585 (1983).

conception divides law into three stages. First, a sovereign enacts a body of laws regulating the persons or events within its territory. This is an exercise of legislative jurisdiction undertaken by the legislature or by the courts in their law-making capacity. Second, an event happens to which the law attaches a legal consequence — the right "vests." Third, a court, in its adjudicative capacity, enforces the right that has previously vested.

For example, a state passes a worker's compensation statute, stating that employers are liable to their employees for injuries received during the course of employment. That is the law, enacted by the legislature. It is not a right, however, upon which a worker may sue until that worker is injured on the job. When the bulldozer veers out of control, crushing the worker's leg, the right to compensation vests. Finally, in order to vindicate the right — to collect the compensation due — the worker brings his case in court, asking the court not to *create* a right to compensation, but rather to enforce a right previously created as a potential cause of action by the legislature and actualized when the bulldozer crushed his leg.

When applied to conflicts law, the vested rights doctrine has historically been linked with a territorial theory of jurisdiction.[18] The territorial theory holds that every sovereign has an exclusive right to regulate persons and things within its territory according to its sovereign will. In other words, all events happening, or having effects, within a sovereign's territory are subject to that sovereign's laws. In a conflicts case a forum applies its own choice of law rules to any case involving other states, because the case itself is an "event" happening within the sovereign's territory. However, at the same time it asserts exclusive jurisdiction within its territory, the forum state recognizes rights created under foreign law. These rights enter not as competing laws, which have no currency on the soil of another sovereign, but rather as "facts" to which forum law is applied. In effect, the forum court treats foreign- and domestically-created rights alike. If a worker from a foreign state sues in the forum state to recover compensation due under a foreign worker's compensation law, and if the right to compensation has duly vested in that worker, the forum court will recognize that foreign-created right as it would recognize a right created by its own legislature. In this way, the concept of exclusive jurisdiction is preserved both for the forum and for the sister state. The forum state preserves its jurisdiction by applying only its law to any case being adjudicated on its soil. At the same time, the forum acknowledges the parallel exclusive jurisdiction of its sister state by accepting the for-

---

18. J. BEALE, TREATISE, *supra* note 5, at 105-113.

eign-created right as a preexisting fact having validity no matter where enforcement is sought.[19]

B. THE FIRST RESTATEMENT

The *First Restatement,* published in 1934 and written in large part by Harvard law professor Joseph Henry Beale, looked to the vested rights doctrine to bring certainty to the field of conflicts. The *Restatement* aimed to set out a body of rules simple in form and capable of easy administration that would promote uniformity of results, enhance predictability, and discourage forum-shopping in multistate cases.[20] The rules elaborated by the *First Restatement* do not constitute an independent body of substantive law to be applied directly to the facts of conflicts cases. Rather, they tell courts which among competing local laws to apply.

The *First Restatement* built upon the central commitment of territorial theory that a conflicts problem has a unique solution — one and only one local law properly governs in a case involving multiple jurisdictions. To find that unique solution, the *Restatement* relies on the doctrine of vested rights, requiring courts to apply the law of the state in which the rights of the parties have vested. How does a court know where a given right has vested? The *Restatement* provides, in effect, that a right vests in the state in which the last act necessary to bring a legal obligation into effect occurs. In torts, as we shall see, the state of the last act is the state where the injury occurs; in contracts, it is the state in which the contract is made; in property, it is the state in which the property is located. On procedural issues, the forum is to apply its own law. The reasons for this substance/procedure dichotomy are sufficiently important to warrant a separate chapter,[21] below.

1. Methodology

The *First Restatement* prescribes a two-step process for determining which local law to apply in a case. First the court must characterize the issue in dispute. Is it a substantive question, to which a foreign law

---

19. The vested rights doctrine parallels the logic, familiar in the area of judgments, of full faith and credit. This doctrine requires that any jurisdiction accord to a valid judgment rendered in a foreign jurisdiction the same force the judgment would have in the rendering forum. *See, e.g.* 1 J. MOORE, J. LUCAS, & T. CURRIER, MOORE'S FEDERAL PRACTICE ¶ 0.406 (2d ed. 1984).

20. Even the RESTATEMENT's critics realized its chief advantage lay in these areas. *See, e.g.,* B. CURRIE, SELECTED ESSAYS IN THE CONFLICT OF LAWS 100-01 (1963). For a recent appraisal of the virtues of rules, see Hill, *The Judicial Function in Choice of Law,* 85 COLUM. L. REV. 1585 (1985).

21. For discussion of substance/procedure distinction, see ch. 8.

might apply, or is it a procedural issue, which is governed automatically by forum law? Further, is the lawsuit a tort, contract, property, or other kind of case? Second, the court must identify the most significant event or element in the case and follow it to a specific jurisdiction. The law of that jurisdiction applies to all substantive issues in the case, even those not involving the foreign jurisdiction. The court ostensibly applies the foreign law without reference to its substantive content or effect. A few examples, taken from the fields of tort and contract, will illustrate the methodology.

a. Torts

According to the *First Restatement* the existence and extent of tort liability is to be determined according to the law of the place of "wrong."[22] Section 377 specifies that "[t]he place of wrong is the state where the last event necessary to make an actor liable for an alleged act takes place."[23] The rationale comes squarely from vested rights theory: the plaintiff does not sue the defendant for the latter's mere negligence, but rather for the injury that the negligence has caused. Since mere negligence that causes no injury is not actionable, the right does not vest until the injury occurs.

An 1892 case, *Alabama Great Southern Railroad v. Carroll,*[24] illustrates the logic of the *First Restatement,* strictly applied. The plaintiff in *Carroll,* a railroad brakeman, was injured when a link between two railway cars broke because of the negligence of his fellow workmen in carrying out inspections in Alabama. The train was travelling from Birmingham, Alabama to Meridian, Mississippi, and both states, Alabama and Mississippi, barred common-law actions for injuries caused by fellow servants. However, Alabama had adopted an employer's liability act that would have given the plaintiff recovery.

The Alabama Supreme Court found the case straightforward: it was a torts case, and liability would be determined by the place of wrong. Though the negligence occurred in Alabama, all parties were from Alabama, and the suit was brought in Alabama, the plaintiff had no cause of action because Mississippi, as the place of injury, supplied the rule of decision in the case.

b. Contracts

In contracts cases the methodology of the *First Restatement* is parallel. Once the action has been characterized as a contracts case the court

---

22. RESTATEMENT OF THE CONFLICT OF LAWS § 378 (1934).
23. RESTATEMENT OF THE CONFLICT OF LAWS § 377 (1934).
24. 97 Ala. 126, 11 So. 803 (1892).

finds the connecting factor and follows it to the governing law of a state. The *First Restatement* distinguishes between issues of validity, which are governed by the local law of the place of contracting,[25] and issues of performance, which are governed by the local law of the place of performance.[26] Validity problems are issues involving formalities of the contract, sufficiency of consideration, the parties' capacity to contract, fraud, illegality, and other defenses making a contract voidable. Performance problems would include sufficiency or manner of performance, excuses for nonperformance, the existence or materiality of breach, questions of damages, and rights to rescind.

Beale claimed that the *First Restatement* applies the "last act" doctrine in contracts, as it does in torts. In his *Treatise on the Conflict of Laws,* Beale stated that the place of contracting is the "place in which the final act was done which made the promise or promises binding."[27] However, Beale's use of the "last act" terminology obscures a significant difference between the *Restatement's* treatment of contracts and torts. Whereas in torts the right does not vest until the injury actually occurs, in contracts, the right vests when the legal relationship is first established. If Beale had rigorously adapted the place of injury rule for contracts cases, the *First Restatement* might have looked not to the place of contracting but rather to the place of breach. Inconsistencies aside, the "last act" in contracts proved easier to describe than to identify, especially since contracts are often negotiated, and defaulted upon, through the mails or over the telephone. Again, case law furnishes vivid examples of the difficulties courts have had in applying the *Restatement's* stark logic.

Milliken v. Pratt,[28] an 1878 case decided by the Supreme Judicial Court of Massachusetts, tells of a contract between the plaintiffs, partners doing business in Portland, Maine, and the defendant Sarah Pratt, wife of Daniel Pratt, both residents of Massachusetts. Daniel wanted to trade with the Milliken company in Maine, so he asked his wife to guarantee a line of credit with the Maine business. Sarah executed the guarantee at her home in Massachusetts and delivered it to her husband, who mailed it to the plaintiffs in Portland. Guarantee in hand, the plaintiffs began trading with Daniel Pratt, who ran up a bill of $860.12, only $300.00 of which he paid. Plaintiffs brought suit in Massachusetts to recover the outstanding balance from Sarah.

Chief Justice Gray opened his opinion in *Milliken* with a statement of the "general rule that the validity of a contract is to be determined

---

25. RESTATEMENT OF THE CONFLICT OF LAWS § 332 (1934).
26. RESTATEMENT OF THE CONFLICT OF LAWS § 358 (1934).
27. 2 J. BEALE, CONFLICT OF LAWS 1045 (1935).
28. 125 Mass. 374 (1878).

by the law of the state in which it is made; if it is valid there, it is deemed valid everywhere, and will sustain an action in the courts of a state whose laws do not permit such a contract."[29] Justice Gray's commitment to vested rights theory was crucial in this case, because Maine allowed married women to contract, and Massachusetts did not. Under the *Restatement,* therefore, the plaintiffs could recover only if the judge decided that the contract was made in Maine. Despite the prevailing "mailbox rule," which specifies that the place of mailing is the place where the contract is posted, the court in *Milliken* found that the contract was not completed until the Milliken company received the guarantee and began shipping goods to Daniel Pratt. Apparently, the court chose to view the agreement as a unilateral contract, involving an exchange of promise and performance, rather than as a bilateral contract, completed with a mutual exchange of promises.

In an updated version of *Milliken,* the Pennsylvania Supreme Court in the 1959 case of *Linn v. Employers Reinsurance Corp.*[30] faced the question of whether a contract accepted by telephone was made in New York, where the acceptance was spoken, or in Pennsylvania, where the words of acceptance were heard. Again, the place of contracting was a crucial issue. New York's Statute of Frauds barred the contract in question, whereas Pennsylvania law allowed it. On analogy with the mailbox rule the Pennsylvania court found that the contract was made in the state from which the accepting party spoke. It therefore applied New York law, barring recovery by the Pennsylvania plaintiffs.

2. Critique

These few cases, from contracts and torts, illustrate the brittle methodology of the *First Restatement.* Examples could be multiplied. The *Restatement*'s sections set out rules for choice of law regarding domicile; marriage, legitimacy, adoption, and custody; corporations; property movable and immovable; recognition of judgments; administration of estates; and the structure of conflicts proceedings. This prolix body of rules early inspired scholarly contempt[31] and judicial frustration. One commentator has summed up the critics' views: "[t]hey condemned the choice-of-law rules as metaphysical in concept, mechanistic in operation, and myopic as to consequences."[32]

---

29. *Id.* at 375.
30. 397 Pa. 153, 153 A.2d 483 (1959).
31. *See, e.g.,* Cook, *The Logical and Legal Bases of the Conflict of Laws* in J. MARTIN, PERSPECTIVES, *supra* note 15, at 11.
32. Rosenberg, *The Comeback of Choice-of-Law Rules,* 81 COLUM. L. REV. 946, 948 (June, 1981).

a. Metaphysical in Concept

The *First Restatement* is metaphysical, because the theory of vested rights must be taken as an article of faith, a logical a priori, if the system is to make any sense at all. If one does not accept the conception of law that undergirds the vested rights theory, the last act doctrine, which gives the *Restatement's* rules their practical application, is completely arbitrary, even in theory.

One might respond that any solution to conflicts problems is bound to rest on some fundamental conception of law. Why is the vested rights doctrine so bad? The answer is that regardless of what one thinks of the theory itself, its operation as the foundation principle of the *First Restatement* is a bit paradoxical. In writing the *Restatement,* Joseph Beale sought not only to bring certainty to the field of conflicts, but to bring certainty of a particular sort. In Beale's view, there are two ways to skin the conflicts cat. One can create an independent body of substantive law, fixed by treaty among sovereigns, to be applied in multistate cases. Beale rejected this type of "alleged international law, upon the terms of which hardly any two [jurists, much less sovereigns] . . . can agree."[33] In its place he offered a system which purportedly solved multistate cases, not according to a separate body of law, but according to "the law of the country in whose court it arises."[34] What Beale failed to recognize, or to acknowledge, is that his system, too, depended on a "superlaw" — the vested rights doctrine — to direct courts to the proper rule of decision in conflicts cases.

b. Mechanistic in Operation

The *First Restatement* is mechanistic, because its rule-making aesthetic produced a body of doctrine too rigid to accommodate the complicated reality of multistate cases. First, as demonstrated by the cases cited above, the methodology of the *Restatement* runs into difficulties at every point. Threshold questions of characterization, which determine which conflicts rules will apply, are often not at all clear. In the seemingly straightforward case of *Carroll,* discussed above, plaintiffs argued that the action should be treated as a contract, rather than as a tort, because the employer was under a contractual duty to the plaintiff by virtue of their employment agreement.[35] Similarly in contracts cases it is often difficult to distinguish a problem of validity from one of performance.

---

33. J. BEALE, TREATISE, *supra* note 5, at 112.
34. *Id.*
35. *See also Levy v. Daniels' U-Drive,* sec. IIB3a *infra.*

The methodology of the *Restatement* does not fare any better on questions of localization. Notwithstanding the *Restatement's* exhaustive prescriptions, it is often difficult in torts cases to pin down the place of wrong in those cases in which the negligence and injury occur in different jurisdictions. It is worth noting that these difficulties did not daunt the authors of the *First Restatement:* "the place of wrong is the place where the harmful force takes effect upon the body."[36] This means that when a person standing in State X fires a gun at a person standing in State Y, the place of wrong is State Y, where the bullet lodges in the victim's body. The *Restatement* even tackles the rather arcane case of injury by poisoning:

> A, in state X, mails to B in state Y a package containing poisoned candy. B eats the candy in state Y and gets on the train to go to state W. After the train has passed into state Z, he becomes ill as a result of the poison and eventually dies from the poison in state W. The place of wrong is state Z.[37]

But such solutions to the localization problem are transparently arbitrary.

Second, the *Restatement's* mechanistic character surfaces in the sometimes fortuitous results it produces. For example, in an automobile accident, parties from State A, driving a car licensed in State A, may be subject to the law of State B merely because they happened to crash there. This is a paradoxical result if one considers that the place of the defendant's conduct may be the more relevant place to look in assigning liability. *Carroll,* discussed above, illustrates this problem. And in contracts cases, even when the place of contracting is clear, it may also be arbitrary. Suppose parties from State A negotiate a contract to be performed in State A, but they happen to reach agreement in a plane flying over State B. The *First Restatement* would apply the law of State B, even though State A's contacts with the case were far more significant. Similarly, in a contract in which the place of contracting differed from the place of performance the *Restatement* would apply different state laws to govern the two sets of issues, even where it is highly unlikely that the parties intended to subject their agreement to two sets of laws.

Finally, the attack on the *First Restatement* as mechanistic refers as much to its spirit as to specific problems of application or result. The notion that judges merely find and apply the law of another jurisdiction without regard to content is a fiction truly difficult to indulge. It is

---

36. RESTATEMENT OF THE CONFLICT OF LAWS § 377, Note 1 (1934).
37. RESTATEMENT OF THE CONFLICT OF LAWS § 377, Note 1, Illustration 2 (1934).

this dogged aesthetic that led a California judge in 1959 to reject the "petrified forest"[38] of the *First Restatement*.

c. Myopic in Result

The *First Restatement* is myopic because the apparatus it supplies for resolving conflicts can work to defeat the reasonable expectations of both parties and interested states. As the *Carroll* case illustrates, the place of wrong methodology may negate the cause of action of parties who had no way of knowing where they might be injured. Because the *First Restatement* restricts a court's attention to certain foreordained connecting factors, it prevents the court from examining other expectations and policies that may be equally, or even more, relevant.

In the 1961 case of *Kilberg v. Northeast Airlines,*[39] the New York Court of Appeals refused to apply the *First Restatement* because of its short-sightedness. Kilberg, a New York domiciliary, purchased in New York a ticket from the defendant airline, incorporated in Massachusetts. Kilberg was flying from New York to Nantucket. The plane crashed in Nantucket, killing Kilberg. Both Massachusetts and New York had wrongful death statutes. The Massachusetts statute limited recovery against a common carrier to $15,000; New York's constitution forbade such limitation. Refusing to apply the law of the place of wrong, the court of appeals insisted that "[m]odern conditions make it unjust and anomalous to subject the traveling citizen of this State to the varying laws of other States through which and over which they move."[40] As *Kilberg* illustrates, the *First Restatement* is doubly myopic. While defeating the reasonable expectations of involved parties, the place of injury rule may also frustrate the policy of the state with the strongest interest in the case. In the view of the *Kilberg* court, New York had as much to lose as Mrs. Kilberg if it deferred to the Massachusetts ceiling on wrongful death benefits.

3. Escape Devices

Because of these anomalies in both application and theory, courts developed a range of escape devices to avoid the *Restatement*'s more troubling consequences.

a. Characterization

One way for the forum to sidestep disadvantageous results is to characterize the case in a way that triggers a favorable rule. For exam-

---

38. Traynor, *Is This Conflict Really Necessary?*, 37 TEX. L. REV. 657, 670 n.35 (1959).
39. 9 N.Y.2d 34, 172 N.E.2d 526, 211 N.Y.S.2d 133 (1961).
40. *Id.* at 39, 172 N.E.2d at 527, 211 N.Y.S.2d at 135.

ple, a forum may characterize the disputed issue in a conflicts case as procedural, rather than substantive, so that it may apply its own law. Or it may alter its characterization of the cause of action to avoid distasteful results.

The 1928 case of *Levy v. Daniels' U-Drive Auto Renting Co.*[41] illustrates this stratagem. The defendant in *Levy* rented a car to a Hartford resident, who set out on a trip through Massachusetts with a fellow Hartford resident, the plaintiff, as passenger. The car was involved in an accident in Massachusetts, which caused the passenger/plaintiff severe injuries. Plaintiff sued the rental company in Connecticut under a statute which made automobile lessors liable "for any damage to any person or property caused by the operation of such motor vehicle while so rented or leased."[42] Massachusetts had no such statute. The defendant claimed that the cause of action was a tort, properly governed by the law of the place of injury. The court disagreed. It found that the purpose of the Connecticut statute was not to compensate injured persons — a tort objective — but rather to promote highway safety by encouraging rental agencies to rent to careful drivers — a contracts objective. In other words, the liability in the case arose out of a contract, not a tort. Therefore the law of Connecticut, as the place of making, governed.

b. Renvoi

Choice of law rules may refer to another state's internal law — the law that would be applied in a purely domestic case without conflicts complications — or to its "whole" law — the internal law plus choice of law rules. To apply the whole law is to apply the law that the other state would apply under its own choice of law rules if actually faced with the multistate problem. Renvoi is illustrated by the 1936 case of *University of Chicago v. Dater.*[43] Plaintiffs sued in Michigan courts on a contract involving property in Chicago. The defendant was Mrs. Price, who was married to Mr. Price at the time the contract was made. Under Michigan law, married women could not contract; under Illinois law they could. The forum court in *Dater* found that the contract was made in Illinois, so it deferred to Illinois law on the issue of Mrs. Price's capacity to contract. However, under the law of Illinois, the case was referred back to Michigan, because Mrs. Price had signed the note there and Illinois applied the "place of contracting" rule to such cases. In other words, the Michigan forum decided that the contract was

41. 108 Conn. 333, 143 A. 163 (1928).
42. *Id.* at 336, 143 A. at 163.
43. 277 Mich. 658, 270 N.W. 175 (1936).

made in Illinois, and then, instead of taking Illinois's law solely on the question of validity, it applied Illinois rule as to where the contract was made. The result was that, while showing great cosmopolitan fervor, the forum could ultimately apply its own law.

Technically, Michigan acted arbitrarily in stopping the renvoi by applying its own law. In fact, a strict logic would mean that no substantive law could ever be settled on in a case of this sort. If Michigan looks to Illinois law to decide a case, and Illinois in turn looks to Michigan law, then each reference to foreign law is at the same time a reference back to domestic law. Because of this "hall of mirrors" problem, the *First Restatement* rejected renvoi except in cases involving title to land or the validity of a decree of divorce.[44]

c. Public Policy

A court's most aggressive means of escape from the strictures of the *First Restatement* is to refuse to apply the prescribed rule because it violates the public policy of the forum. Because the public policy exception is subject to abuse by a court that simply doesn't like foreign law, the standard for refusing to entertain a cause of action on public policy grounds is, in theory, quite stringent. As Judge Cardozo emphasized in *Loucks v. Standard Oil:*

> The Courts are not free to refuse to enforce a foreign right at the pleasure of the judges, to suit the individual notion of expediency or fairness. They do not close their doors, unless help would violate some fundamental principle of justice, some prevalent conception of good morals, some deep-rooted tradition of the common weal.[45]

In keeping with this test, courts properly deny effect to a foreign contract of slavery, as in the 1836 case of *Commonwealth v. Aves,*[46] or perhaps to agreements to subvert a friendly foreign government.[47]

Courts have not always been sparing, however, in their use of the public policy doctrine to defeat foreign actions. In *Kilberg* for example, the New York Court of Appeals used the rhetoric of public policy — "New York's public policy prohibiting the imposition of limits on such damages is strong, clear, and old"[48] — to justify its refusal to apply Massachusetts' lower limit on wrongful death benefits. It is difficult, however, to credit the suggestion that a damages ceiling offends a

---

44. RESTATEMENT OF THE CONFLICT OF LAWS § 8 (1934).

45. 224 N.Y. 99, 120 N.E. 198, 202 (1918).

46. 35 Mass. 193 (1836).

47. *See* Paulsen & Sovern, *"Public Policy" in the Conflict of Laws,* 56 COLUM. L. REV. 969, 980 (1956), citing Oscanyan v. Arms Co., 103 U.S. 261, 277 (1880).

48. Kilberg v. Northeast Airlines, 9 N.Y. at 39, 172 N.E.2d at 528, 211 N.Y.S.2d at 136.

"deep rooted tradition of the common weal." In particular, it is unclear that New York would have been offended by the policy had it been applied to an out-of-stater.

d. Escape Devices in Perspective

Many viewed the escape devices described above as a healthy attempt to convert the rigid rules of the *First Restatement* into a more just and pliable system. However, the escape measures purchased flexibility at the price of the simplicity, certainty, and uniformity the *Restatement* aimed to secure. Furthermore, they fueled the suspicion that judges ostensibly applying hard-and-fast rules were actually deciding cases based on subjective, result-oriented considerations. Rather than shoring up the *Restatement*, then, the supposed "correctives" increased its vulnerability.

III. Interest Analysis

A. Background: The Traditional Approach Unmasked

The "traditional" approach to conflicts began to unravel even before the *First Restatement* achieved final form in 1934. It foundered on more than specific problems of method. The vested rights theory of law, on which the *First Restatement* was grounded, came under "devastating attack"[49] from critics in the 1920s and '30s; and the *Restatement* could only be as secure as its foundation principle. More important, the field of conflicts may not have been ripe for restatement in the 'twenties and 'thirties: the *First Restatement* had imposed a false certainty on an area still in flux.[50]

Responses to the failings of the *First Restatement* took two primary forms. One group of critics rejected not only the specific solutions of the *Restatement*, but also the whole notion of creating a body of choice of law rules to govern multistate cases. This group, led by Duke law professor Brainerd Currie, advocated a policy-oriented approach to conflicts cases — "Interest Analysis" — whereby courts would look to legislative intent to decide among competing laws. The second group agreed with the goals of the *First Restatement* but sought better-

---

49. Reese, *Conflict of Laws and the Restatement Second* in J. Martin, Perspectives, *supra* note 15, at 43. Willis Reese, the reporter of the Restatement (Second) wrote in a 1963 article that "increasing turmoil and doubt had some effect upon the Restatement itself. Judge Goodrich once told the writer that the reason why the original comments are so terse and laconic is that the Advisers frequently disagreed with the reasons advanced by Professor Beale for his rules although they did not object to the rules themselves." *Id.*

50. *Id.*

drawn rules to achieve them. Under the leadership of Columbia law professor Willis Reese, this group set about revising the *First Restatement* in 1952. The product of their work, the *Restatement (Second)*, did not appear until 1971.

The first, more radical, assault gained momentum in a series of articles published in the late fifties and early sixties,[51] wherein Brainerd Currie assaulted the central principles of the *First Restatement* and proposed an alternate conflicts methodology. Currie was convinced that the rules evolved by the *First Restatement* "have not worked and cannot be made to work."[52] It was not that the particular rules were bad; the problem was that "we have such rules at all."[53] To Currie, the rules-oriented approach in multistate cases posed two major problems. First, such rules create conflicts that would not otherwise exist. Second, the "false conflicts" created by the rules are often solved in an irrational way — by defeating the interests of one state without advancing the interests of any others.

Currie explained what he meant by these criticisms in an article considering the case of *Milliken v. Pratt*.[54] You will recall that Mrs. Pratt at her home in Massachusetts executed a guarantee of her husband's credit in favor of a partnership doing business in Portland, Maine. Mr. Pratt proceeded to order goods from the Milliken company, but he failed to pay for much of what he received. Guarantee in hand, the Milliken company sued Mrs. Pratt in Massachusetts to recover the balance due — only to have the lower court inform them that in Massachusetts wives could not contract. On appeal, Mr. Justice Gray found that the contract had been made not in Massachusetts, where it would be void, but rather in Maine, which had emancipated married women. Invoking the traditional conflicts rule that the law of the place of making governs in a contracts case, Mr. Justice Gray judged the guarantee of credit valid under Maine law and found for the plaintiffs.

In his essay *Married Women's Contracts,* Currie built on the *Milliken* facts to lay bare the anomalies of the traditional, rules-oriented methodology. Currie began by pointing out that when legislatures pass laws, they typically say nothing about the reach of those laws in multistate cases, because they tend to have only domestic cases in mind:

---

51. These essays are collected in B. CURRIE, SELECTED ESSAYS ON THE CONFLICT OF LAWS (1963).

52. Currie, *Notes on Methods and Objectives in the Conflict of Laws* in SELECTED ESSAYS, *supra* note 51, at 177, 180.

53. *Id.*

54. Currie, *Married Women's Contracts: A Study in Conflict-of-Laws Method* in SELECTED ESSAYS, *supra* note 51, at 77.

"The domestic case . . . [is] normal, the conflict-of-laws case marginal."[55] Currie argued that although legislatures fail to specify the reach of their laws, purely domestic cases are easy to resolve; it is clear that Massachusetts law applies to a contract involving a Massachusetts married woman, husband, creditor, and transaction. Purely foreign cases are, according to Currie, likewise straightforward; it is unlikely that the Massachusetts legislature intends its married women's laws to apply to cases involving a Maine married woman, husband, creditor, and transaction. It is the range of cases in between — involving any number of different factors connecting the cases to any number of different states — that present conflicts problems.

Currie suggested in his essay that a case like *Milliken* involves four significant factors connecting the case to either Massachusetts or Maine: (1) the domicile, nationality, residence, or place of business of the creditor; (2) the domicile, nationality, or residence of the married woman; (3) the place of the transaction (i.e. the place where the contract was made or the place where it was to be performed); and (4) the place where the action is brought (the forum).[56] Because there are four significant factors, each of which could be either domestic or foreign, there are sixteen possible combinations of the factors — that is, sixteen different cases — a court might face. One of the cases would be purely domestic, if all the factors were domestic, and one would be purely foreign. That leaves fourteen "mixed," or conflict of laws, cases.

Currie began his analysis of the fourteen conflicts cases by examining the legislative policies that underlay the Massachusetts law incapacitating married women. He argued that the policy of the Massachusetts legislature was obvious: Massachusetts wanted to protect married women — that is, Massachusetts married women — from untoward economic influence at the hands of their husbands; and it was willing to subordinate its general policy of insuring the security of commercial transactions in order to do so. Maine, on the other hand, had abandoned any special protection for married women. It protected them only insofar as it protected others, namely by the defenses of fraud, mistake, want of mental capacity, and so on, that it had carved out from a general policy of securing commercial transactions.

Having identified the policies of each state with respect to married women contracts, Currie considered the operation of the traditional conflict of laws rules in relation to those policies. It is this analysis which, according to Currie, exposes the two problems outlined above. The first problem — that the traditional rules create conflicts that do not otherwise exist — is true of ten of the fourteen cases involving a

---

55. *Id.* at 82.
56. *Id.* at 82-83.

mix of domestic and foreign factors. For example, a case in which the married woman is from Maine and all other aspects of the case are linked to Massachusetts does not present a true conflict. Currie illustrated such a case by the following diagram, in which domestic factors are indicated by "D" and foreign factors by "F":[57]

Factors

Residence of the creditor	Residence of the married woman	Place of contracting	Forum
D	F	D	D

According to Currie, even though three of the four factors link the case to Massachusetts, the latter has no interest in applying its law. Massachusetts has no interest because it only seeks to protect Massachusetts married women and the case involves a woman from Maine. Notwithstanding this fact, the *First Restatement* would have Massachusetts apply its own law merely because the place of contracting is domestic. In so doing, the *First Restatement* posited a conflict where none was present.

The second problem — that the traditional rules solve these false conflicts in an irrational way — is best illustrated by the following case:

Residence of the creditor	Residence of the married woman	Place of contracting	Forum
D	D	F	D

No state other than Massachusetts has any interest in the case, because, according to Currie, Maine is not interested in protecting married women, domestic or foreign, and it is not interested in protecting creditors unless they are from Maine. Yet because of the fortuitous circumstance that the contract was made in Maine, the traditional theory requires Massachusetts to go to the trouble of ascertaining and applying foreign law. The result is that Massachusetts defeats its own preferred policy of protecting Massachusetts married women without advancing the interests of any other state.

Applying this kind of factor analysis to each of the fourteen cases involving both domestic and foreign factors, Currie points out that there are ten so-called "false conflicts." Among these, the traditional place-of-making rule produces tolerable results — in the sense that one

---

57. *Id.* at 84. Currie in fact diagramed each of the 16 possible cases in a single chart showing all possible configurations of the four significant factors.

state's interest is advanced without detriment to that of the other — in only four cases. By contrast, in six cases, the traditional approach has the perverse effect of nullifying one state's interest without advancing any interest of the other. Only four cases — in which the creditor is from Maine and the married woman is from Massachusetts — involve a true conflict of interest. The conflict exists because Massachusetts has a legitimate interest in the application of its law whenever a Massachusetts married woman is involved, and Maine has a corresponding legitimate interest in the application of its law whenever a case implicates a Maine creditor. In these cases of genuine conflict, there is no solution that does not subordinate one state's interest to the other. According to Currie, then, the problem with traditional solution to true conflicts is not so much that it produced bad solutions — by definition all solutions are bad for one state or the other — but rather that it "simply strikes down the one interest or the other indiscriminately, arbitrarily, on the basis of fortuitous and irrelevant circumstances."[58]

Currie's point in playing out the *Milliken* scenarios was to demonstrate that, judged by its results, the approach of the *First Restatement* is, at best, arbitrary and, at worst, irrational or perverse. Currie was not content, however, with an act of demolition. In his essay *Methods and Objectives in the Conflict of Laws*,[59] published one year after *Married Women's Contracts,* Currie set forth the basic features of his alternate "government interest" approach to conflict of laws. The paragraphs that follow describe the theory set forth by Currie and by courts applying his method.

B. Theory

As noted, Brainerd Currie objected to traditional conflicts methodology because of its operational failures. It is striking, however, that those "failures" emerge not when the *First Restatement* is analyzed on its own terms, but only when it is examined in light of an alternate assumption — that multistate cases should be decided in terms of the substantive policies underlying legislative enactments. In other words, the *First Restatement* is rational, if not flexible, as a means of enforcing vested rights. It is only irrational if the vested rights principle is rejected and replaced by the assumption that each state's laws aim to benefit domiciliaries. Currie's critique of the *First Restatement,* then, begins only after he has substituted his first principle for that of Joseph Beale.

---

58. *Id.* at 109-110.
59. *Methods and Objectives,* Selected Essays, *supra* note 52, at 177.

Not surprisingly, the opposition between the vested rights and policy-oriented principles grows out of a divergence between their proponents' underlying visions of law. Brainerd Currie took seriously Justice Holmes's well-worn axiom that "[t]he common law is not a brooding omnipresence in the sky but the articulate voice of some sovereign or quasi-sovereign that can be identified."[60] In Currie's realist universe, courts do not apply the law because it is *law*, but rather because it expresses the will of their own sovereign. For Currie, therefore, the act of adjudication, in domestic and multistate cases alike, is not, as with Beale, an occasion for vindicating preexisting rights; rather it is an opportunity to further the objectives of the sovereign. Oversimplifying somewhat, for Beale the territorial theory of sovereignty serves an overarching theory of law; for Currie, the realist theory of law serves an overarching theory of sovereignty.

Two consequences, crucial to interest analysis, follow from Currie's underlying vision of law. First, because he viewed law at bottom as an expression of sovereign will, Currie saw the reach of law not in spatial terms, but rather in terms of the power of a sovereign over its subjects. For Beale's territorialism, then, Currie substitutes a domiciliary theory of jurisdiction. This shift produces his assertion, in the *Milliken* hypothetical, that the Massachusetts policy of protecting married women aimed only to protect *Massachusetts* married women. A territorialist might have read the law to apply to any married woman doing business in Massachusetts.

Second, Currie's view of law as an enactment of sovereign will led him to see a court's adjudication of "true" conflicts as a "political function of a very high order,"[61] to be avoided whenever possible. Judge-made conflict of law rules are anathema to Currie because they constitute an act of high judicial *hubris*. In deciding which law to apply in a multistate case, a court, theoretically the servant of its sovereign, sets itself up as a referee among the competing legitimate interests of sovereign states. To Currie, "[t]his is a function that should not be committed to courts in a democracy."[62] Accordingly, Currie hoped that congressional legislation might someday provide the solution for truly conflicting state interests.[63] However, as Congress had shown little enthusiasm for the task, Currie set about devising a conflicts approach that would tread as softly as possible on sovereign prerogatives.

---

60. Southern Pac. Co. v. Jensen, 244 U.S. 205, 222 (1917).
61. *Methods and Objectives*, Selected Essays, *supra* note 52, at 182.
62. *Id.*
63. *Id.* at 183.

C. METHOD

Currie's "Interest Analysis" method operates at two levels. First, it reduces the number of cases in which courts must decide among competing laws by showing that what appear to be conflict of laws problems are in most instances "false conflicts." Second, whenever courts are required to determine whether the state has a legitimate concern with a case, interest analysis directs that they do so, not by making law or by applying judge-made rules, but rather by the "familiar" method[64] of statutory construction.

Currie once outlined his approach as follows. First, a state should inquire into the policies of the respective laws involved to determine whether it has an interest in application of its law. This is done through statutory construction. It should then apply the law of the only interested state if the case turns out to be a false conflict. If it appears that a true conflict exists, it should reconsider whether both states in fact do have interests. If the conflict is unavoidable, it should then apply its own law.[65]

1. Identifying False Conflicts

As noted in the discussion of Currie's *Milliken* scenarios, a false conflict exists when only one of two or more states with apparently conflicting laws has a legitimate interest in the application of its law. Interest analysis directs courts to uncover false conflicts by examining the substantive policies underlying each state's laws.

The New York Court of Appeals used Currie's method to expose a false conflict in the 1963 case of *Babcock v. Jackson*.[66] The plaintiff in *Babcock,* a New York resident, sued a New York defendant in a New York court to recover for injuries she had received as a passenger in defendant's car during a weekend trip to Ontario. The accident occurred in Ontario when the defendant lost control of his car and crashed into a stone wall. Ontario had a guest statute which barred suits of this sort; New York allowed unlimited recovery.

Faced with an imposing array of New York contacts on one hand and the mere happenstance that the accident took place in Ontario, on the other, the court analyzed the policies underlying the competing laws to see if it was facing a false conflict. New York policy was clear: the legislature had repeatedly refused to enact a statute denying or limiting recovery in guest-host cases. New York, then, had a clear policy of

---

64. *Id.* at 183-84.
65. W. REESE & M. ROSENBERG, CASES AND MATERIALS ON THE CONFLICT OF LAWS 477-78 (8th ed. 1984) paraphrasing Currie.
66. 12 N.Y.2d 473, 240 N.Y.S.2d 743 (1963).

compensating a New York plaintiff for the negligence of a New York driver, driving a car registered in New York. Ontario, by contrast, had "no conceivable interest in denying a remedy to a New York guest against his New York host for injuries suffered in Ontario . . . ."[67] The object of Ontario's guest statute was, in the court's view, to prevent collusive suits between drivers and passengers against insurance companies, and "quite obviously, the fraudulent claims intended to be prevented . . . are those asserted against Ontario defendants and their insurance carriers . . . ."[68]

Once it is assumed that each state intends its laws for its own residents, the conflict dissolves. New York's unlimited liability applies to New York plaintiffs and defendants; Ontario's bar on liability applies to Ontario litigants. Since all parties in *Babcock* hailed from the same state the case presented a classic false conflict.

2. Resolving True Conflicts

When policy analysis uncovers not a false conflict but a genuine clash of interests, Currie instructs a court to apply forum law, even though this outcome defeats the interests of another state. The preference for forum law grows out of Currie's vision of the proper role of courts. Courts are instruments of state policy, and their paradigmatic function is to construe and apply state law. When they decide conflicts cases, they are no longer merely applying state law; rather they are "weighing"[69] their sovereign's law, and its underlying policies, against the law of another sovereign. Currie finds the act of weighing state interests a problematic undertaking for a court; it is doubly disturbing when a court uses the occasion to defeat the policies of its own sovereign. Hence the preference for forum law.

The 1964 Oregon case of *Lilienthal v. Kaufman*[70] shows a court following Currie's approach to decide between competing state interests. The case presented a classic "true conflict," implicating "two jurisdictions, each with several close connections with the transaction, and each with a substantial interest, which will be served or thwarted, depending upon which law is applied."[71] An Oregon spendthrift had gone to San Francisco and persuaded the unsuspecting plaintiff to go into the binocular resale business with him. When the defendant's check for the amount advanced by plaintiff bounced, the plaintiff demanded payment from the defendant's guardian in Oregon. The guard-

---

67. *Id.* at 482, 240 N.Y.S.2d at 750.
68. *Id.* at 483, 240 N.Y.S.2d at 750.
69. *Methods and Objectives* in SELECTED ESSAYS, *supra* note 52, at 182 *et seq.*
70. 239 Or. 1, 395 P.2d 543 (1964).
71. *Id.* at 549.

ian refused to pay, claiming that under Oregon law the notes of a certified spendthrift are void. The plaintiff sued in an Oregon court, but asked that California law be applied. California did not have a law voiding the debts of spendthrifts.

Faced with a direct conflict, the Oregon court had to acknowledge that California's contacts with the case were non-trivial. The plaintiff was a California resident, the defendant had sought him out for the binocular deal in California, the money was loaned in California, and, by the terms of the note, it was to be repaid in California. Oregon's contacts were less impressive: to be sure, the defendant was an Oregon resident and the suit was brought in Oregon, but everything having to do with the transaction took place in California.

Not content to count contacts, however, the Oregon court decided to look behind the competing laws to find the interest each state could claim in the case. Oregon had interests of "some substance."[72] (1) The Oregon spendthrift law was intended to protect the spendthrift's family — presumably an Oregon family. (2) Furthermore, if a spendthrift were "permitted to go unrestrained upon his wasteful way,"[73] it would be the Oregon treasury that must ultimately pay his support through welfare. (3) Oregon also had an interest in protecting commercial transactions and discouraging fraud, but it had apparently decided to subordinate those interests to the policy of protecting spendthrifts and their families. California, on the other hand, had an interest in having its creditor paid. It also had an interest in ensuring that contracts made in its jurisdiction would be enforced. These interests were, in the eyes of the court, "also of substance."[74]

How did the Oregon court break the tie? By following Currie's command to apply forum law in order to vindicate sovereign interests: "Courts are instruments of state policy . . . . In litigation Oregon courts are the appropriate instrument to enforce this policy."[75]

3. Other Methods for Resolving True Conflicts

A number of scholars who subscribe to the basic method of interest analysis have sought to develop sharper instruments than Currie's forum preference rule for resolving true conflicts.

---

72. *Id.*
73. *Id.* at 548.
74. *Id.* at 549.
75. *Id.*

a. Leflar: Choice Influencing Considerations

Robert A. Leflar has proposed that courts confronted with a conflict should select whichever law will best secure justice in the individual case, based on five "choice-influencing" considerations.[76] These are:

(1) Predictability of results
(2) Maintenance of interstate and international order
(3) Simplification of the judicial task
(4) Advancement of governmental interests; and
(5) Application of the better rule of law.

The first three factors import system-wide considerations into the forum court's decisionmaking; the fourth factor adds nothing to Currie's analysis; and the fifth, "better law," consideration is Leflar's innovation, intended to give courts the freedom, not available in purely local cases, to circumvent disfavored local law. The New Hampshire case of *Clark v. Clark*[77] gives lively expression to Leflar's approach:

> We prefer to apply the better rule of law in conflicts cases just as is done in non-conflicts cases, when the choice is open to us. If the law of some other state is outmoded, an unrepealed remnant of a bygone age, "a drag on the coattails of civilization," [citation omitted] . . . we will try to see our way clear to apply our own law instead. If it is our own law that is obsolete or senseless (and it could be) we will try to apply the other state's law.[78]

The better-law approach has been criticized for its subjectivity and for the fact that it puts lower courts in the position of choosing the "better" of two laws, even when these laws have been articulated by superior courts. On the other hand, Leflar's method has been used relatively frequently by courts to displace disfavored laws such as spousal immunity rules, guest statutes, and prohibitions on stacking of uninsured motorist coverage in automobile insurance policies.[79]

b. Baxter: Comparative Impairment

William F. Baxter, writing in 1963, proposed an alternative to Leflar's better-law rule for resolving true conflicts.[80] Baxter argued that the forum should apply the law of the state whose policies would be most impaired if its law weren't applied. Braving its syntactical

---

76. Leflar's theory is summarized in Kay, *Theory Into Practice, supra* note 17, at 562-72. *See also* W. REESE & M. ROSENBERG, CASES AND MATERIALS, *supra* note 65, at 479-80.
77. 107 N.H. 351, 222 A.2d 205 (1966).
78. *Id.* at 355, 222 A.2d at 209.
79. Kay, *Theory Into Practice, supra* note 17, at 571.
80. Baxter, *Choice of Law and the Federal System,* 16 STAN. L. REV. 1 (1963).

pitfalls, the California Supreme Court used this rule to reach its decision in *Bernhard v. Harrah's Club.*[81]

In *Bernhard,* a Nevada tavernkeeper served liquor to an obviously intoxicated California resident who proceeded to drive back into California and into the path of an oncoming motorcycle. The motorcyclist, severely injured, sued Harrah's Club on a proximate-cause theory of liability. California had a statute permitting such an action; Nevada had expressly refused to impose such liability.

Applying a comparative impairment analysis, the court reasoned that California's policy of preventing tavernkeepers from plying obviously intoxicated individuals with alcohol would be impaired if Nevada tavernkeepers could entice customers across the state border and then send them home reeling. Nevada's policy of protecting tavernkeepers from unlimited civil liability would, according to the court, not be comparably impaired if California law were applied. This was so for two reasons. First, Nevada tavernkeepers were already subject to criminal liability for serving alcohol to persons known to be drunk; therefore, applying the California rule in this case would not impose a new duty on them or force them to distinguish among patrons. Second, the California rule extends only to California residents who visit Nevada bars; and it is only fair that Nevada tavernkeepers assume increased economic exposure if they intend to benefit from California business. In short, the court reasoned, Nevada had less to lose than California by the application of the other state's law.

The purpose of the comparative impairment technique was to take courts out of the business of weighing the relative wisdom of state policies and to direct them instead to consider the appropriate scope of competing policies in a multistate context. One is tempted to agree, however, with the *Bernhard* court's observation that "the true function of this methodology can probably be appreciated only casuistically in its application to an endless variety of choice of law problems."[82]

D. Critique

In the vehemence of the criticism his theory has inspired, Brainerd Currie is rivaled only by his arch adversary Joseph Beale. Because interest analysis parts company with territorial theory at the axiomatic level, it was bound to draw fire from those who do not share its fundamental assumptions.

The most straightforward line of criticism points up the practical shortcomings of Currie's approach. As noted above, interest analysis is

---

81. 16 Cal. 3d 313, 546 P.2d 719, 128 Cal. Rptr. 215 (1976).
82. *Id.* at 321, 546 P.2d at 724, 128 Cal. Rptr. at 220.

built on the premise that each state's laws aim to benefit the state's domiciliaries. Yet the theory does not specify how much contact is needed to secure domiciliary status.[83] Is the place of incorporation a domicile? Is "doing business" the standard? Can residence make someone a domiciliary? Nor does interest analysis have a ready solution for the problem of after-acquired domicile, as the recent case of *Allstate Insurance Co. v. Hague*[84] dramatically illustrates.

A second and even more substantial practical failing of interest analysis is the problem of the so-called "unprovided for case" in which neither the forum nor the other state has an interest in the application of its law. The Rhode Island case of *Labree v. Major*[85] illustrates the problem. The defendant in *Labree* was a resident of Rhode Island who set off with her husband to visit friends in Massachusetts. While in Massachusetts, the two couples went sightseeing, taking the Rhode Island visitors' car. While driving along in heavy stop-and-go traffic, the car collided with the rear of a car ahead, injuring the pregnant plaintiff and her unborn child. Massachusetts had a guest statute preventing recovery; Rhode Island allowed recovery. The case was "unprovided for" under the theory of interest analysis because Massachusetts had no interest in applying its guest statute to protect a Rhode Island defendant while denying recovery to a Massachusetts plaintiff. Conversely, Rhode Island had no interest in applying its law to compensate Massachusetts residents injured in Massachusetts. In order to solve the impasse, the Rhode Island court ultimately abandoned the strict domiciliary principle of interest analysis and held that Rhode Island law intended to impose a duty of care on all Rhode Island drivers, regardless of the residence of their guests.[86]

As the *Labree* case demonstrates, interest analysis cannot prescribe a principled solution to the "unprovided-for-case," because it is the method itself that creates the lacuna. Currie, therefore, recommended that the forum apply its own law in the unprovided-for-case since it could not justify applying another state's law.[87]

---

83. John Ely makes much of this point in his recent article, *Choice of Law and the State's Interest in Protecting Its Own*, 23 WM. & MARY L. REV. 173, 173, n.1 (1981), in which he criticizes Currie's particular resident-benefitting theory of jurisdiction.

84. 449 U.S. 302 (1981). *Hague* also illustrates that other factors, such as local employment, may substitute for local domicile. For a detailed discussion of this case, see ch. 9.

85. 306 A.2d 808 (R.I. 1973). *See also* Ely, *Choice of Law, supra* note 83, at 200-206 for a discussion of the problem of the unprovided-for-case.

86. 306 A.2d at 817-18.

87. Currie, *Survival of Actions: Adjudication Versus Automation in the Conflict of Laws* in SELECTED ESSAYS, *supra* note 51, at 128, 153-56.

These practical problems of application do not exhaust the reach of criticism. On the theoretical level, Currie's approach has been assailed on three main grounds. First, as noted by commentators both friendly[88] and hostile,[89] interest analysis depends for survival on the faith that not many "true conflicts" or unprovided-for-cases will arise. This faith is essential because, as demonstrated by the proliferation of alternate methods, interest analysis has not produced a good solution for true conflicts.[90] Of course, all theories have easy cases and hard cases, and like any other approach, interest analysis fares best on cases that are easy on its own terms. But the claim that interest analysis produces fewer hard cases seems unsubstantiated.

The second, more trenchant line of criticism questions the statutory interpretation method avowed by interest analysis. Currie insists that courts should proceed in conflicts cases by the familiar methods of statutory construction and interpretation. This prescription is suspect on two related grounds. First, it assumes that a case with multistate elements presents a court with the same task it would face in a domestic case — to interpret a statute in a way that will effectuate legislative policy. Yet, it is highly unlikely that probing ever deeper into a legislature's substantive policy will illuminate the questions of a statute's geographical reach in a multistate case. It is far more logical to assume that policy analysis in a conflicts case should take account of the values of system coordination and interstate harmony — "policies" states share in a multistate context.[91] Moreover, because most legislatures pass laws without regard to their reach in multistate cases, in a conflicts case there is typically no relevant legislative intent to construe.[92] Currie's interest analysis, then, is less an act of statutory interpretation than an exercise in statutory interpolation.

This point introduces the third criticism of Currie's method: the value it interpolates is a dogged commitment to a domiciliary theory of jurisdiction, and a curious version of the theory at that. Interest analysis is committed not to statutory interpretation in general, but rather

---

88. *See* Sedler, *Interest Analysis and Forum Preference in the Conflict of Laws: A Response to the "New Critics,"* 34 MERCER L. REV. 593, 597-98 (1983) (defending interest analysis in part because it reduces conflicts problems to a relatively few cases).

89. Ely, *Choice of Law, supra* note 83, at 176.

90. *Id.*

91. This criticism is the focus of the 1981 article by Rosenberg, *The Come-back of Choice-of-Law Rules,* 81 COLUM. L. REV. 946 (1981).

92. For an exhaustive discussion of the legislative intent problem in Currie's theory, see Brilmayer, *Interest Analysis and the Myth of Legislative Intent,* 78 MICH. L. REV. 392 (1980). *See also* Kozyris, *Interest Analysis Facing its Critics — And, Incidentally, What Should Be Done About Choice of Law for Products Liability?,* 46 OHIO ST. L.J. 569, 569 (1985).

to a construction of statutes that reveals a legislative policy to benefit a given state's residents. This insistence on a particular brand of legislative intent is demonstrated by Currie's unsupported assertion in his essay *Married Women's Contracts* that the Massachusetts law was intended to benefit only Massachusetts married women, and not, for example, married women entering into contracts in Massachusetts, or married women with property in Massachusetts.[93] John Ely has argued, convincingly, that a system premised on the notion that each state intends its laws to benefit domiciliaries makes neither constitutional nor functional sense.[94] Notwithstanding Currie's claim that his system was constitutionally-compelled,[95] laws that benefit residents to the detriment of out-of-staters have repeatedly run afoul of both the equal protection and privileges and immunities clauses.[96]

Furthermore, it is both illogical and counterproductive to assume that states intend their laws only to benefit domiciliaries and not, for example, to constrain them. It is illogical, because it seems fairly obvious that a state law which creates a cause of action for a plaintiff — for example as a passenger in a car — correspondingly imposes liability on a defendant — the driver. If the plaintiff and defendant are both from the same state, it cannot be said that the law permitting recovery aims only to benefit residents. It is unproductive as the point of departure for solving conflicts cases, because, as has been demonstrated, it does not offer a solution for many types of conflicts. It does not solve the true conflict problem — where the plaintiff is from a plaintiff-protecting state and the defendant is from a defendant-protecting state. It does not solve the problem of the unprovided-for-case, where the plaintiff is from the defendant-protecting state and the defendant is from the plaintiff-protecting state. Finally, it does not even explain the common domicile problem, where a victory for the plaintiff works to the detriment of the local defendant. In such cases, interest analysis works only if it is admitted that a given state's laws are intended to apply to domiciliaries, whether or not the application works to their benefit.[97]

The foregoing arguments all amount to the fundamental claim that Brainerd Currie's avowedly value-neutral policy analysis is actually an elaborate edifice constructed to conceal an a priori commitment to a peculiar — and many would argue perverse — domiciliary theory of

---

93. Brilmayer, *Government Interest Analysis: A House Without Foundations,* 46 Ohio St. L.J. 459 (1985).

94. *See generally,* Ely, *Choice of Law, supra* note 83.

95. *See* Currie, *The Constitution and the Choice of Law: Governmental Interests and the Judicial Function* in Selected Essays, *supra* note 51, at 188.

96. Ely, *Choice of Law, supra* note 83, at 180-199.

97. *Id.* at 208-211.

jurisdiction. In building this edifice, Currie and his followers have not rooted out metaphysics: they have merely altered its first principles.

IV. The Restatement (Second)

The *Restatement (Second)* evolved over the same period as the interest analysis method. But whereas Brainerd Currie sought to bury the traditional approach to conflicts, the authors of the *Restatement (Second)* aimed to refine it.

A. THEORY

The *Restatement (Second)* sought, like its predecessor, to promote uniformity of results, to enhance predictability, and to discourage forum-shopping in multistate cases.[98] But it did not try to achieve those goals through a single, comprehensive set of rules covering every possible conflicts situation; rather, the *Restatement (Second)* adopted a bifurcated approach. In certain precisely defined situations, such as status, corporations, and property, the *Restatement* set out a large number of relatively narrow rules that could be applied easily.[99] In other areas, such as contracts and torts, in which traditional conflicts doctrine was eroding, the *Restatement (Second)* simply laid out broad and flexible rules to guide courts in choosing the applicable law.[100]

Section 6 of the *Restatement (Second)*[101] outlines the general principles to be applied to conflicts arising in ambiguous areas of law. It specifies, first, that where a statute contains a choice-of-law provision for a particular type of case, the courts of the state should follow the statutory directive, subject to constitutional restrictions. Where, as in most cases, there is no statutory directive, the factors relevant to choosing the applicable rule of law include:

(a) The needs of interstate and international systems
(b) The relevant policies of the forum
(c) The relevant policies of other interested states and the relative interests of those states in the determination of a particular issue
(d) The protection of justified expectations
(e) The basic policies underlying the particular field of law
(f) Certainty, predictability, and uniformity of result

---

98. Reese, *Conflict of Laws and the Restatement Second* in J. MARTIN, PERSPECTIVES, *supra* note 15, at 50-51.

99. *Id.* at 44.

100. *Id.* at 45.

101. *Selections from the First and Second Restatement of the Law of Conflict of Laws* in J. MARTIN, PERSPECTIVES, *supra* note 15, at 39.

(g) Ease in the determination and application of the law to be applied.

Note that factors a, d, f, and g retain the basic criteria of the *First Restatement,* whereas factors b, c, and e reflect the values of interest analysis.

B. METHOD

The *Restatement (Second)* rejects the traditional rule that all substantive issues of a case must be governed by the law of a single state; instead, it directs courts to determine which state's law should govern each individual issue in the case. To find the applicable law, the *Restatement* directs courts to focus, not on a single contact, but rather on the state with the "most significant relationship"[102] to a given case, based on a grouping of contacts.

A 1963 case from the Fourth Circuit shows the "most significant relationship" test in operation. In *Lowe's North Wilkesboro Hardware, Inc. v. Fidelity Mutual Life Insurance Co.,*[103] a hardware company located in North Carolina applied to an insurance company in Pennsylvania for a policy on the life of its president, Henry Carl Buchan. The hardware company was the designated beneficiary of the policy. Before the insurance company had completed action on the application Mr. Buchan died. The hardware company then sued the insurance company in a North Carolina federal court, claiming that Fidelity had committed negligent delay in failing to complete the application.

North Carolina law, though not completely clear, would probably have allowed the action for negligent delay; Pennsylvania law did not. The lower court dismissed the action on summary judgment, concluding that Pennsylvania, as the site of Fidelity's home office and of the alleged delay, should have its law applied. The court of appeals affirmed, based on a "flexible approach"[104] which allowed it to inquire "which state has the most significant relationships with the events constituting the alleged tort and with the parties."[105]

North Carolina's claim to a significant relationship relied on the fact that North Carolina was Buchan's residence in life and place of death, the plaintiffs' place of business, and the place where the loss caused by the alleged tort occurred. The court considered these contacts, but it

---

102. *Id.* at 40.
103. 319 F.2d 469 (4th Cir. 1963).
104. *Id.* at 473.
105. *Id.*

judged that Pennsylvania housed "the important events upon which liability, if any, would rest . . . ."[106] The insurance application was sent to Pennsylvania, all information relevant to the application was also sent there, and there the application was processed and acted upon — however slowly. "In sum, it was in Pennsylvania that the alleged delay, the foundation of the cause of action, took place."[107] Noteworthy in this case is the court's isolation of the critical issue — liability — and its weighting of the different contacts according to their relevance to that issue.

C. Critique

Thirteen states have adopted the *Restatement (Second)* as their conflicts approach, but, in the words of one commentator, their commitment to its methodology "varies enormously."[108] The reasons for the uneven usage are not hard to fathom.

First, the compromise between the traditional and policy-oriented approaches reflected in § 6 satisfied zealots of neither school. Those wedded to a rules methodology are distressed when courts use the policy factors specified in §§ 6 (b) and (c) to resolve cases essentially according to a government interest approach.[109] On the other hand, those who favor policy analysis, see the "place of injury" and the "place of conduct" factors, specified as relevant contacts in torts cases,[110] as a disturbing reversion to the vested rights theory.

Second, the method of grouping contacts to determine the state with the most significant relationship to a given issue lists between two extremes — it can either be overly mechanistic or overly subjective. It is too mechanistic if courts simply count the contacts each state has with a case, without considering the relevance of the contacts for the issue in question, distinguishing the weight to be given each contact, or specifying why certain factors are considered while others are not. On the other hand, the grouping of contacts is too subjective if courts simply make conclusory statements about the state with the "most significant relationship" without giving any indication of the basis for that decision.[111]

Third, when a court has weighed the relative significance of each state's relationship to an issue and found the interests evenly divided,

---

106. *Id.* at 474.
107. *Id.*
108. Kay, *Theory Into Practice, supra* note 17, at 561.
109. For examples where courts have done so, *see id.* at 560-62.
110. *See id.* at 559-60 (difficulty in listing relevant contacts under RESTATEMENT (SECOND) approach).
111. *See id.* at 560.

it must turn to an alternate source of values to break the tie. Again, courts tend either to reach for policy analysis or to revert to more traditional rules as the source of those values. Many would argue, therefore, that in all but the most straightforward cases the *Restatement (Second)* fails to resolve the fundamental opposition between a rules- and a policy-oriented approach, and in so doing it fails to provide solutions where they are most needed.

Summary

A leading conflicts scholar, Herma Hill Kay, has recently inventoried the choice of law regimes at use in the fifty states and the District of Columbia.[112] Her study reveals that the intellectual ferment that has raged among conflicts scholars over the past thirty years is amply reflected in the states' multifarious approaches to conflicts problems.

Perhaps surprisingly, the traditional vested rights approach of the *First Restatement* is the theory followed by the largest number of states.[113] A total of twenty-two states use the traditional approach, including sixteen states and the District of Columbia that apply it overall, three states that follow the theory in all but certain types of cases and two states which have not decided a conflicts case in the modern era.[114] Kay emphasizes that though the traditional approach still enjoys a substantial following, its persistence may be due as much to the perceived inadequacies of modern theories as to genuine satisfaction with the traditional approach.[115]

The remaining twenty-nine states have adopted one of six modern approaches. Thirteen, and by some counts fourteen,[116] states follow the *Second Restatement*. However, as noted above, the eclecticism of the *Second Restatement's* methodology obscures a wide variation in the specific approaches used. By contrast, only two states, California and New Jersey, expressly follow Currie's interest analysis[117] method. Interest analysis does, however, figure into other approaches at use in the remaining states. For example, Leflar's better-law approach, used by three states, incorporates aspects of Currie's method for analyzing

---

112. *See id.*

113. *Id.* at 582.

114. *Id.*

115. *Id.* at 583.

116. Thirteen states have explicitly adopted the RESTATEMENT (SECOND) as their approach in conflicts cases. In addition, a federal court has concluded that Vermont follows the RESTATEMENT (SECOND), even though its own courts have not been explicit on their approach. *Id.* at 556, n.224.

117. *Id.* at 544.

conflicts, though it does not adopt his specific solutions. Likewise, the six states that have abandoned the traditional approach but have not committed themselves consistently to any one of the modern theories[118] may use aspects of interest analysis along with the other modern methods.

The remaining four states use one of two additional modern theories. New York and North Dakota follow a "center of gravity" approach — a method that antedated and closely parallels the "most significant relationship" test of the *Second Restatement*.[119] Finally, two states, Kentucky and Michigan, follow a lex fori approach, which directs courts to apply the law of the forum as long as enough contacts can be found to justify the application of local law.[120]

In short, it appears that the fifty states do not each apply "their own set of malleable choice-of-law rules,"[121] as the Supreme Court recently suggested. Rather, state courts currently use, singly or in combination, more like ten different methods.[122] Some variation is to be expected in any common-law area left largely to the states. The multiplicity of choice-of-law approaches, however, can be traced to the fact that any method necessarily offers only imperfect solutions to the irreducible conflicts between the legitimate interests of coexisting — and competing — sovereigns.

---

118. *See id.* at 573.
119. *Id.* at 526.
120. *Id.* at 579.
121. *See* text accompanying note 16.
122. Kay, *Theory Into Practice, supra* note 17, at 585.

Chapter 8

SUBSTANCE AND PROCEDURE

In the preceding chapters, we have seen several situations in which the forum applies a rule of decision it did not generate. States apply federal law, federal courts apply state law, and states apply the law of other states. Yet there are some situations in which the forum has a right to apply certain kinds of rules simply because it is the forum. Typically, it applies its own rules of procedure to regulate the methods of pleading and trying cases.

This practice raises a special class of choice-of-law issues: the choice between forum law and the domestic law of the sovereign that created the cause of action. Usually these are the only two choices. For reasons discussed in the earlier chapter on discriminatory refusal to adjudicate, the forum may not create a distinct and more onerous rule of procedure for application to foreign causes of action, and apply it in lieu of both ordinary local law and the law of the other state. Such discrimination would violate either the supremacy clause (for federal rights) or the full faith and credit clause (for rights created by sister states). A prohibition on discrimination does not resolve the choice-of-law question, however. That choice is instead effected by the categorization of an issue as either "substance" or "procedure."

The need to distinguish between substance and procedure is thus inevitable in several areas of jurisdiction. At first blush, the distinction seems relatively straightforward. Substantive law is law governing actual rights and remedies; it affects the legal implications of conduct outside the courtroom. Procedural law, by contrast, governs the structure of litigation; it dictates the rules within the courtroom. This classification, although theoretically simple, breaks down in practice, largely because of the existence of a substantial gray area. Laws dealing with evidentiary privilege, statutes of limitations, and burdens of proof, for example, clearly affect the conduct of litigation, but they have a discernible impact on out-of-court rights as well. Such laws do not admit of easy classification as either substance or procedure.

Moreover, the classification of a law may depend not only on the subject matter of the law itself, but on the context in which the classification is being made. A state applying another state's law presents a conflict of laws problem. A federal court applying state law raises an *Erie Railroad* problem. When state courts enforce federal rights, the problem is called "converse *Erie.*" Furthermore, the substance/procedure line-drawing may be determined by the context in which the line is being drawn. This concept is troubling because the substance/procedure distinction seems to be a natural distinction that somehow arises out of the nature of law itself. Thus the line would seem to be something which is properly "discovered," not drawn. It has become increasingly apparent, however, that the distinction between substance and procedure is context dependent. Once this point is accepted, it is rather easy to accept, as well, the conclusion that the line which separates the two must be drawn differently in different legal contexts.

I. The Substance/Procedure Labels

Courts distinguish substance from procedure in order to differentiate those things which the forum has a legitimate interest in regulating from those that are more properly the concern of the sovereign that created the cause of action. Even if the forum is willing to lend its courts to the enforcement of a foreign cause of action, it may balk at attempting to mimic all of the foreign court system's procedural technicalities. Furthermore, it is not clear that having the forum do so would advance a foreign state's interests in any way. If procedural rules are designed only to enhance the efficient conduct of litigation, then each court should conduct its litigation as it sees fit.

One test frequently invoked to distinguish between substance and procedure centers on the concept of primary conduct. This test classifies as substantive those laws which have an effect on primary conduct, on transactions and relationships apart from the courtroom setting. Those laws which affect only the conduct within the litigation are classified as procedural. To choose a fairly clear example, the speed limit is a substantive rule because it regulates activities on the highway. A rule allowing thirty days in which to appeal a trial court decision regulates only in-court activities, and is therefore procedural.

At first glance, this test, like many of the substance/procedure tests, seems easy to apply. The test reveals itself as more problematic, however, when one asks exactly what is meant by an effect on primary conduct. Sometimes it is hard to tell whether even plainly substantive rules are effective in influencing conduct; the empirical consequences of the law are difficult to verify. Furthermore, many rules regulating in-court activities such as the introduction of evidence arguably do have such an effect. For example, a rule of evidentiary privilege may influence the determination of whether or not to disclose a confidence.

Critics can also object to this test's apparent disregard of the legislative purpose behind passage of a law as distinct from its empirical consequences. If legislators had a significant non-litigation purpose in mind in enacting a law, so the argument goes, the law should be classified as substantive, even if the impact on primary conduct is not empirically demonstrated. Thus, for example, since one asserted purpose for the enactment of statutes of limitations is to enable a potential defendant to be put at ease after a certain period of time, and freed from doubt and worry about prospective litigation, statutes of limitation should be classified as substantive. Of course, the legislative purpose test is subject to the vagaries of investigating legislative intent; and as any student of legislative history knows, such vagaries ought not be taken lightly. Legislative intent is often impossible to ascertain. This is particularly true with respect to state procedural laws, which may have no ascertainable legislative history at all, much less an explanation of substantive motivations which the legislators considered to be important.

Recognizing these difficulties, John Ely has tried to devise a classification test[1] that avoids the use of legislative intent as a determinant. Ely defines a rule as procedural if it is designed to improve the fairness or efficiency of the litigation process. A rule is substantive if it is enacted for one or more nonprocedural reasons, for some purpose or purposes not having to do with the fairness or efficiency of the litigation process.[2] This definition does a fairly good job of shadowing the generic concepts of substance and procedure, but, ironically, only by retaining some measure of legislative intent. As noted above, it is notoriously difficult to ascertain the purposes for which a rule was enacted, particularly a procedural rule.

Moreover, since procedural rules arguably can and do affect substantive rights, a law may be both substantive and procedural under many of the above definitions. Thus a rule may directly regulate courtroom procedure, even though it was enacted to establish a substantive right and to deal with a concern quite apart from truth or fairness in the litigation process itself. For example, a rule of privilege, such as spousal privilege, might speak solely in terms of the introduction of evidence in court. However, the privilege itself is more easily explained as the product of substantive concerns: the privacy of marriage, a concept of the marital unit as a single entity, or a view that state compulsion is an inappropriate invasion of the familial relationship. Indeed, it is not at all clear that privilege as a procedural rule is designed to get at truth or increase litigation efficiency; in fact, quite the opposite seems to be true.

Given that the basic goal is clear — to allow the forum to regulate the litigation while the state that established substantive rights regulates primary conduct — the main difficulty concerns a substantial area of overlap. Some rules influence (or were designed to influence) both in-court and out-of-court behavior. Or, they impose limits on what

---

1. Ely, *The Irrepressible Myth of Erie*, 87 HARV. L. REV. 693 (1974).
2. *Id.* at 724-25.

can be done in court (as with the husband/wife evidentiary privilege) in order to influence what happens in a substantive relationship outside of court. Such "mixed cases" are the bane of the substance/procedure distinction. How these problem cases are resolved depends on whether the distinction is being used in the *Erie,* conflicts, or converse *Erie* context.

II. The Erie Doctrine

The substance/procedure distinction has received the most attention by far in connection with the application of the *Erie* doctrine in federal court. Choice of law in federal court is governed by the Rules of Decision Act, which has been in existence since 1789. The Rules of Decision Act provides:

> The laws of the several states, except where the Constitution or treaties of the United States or Acts of Congress otherwise require or provide, shall be regarded as rules of decision in civil actions in the courts of the United States, in cases where they apply.[3]

Before *Erie* the Supreme Court had interpreted the Rules of Decision Act as requiring that state statutory law be applied, where relevant, in diversity cases, but where common law governed, a court was supposed to look to "general federal common law."[4] This holding was finally rejected in *Erie.* The *Erie* Court held that a federal court sits, in a diversity case, as a court of the state in which it is located. Therefore, in matters of substantive law, whether statutory or decisional, the state law is to govern.

The Rules of Decision Act does not apply to procedural laws, however; in matters of procedure the federal courts apply federal procedural law. This is because the federal courts were explicitly authorized by statute to formulate federal rules of procedure.[5] While *Erie* thus put an end to the creation of general federal common law, it left the federal courts with a new task: to explore the distinction between substance and procedure. *Erie* provides a guide for that exploration. In fashioning an appropriate test to determine what is substance and what is procedure, courts have looked to the "twin aims of *Erie*": the equitable administration of laws between residents and nonresidents, and the discouragement of forum-shopping.

---

3. 28 U.S.C. § 1652.

4. Swift v. Tyson, 41 U.S. (16 Pet.) 1 (1842).

5. The Rules Enabling Act, 28 U.S.C. § 2072; *see also* 28 U.S.C. § 2071, 18 U.S.C. §§ 3771, 3772.

The first step in applying the policy considerations of *Erie* to the substance/procedure distinction was taken in *Guaranty Trust Co. v. York.*[6] *York,* a statute of limitations case, fashioned the so-called outcome determinative test. Refusing to confine itself to abstract principles of substance and procedure, the *York* Court determined that the considerations of Erie required application of state law whenever the outcome of the suit would be significantly different depending on whether state or federal law were applied. For *Erie* purposes, at least, substantive matters were those which affected the outcome of the case. This rule makes a certain amount of sense, because the state which formulated the substantive rules would presumably not be offended if a federal court did not interfere with the substantive outcome the state intended. Similarly, rules would not motivate forum shopping if they did not affect the outcome.

But the outcome determinative test of *York* is troubling in several respects. First, it is over-inclusive; almost any rule of law can and will affect the outcome of a case, especially if it is broken. Even filing fees, or regulations on the color of brief covers may result in a case being dismissed. Second, the outcome determinative test ignores the policy justifications inherent in the adoption of a procedural rule; procedural rules as well as substantive ones reflect a value choice, which should not automatically be ignored. Third, the test fails to acknowledge the genuine differences between a state and a federal forum. The fact that some difference may be desirable is established by the very existence of diversity jurisdiction.

The Supreme Court recognized these problems, and in *Byrd v. Blue Ridge Electric Cooperative Inc.,*[7] the Court indicated the appropriateness of broader considerations. *Byrd* was a case involving a suit against an employer for injuries resulting from alleged negligence. The employer asserted as a defense that the plaintiff's exclusive remedy lay under the Worker's Compensation Law. State law made the ruling on such a defense a matter for the judge alone, but federal law required issues of fact relevant to a defense to be tried to the jury. The *Byrd* Court analyzed the state rule, and noted that the outcome of the case might be substantially affected by whether the issue was decided by the judge or by the jury. "Therefore were 'outcome' the only consideration, a strong case might appear for saying that the federal court should follow the state practice."[8]

But the Court held that outcome determination was not the only factor to be considered. State and federal policies behind the conflicting

6. 320 U.S. 99 (1945).
7. 356 U.S. 525 (1958).
8. *Id.*

253

laws must also be examined. The Court conducted such an examination and determined that the federal law was based on the seventh amendment right to a jury trial, while the state law was merely grounded in custom and convenience. It therefore decided that the state rule had to yield to the strong federal procedural policy, in spite of the possibility that application of the federal law might result in a different outcome. *Byrd* works a limited modification of the outcome determinative test to the extent that the policy behind the federal rule is strong, and the state rule is not intimately bound up with substantive rights and obligations.

In *Hanna v. Plumer,*[9] the Court's attention was redirected to more abstract concepts of substance and procedure. *Hanna* involved a direct conflict between a state rule for service of process, and federal policy as embodied in Rule 4 of the Federal Rules of Civil Procedure. The *Hanna* Court reaffirmed the fact that the outcome determinative test is not a talisman, and that choice of law should not be made by any automatic criterion but by reference to the underlying policies of the conflicting laws. The Court then determined that in the event of a conflict between a state law and a federal rule, the federal rule applies, if it is valid. The Court did not indicate clearly whether this was a modification of the *Erie* doctrine, or whether *Erie* simply did not apply to federal law embodied in a federal rule. The conclusion, however, was that valid federal rules, since they are promulgated under the Rules Enabling Act, are procedural. The Rules Enabling Act provides in part:

> The Supreme Court shall have the power to prescribe by general rules . . . the practice and procedure in civil actions . . . . Such rules shall neither abridge, enlarge, or modify the substantive right [of any litigant.][10]

Additionally, the Court found that *Erie* and its offspring cast no doubt on the long-recognized power of Congress to prescribe such housekeeping rules for federal courts, and that the *Erie* rule was created to serve another purpose all together.

Because *Hanna* involves the direct conflict of a state law with a federal rule, and relies on the restrictions of the Rules Enabling Act to conclude that any valid federal rule is procedural, it raises some interesting questions about the character of the rules. The Court in *Hanna* relied on the first sentence of the Rules Enabling Act for the principle that the federal rules are indeed procedural. But the Rules Enabling Act goes on to require that the rules not abridge, enlarge, or modify substantive rights. To take this limitation seriously might create real

---

9. 380 U.S. 460 (1965).
10. 28 U.S.C. § 2072.

difficulty with the validity of the rules, because it is possible to attribute a substantive purpose to every subject governed by a rule.[11] The Rules Enabling Act would thus arguably seem to require a stricter standard than merely finding that the rules govern "procedure." In fact, the standard apparently mandated by the second sentence of the Rules Enabling Act is similar to that created by broad readings of *Erie;* both cases seem to demand that a rule which has a material substantive impact be held to be substantive, even if the rule is concerned additionally with procedure.

This conclusion is borne out by a recent Supreme Court case, *Walker v. Armco Steel Co.,*[12] and by several courts of appeals decisions. In *Walker,* the plaintiff in a diversity case who had failed to bring his tort action within the time period specified by the relevant Oklahoma statute of limitations and accompanying service of process rule appealed the dismissal of his case under Oklahoma law on the ground that Federal Rule 3, and not the state service of process rule, ought to govern the timing of his action. The Supreme Court upheld the dismissal on the ground that the state requirement of actual service "is an integral part of the several policies served by the statute of limitations"[13] and therefore substantive under *Erie.* By contrast, the Court found that Federal Rule 3, which states that "a civil action is commenced by filing a complaint with the court,"[14] is strictly procedural; it simply governs the date from which various timing requirements of the federal rules begin to run.

Under this analysis, a federal court sitting in diversity would indeed apply Rule 3, because it is plainly procedural; but the Court found that the application of the rule did not toll the state statute of limitations. Unlike *Hanna,* then, the *Walker* case did not pose a direct conflict between state and federal rules; rather it involved the coexistence of two rules that did not overlap in scope. The Court in *Walker* held that the federal court must apply each rule in its proper context; and if the plaintiff's action could not fulfill state statute of limitations requirements, it could not survive long enough to come under the timing rules of the federal court.

---

11. Compare the misgivings of Justices Black and Douglas, expressed at 374 U.S. at 865-66 (many of the federal rules substantially affect the rights of litigants).

12. 446 U.S. 740 (1980).

13. *Id.* at 751.

14. *Id.*

In cases that predated *Walker,* several circuit courts had similarly stated that a state procedural law which has a direct substantive impact prevails over a conflicting Federal Rule of Civil Procedure.[15] In *Marshall v. Mulrenin,*[16] the First Circuit interpreted *Hanna v. Plumer* as addressing merely a procedural conflict. The federal rule should "not . . . be applied to the extent, if any, that it would defeat rights arising from state substantive law as distinguished from state procedure."[17] This approach prevents displacement of a state substantive right, and also achieves a reasonable balance of state and federal policies. However, the *Marshall* resolution of this *Erie* conflict again requires the classification of the state law as substantive or procedural. Further, this classification is complicated by the fact that the court in *Marshall* explicitly recognized that such a characterization could not be made solely dependent on the state's labeling of the law as procedural.

III. Conflict of Laws

While both the principles behind the *Erie* doctrine and the Rules Enabling Act seem to require that the majority of mixed or borderline rules be classified as substantive, these principles are not universal to the substance/procedure distinction. In the state/state conflict of laws areas, the line has been drawn in a different place.

In conflicts cases a state court applies foreign substantive law, but local procedural law. The need for classification seems analogous to the *Erie* situation, yet in the conflicts area, courts have, in general, held less firmly to the notion that the outcome must be the same as it would have been in the other forum. In other words, many rules which for *Erie* purposes would be substantive are, in the conflicts area, procedural. Presumptions, burdens of proof, and statutes of limitations, to name a few, have all been treated as procedural for conflicts purposes, although they have been held to be substantive for *Erie* purposes.[18] The

---

15. *See, e.g.,* Sylvestri v. Warner & Swasey Co., 398 F.2d 598, 604-606 (2d Cir. 1968) (deciding that the state law did not have a direct substantive effect, and that therefore the federal rule prevailed). *Cf.* Welch v. Louisiana Power & Light Co., 466 F.2d 1344, 1345 (5th Cir. 1972) (establishing "strong presumption" that federal rules rather than state law should apply in matters that are "arguably" procedural).

16. 508 F.2d 39 (1st Cir. 1974).

17. *Id.* at 44.

18. *See, e.g.,* Levy v. Steiger, 233 Mass. 600, 124 N.E. 477 (1919). "It is elementary that the law of the place where the injury was received determines whether a right of action exists, and that the law of the place where the action is brought regulates the remedy and its incidents, such as pleading, evidence and practice." *See generally* R. WEINTRAUB, COMMENTARY ON THE CONFLICTS OF LAWS 56-57 (2d ed. 1980) (collecting cases).

general rule is a rather loose standard: procedural rules should be classified as those which concern the method of presenting facts to the court; substantive rules concern the legal effect of those facts.[19]

This principle is subject to an important exception: where the foreign procedural rule is intimately bound up with the substantive right, such that it serves to limit or qualify the right, a foreign procedural rule will usually supplant a forum's own rule.[20] The reason behind this exception is clear enough. Assume that a state adopts a particularly generous substantive law, such as a tort cause of action with punitive damages for infliction of emotional distress. To be fair, it prescribes a shorter statute of limitations than that applied to other types of tort actions. If another state enforces the cause of action but applies its longer statute of limitations, it will effectuate a result that the first state never intended. The shorter statute of limitations was a quid pro quo for a generous liability rule. As can be imagined, however, it is not always easy to determine whether a procedure was intimately bound up with the cause of action. Perhaps it is helpful to note that rules which apply to a wide range of causes of action are probably procedural, while those that address only a specific cause of action may be found to be substantive.[21]

One commentator[22] has suggested that applying the procedural category more loosely in conflicts cases is inappropriate, and that the same principles which support an outcome determinative test for *Erie* purposes would support such a test in the conflicts area. After all, it is urged, the forum which applies foreign substantive law is really acting as a court of convenience, and it arguably has no interest in the rights and liabilities involved in the case. The ideal situation is where the court which has the substantive interest also serves as the forum. But where this is not so, the forum of convenience should be acting, as far as possible, as the interested forum would act. Therefore it seems appropriate to incorporate as much of the foreign law as possible. Although, as in the *Erie* area, practical considerations may prevent a court from adopting every procedural peculiarity of the foreign court, the forum should be at least as reluctant as in *Erie* cases to use rules that would change the outcome of the case.[23]

This argument implicitly assumes however that the rationale for applying state law in an *Erie* case is substantially the same as the

19. G. STUMBERG, PRINCIPLES OF CONFLICT OF LAWS 133 (3d ed. 1963).

20. R. WEINTRAUB, *supra* note 18, at 59-61 (statute of limitations).

21. *Cf.* Davis v. Mills, 194 U.S. 451, 454 (1904) (applying the specificity test).

22. *See* Sedler, *The Erie Outcome Test as a Guide to Substance and Procedure in the Conflict of Laws,* 37 N.Y.U. L. REV. 813 (1962).

23. *Id.*

rationale for applying foreign law in a conflicts case. This is not necessarily the case. There are, rather, important differences between the choice of law in the state/state context and in the federal/state *Erie* context.

First, recall that the difficult cases are those involving rules with both substantive and procedural purposes. In the *Erie* context, these are resolved in favor of state law, in part because the Rules Enabling Act requires that substantive rights not be abridged. Absence of substantive impact, not presence of procedural purpose, is the important test. *Byrd v. Blue Ridge* was an exception, because the right to a jury trial in federal court is constitutional in stature, and therefore obviously need not satisfy the Rules Enabling Act. But in the conflict of laws context, all that a sister state needs is some reasonable basis for regulation, for constitutional reasons that will be addressed in a subsequent chapter.[24] One state's substantive interest is not automatically more important than another state's procedural interest. Forum rules that have both types of purposes can be applied because the test is presence of procedural purpose, not absence of substantive impact.

Second, the federal/state analysis is different because of the special nature of the federal/state relationship. States exist as co-equal sovereigns, and state courts have equivalent rules and regulations in both substantive and procedural areas. Federal courts, however, are courts of limited powers, with jurisdiction over cases only as provided by article III. Further, there is no general federal common law. Federal law contains large gaps between areas of federal legislation. And federal courts turn, as a matter of routine, to state law to fill in those gaps. In a purely local state case, Connecticut will not turn to New York law to define property, or to determine the burden of proof for contributory negligence. Yet federal courts often look to the law of the state in which they sit, not merely in diversity cases, but in federal question cases as well, when they lack an appropriate expression of federal law.[25]

Thus, where the Federal Rules of Civil Procedure are silent, it is reasonable to turn to pre-existing state law. The alternative would be for the federal court to create a new rule; unlike other state courts, they do not possess a body of analogous rules designed for purely local consumption. Given that state rules need not compete with pre-existing rules (as they must in the context of the conflict of laws) it seems all the more reasonable to apply them to any problems where they are pertinent.

---

24. Chapter 9.
25. This is a direct consequence of the Rules of Decision Act, discussed in sec. II of this chapter.

IV. *Converse* Erie

The line between substance and procedure must be drawn in any context in which the courts of one sovereign must decide whether or not to apply the laws of another sovereign.[26] Having addressed the federal/state and state/state versions of the distinction, one variation still remains: the state/federal context. Cases in this final section are sometimes termed converse-*Erie* cases,[27] because they present the converse of the *Erie* situation: federal substantive law applied in state court. The question in converse-*Erie* cases is to what extent state courts may apply their own procedural rules when those rules conflict with the procedural rules generally applied by the federal courts, and thus to what extent state courts may decline to apply federal law.

Cases where a federal right is vindicated in state court are of two forms: one where the federal law is the basis for the action, and the other where it provides a defense to a state-law action. Most discussion of the converse-*Erie* problem focuses on the former,[28] although as we shall see there are analogous issues when state courts entertain federal defenses. State courts are obliged to hear actions under federal as well as state law,[29] and they must enforce federal substantive law, where applicable, under the supremacy clause. The conflict arises in the application of procedural rules. On the one hand it would be a harsh intrusion upon the autonomy of state government and the state courts to require the state courts to adopt every jot and title of federal

---

26. Another main area in which the substance/procedure distinction is important is in the constitutional prohibition of retroactive laws. This prohibition applies only to substantive laws and not to those which only affect procedure. Related to this are cases involving ex post facto laws or the impairment of contracts. For an illustration of the different uses of the distinction in the jurisdictional and retroactivity contexts, contrast Levy v. Steiger, 233 Mass. 600, 124 N.E. 477 (1919) with Duggan v. Bay State St. Ry., 230 Mass. 370, 119 N.E. 757 (1918). The distinction between substance and procedure in these areas is concerned with the theory that it is not fair to alter vested or substantive rights by subsequent legislative enactment, but that individuals have no legitimate expectation that the judicial machinery for enforcement of these rights will remain unchanged. In a sense, these limits are jurisdictional because they address the allocation of the power of courts or legislatures over time.

27. The term "Converse Erie" was first used in Hill, *Substance and Procedure in State FELA Actions — The Converse of the Erie Problem?*, 17 Ohio St. L.J. 384 (1956).

28. Cases involving a federal defense to a state action may, however, present a more compelling argument for application of federal law. A federal claim may generally be brought in either state or federal court, while the defendant in a state action cannot ordinarily remove a case from state to federal court on the basis of a federal defense.

29. Testa v. Katt, 330 U.S. 386 (1947) (holding that state courts have a duty to enforce federal statutes — even penal statutes — where the same type of claim arising under state law would be enforced in the courts of the state).

procedure when hearing federal cases. In fact, some authority suggests that "federal law takes the state courts as it finds them."[30] For instance, as noted in an earlier chapter, a state may simply fail to provide a court of competent jurisdiction so long as it does not discriminate.[31]

On the other hand, the supremacy clause applies to all federal law, and if the federal procedural rule is instrumental in effecting the purpose of the substantive law, its application seems to be mandated by the Constitution. If a state court has a court competent to hear the action, it must determine the rights according to the proper rules laid down by Congress. Under this view, the important questions are whether Congress intended the rule in question to apply in state courts, and whether this intention is an appropriate exercise of a valid federal substantive power. The problem, therefore, is to detect those federal procedural rules which further the federal policy behind the substantive law, and which should thus be treated as substantive for converse-*Erie* purposes.

There has been some tendency to use an *Erie*-type outcome determinative test in converse-*Erie* cases. Such a test was used in *Brown v. Western Railway of Alabama*[32] to classify a state pleading rule as substantive in a Federal Employers' Liability Act (FELA) case.[33] The Court held that the state rule could not be used to defeat FELA liability: "[s]trict local rules of pleading cannot be used to impose unnecessary burdens upon rights of recovery authorized by federal laws."[34] Although a rule of pleading is generally classified as procedural, its ability in *Brown* to defeat recovery led to the opposite classification.

In other cases the Court has placed more emphasis on the purpose behind the federal law, and has attempted to discern congressional intent as to which federal procedural rules should be incorporated within the federal law. This approach is particularly apparent in the cases involving the federal right to a jury trial. In *Dice v. Akron, Canton & Youngstown R.R.*,[35] the most well known of these cases,[36] the

---

30. Hart, *The Relations Between State and Federal Law,* 54 COLUM. L. REV. 489, 508 (1954); Brown v. Gerdes, 321 U.S. 178, 190 (1944) (Frankfurter, J., concurring).

31. Chapter 4, sec. I.

32. 338 U.S. 294 (1949).

33. The main body of converse-*Erie* case law is composed of FELA cases, for reasons that remain somewhat obscure. *But see also* Federal Energy Regulatory Comm'n v. Mississippi, 456 U.S. 742 (1982) (upholding federal statute prescribing procedural provisions for intervention, standing, and appeal in state courts).

34. 338 U.S. at 298 (1949).

35. 342 U.S. 359 (1952).

36. *See also* Minneapolis & St. Louis R.R. v. Bombolis, 241 U.S. 211 (1916); Chesapeake & Ohio Ry. v. Carnahan, 241 U.S. 241 (1916); Wilkerson v. McCarthy, 336 U.S. 53 (1949).

Court considered the extent to which a jury trial is a part of the remedy afforded by the FELA. The Court in *Dice* determined that the right to trial by jury was "part and parcel of the remedy" provided by the FELA. It was therefore held that trial by jury was "too substantial a part of the rights accorded by the Act to permit it to be classified as a mere 'local rule of procedure' . . . ."[37] This test is reminiscent of the conflict of laws doctrine for procedural rights that are closely bound up with the substantive cause of action. The difference however is that states need not recognize such procedural rights in the choice-of-law context,[38] although they commonly do. In the converse-*Erie* context, recognition of such procedural rules is obligatory under the supremacy clause.

The Court's reasoning in *Dice* is also somewhat similar to that in *Byrd v. Blue Ridge, supra.* In both cases, the Court found that the purpose behind the federal right to a jury trial was more important than state custom or convenience. Although this decision resulted in the right being classified as procedural for *Erie* purposes and as substantive for converse-*Erie* purposes, in both instances the test involved the examination of the purpose behind an arguably procedural rule, and the weighing of this purpose against that of the conflicting rule. The difference between them is that in *Dice* the interest in a jury trial arose out of substantive concerns about the proper implementation of a particular substantive right. In *Byrd,* it arose out of an interest of the forum as such, by virtue of the seventh amendment. Furthermore, in both instances a legitimate federal interest was uncovered; the cases are consistent with each other and with the supremacy clause in that a valid federal interest prevailed.

There are reasons for the similarity between *Erie* and converse-*Erie* line drawing. Both types of cases implicate concerns about the twin aims of *Erie,* avoiding arbitrary differences based on choice of forum and eliminating forum-shopping. Additionally both involve the conflict between the state and federal sovereigns, a conflict which recalls traditional federalism concerns. The situations are symmetric in that state substantive law preempts conflicting federal rules in the *Erie* context because of the Rules Enabling Act, while federal substantive law preempts conflicting state rules in the converse-*Erie* context under the supremacy clause. In both contexts, the sovereign that created the cause of action is paramount in mixed or borderline cases.[39]

---

37. 342 U.S. at 363.

38. Wells v. Simonds Abrasive Co., 345 U.S. 514, 518 (1953) (such distinctions "too unsubstantial" to constitute full faith and credit doctrine).

39. *Byrd v. Blue Ridge* is not a counter-example so much as an exception. The Rules Enabling Act is not pertinent as to a constitutionally created right to a jury trial, even if it does "abridge, enlarge, or modify" substantive rights.

Yet the two areas are not identical, and the desire to borrow the *Erie* test in the converse-*Erie* area is subject to a note of caution. Where there is a federal cause of action, there is no problem of discrimination based on the citizenship of the parties because non-diverse parties can bring the case in federal court. Thus, one of the underlying rationales of *Erie* is inapplicable. Converse-*Erie* cases, in addition, involve application of federal law in the courts of many jurisdictions. This creates a need for uniformity that is arguably more compelling than exists in the *Erie* context. One of the purposes of the FELA, for example, was to create uniformity throughout the Union with respect to the financial responsibility of railroads for injuries to their employees.[40] While the strict outcome-determinative test seems harsh and mechanical in *Erie* cases, the need for uniformity of federal law might make such a test more appropriate for converse-*Erie* cases. Finally, where a state procedural rule operates to defeat a federal right it is also in direct conflict with the judicial mechanism set up by Congress. Arguably this situation is automatically one of conflict, and the constitutional solution to such conflicts is the supremacy clause. In contrast, we noted earlier that in the *Erie* context one reason for deference to the state rule is the absence of a pre-existing federal rule in competition.

These arguments suggest that the states ought almost automatically to be required to apply federal law in converse-*Erie* cases. Fairness, however, requires recognition of competing considerations. In setting up an enforcement system that provides for concurrent jurisdiction of the state and federal courts, Congress must usually be presumed to have contemplated that the "ordinary incidents of state procedure" would apply.[41] It therefore seems wrong to presume that Congress intended the uniform application of federal procedure. Were that the case, Congress could have provided for exclusive federal court jurisdiction. Additionally there may be constitutional limits on the ability of Congress to remake the judicial machinery of the states.[42] Insofar as the state courts may not simply decline to hear cases of federal law, the requirement that the courts apply federal procedure rules would permit congressional intrusion into the heart of state government. While federalism principles underlying *Erie* safeguard for the state those areas in which the federal legislature has chosen not to act, in con-

---

40. *See* Norfolk & W.R.R. v. Liepelt, 444 U.S. 490, 493 (1980), citing H.R. Rep. No. 1386, 60th Cong., 1st Sess. 3 (1908).

41. Dickenson v. Stiles, 246 U.S. 631, 633 (1918).

42. Hill, *supra* note 27, at 413. *Cf. Federal Energy Regulatory Comm'n v. Mississippi, supra,* note 33, and C. WRIGHT, FEDERAL COURTS 272-73 (4th ed. 1983) ("even if the FELA cases are unique, they stand for the proposition that Congress has constitutional power to control the incidents of a state trial of a federal claim").

verse-*Erie* cases it serves as a reminder that there may be areas in which the federal government cannot intrude even if it chooses.

V. *Converse* Erie *and Federal Defenses*

An analogous situation arises where federal law provides not an entire cause of action, but rather a federal defense to a state-law action. This sometimes happens in civil actions: for instance, a defendant may wish to raise the objection that the state cannot exercise personal jurisdiction consistent with the due process clause. This situation arises with particular frequency, however, in criminal cases, because the Constitution provides many defenses such as double jeopardy, exclusion of illegally seized evidence, and so forth. The issue in these cases is to what extent the state may impose its own procedural rules upon a federal substantive defense, thereby limiting use of the defense. The usual rule is that the state has a right to apply its own rules of procedure. These procedural rules are respected during Supreme Court review by the "adequate and independent state ground doctrine."[43]

One example of this sort of state procedural limitation is state forfeiture rules. State forfeiture rules involve limitations on the time and manner in which a defendant can object to the introduction of evidence, challenge the composition of the jury, or similarly vindicate federal, and often constitutional, rights. The rules, which are most often challenged in the criminal context, are generally treated as procedural; that is, states apply their own rules. At some points the case law has seemed inconsistent in the level of inquiry to which it subjects these rules. In *Henry v. Mississippi*,[44] the Court seemed on the verge of establishing a totally different test for state procedural laws. *Henry* recognized that the use of a procedural default or noncompliance serves to bar vindication of a federal right.[45] In elaborate dicta the Court concluded that "the question of when and how defaults in compliance with state procedural rules can preclude our consideration of a federal question is itself a federal question."[46] The case was seen as a serious

---

43. An independent and adequate state-law basis for a decision may be provided by either a state substantive law or a state procedural law. *See* ch. 2, sec. IIIB. For a general discussion of applying state procedural rules to federal defenses, see Meltzer, *State Court Forfeitures of Federal Rights,* 99 HARV. L. REV. 1128 (1986).

44. 379 U.S. 443 (1965).

45. In contrast, when the adequate state ground is substantive, reversal on the federal issue will not change the outcome of the case, making Supreme Court review advisory.

46. *Id.* at 447.

departure from the precedents at the time, and despite its intellectual interest it has scarcely been followed since.[47]

The notion in *Henry* that federal law governs the way that federal rights are asserted may stem from the resemblance to a different but related problem. Some "waiver" rules are treated as federal issues when federal rights are at stake. For example, a defendant has a choice between exercising the right to a trial and pleading guilty. There is a federal standard for determining proper waiver of such a right: "intentional relinquishment or abandonment of a known right".[48] If the defendant later claims that he or she did not know such a right existed at the time of the guilty plea, this presents a federal issue. This is so even though the waiver seems to involve a procedural question about the assertion of a legal claim in court. Why is it not, then, decided under state procedural law, as would be the "waiver" of a right to protest personal jurisdiction?[49]

The Supreme Court's evident confusion over this issue is amply illustrated by *International Longshoremen's Ass'n, AFL-CIO v. Davis*.[50] An Alabama state court was called upon to adjudicate a labor dispute, even though exclusive jurisdiction over the dispute was arguably vested in the National Labor Relations Board. For the first time in its motion for judgment not withstanding the verdict, the union raised the pre-emption issue. The trial court denied the motion without opinion, and the state supreme court affirmed on the ground that as a waivable defense pre-emption had to be affirmatively pleaded. Despite this reliance on Alabama law, the Supreme Court held that no adequate and independent state ground barred its exercise of jurisdiction. Its rationale was unclear.

> [T]he point is not whether *state* law gives the state courts jurisdiction over particular controversies but whether jurisdiction provided by state law is itself pre-empted by *federal* law . . . . It is clearly within Congress' powers to establish an exclusive federal forum to adjudicate issues of federal law . . . . Whether it has done so in a specific case is the question that must be answered . . . [and] such a determination of congressional intent and the boundaries and character of a pre-empting congressional enactment is one of federal law.[51]

---

47. *See, e.g.,* Wainwright v. Sykes, 433 U.S. 72 (1977).

48. Johnson v. Zerbst, 304 U.S. 458, 464 (1938).

49. States typically treat absence of a protest against personal jurisdiction as consent, regardless of whether the defendant knew of the due process right to challenge the state's authority. *See* ch. 1.

50. 106 S. Ct. 1904 (1986).

51. *Id.* at 1910.

If so, the Court continued, the state law is not an independent and adequate state ground. It concluded, therefore, that whether pre-emption is a waivable affirmative defense was a federal question, and that the pre-emption claim was not waivable.

The confusion stems from the existence of two pre-emption claims in the same case. The issue of whether the labor board's jurisdiction pre-empted the state court was admittedly federal; no one argued otherwise and the Court's emphasis of this point was misdirected. The difficult issue was instead whether the state's rule for pleading this admittedly federal defense was also pre-empted. As the example of personal jurisdiction defenses illustrates, there are many circumstances in which a state court would lack power to adjudicate, but for the fact that the defendant neglected to raise its lack of power under the applicable state rules. Clearly the state has a valid procedural purpose in requiring the defendant to raise such claims at the outset, namely the conservation of judicial resources provided by dismissing such cases at the earliest opportunity. The state procedural rule on the issue was thus a reasonable one. The question is, why is assertion of some rights characterized as "waiver," so that federal law pre-empts state rules governing the assertion, while assertion of others is not, so that state law prevails.[52] This is the issue which the Court failed to illuminate.

VI. Conclusion

The differing contours of the substance/procedure distinction depend to a large degree on different constitutional and statutory considerations. In all of these areas, a rule that has only procedural purposes and no substantive impact at all is governed by forum law. A rule that has no procedural justification but only substantive purposes should be governed by the law that creates the underlying right. The difficulties involve deciding what constitutes a procedural (or substantive) interest and what to do about rules with both objectives. In conflicts, any procedural purpose is adequate, even if there is also substantive impact. In *Erie* and in converse-*Erie* cases, the existence of additional substantive impact may prevent application of forum law, under the Rules Enabling Act, the Rules of Decision Act, the *Erie* doctrine, or the supremacy clause.

---

52. *See* Meltzer, *supra* note 43, at 1201 n.369.

Chapter 9

CONSTITUTIONAL LIMITS ON CHOICE OF LAW

Here we address a very important question in a multi-sovereign system like that of the United States: what are the constitutional limits on application of local law to a case that has elements involving more than one sovereign? As the word "limits" indicates, this inquiry concerns only whether or not it is constitutionally *permissible* for the forum to apply its own substantive law to a case, not the theoretically best resolution of a mixed case.

The earlier discussion of choice-of-law theories indicates that there is tremendous ground for disagreement about the most desirable result when a forum is faced with a case in which two or more sovereigns have an interest. One might think, then, that the question of a permissible choice of law is relatively simple and uncontroversial. Recent Supreme Court decisions, however, demonstrate just how uncertain and ephemeral those limits are.

As in other areas of jurisdiction, such as the right to adjudicate, the need to protect each state in the federal system from overreaching by other states and the need to protect the litigants are of paramount importance. At least four constitutional provisions potentially come into play: the due process, full faith and credit, equal protection, and privileges and immunities clauses. Because there are several constitutional policies and provisions involved, it becomes difficult to account for the results in cases that do not explain their reasons fully. In addition, the various doctrines of constitutional limits on choice of law have changed drastically over the last fifty years.

Beginning with a rough synopsis of the connecting factors that have been relevant to constitutional limits on choice of law, we then describe the values that constitutional limits on choice of law are designed to promote. At that point an effort will be made to describe how different constitutional concerns fit into the general scheme.

I. Contacts Relevant to Constitutional Choice of Law

One recent case referred to a "significant aggregation of contacts, creating state interests"[1] as justifying application of forum law. Although the list below suggests that some factors are sufficient or insufficient to withstand a constitutional challenge to the application of forum law, it is important to remember that each of these factors was important *in the context of a particular case*. Conflicts of law is a fact-

---

1. Allstate Ins. Co. v. Hague, 449 U.S. 302, 313 (1981).

dependent field, and consequently, although a contact may be sufficient in one case, it may not be in a slightly different case. With this caution, however, one can find limited guidance from the Court as to what sort of contacts are sufficient to justify imposition of the forum's substantive law. The factors which have been deemed sufficient in the past include:

A. The Loss or Injury Occurred in the Forum

The clearest example of this factor is found in *Watson v. Employers Liability Assurance Corp.,*[2] where a Louisiana woman was injured by a Toni home permanent which she had purchased in Louisiana and used at home. The Supreme Court upheld application of Louisiana's direct action statute, relying primarily on the fact that the injury occurred within the forum state, even though the insurance policy sued on was negotiated, issued and delivered in Massachusetts. The Court also pointed to plaintiff's long-time residence in the forum and to the national coverage specified in the disputed insurance contract.

Other cases have also suggested that the place of injury is relevant. *Clay v. Sun Insurance Co.,*[3] discussed below, relied on the fact that the loss occurred in the forum; as did *Pacific Employers Insurance Co. v. Industrial Accident Commission.*[4] In *Day & Zimmerman, Inc. v. Challoner,*[5] the plaintiff had been injured in Cambodia by a defective mortar. Suing in Texas federal court, he convinced the lower court not to apply the Texas "place of injury" rule on the grounds that Cambodia had no interest in the dispute. In reversing this decision, the Supreme Court held that the choice-of-law rules of Texas must be applied. Although the Court did not explicitly address the constitutionality of applying Cambodian law, the reason is probably that application of Cambodian law was so clearly constitutional that no one thought to raise the issue.

B. The Carrying on of Business by the Defendant in the Forum

Doing business in the forum appears to be a persuasive factor in the choice-of-law context, as it is in personal jurisdiction. *Watson* relied in part on this element, as did *Clay v. Sun Insurance Office Ltd.*[6] Both cases involved a loss in the forum; however, the *Clay* Court also consid-

---

2. 348 U.S. 66 (1954).
3. 377 U.S. 179 (1964).
4. 306 U.S. 493 (1939).
5. 423 U.S. 3 (1975) (per curiam).
6. 377 U.S. 179 (1964).

ered the fact that the defendant insurance company was licensed to do and was doing business in the state.[7] The notice given to defendant by its business activities in the forum, when coupled with the plaintiff's sustained residence in the forum, and the "ambulatory" nature of the insurance contract, was sufficient for application of Florida (forum) law.

Allstate Insurance Co. v. Hague,[8] discussed at greater length below, also relied upon the fact that the defendant carried on business in the forum.[9] "By virtue of its presence, Allstate can hardly claim unfamiliarity with the laws of the host jurisdiction. It is no surprise that the state courts might apply forum law to litigation in which the company is involved."[10] However, the plurality opinion relied also on a number of other factors and suggested that no one of them would have been sufficient by itself.

C. LOCAL DOMICILE OF THE PARTY PROTESTING APPLICATION OF THE LAW

In *Skiriotes v. Florida*,[11] the criminal defendant's residence in the state, coupled with his business activities there (as a professional sponge diver), sufficed to permit application of Florida criminal law to activities occurring beyond the territorial waters.[12] "There is nothing novel in the doctrine that a state may exercise its authority over its citizens on the high seas."[13] An unstated assumption of the case seems to be that the defendant's residence and local business activities constituted notice to him that forum law might be applied to his actions. *Skiriotes* cited *Blackmer v. United States*,[14] which had held that an American in Paris might be required to return to the United States to answer a subpoena. The common rationale of these cases is that a citizen may validly be subjected to the commands of his or her own government.[15]

Bigelow v. Virginia,[16] casts some doubt on this however. In *Bigelow*, the Court held that Virginia could not prevent a Virginia newspaper from advertising a New York abortion clinic. The opinion suggests that

---

7. *Id.* at 180, 182.
8. 449 U.S. 302 (1981).
9. *Id.* at 317-18.
10. *Id.*
11. 313 U.S. 69 (1941).
12. *Id.* at 77.
13. *Cf.* Allstate Ins. Co. v. Hague, 449 U.S. at 317-18 (corporation's presence in state through doing business there constitutes notice that forum law might be applied to it).
14. 284 U.S. 421 (1932).
15. *Id.* at 437.
16. 421 U.S. 809, 824 (1975).

Virginia cannot regulate its residents who obtained abortions in other states even if the local rules it imposes are valid health-related regulations. The case may perhaps be explained in terms of the Court's protection of the right of abortion, but it arguably holds that a state cannot command its citizens to perform or abstain from other actions in other states of the United States. The rationale for such a distinction would be that, when in other states, the citizens have an overriding obligation to adhere to that state's laws, which the forum must respect. Perhaps the best explanation for the case, however, is one that reconciles it with *Skiriotes*. The Court may have been indicating merely that residents from other states cannot be prevented from giving Virginia residents information about abortions; in other words, that Virginia had no right to regulate nonresidents.[17]

D. EMPLOYMENT IN THE FORUM

Under some circumstances, employment in the forum may be a sufficient factor to allow the forum to apply its substantive law. In *Cardillo v. Liberty Mutual Insurance Co.*,[18] the fact that plaintiff's decedent had been hired in the District of Columbia, that he resided there, and that he commuted daily from the District of Columbia to Virginia on temporary work assignment provided a sufficient basis for the District of Columbia to apply its law to the case, even though the decedent had been killed in Virginia during the course of his daily commute.

The most famous, if not infamous, use of employment in the forum as a sufficient factor to justify the forum's choice of law is in *Allstate Insurance Co. v. Hague*,[19] which is discussed at greater length below. What is striking about *Allstate* is that the decedent's employment in the forum was deemed to be "a very important contact," despite the fact that decedent was killed outside of the forum and was not involved in any business activity — not even his daily commute — at the time of the accident.[20]

E. THE EMPLOYMENT CONTRACT WAS FORMED IN THE FORUM

Some courts have found the existence, or nonexistence, of an employment contract formed in the forum to be decisive. Obviously, this factor is likely to overlap with the previous one, since persons typically work

---

17. *Id.* at 824-25 ("It may not under the guise of its police powers, bar a citizen of another State from disseminating information about an activity that is legal in that State."); *see also* discussion in ch. 11, sec. I.

18. 330 U.S. 469, 474-75 (1947).

19. 449 U.S. 302 (1981).

20. *Id.* at 313-14.

at the place where the employment relationship was formed. In *Alaska Packers Association v. Industrial Accident Commission,*[21] however, the claimant under the California worker's compensation statute was employed in California for work in Alaska where he was injured. Interestingly, he was not a California domiciliary, which underscores the importance of the local formation of the employment contract.

In *McCluney v. Jos. Schlitz Brewing Co.,*[22] the court refused to allow the plaintiff the benefit of forum law in an employment suit even though the original employment contract and employment relationship had been formed there. Since that time, the plaintiff had been promoted a number of times to jobs outside the forum. The performance of the contract therefore occurred primarily outside of the forum, and both of the parties were domiciled elsewhere at the time of performance. The court reasoned that each promotion constituted a new job and therefore the original contract was not a relevant contact.

F. RESIDENCE OF THE BENEFITTING PARTY

The local residence of the party who would benefit by application of local law is a factor that has been cited as relevant in conjunction with other factors. For example, *Watson* relied in part on the local domicile of the plaintiff,[23] and *Pacific Employers* mentioned in dictum the right to protect local residents. However, the Court has also indicated that mere technical residence of the plaintiff does not in and of itself suffice to make application of that state's law constitutional.[24] However, this does not answer the question of whether "true" residence would be sufficient, or what the difference between "technical" and other residence might be.

The Court has held that post-occurrence change of residence of a party does not by itself give the forum authority to impose its substantive law. In *John Hancock Mutual Life Insurance Co. v. Yates,*[25] the Court refused to allow Georgia to apply its law to a suit concerning an insurance policy issued in New York on a New York insured with a New York beneficiary. The sole connection with Georgia was the fact

---

21. 294 U.S. 532, 541 (1935). "The fact that the contract is to be performed elsewhere does not of itself put these incidents beyond reach of the power which a state may constitutionally exercise."

22. 649 F.2d 578 (8th Cir. 1981), *aff'd,* 454 U.S. 1071 (1981). "The simple fact that McCluney was originally hired in Missouri, in light of his subsequent employment history . . . is not controlling." *Id.* at 583.

23. 348 U.S. 66, 72-73 (1954).

24. Allstate Ins. Co. v. Hague, 449 U.S. 302, 311 (1981) citing Home Ins. v. Dick, 281 U.S. 397 (1930).

25. 299 U.S. 178 (1936).

that after the death of the insured, the beneficiary moved to Georgia. Application of Georgia law to such a policy, the Court held, violated the full faith and credit clause and the due process clause because, quite simply, "there was no occurrence, nothing done, to which the law of Georgia could apply."[26] The Court did rely on post-transaction change in domicile in *Allstate Insurance Co. v. Hague,* although it seemingly reaffirmed *Yate's* holding that standing alone that factor would not suffice.[27]

G. The Situs of Land

In at least one case, albeit an old one, the Court has recognized the right of a court to apply its own law when it was the situs of the land that was the subject of the suit. *Kryger v. Wilson*[28] allowed application of North Dakota law to a quiet title action involving land there situated, despite the fact that the contract for purchase had been entered into elsewhere.

H. Law of the Forum

The simple contact of being the forum may also count in the constitutional choice-of-law analysis. Justice Stevens, for instance, has indicated his opinion that application of forum law would rarely be unconstitutional because it is reasonable for a court to want to apply its own law with which it is more familiar.[29]

In certain circumstances, the fact that the chosen law is forum law may indeed be dispositive. This occurs chiefly with procedural issues, mirroring the traditional choice-of-law rule that the forum applies its own rules on matters of procedure.[30] While the Supreme Court will not automatically accept a state's characterization of an issue as "procedural,"[31] it has allowed the forum to apply its own rule on a classic example of a procedural rule, namely the statute of limitations.[32] Some

---

26. *Id.* at 182.

27. 449 U.S. 302, 318-19 (1981).

28. 242 U.S. 171 (1916).

29. Allstate Ins. Co. v. Hague, 449 U.S. 302, 326 (1981) (Stevens, J., concurring). "The forum State's interest in the fair and efficient administration of justice is therefore sufficient, in my judgment to attach a presumption of validity to a forum State's decision to apply its own law to a dispute over which it has jurisdiction."

30. *See, e.g.,* Kansas ex rel. Winkle Terra Cotta Co. v. United States Fid. & Guar. Co., 322 Mo. 121, 14 S.W.2d 576 (1928) ("In all matters of procedure courts are governed by the laws of the jurisdiction in which they sit, without any regard to the domicile of the parties, the origin of the right or the country of the act."), *id.* at 581 (citations omitted); RESTATEMENT (FIRST) OF CONFLICT OF LAWS §§ 584-85 (1934).

31. Home Ins. Co. v. Dick, 281 U.S. 397, 405-07 (1930).

32. McElmoyle v. Cohen, 38 U.S. 312 (1839) and, more recently, Wells v. Simonds Abrasive Co., 345 U.S. 514 (1953).

authors have argued that it makes more sense for a forum to apply its own *shorter* statute of limitations, but not its *longer* one.[33] The rationale is that applying a shorter statute leaves the plaintiff free to try to find another forum, and that the forum court has an interest in not adjudicating stale claims. The Court has yet to adopt this distinction, however.

The contact of being the forum is clearly not always decisive. A recent case suggests that it has little if any weight in determining the permissibility of applying forum substantive law to claims unrelated to the forum. In *Phillips Petroleum Co. v. Shutts,* the Court determined that although the state court had adjudicative jurisdiction over all the non-resident class action plaintiffs, the forum state did not thereby have the "significant contact or aggregation of contacts" to the claims that is necessary to support the application of forum law to all the claims.[34]

II. Underlying Theory

It should be clear by now that the relevant factual contacts for purposes of constitutional and common-law limits on choice of law are similar. This should not come as a surprise. What is more puzzling is the theoretical relationship between the mutually contradictory common-law choice-of-law methodologies and the constitutional limitations.

Early constitutional decisions manifest a clear reliance on the vested rights approach to choice of law. Some such cases explicitly employ the language of vested rights.[35] Furthermore, these cases rely heavily on traditional connecting factors such as the place of contracting, sometimes engaging in a highly refined analysis of where the acceptance occurred that is strongly reminiscent of common-law cases such as *Milliken v. Pratt.*[36] In addition, these cases seemed to assume (as did the vested rights approach) that only one state might legitimately apply its own law. For this reason, the Supreme Court during this

---

33. Martin, *Statutes of Limitations and Rationality in the Conflict of Laws,* 19 WASHBURN L. REV. 405, 415-21 (1980).

34. 105 S. Ct. 2965, 2980 (1985).

35. *See, e.g.,* Hartford Accident & Indem. Co. v. Delta & Pine Land Co., 292 U.S. 143, 150 (1934) (a state "may not, on grounds of policy, ignore a right which has lawfully vested elsewhere, if, as here, the interest of the forum has but slight connection with the substance of the contract obligations"); Mutual Life Ins. Co. v. Liebing, 259 U.S. 209, 213-14 (1922) ("law of the place where a contract is made . . . determine the validity and the legal consequences of the act"); New York Life Ins. v. Dodge, 246 U.S. 357, 376-77 (1918).

36. 125 Mass. 374 (1878). *See* ch. 7.

period has been accused of attempting to enshrine vested rights as a constitutional doctrine.[37]

Later cases demonstrated an awareness that more than one state might legitimately apply its law, so that the result would depend on where suit was brought.[38] This has now been explicitly acknowledged by the Court.[39] Moreover, the Court has ceased talking in terms of vested rights. Instead, for about the last forty years it has also spoken in terms of "interests."[40] Its most recent formulation speaks of "a significant aggregation of contacts, creating state interests"[41] which seems deliberately to avoid choosing one theoretical camp over another. Certainly that language does not mandate governmental interest analysis. Despite the Court's acknowledgement that interest analysis predominates as a matter of state law,[42] an assertion that even some interest analysts concede to be incorrect,[43] the claim that interest analysis is constitutionally required is, in the words of one author, "so plainly the result of wishful thinking as not to merit extended rejoinder."[44] For one thing, the Court's continued reliance on traditional connecting factors such as the place of contracting or injury manifests divergence from the governmental interest approach. For another, no case using the term "interest" has employed it as Brainerd Currie would have.[45] The Court has simply shown no inclination to invalidate as unconstitutional the application of traditional choice-of-law rules, and there is no groundswell of that sort in the lower courts, either.

Thus it seems that the Court has simply moved from preference for vested rights analysis to a more neutral approach. What does that neutral approach consist of? The two general themes are fairness to the protesting litigant and the interests (or lack of interests) of the forum.

---

37. R. WEINTRAUB, COMMENTARY ON THE CONFLICT OF LAWS 495 (2d ed. 1980).

38. Watson v. Employers Liab. Assurance Corp., 348 U.S. 66, 72-73 (1954); Clay v. Sun Ins. Office, Ltd., 377 U.S. 179, 181-82 (1964).

39. Allstate Ins. Co. v. Hague, 449 U.S. 302, 307 (1981).

40. See, e.g., Alaska Packers Ass'n v. Industrial Accident Comm'n, 294 U.S. 532, 542-43 (1935) (California had a legitimate interest in regulating California employer-employee business relationship by applying its worker's compensation law); Carroll v. Lanza, 349 U.S. 408, 412-23 (1955) ("The State of the forum also has interests to serve and to protect . . . [t]he State where the tort occurs certainly has a concern in the problems following in the wake of the injury.").

41. Allstate Ins. Co. v. Hague, 449 U.S. 302, 320 (1981).

42. Id. at 308-09 n.11.

43. Kay, Theory Into Practice Choice of Law in the Courts, 34 MERCER L. REV. 521, 544 (1983).

44. Ely, Choice of Law and the State's Interest in Protecting Its Own, 23 WM. & MARY L. REV. 173, 180 (1981).

45. Id. For discussion of Currie's method of interest analysis, see ch. 7, sec. III.

Fairness to the litigant has been seen as involving primarily the avoidance of unfair surprise. One can easily explain the unwillingness to rely solely on a post-transaction change in domicile in these terms. If a litigant might obtain a change in law through the simple expedient of moving, this would give the defendant no way to anticipate which law would apply to his or her case. Conversely, the Court has on numerous occasions explained its reliance on particular connecting factors by noting that the factor allowed the defendant to anticipate application of local law. For instance, in *Skiriotes v. Florida,* cited earlier, the defendant's Florida residence enabled him to familiarize himself with Florida law and to anticipate its application.[46] Similarly, the opinion in *Clay v. Sun Insurance Office, Ltd.* pointed out that the insurance policy was sold with the knowledge that the plaintiff's property would be protected no matter where in the world he took it, and did not contain a choice-of-law clause barring application of other states' laws. The company knew he had taken his property to Florida, and since it was licensed to do business there, it might have expected to be sued there.[47] Other cases have also relied on unrelated local business as proof that the defendant would not be unfairly surprised by application of local law.[48]

Unfair surprise is also a primary evil to be avoided in other contexts, such as the constitutional limits on adjudicative jurisdiction.[49] While unfair surprise seems a plausible concern, brief examination shows that it is a slipperier concept than first appears, and may not even make much sense at all. For example, in *World-Wide Volkswagen v. Woodson,* the Court invalidated on foreseeability grounds an assertion of jurisdiction over an out-of-state car dealer who sold a car that was taken into the state by the buyer. The dealer could not reasonably have been expected to anticipate being haled into court there.[50] Contrast *Clay* where the insurance company supposedly had reason to anticipate application of forum law simply because it must have been aware that the plaintiff might take his property into the forum.

One also wonders how and at what point foreseeability must be measured. In some sense a potential defendant will expect that if he or she ever gets involved in litigation that the future plaintiff will shop for the most attractive forum. If for instance California has the most

---

46. 313 U.S. 69, 72 (1941).
47. 377 U.S. 179, 182 (1964).
48. *See, e.g.,* Allstate Ins. Co. v. Hague, 449 U.S. 302, 317-18 (1981).
49. World-Wide Volkswagen Corp. v. Woodson, 444 U.S. 286, 297 (1980); *see also* Shaffer v. Heitner, 433 U.S. 186, 213-17 (1977). *See generally* discussion at ch. 1, sec. IIA.
50. 444 U.S. at 297-99 (1980).

lenient products liability law in the country, does this mean that every manufacturer should expect application of California law, and therefore that California law may be validly applied? If the state of California sent letters to manufacturers notifying them of an intention to apply California law, would that solve any constitutional problem? Presumably not — the defendant simply *should not be obliged* to expect being either haled into court or subjected to California law on such a basis. The real question is what the defendant ought to be required to expect, which is a function of substantive standards and not forseeability.

The second consideration is "interests", an equally mysterious concept. In some worker's compensation cases, states have acquired an interest by being the state in which the injury occurred.[51] In others, being the state where the contract was entered into created an interest.[52] There are some indications that interests may arise where there are local medical creditors to be paid,[53] although the Court has explicitly refused in making this argument to ask whether in fact any such local creditors exist.[54] In *Watson v. Employers Liability Assurance Corp.*, there was an interest in providing compensation for a local woman injured locally by a product purchased locally. In *Allstate Insurance Co. v. Hague*, the forum acquired an interest (albeit a not very profound one)[55] through the coincidence that the plaintiff's decedent was employed there. This was true even though the employment relationship was in no way relevant to the case. The Court has never given the slightest indication of how to go about deciding whether a contact creates an interest or not; "interest" seems to be a label tailored to fit a conclusion.

The considerations of foreseeability and interests have figured in lines of cases arising under several different constitutional provisions. The constitutional provisions relied upon most frequently in choice of

---

51. Pacific Employers Ins. Co. v. Industrial Accident Comm'n, 306 U.S. 493 (1939); Carroll v. Lanza, 349 U.S. 408, 412-13 (1955).

52. *See, e.g.*, Alaska Packers Ass'n v. Industrial Accident Comm'n, 294 U.S. 532 (1935) (although worker was injured in Alaska, he would recover under California worker's compensation law in a California court because employment relationship had been formed there).

53. Carroll v. Lanza, 349 U.S. 408, 413 (1955); Pacific Employers Ins. Co. v. Industrial Accident Comm'n, 306 U.S. 493, 501 (1939); Allstate Ins. Co. v. Hague, 449 U.S. 302, 316 n.22 (1981).

54. Carroll v. Lanza, 349 U.S. 408, 413 (1955) ("Arkansas therefore has a legitimate interest in opening her courts to suits of this nature, even though in this case Carroll's injury may have cast no burden on her or her institutions").

55. Allstate Ins. Co. v. Hague, 449 U.S. 302, 314 (1981) ("While employment status may implicate a state interest less substantial than does resident status, that interest is nevertheless important.").

law analysis are the due process and full faith and credit clauses, although equal protection and privileges and immunities might also in theory play a role. The respective functions of these clauses are unclear; due process and full faith and credit, in particular, may be interchangeable. Nevertheless, we separate their discussion because certain precedents purport to rely on one clause rather than another.

A. DUE PROCESS

The due process clause states that "[no] State [shall] deprive any person of life, liberty, or property, without due process of law . . . ."[56] A good example of how the clause has been applied is *Home Insurance Co. v. Dick*.[57] Dick brought suit in Texas state court to recover on a fire insurance policy. The policy in dispute had been issued in Mexico to a Mexican citizen to cover a boat only in certain Mexican waters. The policy explicitly required that all claims be filed within one year after a loss. Plaintiff, a Texas domiciliary to whom the policy had been assigned prior to the loss, brought suit in Texas more than one year after the loss. Under Texas law, the one year limitation in the policy would be invalid and thus would not bar Dick's suit. However, under Mexican law, such a limitation was valid. The question facing the Texas court was clear — should it apply its own local law to the controversy, or should it apply Mexican law which would require dismissal of the suit? The Texas courts applied local law and sustained the claim. On appeal, the Supreme Court held that Texas had too little connection to the case to allow it to apply its own substantive law.

The Court looked to the due process clause for guidance in its decision. Keeping in mind the dangers of overreaching by the forum and the need for fairness to the litigants, the Court quickly rejected plaintiff's attempt to characterize the policy's filing limitation as a matter of procedure to which the forum was entitled to apply its own local law. Such a shifting of labels could not obscure the fact that the Texas statute sought to "create rights and obligations," the Court stated, thereby triggering the due process clause. Turning to the contacts Texas had with the case, the Court found none of any significance. By trying to impose its local substantive law on contracts in which it had no real interest, Texas had violated the notion of fundamental fairness embodied in the due process clause.

---

56. U.S. CONST. amend. XIV, § 1.
57. 281 U.S. 397 (1930).

The most recent Supreme Court decision on due process as a constitutional limit on the choice of forum law is the controversial case of *Allstate Insurance Co. v. Hague*.[58] *Hague* involved a suit in Minnesota state court seeking recovery under an auto insurance policy. Plaintiff's first husband was killed by an uninsured car in Wisconsin where he and his family had lived for many years. The insurance was issued by a national company in Wisconsin to plaintiff's decedent (a Wisconsin resident), covering three vehicles garaged in Wisconsin.

After her first husband's death, plaintiff moved to Minnesota, married a Minnesotan, and filed suit on behalf of her first husband's estate. Under Minnesota law, the uninsured motorist provisions of all three vehicles could be "stacked" to allow recovery of $45,000. Under Wisconsin law, stacking was not permitted, thereby limiting her recovery to $15,000. The Minnesota trial court applied the Minnesota law, and was affirmed in that decision by the state supreme court and the United States Supreme Court.

What contact with Minnesota could justify such a result? The Supreme Court plurality (there were three opinions) saw three factors which, when aggregated, were "significant," and constitutionally sufficient. The first factor was plaintiff's post-transaction move to the forum, which the plurality conceded would in and of itself be insufficient under *Yates*. Second, the Court pointed to the insurance company's continuing business presence in the forum state, suggesting that there could be no notice or fairness problems in applying Minnesota law in this case since defendant clearly knew Minnesota law would be applied in some cases to which it was party. The final, and most important factor was the employment of plaintiff's decedent in the forum. The fact that he was not killed in the course of his employment, or even during his daily commute, did not appear to bother the plurality.

Justice Stevens thought that the case should be analyzed according to both due process and full faith and credit, but agreed with the plurality's result.[59] The dissent agreed with the plurality that "the Court should invalidate a forum state's decision to apply its own law only when there are no significant contacts between the state and the litigation." However, the dissenters simply saw no significant contacts of any kind between Minnesota and Mrs. Hague's case.[60] In particular, they argued that the "very significant employment contact" was totally irrelevant to the dispute, thus distinguishing cases the plurality had relied upon. Those cases, although mentioning local employment, were worker's compensation cases.

---

58. 449 U.S. 302 (1981).
59. *Id.* at 320-32 (Stevens, J., concurring).
60. *Id.* at 332 (Powell, J., dissenting).

There has been a great deal of scholarly criticism of the *Hague* decision,[61] much of it suggesting that given the minimal nature of the contact between the forum and the litigation there declare sufficient, the Supreme Court will refuse to consider seriously any constitutional limits to the application of forum law. The case raises doubts about whether there can ever be a due process violation if there are "minimum contacts" sufficient to justify adjudicative jurisdiction and if the local law itself does not violate any constitutional provision.

Other scholars have embraced the *Hague* decision, in contrast, on the precise grounds that there is no need for more than "minimal scrutiny" of the forum's application of its own law once "minimum contacts" for adjudicative jurisdiction have been established.[62] The argument is that if the law itself is constitutional, and if the defendant is properly haled into a court which has proper jurisdiction to hear the case, then there can be no due process violation if forum law is applied.

There are several problems with this point of view. For one thing, it is not clear that bases for jurisdiction such as mere physical presence are now constitutionally invalid.[63] Adjudicative jurisdiction premised on such factors seems to give rise to no right to apply forum law. More generally, the fact that the forum is a convenient place to adjudicate does not necessarily make application of forum law fair. For example, a company may do business in many states, making it subject to suit in all of them. That does not necessarily mean that all of the company's legal problems, nationwide, ought to be governed by that state's law which is least advantageous to it. But if minimum contacts for suit also satisfies the choice-of-law test, then plaintiffs will all sue the company in the state with the most pro-plaintiff law. In effect, the price of doing business in a state would be to submit to all of its laws for all of one's activities.

The Court appears to have acknowledged this danger in the recent case of *Phillips Petroleum Co. v. Shutts*, where it held that the applica-

---

61. *See, e.g.,* Symposium, 10 HOFSTRA L. REV. 1 (1981). Martin, *Personal Jurisdiction and Choice of Law,* 78 MICH. L. REV. 872, 873 (1980) (written before the Court's decision in *Allstate,* and arguing that the Court should require that the state have at least "minimum contacts" related to the substance of the case in order to support the application of forum law); E. SCOLES & P. HAY, CONFLICT OF LAWS 85-87 (1982) (citing to the large literature).

62. *See, e.g.,* Weinberg, *Choice of Law and Minimal Scrutiny,* 49 U. CHI. L. REV. 440 (1982).

63. International Shoe Co. v. Washington, 326 U.S. 310, 316 (1945) ("due process requires only that in order to subject a defendant to a judgment *in personam,* if he be not present within the territory of the forum, he have certain minimum contacts with it such that the maintenance of the suit does not offend 'traditional notions of fair play and substantial justice'") (citations omitted).

tion of forum law to all claims in a complex multistate class action was "sufficiently arbitrary and unfair as to exceed constitutional limits."[64] The defendant in *Phillips Petroleum* did do business in the forum and some members of the plaintiff class resided there, making jurisdiction over the action and all the parties appropriate. However, the Court noted, the majority of the plaintiff class lived outside the forum and there was "no indication" that the parties had any idea that forum law would control all the royalty claims.[65] In light of the unfair surprise to the parties and the forum's lack of contacts with many of the transactions, the Court held that on such facts the forum was not free to apply forum law to the transactions involving persons and property outside of the state.

Shutts suggests that the Court may be retreating from the leniency of *Allstate,* especially when one considers the near unanimity of the *Shutts* opinion. Only Justice Stevens dissented on the conflict of laws portion, reiterating the points made in his concurrence in *Allstate.*[66] It remains to be seen whether *Shutts* represents a significant revitalization of the constitutional limits on the application of forum law, or whether its holding will be confined to the special category of nationwide class action suits.

B. The Full Faith and Credit Clause

The due process clause deals with the dual issues of the reach of state power and the fairness to parties over whom that power is exercised. In contrast, the full faith and credit clause deals expressly with the conflicting interests of separate states within a federal system; indeed, unlike due process, it applies only where the competing sovereign is a state, and not a foreign nation.[67] The clause states: "Full Faith and Credit shall be given in each State to the public Acts, Records, and judicial Proceedings of every other State. And the Congress may by general Laws prescribe the Manner in which such Acts, Records and Proceedings shall be proved, and the Effect thereof."[68] Although the clause does not explicitly mention choice of law, its words have great potential relevance to one of the two prime concerns in choice of law — the preservation of the federal system by the prevention of overreaching by any one state.

---

64. 105 S. Ct. 2965, 2980 (1985).

65. *Id.*

66. *Id.* at 2981-92, esp. 2291-92 (Stevens, J., concurring in part and dissenting in part).

67. Aetna Life Ins. Co. v. Tremblay, 223 U.S. 185, 190 (1912) (no constitutional provision requires state recognition of judgments of foreign nations); Home Ins. Co. v. Dick, 281 U.S. 397, 410-11 (1930).

68. U.S. Const. art. IV, § 1.

Some commentators have argued that the full faith and credit clause, with its clear focus on the relationship between sovereign states in a federal system, should play a more active role in choice of law.[69] However, that call has gone unheeded. Despite the rather different analysis suggested by both the wording and the underlying focus of the full faith and credit clause, the Supreme Court has merged its requirements with those of due process. The ease with which the plurality in *Allstate* and the majority in *Shutts* combined the due process and full faith and credit requirements,[70] despite the protests of Justice Stevens,[71] raises the question of why full faith and credit no longer has any independent vitality in choice of law. Whatever the reason, full faith and credit has been confined primarily to judgments cases.[72]

In one early Supreme Court case considering full faith and credit in choice of law, the Court held that the clause placed an affirmative requirement on the forum state (New Hampshire) where the accident had occurred to defer to the worker's compensation law of another interested state (Vermont) where the decedent had been hired.[73] Only three years later, however, this holding was severely undercut. In *Alaska Packers Association v. Industrial Accident Commission*, the Court ruled that the forum state was entitled to apply its exclusive worker's compensation law, despite the claims of defendant that the law of the state of the injury should control. The Court noted that the full faith and credit clause does not always require the forum state to apply the other state's law in a mixed case. Otherwise, the Court reasoned, the clause would lead to the absurd result that in mixed cases, State A's law would be applied only by State B, and vice versa. The rule set forward by the Court in *Alaska Packers* read the full faith and credit clause to require deference by the forum only in those in-

---

69. *E.g.*, Hay, *Full Faith and Credit and Federalism in Choice of Law*, 34 MERCER L. REV. 709 (1983) (not only minimum contacts, but also a substantial connection between the parties, the forum and the transaction should inform choice of law as means of fulfilling full faith and credit requirements).

70. Allstate Ins. Co. v. Hague, 449 U.S. 302, 308 n.10 (1981) ("This Court has taken a similar approach in deciding choice-of-law cases under both the Due Process Clause and the Full Faith and Credit Clause.").

71. Allstate Ins. Co. v. Hague, 449 U.S. at 321-31 (Stevens, J., concurring); Phillips Petroleum Co. v. Shutts, 105 S. Ct. at 2986-91 (Stevens, J., concurring in part and dissenting in part).

72. For a general discussion of the distinction, see Brilmayer, *Credit Due Judgments and Credit Due Laws: The Respective Roles of Due Process and Full Faith and Credit in the Inter State Context*, 70 IOWA L. REV. 95 (1984).

73. Bradford Elec. Light Co. v. Clapper, 286 U.S. 145 (1935).

stances where its own interests are outweighed by those of the other state.[74] The Court left to itself the ultimate task of weighing those competing interests.

In the next major full faith and credit case, *Pacific Employers Insurance Co. v. Industrial Accident Commission,*[75] the Supreme Court focused on the weighing of governmental interests. Although the Court recognized that Massachusetts, the state where plaintiff resided and where his employment contract was formed, had an interest in the case, it held flatly that such an interest could not "override the constitutional authority of another state to legislate for the bodily safety and economic protection of employees injured within it."[76] Despite the fact that the employment relationship had been created outside of the forum state — a factor that had seemed important in *Alaska Packers* — the Court held that full faith and credit allowed the forum to apply its own law. The injured worker was able to persuade the Court that the fact that his injury within the state, coupled with a forum statute which purported to cover all employment injuries within the state, was sufficient to overcome any full faith and credit challenges to the application of forum law.

In *Carroll v. Lanza,* the Court again held that injury within the state provided a sufficient justification for application of forum law.[77] The Court definitively rejected defendant's contention that full faith and credit *required* the forum to apply the law of the other interested state, holding that where the forum's interests are "large and considerable," the law of the forum could constitutionally be applied.[78] This focus on the interest of the forum state in applying its law was reiterated in *Richards v. United States:*

> Where more than one State has sufficiently substantial contact with the activity in question, the forum State, by analysis of the interests possessed by the States involved, could constitutionally apply to the decision of the case the law of one or another state having such interest in the multistate activity.[79]

As this quotation indicates, the constitutional restrictions have been significantly loosened. The evolution of the case law concerning the full faith and credit clause indicated the general movement of the Supreme Court towards allowing the forum very extensive freedom to apply its own or even another interested forum's law to mixed cases.

---

74. 294 U.S. 532, 547-48 (1935).
75. 306 U.S. 493 (1939).
76. *Id.* at 503.
77. 349 U.S. 408 (1955).
78. *Id.* at 413.
79. 369 U.S. 1, 15 (1962).

C. EQUAL PROTECTION AND PRIVILEGES AND IMMUNITIES

While the due process clause has held the premier position in delineating the outer bounds of what the Constitution permits in choice of law, and full faith and credit has played a somewhat less important role, the equal protection and the privileges and immunities clauses have been often discussed in the literature, but almost totally overlooked by the case decisions as sources of constitutional limits to state choice of law. The equal protection clause, which commands every state to provide "to any person within its jurisdiction the equal protection of the laws,"[80] makes no specific mention of multistate situations, although it applies to differentiations of all sorts and therefore to different treatment based on state residence. The privileges and immunities clause provides that "the Citizens of each State shall be entitled to all the Privileges and Immunities of Citizens in the several States."[81]

These two clauses question the state's power to make classifications based on citizenship or residency. Underlying privileges and immunities, especially, is the recognition that for the federal system to survive and prosper, states must treat individuals from other states equally. Difficulties arise, however, in determining just what it means to treat individuals equally. With whom is one to be treated equally? Two possible interpretations immediately come to mind. First, in the choice-of-law context, treating residents and nonresidents equally could mean that any benefits or burdens that the local law extends to its citizens and residents must also be extended to nonresidents.

Alternatively, treating all persons equally could mean that each state treats residents of other states as would the home state of those individuals. This latter interpretation relies on a presumption that each state has the authority to and does protect its own residents by laws which it deems to be appropriate and constitutional. Accordingly, for the forum to apply the law of the out-of-state resident to that person would arguably be the most "equal" and fair result.

Brainerd Currie and Herma Hill Kay used the equal protection and privileges and immunities clauses to support the argument that conflicts of law issues should be resolved by governmental interest analysis. Whereas the traditional choice-of-law rules had obscured the "inherent" problems of discrimination, Currie and Kay argued, interest analysis would bring those problems out into the open. In their words, interest analysis:

---

80. U.S. CONST. amend. XIV, § 1.
81. U.S. CONST. art. IV, § 2, cl. 1.

counsels the rational, moderate, and controlled pursuit of self-interest; it also counsels that self-interest should be subordinated freely, and even gladly, to the constitutional restraints required and made possible by a federal union.[82]

For Professors Currie and Kay, equal protection and privileges and immunities have an important role to play in restraining the forum from "provincial and short-sighted pursuit of domestic interests."[83]

Recently, there has been a resurgence of interest in a more active role for these two clauses as constitutional limitations in choice of law. Dean Ely has suggested recently that Currie and Kay were mistaken in placing sole emphasis on the *benefits* to local residents, rather than recognizing that states may also have a special interest in burdening locals.[84] Criminal law would, for instance, be an example of a forum law that arguably burdens those residing within the territory. Ely argues that the clear purpose of the privileges and immunities clause is to "protect people from being disadvantaged by legislatures they lack any say in electing," thus privileges and immunities in the choice-of-law context ought to be satisfied if everyone is provided the protection and benefits of his or her home state's law.[85]

In contrast, Professor Weinberg argues that the real danger of discrimination is not that of denying local benefits to out-of-staters, but rather of discriminating between similarly situated locals when the forum chooses to depart from forum law.[86] Her argument with Ely stems from the belief that it is often, if not always, "rational" for a state to distinguish between residents and nonresidents in the formulation of its laws. Indeed, it is argued to be unconstitutional for a state to differentiate between its own residents on such an irrational basis as where the cause of action arose.

It is helpful to compare two cases which deal in different ways with the issue of what constitutes a legitimate state interest in making distinctions between its residents and nonresidents. The first of these cases is *Truax v. Raich*, decided by the Supreme Court in 1915.[87] The plaintiff, a resident of Arizona and legal alien, challenged on equal protection grounds an Arizona law severely limiting employment of aliens. The Court agreed with the plaintiff, holding first that aliens are protected by the equal protection clause, and second that although

---

82. Currie & Schreter (Kay), *Unconstitutional Discrimination in the Conflicts of Laws: Privileges and Immunities*, 69 YALE L.J. 1323, 1391 (1960).

83. Currie & Schreter (Kay), *Unconstitutional Discrimination in the Conflicts of Laws: Equal Protection*, 28 U. CHI. L. REV. 1, 52 (1960).

84. Ely, *supra* note 44, at 81 (1981).

85. *Id.* at 190.

86. Weinberg, *On Departing from Forum Law*, 35 MERCER L. REV. 595, 596 (1984).

87. 239 U.S. 33 (1915).

Arizona was entitled to make reasonable legislative classifications to promote health, safety, morals, and public welfare, the Act in question went beyond what was constitutionally permissible by denying lawful inhabitants of their ability to earn a living. Many other cases have invalidated different treatment of locals and foreigners.[88]

In contrast, *Kilberg v. Northeast Airlines* shows just how far courts are willing to go to protect local residents.[89] *Kilberg* involved a suit by a New York resident in New York to recover damages under a wrongful death act for an airplane crash in Massachusetts. The problem was that under New York law, there was no limit on the damages plaintiff could collect. Under Massachusetts law, damages were limited to $15,000. Normally, the place of the accident dictated which wrongful death statute should apply, seeming here to call for application of the limited Massachusetts act. Nevertheless, the New York court applied the Massachusetts act, without the damages limitation. In the words of Justice Desmond, "Our courts should if possible provide protection for our own State's people against unfair and anachronistic treatment of the lawsuits which result from these disasters."[90]

How are we to understand these two cases? Perhaps the salient difference is that in *Kilberg* the result of not applying the favorable local law would be to apply the law of a competing state. In the typical equal protection case, in contrast, the consequence of not granting the benefit to the foreigner is to deny any remedy at all (or to grant some diminished level of benefits provided by local law). Cases like *Truax*, after all, are not really choice-of-law cases. There is no alternative but to apply local law, with local law specifying different amounts of protection for insiders and outsiders.[91] Thus, in choice-of-law cases such as *Kilberg*, the discrimination can be explained as deference to another sovereign. It is not that the forum is deliberately offering less to outsiders; it is that the forum recognizes that outsiders ought to be governed by their home state's law.

This explanation is only partially convincing, given that the forum does not *always* defer to the home state's law. It applies forum law in many cases involving outsiders. In fact, under interest analysis the

---

88. For general treatments, see Simson, *Discrimination Against Non Residents and the Privileges and Immunities Clause of Article IV*, 128 U. PA. L. REV. 379 (1979), J. ELY, DEMOCRACY AND DISTRUST (1980), and L. TRIBE, AMERICAN CONSTITUTIONAL LAW 1052-56 (1978); Sunstein, *Naked Preferences and the Constitution*, 84 COLUM. L. REV. 1689, 1705-10 (1984).

89. 9 N.Y.2d 34, 172 N.E.2d 526 (1961).

90. *Id.* at 527-28.

91. For a comparison of discrimination in the interstate and intrastate contexts, see Brilmayer, *Carolene, Conflicts, and the Fate of the Inside Outsiders*, forthcoming June 1986 Pennsylvania Law Review.

forum will *always* subject outsiders to forum law when forum law is advantageous to the resident, because then the forum has an interest in providing the advantage to its resident. The deference to the other state occurs only in those cases where the state has nothing to gain by application of forum law anyway.

In this context it should be pointed out that not all choice-of-law rules relying on domiciliary connecting factors have this problem. For instance, a state might apply its law of intestate succession to anyone who dies domiciled within the state; where the decedent is a foreign domiciliary, the state defers to that foreign state's law. This rule does not discriminate in the same way because it cannot be anticipated whether local law is more or less generous. The state does not limit its deference to situations where the deference is to the disadvantage of the outsider, which is precisely the problem that modern interest analysis encounters.

D. COMMERCE CLAUSE

In several cases, the Court has recognized that the commerce clause might apply to the choice-of-law process. In *Edgar v. MITE Corp.*,[92] the Court invalidated an Illinois statute that purported to give greater protection to Illinois shareholders in takeover battles than is accorded under the federal securities laws. While conceding that it might be a legitimate goal for Illinois to provide protection to local shareholders, the majority found that the act did not in fact focus on Illinois shareholders, but rather on takeovers occurring nationwide. *That,* the Court implied, is a "goal" that violates the commerce clause and the federal securities laws. The Court analogized the Illinois Business Take-Over Act to the attachment statute in *Shaffer v. Heitner,* where "any attempt 'directly' to assert extraterritorial jurisdiction over persons or property would offend sister States and exceed the inherent limits of the State's power."[93]

A similar result was reached in *Brown-Forman Distillers Corp. v. New York State Liquor Authority.*[94] The state of New York required liquor distillers or producers selling to wholesalers within the state to sell at a price no higher than the lowest price charged to wholesalers elsewhere in the country. The price schedule was required to be posted before the twenty-fifth day of each month, and went into effect on the first day of the second following month. Changes in that price schedule required approval by the New York board. The practical consequence

---

92. 457 U.S. 624 (1982).
93. *Id.* at 643, quoting Shaffer v. Heitner, 433 U.S. 186, 197 (1977).
94. 54 U.S.L.W. 4567 (6-3-86).

of the law was that the distiller might not thereafter lower the prices charged in other states, because it would then be selling at a price lower than the schedule posted for New York. The Court recognized that New York had a valid interest in seeking the lowest possible prices for its consumers.[95] Citing *Mite,* however, the Court stated that "[f]orcing a merchant to seek regulatory approval in one State before undertaking a transaction in another directly regulates interstate commerce. . . . New York . . . may not 'project its legislation into [other states] by regulating the price to be paid' for liquor in those States."[96] For essentially the same reason, New York's action was not validated by the twenty first amendment.[97] As in *Mite,* a statute promoting valid local interests foundered on commerce clause objections because of its extraterritorial implications.

The Court has never tried to reconcile this new commerce clause jurisprudence with its due process holdings concerning choice of law. Recalling *Allstate Insurance Co. v. Hague,* one wonders what would have happened if Minnesota had required all insurance companies doing business in the state to refrain from placing anti-stacking clauses in insurance policies issued to residents of the other states. Presumably under *Brown-Forman* this would violate the commerce clause. Yet the *Hague* decision had essentially this extraterritorial impact when it allowed Minnesota to invalidate a clause written in another state, and covering accidents occuring elsewhere. Perhaps the demise of the due process clause as a limit on choice of law is to be followed by a comparable policing of extraterritoriality under a commerce clause rubric.

III. *Conclusion*

In conclusion, there are several trends worth noting in the often confusing area of constitutional limits on choice of law. First, the Court has moved progressively away from the view that there must be any one pertinent key factor, such as the place of contracting, which will determine the applicable law. Over the years the Court has come to look at a much broader range of factors, explicitly considering such elements as the interests of the forum, fairness to the defendant, and the relationship of the forum to the action.

Second, the Court has not only broadened its vision of what can be considered in determining the constitutionality of a state's application of local law to a mixed case, but it has also considerably relaxed its

---

95. *Id.* at 4569 ("a State may seek lower prices for its consumers").
96. *Id.*
97. *Id.* at 4570.

standard of review. *Allstate v. Hague* stands as an example of just how far the Court is willing to go in allowing the forum to apply its local substantive law to any mixed case that has even the most tangential connection to the forum. Although there is a great deal of scholarly criticism of the *Allstate* reasoning and result, the case is a clear sign of the Court's unwillingness to nullify the choice of forum law unless that choice is completely without a rational basis.

The *Shutts* decision may indicate that the Court will not permit the application of forum law to specific claims that are easily identifiable as totally unrelated to the forum. Whether the case stands for this proposition or more remains to be seen. Apparently the application of forum law to nonresident plaintiffs in *Shutts* exceeded that requirement of minimal rationality. It is as yet unclear whether the Court would invalidate the application of forum law to a plaintiff who was resident in the forum.

In considering the future of constitutional limits on choice of law, the reader should keep in mind the relationship between adjudicative and legislative jurisdiction. If the Court abides by the implied message of *Allstate* — namely that the forum has extensive freedom to apply its law to multistate cases — then one would expect to see more intense interest in the preliminary question of whether the court chosen by the plaintiff has jurisdiction to hear the case. A loosening of constitutional requirements in one area is almost certain to bring calls for restrictions in the other.

Chapter 10

JURISDICTION OVER INTERNATIONAL TRANSACTIONS

The international character of a transaction resulting in litigation affects the different jurisdictional questions (personal jurisdiction, subject matter jurisdiction, choice of law and enforcement of judgments) in various ways and degrees. The reasons behind the range of effects is interesting in itself. International jurisdictional problems raise different issues than domestic questions for at least three interrelated reasons: institutional considerations, judicial competence and judicial resources.

There is no international judicial body that operates like the United States Supreme Court. The Supreme Court has the capacity to resolve the tension which results when judicial activity on the part of one state interferes with an important interest of another. When conflicts surface between nation-states, on the other hand, their resolution is primarily a matter of diplomacy. Foreign relations is the business of an executive rather than the courts. The resolution of these conflicts is a particularly delicate matter because the confrontation between laws and policies of the United States and foreign states are often sharper and more complex than any analogous showdown between two states. Simply put, overly aggressive adjudication can disrupt commerce and peace between nations much more than it can between states. Institutional considerations thus will often urge or require the courts to defer to the executive or the legislature.

Second, the international aspects of a case may raise problems of judicial efficacy and competence. There is no international full faith and credit clause to ensure that the judgment of an American court will receive its due respect around the world as it would around this country. Thus, judges are understandably reluctant to render opinions that are likely to be ineffective. Furthermore, the location of crucial evidence in foreign countries that may have an interest in keeping that evidence out of an American court may make reasonably competent adjudication impossible. A general policy of self restraint may act as a key to unlocking barriers foreign authorities may erect against the process of adjudication and the enforcement of judgments.

Finally, there is the problem of scarce judicial resources. When most of the important aspects of a case are unrelated to the sovereign asked to decide it, that sovereign might sensibly conclude that it does not have an interest in intervening. Of course, the same is true of a state court asked to resolve a controversy that occurred in another state. But state courts are typically bound by the full faith and credit clause to consider disputes from other states.[1] An American court, on the other hand, can decline to expend its resources on an alien dispute with a clear constitutional conscience.[2]

Interstate conflict of laws problems involve the competing claims of different states, mediated by the Constitution. In contrast, international conflict of laws problems are of two types: conflicts between a state and a foreign nation, and conflicts between the federal government and another nation. Such conflicts may be broken down further according to whether the problems they raise concern adjudicative jurisdiction or choice of law. The result is four categories of problems, which we will consider separately.

	state law	federal law
adjudicative	state long-arm statutes in the international context	federal adjudicative authority in the international context
choice of law	the reach of state law overseas	the reach of American law overseas

The discussion of adjudicative jurisdiction will be brief (as befitting our primary interest here in Part II in legislative jurisdiction) because the fact that the dispute is international rather than interstate makes little difference. After considering these categories in order, we conclude with a few remarks about enforcement of judgments in the interstate context.

I. Personal Jurisdiction

A. Personal Jurisdiction over Foreign Defendants in State Courts

A recent Supreme Court decision regarding due process limitations on state assertions of personal jurisdiction over nonresident defendants indicates that nonresident alien defendants receive the same protection from the long arm of a state court as residents of other states do. *Helicopteros Nacionales de Colombia* v. *Hall*[3] was a wrongful death

---

1. See, Hughes v. Fetter, 341 U.S. 609 (1953) discussed at ch. 4, sec. IB.

2. The full faith and credit clause does not apply to the laws of other nations. *See* Allstate Ins. Co. v. Hague, 449 U.S. 302, 321, n.4 (Stevens, J., concurring); Home Ins. Co. v. Dick, 281 U.S. 397, 411 (1930).

3. 466 U.S. 408 (1984).

action brought in a Texas state court. The suit was grounded on a helicopter crash in which four employees of the defendant, Helicol, perished. Helicol was a Colombian corporation that provided helicopter services in Peru to the decedent's employer, joint venture headquartered in Texas. The contract for the provision of helicopter services was negotiated in Texas, but signed in Peru. Helicol's only other contact with Texas was that, over the course of several years, it had purchased helicopters from a Texas corporation and had its pilots trained there. Helicol was not authorized to do business in Texas, nor had it appointed an agent there for service of process.[4] The Supreme Court of Texas held that the long-arm statute extended its reach to the limits of the United States Constitution. Thus, because it deemed the assertion of jurisdiction over Helicol to be constitutionally permissible, it affirmed a judgment in favor of the plaintiffs.[5]

The United States Supreme Court reversed. The Court held that the purchase of goods in a state, coupled with the provision of ancillary services, such as personnel training, was constitutionally insufficient to assert jurisdiction over a non-resident defendant. The mere negotiation of the sale and service contract in Texas was not enough to tip the balance in plaintiff's favor. An eight-Justice majority characterized the action by Texas courts as an attempt to assert "general jurisdiction" over Helicol, since the plaintiff failed to claim that Helicol's contacts with Texas were the basis of the cause of action.[6] Helicol thus did not have sufficient contacts with Texas and the case was dismissed.

The reader who recalls the earlier discussion of personal jurisdiction will recognize that this analysis is thoroughly ordinary. Nothing was made of the fact that the relevant events and parties occurred outside of the United States. Indeed, we could substitute "Pennsylvania" for "Peru" and "Connecticut" for "Colombia" in the opinion and nothing would seem out of place. This is remarkable because the petition for certiorari specifically presented the question of whether the due process clause afforded *less* protection to alien nonresident defendants than to domestic ones.[7] In ignoring that question completely, the Court implicitly answered it in the negative. On the other hand, both Helicol and the United States argued that alien defendants should be afforded

---

4. *Id.* at 408-12.

5. Hall v. Helicopteros Nacionales de Colombia, 638 S.W.2d 870, 872-874 (Tex. 1982).

6. 466 U.S. at 415-16 & n.10. It is worth noting that one Justice saw the case as possibly amenable to specific jurisdiction analysis. See *id.* at 424 (Brennan, J., dissenting). The Court's refusal to consider the question of specific jurisdiction was said to have been the result of the plaintiff's failure to raise the argument. *See id.* at 415 n.10 citing to Brief for Respondents at 14; Tr. of Oral Arg. at 26-27, 30-31.

7. Petition for Writ of Certiorari at i-ii, Hall v. Helicopteros, 466 U.S. 408 (1984).

more protection than domestic defendants. They emphasized the harm that upholding Texas' assertion of jurisdiction might inflict on government efforts to promote the exportation of American goods,[8] and pointed to the trouble the Court might have in enforcing any judgment it might issue in the case.[9] The failure to address these problems of foreign trade and enforceability of judgments, which were patently presented, suggests that the Court is not any more interested in affording greater protection to alien nonresident defendants than it is in affording less protection.

The constitutional irrelevance of the alien status of a defendant is mirrored by state long-arm statutes which generally fail to distinguish between domestic and foreign defendants. Indeed, it is questionable whether application of a lower standard would meet current constitutional standards relating to the treatment of aliens.[10] Thus, both as a matter of theory and practice, the international character of a transaction seemingly does not affect the states' ability to assert personal jurisdiction over nonresidents.[11]

B. PERSONAL JURISDICTION OVER FOREIGN DEFENDANTS IN FEDERAL COURTS

The Federal Rules of Civil Procedure require federal courts to apply the long-arm statute of the states in which they sit.[12] In determining whether jurisdiction is permissible under that statute, contacts with the forum state are generally the only ones considered. However, a problem may arise when plaintiffs invoke a federal court's federal question jurisdiction. The fifth, rather than the fourteenth, amendment governs the assertion of jurisdiction by federal courts.[13] Some courts have debated whether the alien defendant's contacts should in-

---

8. Brief for Petitioner at 23-24, Hall v. Helicopteros, 466 U.S. 408 (1984); Brief for United States as Amicus Curiae at 11-13, Hall v. Helicopteros, 466 U.S. 408 (1984).

9. Brief for Petitioners at 24, Hall v. Helicopteros, 466 U.S. 408 (1984).

10. *Cf.* Plyler v. Doe, 457 U.S. 202 (1982) (striking down Texas law barring students from public education based on alien status); Zschernig v. Miller, 389 U.S. 429 (1968) (striking down on separation of powers grounds a statute which denied aliens their rights to property).

11. One possible exception to the assertion in the text is the so-called doctrine of "jurisdiction by necessity" discussed at ch. 1, sec. IIB. The Supreme Court explicitly refused to consider the constitutionality of jurisdiction by necessity for lack of a complete record on the subject. The majority referred to the doctrine as "a potentially far reaching *modification* of existing law." 466 U.S. at 419 n.13 (emphasis supplied). It is arguable that if such a doctrine were recognized, it would apply more forcefully in the international context.

12. Fed. R. Civ. P. 4(e).

13. *See, e.g.,* Cryomedics, Inc. v. Spembly Ltd., 397 F. Supp. 287, 288 n.3 (D. Conn. 1975).

clude only those with the forum state, or whether the aggregate of the defendant's contacts with the United States may be considered. An aggregation of contacts is plausible because federal courts are agents of a single sovereign whose jurisdiction extends uniformly across the United States and for whom state boundaries may be constitutionally irrelevant.[14]

In actions where Congress has provided for nationwide service of process, federal courts generally agree that the aggregation of an alien defendant's contacts with the United States as a whole is appropriate.[15] Provisions for nationwide service of process generally imply a desire on the part of Congress to treat the United States as a single sovereign body. Under these statutes, American defendants are amenable to personal jurisdiction in all federal courts and the specific location of their contacts inside the United States is irrelevant to the question of jurisdiction.[16] In these cases, to prohibit aggregation of an alien defendant's contacts would afford them more protection than is available to American defendants. Permitting aggregation establishes a kind of jurisdictional parity between alien and out-of-state defendants.

Some courts, however, aggregate the contacts of an alien defendant even in cases where nationwide service of American defendants is not available.[17] In these situations an alien defendant may be susceptible to personal jurisdiction in a forum where an analogous domestic defendant would not. Courts favoring this differential treatment advance two justifications. First, without aggregation alien defendants who conduct affairs in several states without having minimum contacts in any one state could not be sued anywhere in the United States.[18] This may greatly inconvenience the plaintiff. Although American defendants might also not do sufficient business to establish minimum contacts with any one state, they would generally be subject to the jurisdiction of at least one United States forum, such as the state of citizen-

---

14. Edward J. Moriarty & Co. v. General Tire & Rubber Co., 289 F. Supp. 381, 390 (S.D. Ohio 1967); see generally Cryomedics v. Spembly, 397 F. Supp. at 290-91.

15. See, e.g., Staffin v. Greenberg, 509 F. Supp. 825, 831 (E.D. Pa. 1981); Cryomedics v. Spembly, 397 F. Supp. at 287; Moriarty v. General Tire & Rubber Co., 289 F. Supp. at 381; see generally R. CASAD, JURISDICTION IN CIVIL ACTIONS ¶ 4.06[5] & n.345 (1983) (hereinafter cited as CASAD); von Merhen & Trautman, Jurisdiction to Adjudicate: A Suggested Analysis, 79 HARV. L. REV. 1121, 1123-25 n.6 (1966).

16. See, e.g., Staffin v. Greenberg, 509 F. Supp. at 831 (E.D. Pa. 1981); Cryomedics v. Spembly, 397 F. Supp. at 287; Moriarty v. General Tire & Rubber Co., 289 F. Supp. at 381; see generally CASAD, supra note 15, at ¶ 4.06[5], von Merhen & Trautman, supra note 15, at 1123-25 n.6 (1966) (questions of venue and forum non conveniens remain relevant).

17. See, e.g., Centronics Data Computer Corp. v. Mannesmann A.G., 432 F. Supp. 659 (D.N.H. 1977) (defendant's alien status a substantial factor in finding jurisdiction); see generally CASAD, supra note 15, ¶ 4.06[5] & n.346.

18. See Centronics v. Mannesmann, supra note 17, at 664.

ship or incorporation. It can be argued, however, that it is not the convenience of the plaintiff which ought to be at issue in deciding jurisdictional questions but rather fairness to the defendant.

The second justification for aggregation of an alien defendant's contacts relates to the inconvenience of the defendant. Some courts argue that the convenience of the forum is more significant to American defendants than it is to alien defendants, for whom all American jurisdictions are, in a sense, equally distant and inconvenient.[19] Courts that advance this convenience rationale are, in effect, arguing that since it is already burdensome for alien defendants to come to the United States, the incremental burden of litigating in a particularly remote state should not matter. This rationale is questionable, however. First, it depends on litigation in American courts being more inconvenient for alien defendants than it is for American defendants. This is often not the case. Moreover, it is not clear that an initial disadvantage should justify a further disadvantage.

Most courts, for some or all of these reasons, have refused to aggregate an alien defendant's contacts unless Congress has provided for nationwide service of process for domestic defendants.[20] They base this decision on the fact that the Federal Rules of Civil Procedure specify that when service of process is based on a state long-arm statute, such service must be appropriate according to that statute. Thus, since states applying their long-arm statutes cannot aggregate a defendant's national contacts neither can federal courts using those statutes. This reading of the Federal Rules gains support from the fact that the rules do not distinguish between the use of state long-arm statutes in diversity cases and their use in federal question cases. Unless federal courts were willing to extend the aggregation theory into the diversity context, thus risking offense to the principles underlying *Erie Railroad*,[21] their selective application of the theory to federal question cases would contradict the unitary treatment that the rules apparently envision.

II. Choice of Law

A. LIMITATIONS ON THE EXTRATERRITORIAL APPLICATION OF STATE LAW

Federal constitutional limitations on the extraterritorial application of state laws have been described elsewhere in this the book. These due

---

19. *See, e.g.,* Cryomedics v. Spembly, *supra* note 13, at 292.

20. *See, e.g.,* De James v. Magnificance Carriers, 491 F. Supp. 1276, 1284 (D.N.J. 1980), *aff'd on other grounds,* 654 F.2d 280 (3d Cir. 1981); Wells Fargo & Co. v. Wells Fargo Express, 556 F.2d 406, 417-18 (9th Cir. 1977).

21. For a discussion of *Erie,* and its underlying principles of equal treatment and avoidance of forum shopping, see ch. 6.

process limitations apply to international cases as well as interstate cases. *Home Insurance Co. v. Dick*[22] is instructive on this point. Dick, a Texas citizen, brought suit in Texas against a Mexican insurance company. The loss by fire of a tugboat occasioned the suit. An insurance policy on the boat was issued in Mexico and assigned to Dick there. The policy covered the boat only in certain Mexican waters and provided for the application of Mexican law. Dick was residing in Mexico at all relevant times. Dick filed suit in Texas by garnishing Texas assets of New York corporations that had entered into reinsurance contracts with the Mexican company relating to the insurance policy that he held. The reinsurance contracts arose through correspondences between Mexico and New York.[23]

The conflict in the case centered on a clause in the policy that required Dick to make a claim under the policy within one year of the occurrence of damages upon which the claim was based.[24] This requirement was valid under Mexican law, but not under Texas law, which provided that such clauses were void if they provided less than a two-year period of limitation.[25] The United States Supreme Court, reversing the decisions of the state courts, held that application of Texas law to the policy violated the due process clause because neither the formation of the contract nor the events leading to the claim were related to Texas.[26] Dick's Texas citizenship could not by itself justify protectionism by Texas courts and his case was dismissed.[27]

The significance of the opinion lies in the fact that a claim for the application of a foreign nation's law triumphed over a competing claim for the application of a state law. One arguable constitutional difference between international and domestic conflicts cases turns on the fact that the full faith and credit clause is not internationally applicable. The due process clause does however protect alien defendants.[28] Therefore, because the Supreme Court has stated that the due process clause imposes the same limitations as the full faith and credit clause, this becomes a distinction without a difference.[29] In short, the Constitution seemingly restricts the states as much in the international context as it does in the interstate context.

---

22. 281 U.S. 397 (1930).
23. *Id.* at 402-04.
24. *Id.* at 403.
25. *Id.* at 404-05.
26. *Id.* at 407-11.
27. *Id.* at 408.
28. *Id.* at 411 (fourteenth amendment protections apply to aliens).
29. *See* Allstate Ins. Co. v. Hague, 449 U.S. at 308. *But see id.* at 320-332 (Stevens, J., concurring) (distinguishing between the due process and full faith and credit clauses).

B. EXTRATERRITORIAL APPLICATION OF FEDERAL LAW

1. *Subject Matter Jurisdiction and Conflict of Laws in Federal Adjudications of Private International Controversies*

The question of the extraterritorial reach of federal law is more complicated because of its close connection with the question of the federal court's authority to adjudicate the case. This relationship is illustrated by the often-cited case of *Lauritzen v. Larsen.*[30] Larsen was a Danish seaman crewing on a Danish ship. He signed articles of employment, which contained a Danish choice-of-law clause, in New York. He later suffered injury as a result of negligence in the harbor of Havana, Cuba. Larsen sued in federal court in New York under the Jones Act. The shipowner, joined by the Danish government, contended that Danish law applied and that Larsen had received his due under that law.[31] The trial court permitted Larsen's suit under the Jones Act. The Second Circuit affirmed the jury verdict in his favor.

The Supreme Court reversed. The majority stated that the United States' shipping laws would apply "only to areas and transactions in which American Law would be considered operative under prevalent doctrines of international law."[32] The Court then performed a conflicts of law analysis that considered seven factors[33] and concluded that Danish law rather than the Jones Act governed the case. This did not mean however that an American federal court would necessarily apply that law. Rather, without a proper basis for federal adjudicative jurisdiction, the case would have to be dismissed from federal court; and Larsen would be sent to his Scandinavian remedy.[34]

Contrast this outcome with the treatment of interstate disputes. Under *Hughes v. Fetter,*[35] it is unconstitutional for a state court to dismiss a suit merely because it has determined that the law of another state applies. Thus, in interstate cases, the courts of one state must apply a sister state's law after it has determined that law to apply to the case. Yet in *Lauritzen,* the Court left no room for the federal court applica-

---

30. 345 U.S. 571 (1953).

31. *Id.* at 575.

32. *Id.* at 577.

33. The factors are discussed in 345 U.S. at 583-91. They include the place of the wrongful act; the law of the flag; allegiance or domicile of the victim; allegiance of the shipowner; place of contracting; availability of foreign forum; and the law of the forum.

34. The Court did not actually dismiss the action but remanded the case to the district court for proceedings consistent with the opinion. 345 U.S. at 593. The description of Danish law that the Court gave provided for presentation of claims through a Danish consulate and administrative remedies. *Id.* at 575. This indicates that the only proceeding consistent with the application of Danish law would be dismissal from the United States forum.

35. 341 U.S. at 609 discussed *supra,* ch. 4, sec. IB.

tion of Danish compensation principles. The reason for this result apparently was that after determining that American law did not apply, the Court was forced to conclude that there was no basis for federal adjudicative jurisdiction. Thus, in cases involving the application of a federal statute to an international transaction, a federal court must perform its conflicts analysis before determining that it has subject matter jurisdiction. Thus, international law problems bear a resemblance to the special problems discussed in Part III, where adjudicative and legislative jurisdictional analysis intersect. Or, at least they do when a case is brought in an article III court and no other basis for subject matter jurisdiction, such as diversity, can be found.

As one judge has observed in relation to the extraterritorial application of the Sherman Act, this role of the conflicts rules has not been made explicit in many cases.[36] The role of conflict of laws in determining the subject matter jurisdiction of American courts is nevertheless a direct result of the limited grant of authority to federal courts under article III.[37]

2. The Recognized Bases for Extraterritorial Application of Federal Law

The role that the Constitution plays in determining the extraterritorial application of federal law is extremely ambiguous. As discussed earlier in the chapter, the full faith and credit clause does not apply to the international choice-of-law question. Although some courts have hinted that the Constitution might limit the extraterritorial application of federal law,[38] no court has ever held the application of American law to an international controversy violative of due process. Thus, on a practical level, there have been no constitutional limits on the extraterritorial application of federal law. However, it is difficult to believe that a federal court would refrain from imposing such a limitation in an extreme case, given that such limitations have been applied to exercises of personal jurisdiction by state and federal courts and to the extraterritorial application of state law.[39]

---

36. *See* Mannington Mills, Inc. v. Congoleum Corp., 595 F.2d 1287, 1301 (3d Cir. 1979) (Adams, J., concurring).

37. *See, e.g.,* United States v. Alcoa, 148 F.2d 416 at 443 (2d Cir. 1945) (noting in passing the applicability of the Constitution).

38. *See, e.g.,* Leasco Data Processing Equip. Corp. v. Maxwell, 468 F.2d 1326, 1334 (2d Cir. 1972); United States v. Alcoa, 148 F.2d 416, 443 (2d Cir. 1945).

39. For a more extended discussion of this problem, see Brilmayer, *Extraterritorial Application of American Law: A Methodological Overview* (forthcoming, Law and Contemp. Probs.).

Federal courts have also held that principles of international law do not constrain the extraterritorial application of federal law.[40] Rather, international law merely serves as a guide to courts in interpreting the extent to which an *ambiguous* federal statute reaches beyond American boundaries.[41] An interpretative guide, however, is not the same thing as a normative limit. Thus, if Congress were sufficiently explicit, it seemingly could give extraterritorial effect to one of its laws even where such an effect would violate international law.[42]

Free from the limiting impact of both constitutional and international law, federal courts frame their inquiry into the extraterritorial reach of federal law in terms of congressional intent. This is not surprising given the politically sensitive nature of many international controversies. Federal courts have developed three different standards, or circumstances, in which the extraterritorial application of federal law is appropriate. The *Restatement (Revised) of Foreign Relations Law (Restatement (Revised))* articulates these standards explicitly. The rules in the *Restatement (Revised)* are not abstract derivations of "proper standards." Rather, they were gleaned from the practical experiences of federal courts struggling with the question of how far Congress would want federal law to reach in cases where its legislation is silent, or speaks ambiguously about the issue of extraterritoriality. The three categories of extraterritorial application of American law often go under the names of "regulation of nationals," "act territoriality," and "impact territoriality".

The first basis of extraterritorial jurisdiction — that based on the nationality of the parties involved — is broad in its application but narrow in the range of parties to which it applies. Section 402 of the *Restatement (Revised)* recognizes jurisdiction to prescribe a rule of law attaching legal consequences to activities, status, interests or relations of a national of the state wherever located.[43] The United States has jurisdiction over the activities of its nationals regardless of where the acts occur or whether the acts produce effects within its territories.

Nationality as a sufficient basis for legislative jurisdiction seems unexceptionable in most cases involving jurisdiction to *restrict* the

---

40. *See, e.g.,* Timberlane Lumber Co. v. Bank of America, 549 F.2d 597, 609 (7th Cir. 1976); Leasco v. Maxwell, 468 F.2d at 1334; United States v. Alcoa, 148 F.2d at 443.

41. *See, e.g.,* Timberlane v. Bank of America, 549 F.2d at 611-15; Leasco v. Maxwell, 468 F.2d at 1334-35.

42. Leasco v. Maxwell, 468 F.2d at 1334; United States v. Alcoa, 148 F.2d at 443.

43. RESTATEMENT (SECOND) OF FOREIGN RELATIONS LAW OF THE UNITED STATES § 30(1)(a) (1964) (hereinafter cited as RESTATEMENT); RESTATEMENT OF THE FOREIGN RELATIONS LAW OF THE UNITED STATES (REVISED) § 402(2), Tentative Draft No. 6 (1985) (hereinafter cited as RESTATEMENT (REVISED)).

activities of nationals abroad. Parties who wish to act abroad in a manner which is unacceptable to their sovereign are free to renounce that nationality. The legitimacy of nationality as a basis for extraterritorial jurisdiction could conceivably be strained if the sovereign did not have a sufficient interest in the actions of its national to warrant jurisdiction. No court, however, has been confronted with such an extreme case. The more likely problem is that the United States' legitimate interest in regulating the behavior of its nationals abroad conflicts with the foreign sovereign's interest in subjecting the American to its laws. For example, American law may instruct a citizen to produce documents for discovery that are secret or privileged under another nation's laws.

The situation is different where nationality is used as a means of conferring the *benefit,* rather than the burden, of American laws to an American extraterritorially. These cases involve sanctioning the conduct of a party that is not American, because if the restricted party were also American then extraterritorial jurisdiction could be based on that party's nationality. This results in American law regulating non-nationals. A policy of giving effect to congressional legislation based solely on the fact that it benefits an American citizen would thus impose American regulation on foreigners abroad merely because they dealt with an American. Such a policy would generate tensions between the United States and other sovereigns. Accordingly, some United States courts have recognized that injury to a United States national is not a sufficient condition for the extraterritorial application of American law.[44] The *Restatement (Revised)* affirms this principle.[45]

The second and most obvious basis for the extraterritorial application of American law is act territoriality.[46] The rule attaches legal consequences to conduct which occurs within United States territory regardless of whether the effect of that conduct occurs locally.[47] Thus, for example, it would be possible under this theory to apply American laws governing business fraud to cases where the fraudulent representations occur locally but lead to wholly extraterritorial injury to the victim. The United States has a legitimate interest in proscribing or regulating local acts or omissions that produce unwanted results even if those results transpire elsewhere.

---

44. *See, e.g.,* United States v. Columbia-Colella, 604 F.2d 356 (5th Cir. 1979) (reversing conviction for receiving stolen goods because only connection to the United States was that goods were stolen from a United States national).

45. RESTATEMENT, *supra* note 43, at § 30(2); RESTATEMENT (REVISED), *supra* note 43, at § 403.

46. M. McDOUGAL & W. REISMAN, INTERNATIONAL LAW IN A CONTEMPORARY PERSPECTIVE 1295 (1981).

47. RESTATEMENT, *supra* note 43, at § 17(a); RESTATEMENT (REVISED), *supra* note 43, at § 402(1)(a).

The final basis on which a court can apply federal law to an international controversy — "impact territoriality" — is the inverse of act territoriality. Under this theory, federal law may apply to conduct that occurs outside the United States which has effects within its territory. The *Restatement (Revised)* now requires that the effects within the United States be substantial and that they be a direct and foreseeable result of the extraterritorial activity in question.[48] As we shall see, however, the requirement that the effects be direct, foreseeable and substantial has not constrained the extraterritorial reach of American laws to any meaningful degree. Cases in which American courts have applied unmitigated impact theories of jurisdiction, most notably antitrust, have led to the most expansive extraterritorial application of American law and, consequently, to the greatest conflicts with the policies of other nations. American courts have responded to this problem by tempering impact territoriality either with elements of the act and nationality theories of extraterritoriality or by developing doctrines of abstention.

3. Applications of the Principles of Subject Matter Jurisdiction and Choice of Law

The bases of jurisdiction outlined above define different connecting factors that might indicate congressional intent to have a law applied extraterritorially. But how is one to know, in the context of a particular statute, which of these connecting factors is relevant? Congress does not generally specify that one of the bases is applicable to a particular statute. Indeed, Congress is generally altogether silent on the question of extraterritorial application. It is therefore up to the courts to define the extraterritorial reach of American law.

Courts limit the extraterritorial application of federal law with a presumption that legislation is territorial unless it is clearly stated otherwise. In this way, courts may avoid the expansive possibilities of jurisdiction based upon impact within the territory. As just mentioned, the impact basis of jurisdiction has created the most severe tensions between the United States and foreign nations. The combination of approaches that courts employ when applying federal law in the international context leads to an interesting irony when compared to the behavior of state courts determining the interstate reaches of their law. Both analyses rely heavily on notions of legislative intent, but in the international context territoriality is the norm and protection of locals is considered a highly controversial basis for jurisdiction. The

---

48. RESTATEMENT, *supra* note 43, at § 18(b); RESTATEMENT (REVISED), *supra* note 43, at § 402(1)(C).

reverse is true in the domestic context, as our earlier discussion of modern choice-of-law theory demonstrated.[49]

This presumption of territoriality, however, does not always govern in international law. For some statutes, the relevant principles have been nationality or impact territoriality. To illustrate how departures from act territoriality have been justified, we first consider examples of the presumption of territoriality, then cases where nationality has been the guiding principle, and finally discuss applications of the principle of impact territoriality.

a. Act Territoriality

In *Foley Brothers, Inc. v. Filardo*,[50] the Supreme Court faced the question of the extraterritorial reach of the eight-hour employment law.[51] That statute required that "every contract made to which the United States is a party" would limit a wage earner's work day to eight hours or provide for overtime pay.[52] Foley Brothers contracted with the United States to build public works in Iraq and Iran. The company then refused to pay overtime rates to an American citizen working on the project in Iraq and Iran. Writing for the Court, Justice Hughes assumed that Congress could give the law extraterritorial effect if it wished.[53] However, all legislation carries a presumption of territoriality. The statute stated that it applied to "every contract" to which the United States was party. But even a word as broad as "every" had to be construed against a territorial presumption. Therefore, because the statute made no reference to foreign application, its force was confined to labor contracts executed within the United States' borders. That the United States was a direct beneficiary of the contract, and both the employer and employee were American, did not legitimate the extraterritorial application of American law absent a reasonably clear congressional directive.[54]

It is illuminating to contrast *Foley Brothers* to a case where the Supreme Court gave foreign effect to a federal labor law. In *Vermilya-Brown Co. v. Connell*,[55] a case distinguished in *Foley Brothers*, the Supreme Court applied the Fair Labor Standards Act to employees of a contractor for military installation on land in Bermuda.[56] The United

---

49. *See* ch. 7, sec. III (discussing governmental interest analysis).
50. 336 U.S. 281 (1949).
51. *Id.* at 282, n.1 citing 27 Stat. 340, as amended 40 U.S.C. §§ 321-326.
52. *Id.* at 282.
53. *Id.* at 284-85 (plaintiffs conceded this point).
54. *Id.* at 285.
55. 335 U.S. 377 (1948).
56. *Id.* at 379 n.1 citing 55 Stat. 1560, 1572, 1576, 1590.

States held the land on a ninety-nine year lease from the United Kingdom. Although the Court cited the compelling interest of the United States government, this interest was not a sufficient condition for the application of American law to territory subject to British sovereignty absent some legislative authority. The Court found such authority, however, in the fact that Congress had made the act applicable to "possessions" of the United States.[57] The Court interpreted this reference in the statute to possessions to be a legislative mandate for extraterritorial application of the Fair Labor Standards Act.[58] The term possession could have been construed narrowly to apply only to possessions outside the United States boundaries over which the United States had actual sovereignty rather than a mere leasehold. Nonetheless, the Court, having found language in the Act mandating some extraterritorial application, analyzed the extent of the foreign reach in terms of the purposes of the act.[59] Because the Act's purpose would be served by extraterritorial application, its standards were applied.[60] Thus, the presumption of territoriality apparently applies only to the threshold question of whether the act should have *any* extraterritorial effect.[61] It does not contain a corresponding principle of narrow construction once some congressional intent for extraterritoriality has been found.

b. Nationality as a Basis for Extraterritoriality

Federal courts are willing to give the broadest of extraterritorial effect to congressional statutes when they impose obligations on United States nationals. In these cases, courts generally concern themselves only with the traditional due process requirements of notice and an opportunity to be heard. The Supreme Court's decision in *Blackmer v. United States*[62] illustrates this point well. Blackmer was a United States citizen residing in France. He was held in contempt of court for failing to respond to a subpoena requiring him to appear as a witness in a criminal proceeding. The subpoena issued in accordance with a statute requiring United States citizens living abroad to honor subpoenas commanding their appearance in United States courts.[63]

Blackmer challenged the contempt order on fifth amendment due process grounds. Denying Blackmer's claim, the Court held that, al-

---

57. *Id.* at 386.
58. *Id.* at 386-90.
59. *Id.* at 390.
60. *Id.*
61. *Id.*
62. Blackmer v. United States, 284 U.S. 421 (1932).
63. *Id.* at 433 citing 28 U.S.C. §§ 711-18.

though American laws are *presumed* to have only territorial effect, "the question of [an American law's] application, so far as citizens of the United States in foreign countries are concerned, is one of construction, not of legislative power."[64] The relevant law provided specifically for foreign application.[65] Therefore, because Blackmer had notice of the subpoena, he did not merit constitutional protection from the contempt order.[66] *Blackmer* did not raise the issue of personal jurisdiction because Blackmer was merely a witness rather than a party to the court proceedings. The case instead illustrates the breadth of Congressional power to regulate the substantive conduct of its citizens living abroad. The courts have also given broad extraterritorial effect to American laws as applied to American nationals in cases involving substantive statutes such as the Lanham Act and Title VII of the Civil Rights Act of 1964.[67]

Federal courts do not assume, however, that congressional statutes apply to American nationals situated abroad merely because nationality is a potential basis for legislative jurisdiction. Unless there is a clear articulation of legislative intent for the statute to apply extraterritoriality, the presumption of territoriality applies even when an American national is involved. In *United States v. Mitchell*,[68] for example, the Court of Appeals for the Fifth Circuit reversed Mitchell's conviction for violating the Marine Mammal Protection Act of 1972.[69] Mitchell, an American national, had captured dolphins within Bahamian territorial waters. Although the court conceded that Congress could have prohibited Mitchell from taking dolphins from Bahamian waters, because there was no clear articulation of legislative intent to issue such a prohibition, they reversed Mitchell's conviction.[70]

c. Impact Territoriality and the Antitrust Laws

Sections 1 and 2 of the Sherman Act explicitly proscribe conspiracies in restraint of trade and monopolization of trade and commerce with "foreign nations."[71] There is little in the legislative history of the Act

---

64. *Id.* at 437.

65. *Id.* at 433, n.1.

66. *Id.* at 439-42.

67. *See, e.g.,* Steele v. Bulova Watch Co., 344 U.S. 280 (1956) (Lanham Act applied to United States citizen for activities in Mexico); Bryant v. International School Servs. Inc., 502 F. Supp. 472, 482, 483 (D.N.J. (1980)), *rev'd on other grounds,* 675 F.2d 562 (3d Cir. 1982) (Title VII applied to American company for activities in Iran).

68. 553 F.2d 996 (5th Cir. 1977).

69. 16 U.S.C. §§ 1361 *et seq.*

70. 553 F.2d at 1001, 1003-05.

71. 15 U.S.C. §§ 1, 2.

to guide a court in determining just how far Congress meant this regulation of extraterritorial activity to reach. The history of construction of the Act's extraterritorial provisions spans a wide range of approaches to the problem of subject matter jurisdiction over international transactions and provides interesting illustrations of how courts react to the institutional concerns implicated in adjudicating transnational controversies.

(i) The Age of Act Territorialism: *American Banana*

The Supreme Court's first confrontation with the foreign trade provisions of the Sherman Act resulted in a remarkably restrained interpretation of the extraterritorial reach of American antitrust law. In *American Banana Co.* v. *United Fruit Co.*[72] the American Banana Company alleged that the United Fruit Company had monopolized the banana trade between the United States and Central America. American Banana claimed that United Fruit had accomplished this goal by inducing the Costa Rican army to evict American from its plantation and by deliberately overbidding in purchasing bananas to eliminate competition in the buyer's market.[73] The trial court dismissed the complaint for failure to state a cause of action and the court of appeals affirmed.[74]

The Supreme Court, speaking through Justice Holmes, affirmed this judgment. Justice Holmes found it "surprising to hear it argued"[75] that the acts that served as the basis of the complaint, all of which took place outside of United States' boundaries, should be governed by United States law. While acknowledging that Congress could prescribe locally enforceable rules of law governing wholly extraterritorial acts "in cases immediately affecting national interests,"[76] Holmes voiced the common concern that an expansive interpretation of penal legislation would offend the comity of nations. For this reason, the Court would construe an ambiguous statute to confine its operation and effect "to the territorial limits over which the lawmaker has general and legitimate power."[77] "All legislation is *prima facie* territorial,"[78] Justice Holmes wrote, and universal terms such as "Every contract in restraint of trade" or "Every person who shall monopolize" were not sufficient to overcome the presumption. The acts in question were

---

72. 213 U.S. 347 (1909).
73. *Id.* at 354-55.
74. *Id.* at 353-55.
75. *Id.* at 355.
76. *Id.* at 356.
77. *Id.* at 357.
78. *Id.* citing Ex parte Bain, In re Sawers, 12 Ch. Div. 522, 528; State v. Carter, 27 N.J. (3 Dutcher) 499; People v. Merrill, 2 Parker Crim. Rep. 590, 596.

therefore to be governed by the law of Costa Rica and were not a matter for the United States' concern.[79]

Justice Holmes' requirement that an antitrust complaint include some local illegal act was consistent with the lex loci approach to the conflict of laws that characterized his day. It is significant, however, that he did not approach the problem in terms of the abstract notion of vested rights on which Beale was to ground lex loci.[80] Rather, principles of territoriality served as guides in interpreting the will of the legislature to which the judged owed obedience.[81]

(ii) The Decline of a Pure-Act Test and the Rise of the Effects Test

The pure-act territorialism of *American Banana* caused problems because it did not afford American markets protection from extraterritorial anticompetitive behavior that had real effects within the United States. These problems were exacerbated by this century's rapid growth in interdependence within the world economy. The equally rapid growth of American influence in the realm of world economics and politics led to an aggressive solution. Almost immediately after *American Banana* was decided, the Supreme Court began to limit its holding. In the years following *American Banana* the Court applied the Sherman Act's conspiracy provisions to cases involving a foreign conspiracy designed to divide up both American and foreign markets,[82] to a conspiracy to fortify an unlawful domestic monopoly,[83] and to conspiracies formed abroad that were put into operation locally.[84] Significantly, all of these cases were criminal actions brought by the United States, rather than civil actions by aggrieved competitors.[85] Thus, the move away from pure-act territorialism came in steps directly guided by the executive branch. Moreover, all of these cases had some territorial or personal nexus with the United States.[86]

It was not until *United States v. Alcoa*[87] that an American court was faced with the application of the Sherman Act to an extraterritorial

---

79. *Id.* at 357-59.

80. *See* ch. 7, sec. I.

81. 213 U.S. at 357.

82. United States v. American Tobacco Co., 221 U.S. 106 (1911).

83. United States v. Pacific & Arctic Ry. & Nav. Co., 228 U.S. 87 (1913).

84. United States v. Sisal Sales Corp., 274 U.S. 268 (1927).

85. *Compare* American Banana Co. v. United Fruit Co., 213 U.S. at 347 (action brought by an aggrieved competitor).

86. The cases involved both American companies (*see supra* notes 71-73) and either mixed foreign and domestic markets (*see supra* note 71) or relevant acts within the United States (*see supra* note 72).

87. 148 F.2d 416 (2d Cir. 1945). The case has a peculiar procedural history. It was brought before the Supreme Court, but more than half of the Justices disqualified themselves. The case was then certified to the Second Circuit for a final decision. Because of this unusual process, the decision is binding in all circuits.

conspiracy wholly between foreign parties. The case involved an alleged conspiracy between Aluminum Limited and European producers of aluminum. Aluminum Limited was a Canadian company. Aluminum Limited had been a subsidiary of Alcoa, an American corporation. However, at the time of the suit, Aluminum Limited was acting independently from Alcoa. The United States government accused Aluminum Limited of agreeing to production quotas which applied to that portion of its production that ordinarily found its way into American markets.[88]

Judge Learned Hand wrote the opinion for the Court. Like Justice Holmes, Judge Hand viewed the problem solely as one concerning the intent of Congress in passing the Act.[89] Indeed, he was even more explicit in his blind obedience to congressional will, writing that

> we are concerned only with whether Congress chose to attach liability to the conduct outside the United States of persons not in allegiance to it. That being so, the only question open is whether Congress intended to impose the liability, and whether our own Constitution permits it to do so: as a court of the United States, we cannot look beyond our own law.[90]

Judge Hand's interpretive tunnel vision thus precluded any analysis of international law as limiting congressional will.[91] Like Holmes, however, Hand believed that he should construe the "general terms" of the Sherman Act in the light of "limitations customarily observed by nations upon the exercise of their powers; limitations which generally correspond to those fixed by the 'conflict of laws.'"[92]

Not surprisingly, this conflict of laws analogy produced a far more extensive application of the Sherman Act in 1945 than it had in 1909. Judge Hand concluded that the Sherman Act reached foreign defendants and acts whenever those acts were intended to affect American markets and actually had some effect on those markets.[93] This standard embraces a pure-impact theory of jurisdiction. Applying this stan-

---

88. 148 F.2d 439-441. Aluminum Limited's European dealings was only one issue in a complicated case that the government brought to break up Alcoa's domestic aluminum monopoly. *See* J. ATWOOD & K. BREWSTER, ANTITRUST AND AMERICAN BUSINESS ABROAD 147 (2d ed. 1981) (hereinafter cited as ATWOOD & BREWSTER).

89. 148 F.2d at 443.

90. *Id.*

91. *But see* Pacific Seafarers, Inc. v. Pacific Far East Line, Inc., 404 F.2d 804, 814, & n.36 (D.C. Cir. 1968), *cert. denied,* 393 U.S. 1093 (1969) ("It may fairly be inferred, in the absence of clear showing to the contrary, that Congress did not intend an application [of the Sherman Act] that would violate principles of international law.").

92. 148 F.2d at 443.

93. *Id.* at 444-45. The Supreme Court first approved the Alcoa test in Steele v. Bulova Watch, 344 U.S. 280 (1952), a Lanham Act case.

dard to the facts of *Alcoa,* he concluded that Aluminum Limited had violated American law.[94] Thus, in *Alcoa,* American law was applied to the extraterritorial acts of a foreign corporation.

Commentators have observed that the test Judge Hand fashioned in *Alcoa* was far more expansive than was necessary to reach the conduct of Aluminum Limited.[95] It is worth inquiring into the conditions that led to the acceptance of pure-impact territoriality as a legitimate basis of Sherman Act jurisdiction over foreign transactions. Plainly, the times were a factor. The decision came at the end of the Second World War, when the United States' influence in world affairs was near its historic zenith. But institutional as well as situational conditions lead to the outcome. The case was brought by the United States government, rather than by a private party. It should therefore not be surprising that Judge Hand was willing to give an expansive reading to the Sherman Act. The fact that the action was brought by the executive indicates that American markets, in fact, probably had suffered harm. Moreover, when the executive brings the suit, the general concern over interference with the foreign policymaking function disappears. The executive, by bringing the suit in the first place, signals approval that the suit go forward. Thus, when the executive initiates a suit, refusal to adjudicate may interfere with the executive function more than the assertion of jurisdiction. These institutional considerations serve to legitimate the application of American law.

(iii) The Problems in *Alcoa*

The United States government, however, is not the only plaintiff that benefits from the *Alcoa* standard. Application of the standard does not depend on the United States bringing suit. Thus, the decision in *Alcoa* has made it far easier for private plaintiffs to bring suit in the United States solely on the basis of foreign activity. Ambiguities in both the *intended* and *actual* aspects of the effects requirement have contributed to this problem. Courts have not held that a plaintiff must show a specific and subjective intent to affect American markets in order to invoke the protection of the American antitrust laws.[96] Indeed, some have stated that this intent requirement can be met by the rule

---

94. *Id.* at 445.

95. *See, e.g.,* ATWOOD & BREWSTER, *supra* note 88, at 148-49.

96. Recently, in fact, some courts have held that general intent (which includes the idea of natural consequences) is all that need be shown. *See* Zenith Radio Corp. v. Matsushita Elec. Indus. Co., 494 F. Supp. 1161 (E.D. Pa. 1980); Fleischmann Distilling Corp. v. Distillers Co., 395 F. Supp. 221, 227 (S.D.N.Y. 1975).

that persons are presumed to intend *all* the natural consequences of their actions.[97] While it is unclear whether Hand meant to establish this broad notion of intent as the one relevant to the jurisdictional inquiry, the notion of intended effect loses much of its significance when it is argued that people (and, presumably, corporations) intend all the natural consequence of their actions. The intent requirement thus does very little to limit Alcoa's impact territorialism.

Similar problems plague the actual-effects requirement. In *Alcoa,* Judge Hand required that after the plaintiffs prove intent, the burden then shifts to the defendants to prove the absence of an actual effect on American markets.[98] This rule serves to infer actual effects from intent. Given the complexity and interrelatedness of the world economy, it seems that such a burden simply cannot be carried. Although not all courts have accepted Judge Hand's inference of actual effects from intent, most have allowed plaintiffs to prove actual effects from the nature of the illegal agreement or the economic power of the participants in the alleged conspiracy. In *United States v. General Electric,*[99] for example, the court inferred that a European conspiracy to restrain trade in incandescent products had substantial effects on American markets from the fact that General Electric, one of the conspirators, held the dominant position in the United States market. These difficulties in limiting the concepts of intended and actual effects have drawn the impact theory of jurisdiction into extreme controversy and the application of American antitrust law has come perilously close to becoming a theory of universal jurisdiction.

(iv) Tempering *Aloca: Timberlane* and *Mannington Mills*

Not surprisingly, this universal application of American antitrust law has angered foreign nations. Some nations have gone so far as to provide for the recapture of certain antitrust damages collected in American courts through the attachment of assets that the plaintiffs hold in that country.[100] Foreign countries have also shown official reluctance to assisting American courts in the processing of antitrust disputes.[101] Thus, the crisis reaches beyond the courtroom and into the oval rooms where executives conduct foreign policy.

---

97. *Id.*

98. 148 F.2d at 444.

99. 82 F. Supp. 753, 891 (D. N.J. 1949).

100. *See, e.g.,* Protection of Trading Interests Act, 1980 ch. 11, § 6. (Great Britain). Section 5 of this act also provides that treble damages awards are unregistered in British courts for the purpose of enforcement. Such provisions commonly are called "clawback" statutes.

101. *See, e.g.,* Protection of Trading Interests Act, 1980 ch. 11 § 2(1) (Great Britain). These provisions are sometimes called "blocking" statutes. For a general guide to

Some American courts have responded to this problem by considering factors other than the intended and actual effects of foreign activity on domestic markets in deciding whether American antitrust law should be applied to a case. In *Timberlane Lumber Co. v. Bank of America*,[102] the Ninth Circuit reversed a lower court's dismissal of an antitrust action based upon alleged anticompetitive behavior in Honduras. The lower court relied on *American Banana* in dismissing the actions. In remanding the case, Judge Choy ordered the trial judge to determine the existence of a direct and foreseeable anticompetitive effect on American markets. But he went further and required the trial court to consider several additional factors beyond those required by *Alcoa* before deciding actually to assert jurisdiction. These factors included: (1) the degree of conflict with foreign law or policy; (2) the nationality of the parties; (3) the locations and principal places of business of corporations; (4) the extent to which either nation involved can expect to see its judgment enforced; (5) the relative significance of the effects on United States commerce and that of foreign nations; (6) the explicitness of the intent to harm American commerce; and (7) the relative importance to the violations of foreign and domestic conduct.[103] Although Judge Choy wrote that principles of international law could not require an American court to abstain from jurisdiction, in cases where foreign interests outweighed American ones a *prudentially* based abstention policy should counsel a court from asserting jurisdiction. This serves to protect American interests and contributes to comity between nations.[104]

The Third Circuit in *Mannington Mills v. Congoleum Corp.*[105] gave a different list of factors it deemed to be relevant in deciding when a court should abstain from exercising its valid jurisdiction. The *Mannington* court listed, among others, the following factors: the possible effect of an exercise of jurisdiction on foreign relations; the possibility that the American court's judgment might require one of the parties to perform an act illegal under the laws of another country; the availability of foreign remedies; and the existence of treaties addressing the issue.[106]

---

foreign legislative reactions to United States antitrust laws, see A. LOWE, EXTRATERRITORIAL JURISDICTION 79-225 (1983). For a discussion of recent cases that have exacerbated the controversy with foreign governments, see Note, *Forum Non Conveniens and the Extraterritorial Application of United States Antitrust Law,* 94 YALE L.J. 1694 (1984).

102. 549 F.2d 597 (9th Cir. 1976).
103. *Id.* at 614.
104. *Id.* at 608, 610, 615.
105. 595 F.2d 1287 (3d Cir. 1979).
106. *Id.* at 1297-98.

Timberlane and *Mannington Mills* were both private suits under the antitrust laws. Although the *Restatement (Revised)* argues that private and criminal actions should be treated identically for jurisdictional purposes,[107] separation of powers concerns provide one basis for treating them differently. As discussed previously, actions that have the stamp of executive approval provide occasions for courts to expand the reach of the antitrust laws without exposing themselves to charges of interfering with the executive function in foreign policymaking. Similarly, actions that proceed without express approval of the executive give courts an opportunity to defuse some of the more explosive aspects of a doctrine that threatens the sovereignty of foreign nations.

These cases are apt illustrations of conflict of laws issues that are peculiar to international — as opposed to interstate — conflicts. As we said at the beginning of the chapter, institutional considerations are different in the international context. In both kinds of conflicts, courts look to the degree of conflict with nondomestic laws or policies. However, in international cases, this inquiry reflects a desire to avoid exercising jurisdiction in cases that are most likely to have discordant diplomatic implications. Within our constitutional structure, foreign policymaking is an executive function. This desire not to interfere with the executive function finds explicit expression in *Mannington Mills'* ruling that possible effects on foreign relations and the existence of relevant treaties with affected nations are factors relevant to the court's decision whether to assert jurisdiction. The degree of diplomatic tension accompanying an exercise of jurisdiction is likely to be highest when such an exercise might result in an order that could not be squared with another nation's law. The *Mannington Mills* court responded to this problem by ordering lower courts to consider the possibility that its judgment would require an act made illegal by another sovereign.

The other concerns that distinguish international from interstate conflicts cases — particularly the problems of judicial competence and scarce judicial resources — are also reflected in these cases. The *Timberlane* and *Mannington Mills* courts both listed the enforceability of judgments as a relevant concern in deciding whether to abstain from subject matter jurisdiction. Finally, the consideration of available foreign remedies and the pendency of litigation in other forums may reflect a desire to economize on scarce judicial resources; even when there is a prima facie case for jurisdiction, abstention may be wise when a transaction has only peripheral connections with the United States, and another country is willing to exercise some kind of control

---

107. RESTATEMENT (REVISED) *supra* note 43, at § 402 comment f.

over the anticompetitive behavior. The requirement that courts look to the existence of foreign remedies and proceedings also reflects a general desire to achieve comity and cooperation. Foreign nations are likely to be especially offended by American assertions of jurisdiction in cases where they have mechanisms for dealing with the problem and may in fact be addressing it.[108]

The abstention doctrine of *Timberlane* and *Mannington Mills* has met with a mixed reception. Several executive departments and academic commentators praise the approach for allowing courts to achieve a proper balance between the need to protect American courts from foreign anticompetitive behavior and the desire to avoid unnecessary disruptions to diplomatic relations and the international community.[109] Congress has indicated tolerance for the abstention model. Recently, Congress modified the Sherman Act to require that before the Act is applied extraterritorially, the effect on foreign commerce or trade must be direct, substantial and reasonably foreseeable. A House report accompanying the legislation acknowledged the balancing approach employed in *Timberlane* and stated that the legislation was meant neither to encourage nor discourage abstention analysis in cases where the jurisdictional threshold established by *Alcoa* is met.[110]

Abstention also has its critics. Some courts have refused to alter the pure-effects test of *Alcoa* without a clear legislative mandate.[111] Beyond the question of legislative approval, several analysts believe that the balancing implicit in the abstention doctrine is unsound in principle. The critics claim that the factors utilized in the abstention calculus threaten the legitimacy of the courts by forcing them to weigh competing political interests, a function for which they are ill-equipped, and by generally requiring them to engage in areas where judicially manageable standards are not available.[112] But many who have rejected abstention nevertheless have recognized the need to put some limit on open-ended application of the *Alcoa* test. Suggestions for

---

108. *See* ATWOOD & BREWSTER, *supra* note 88, at 162.

109. *See, e.g.,* Antitrust Division, United States Department of Justice, Antitrust Guide for International Operations 6-7 (1977); Ongman, *"Be No Longer a Chaos": Constructing a Normative Theory of the Sherman Act's Extraterritorial Scope,* 71 Nw. U.L. REV. 733 (1977).

110. H.R. Rep. No. 686, 97th Cong., 2d Sess. 13, reprinted in 1982 U.S. Code Cong. & Admin. News 2487-500. It is not yet clear what effect this amendment will have on the expansiveness of the *Alcoa* test.

111. *See* Laker Airways v. Sabena, Belgian World Airlines, 731 F.2d 909, 949-51 (D.C. Cir. 1984); *see also* In re Uranium Antitrust Litig., 617 F.2d 1248, 1255 (7th Cir. 1980); Grippando, *Declining to Exercise Extraterritorial Antitrust Jurisdiction on Grounds of International Comity: An Illegitimate Extension of the Judicial Abstention Doctrine,* 23 VA. J. INT'L L. 395 (1983).

112. *See, e.g.,* Note, *supra* note 101, at 1702-06; Grippando, *supra* note 111.

reform have included the establishment of international standards by treaty and the employment of forum non conveniens analysis to dismiss cases with only tenuous connections with the United States.[113]

Confrontations between American antitrust policy and foreign practices have produced the most panoramic expansions of American law. Thus, if one were to attempt to draw the entire picture of the modern judicial view of America's legislative jurisdiction abroad from its interpretation of the Sherman Act, this would yield a very distorted view. Courts paint with a narrower brush when interpreting most statutes. We next consider the extraterritorial application of statutes regulating securities as an example of the continued importance of act territoriality in interpreting modern regulatory acts.

4. Statutes Regulating Securities: The Continuing Importance of Act Territoriality

Any attempt at generalization about the extent to which federal courts give extraterritorial effects to federal securities law in terms of rules or standards would be fruitless and misleading. There are almost as many standards for determining the applicability of American securities laws to largely foreign transactions as there are courts that have addressed the problem. Furthermore, the enunciated standards may be broader than necessitated by the facts of the cases in which the courts actually assert jurisdiction. Thus, the courts often state that mere impact on domestic markets would suffice to apply American securities law to a foreign transaction. However, the courts actually have asserted jurisdiction in cases which either involved some conduct in the United States or which involved the application of the securities laws to American nationals. Thus, in practice, the courts have developed a series of jurisdictional tests that are a hybrid of impact territoriality and other bases of jurisdiction.

a. Commodities Exchange Act

It is arguable that subject matter jurisdiction should be available under the Commodities Exchange Act on either act or impact territoriality. But in practice, courts have applied the Act to cases where at least part of the activity giving rise to the complaint took place within United States territory. In *Psimenos v. E.F. Hutton & Co.,*[114] for example, the Second Circuit applied the act in a suit by a Greek citizen against a United States citizen based upon fraudulent procurement and management of his commodities trading account. The

---

113. *See, e.g.,* Note, *supra* note 101, at 1706-14.
114. 722 F.2d 1041, 1045 (2d Cir. 1983).

court grounded its assertion of jurisdiction on the fact that literature inducing the transaction and the futures contracts themselves emanated from within the United States.[115] These local events were sufficiently linked to the cause of action to justify application of the Act, even though the account that was the subject of the relevant transactions was located in Athens.[116] In *Tameri v. Bache & Co.*,[117] the Seventh Circuit applied the Act in a suit by Lebanese citizens against a Lebanese corporation. The Court indicated that an effect on American securities markets would suffice to legitimate the assertion of jurisdiction.[118] The court emphasized, however, that the fraudulent scheme depended in part on the transmission of commodity futures orders to the United States and the conduct of futures trading in United States markets.[119] Thus, while conceding the potential for an expansive reading of the act, courts have, in fact, relied on a form of act territoriality, the most traditional basis for legislative jurisdiction.

The limits of the Commodity Exchange Act's extraterritorial reach were announced in *Commodity Futures Trading Commission v. Nahas*.[120] In that case, the Commodity Futures Trading Commission sought a contempt order against a Brazilian citizen for failing to respond to a subpoena served on him in Brazil. The district court granted the order; but the court of appeals reversed.[121] The case is a vivid example of how prudent statutory construction can temper the extraterritorial reach of federal law. The court did not even discuss possible constitutional limits on the extraterritorial reach of the Act, and flatly declared that "federal courts must give effect to a valid, unambiguous congressional mandate, even if such effect would . . . violate international law."[122] Nevertheless, the various provisions of the Act were presumed to have effect only within United States territory unless there appeared a clear congressional intent to the contrary.[123]

b. Securities and Exchange Act

By now it should not be surprising that the reach of the Securities and Exchange Act is viewed as a question of congressional intent. The pattern of doctrinal development in the Securities and Exchange Act

---

115. *Id.* at 1046.
116. *Id.* at 1043.
117. 730 F.2d 1103 (7th Cir. 1984).
118. *Id.* at 1107.
119. *Id.* at 1108.
120. 738 F.2d 487 (D.C. Cir. 1984).
121. *Id.* at 489.
122. *Id.* at 495.
123. *Id.*

replicates that of the Commodity Exchange Act. There is, however, an interesting variation in the case of the Securities and Exchange Act. At least one court has viewed the question as one of whether Congress desired to expend scarce judicial resources in the adjudication of a foreign controversy.[124] In theory, courts have recognized both act and impact theories as legitimate bases for asserting subject matter jurisdiction over largely foreign transactions.[125] Commentators have criticized the courts for extending the reach of the Act by adopting a pure-effects test.[126]

As with the commodities acts, however, the courts' extraterritorial rhetoric is far more expansive than its practice. Those cases which have articulated an effects test for extraterritorial application of the Securities and Exchange Act have in fact involved either American nationals as defendants or transactions in which some part of the controverted conduct occurred within United States territory.[127]

5. Assessing Extraterritoriality

There is no shortage of academics and other observers who are willing to find a crisis in the aggressive exportation of American law.[128] Courts are viewed as willing to apply federal law at the drop of a plaintiff's hat. Fundamental methodological reform, by way of legislation, treaty, or judicial restraint is viewed as necessary and urgent.

Although there may be some cause for concern, much of the criticism and alarm seems exaggerated. We have seen, in effect, two basic approaches to the analysis of federal legislative jurisdiction abroad. In the antitrust area, some courts have taken impact territoriality to

---

124. Bersch v. Drexel Firestone, Inc., 519 F.2d 974, 985 (2d Cir. 1975).

125. *See, e.g.,* Continental Grain (Australia) Pty., Ltd. v. Pacific Oilseeds, Inc., 592 F.2d 409, 417 (8th Cir. 1979); Schoenbaum Oilseeds v. Firstbrook, 405 F.2d 200, 206-09 (2d Cir.), *rev'd in part on other grounds en banc,* 405 F.2d 215, *cert. denied,* 395 U.S. 906 (1969).

126. *See* Note, *American Adjudication of Transnational Securities Fraud,* 89 HARV. L. REV. 553, 563-568 (1976); *see also* Note, *Predictability and Comity: Toward Common Principles of Extraterritorial Jurisdiction,* 98 HARV. L. REV. 1310, 1314-16 (1985).

127. *See* Grunethal GmbH v. Hotz, 712 F.2d 421, 422 (9th Cir. 1983) (fraudulent conduct within United States); Continental Grain v. Pacific Oilseeds, 592 F.2d at 411, 415 (fraudulent use of United States mails); Des Brisay v. Goldfield Corp., 549 F.2d 133, 136 (9th Cir. 1977) (defendant American corporation); IIT v. Vencap, Ltd., 519 F.2d 1001, 1015-1018 (use of New York office as base of defendants' allegedly fraudulent conduct); Bersch v. Drexel Firestone, 519 F.2d at 990-93 (fraudulent stock sale in United States territory); Leasco v. Maxwell, 468 F.2d at 1330-35 (fraudulent conduct within United States); Roth v. Fund of Funds Ltd., 405 F.2d 421, 422 (2d Cir. 1969) (short-swing profit on stock purchased in United States using United States brokers); Schoenbaum v. Firstbrook, 405 F.2d at 206-07 (stock purchased on American Exchange).

128. *See, e.g.,* Note, *supra* note 86.

extremes. Cases involving no relevant local conduct often go forward. It is in these cases that courts have found it most necessary to struggle with a limiting principle such as that found in the abstention doctrine. In the securities area, on the other hand, we see that impact territoriality basis of jurisdiction is tempered by act territoriality and nationality jurisdiction. These hybrid bases of legislative jurisdiction are inherently more limited than the pure-effects test expressed in *Alcoa* and applied to antitrust cases. These hybrid tests have not caused sufficiently drastic results to require the development of an external constraint such as abstention.

It is interesting that the area in which expansive interpretations have prevailed is the antitrust area. Antitrust violations are perceived to affect economic markets. Therefore, courts may be particularly wary of a foreign antitrust conspiracy's potential effect on the American market since that effect has a measure of permanence. This view of an antitrust violation's affect on the economic market may explain the choice of an expansive-effects test tempered by case-by-case considerations of abstention. Of course, there may be cases of securities fraud that have as much or more effect on the securities markets as some antitrust violations have on the economic market for goods. Typically, however, securities cases allege injury to a limited group of plaintiffs over a finite period of time. The jurisdictional doctrines developed under each statute, for this reason, seem likely responses to the different characteristics of the respective consequence of violation.

III. Judgments: The Role of Comity

Policy issues similar to those raised by the extraterritorial application of American law also affect the decisions of American courts to enforce foreign judgments. The full faith and credit clause does not apply to judgments rendered by foreign courts.[129] Thus, American courts generally apply a flexible comity analysis when deciding whether to enforce foreign judgments of a foreign court.[130] One significant question in this area is the role that reciprocity should play in this analysis whether to enforce foreign judgments. Should an American court enforce the judicial judgments of a foreign nation only when that country would enforce an analogous judgment by an American court?

---

129. *See* Allstate Ins. Co. v. Hague, 449 U.S. at 321 n.4 (Stevens J., concurring).

130. *See, e.g.,* Sangiovanni Hernandez v. Dominica De Avacion, 556 F.2d 611, 614-15 (1st Cir. 1977); Somportex Ltd. v. Philadelphia Chewing Gum Corp., 453 F.2d 435, 440-41 (3d Cir. 1972); Montemurro v. Immigration & Naturalization Serv., 409 F.2d 832, 833 (9th Cir. 1969).

The Supreme Court answered this question affirmatively in the case of *Hilton v. Guyot*.[131] But recent Supreme Court cases, though not formally overruling the reciprocity requirement, have expressed some reservations about its continuing vitality and have refused to extend the principle.[132] Lower courts have gone further than the Supreme Court and routinely enforce foreign judgments without a finding of reciprocity.[133]

Reasons for abandoning a strict reciprocity requirement are not hard to find. One argument against a reciprocity requirement turns on the unfairness of making litigants suffer for the policies of the country in which the judgment was obtained. Although there is some attraction to this argument, any system involving comity will lead to some unfairness to particular litigants, since it focuses not on fairness to litigants but on relations with other states. Given that focus, the litigants will always be innocent bystanders. An additional theoretical argument against reciprocity, however, might be that if such a requirement were adopted by all the sovereigns on an international system, no judgment would ever be enforceable in a foreign court. A court would not enforce a foreign court's judgment unless that court had *already* enforced a similar judgment. The system might produce a kind of judgment paralysis, since no court would be willing to go first.

It is possible that a reciprocity requirement could escape this problem by assuming that a foreign court would reciprocate in the absence of clear evidence that it would not. However, this would not solve all of the problems associated with a reciprocity requirement. For example, two judicial systems that had not been honoring each other's judgments could not change their policy and begin to cooperate unless one of them were willing to invite such a change by beginning to honor the other court's judgments. Such a practice would not be consistent with a reciprocity requirement, even as tempered by a presumption of reciprocity. A flexible system of comity, on the other hand, allows for the development of mutual cooperation among courts of various countries in giving effect to their respective judgments.

International law has both important similarities with and important differences from interstate choice of law. The similarities should

---

131. 159 U.S. 113, 226-28 (1895).

132. *See* Banco Nacional de Cuba v. Sabbatino, 376 U.S. 398, 411-12.

133. *See, e.g.,* Tahan v. Hodgson, 662 F.2d 862, 867-88 (D.C. Cir. 1981) (enforcing foreign judgment without finding of reciprocity and stating that, "[i]t is unlikely that reciprocity is any longer a federally mandated requirement for enforcement of foreign judgments"); Bank of Montreal v. Kough, 612 F.2d 467, 471-72 (9th Cir. 1980) (no reciprocity under Uniform Enforcement of Money Judgments Act because such a requirement is not explicitly stated).

not be surprising, given the common underlying analytical structures.[134] The differences relate primarily to the overriding importance of politics, and executive branch diplomacy in foreign relations. There being no "legal" method for settling international disputes, given the absence of any overarching judicial authority, issues of international comity are resolved primarily through political give and take. What is perhaps surprising is that the outcome of these political processes is as influenced by principle as it appears to be.

---

134. *See generally* Brilmayer, *supra* note 39.

PART III

SOME SPECIAL PROBLEMS AT THE INTERSECTION OF ADJUDICATIVE AND LEGISLATIVE JURISDICTION

To this point we have more or less divorced questions of legislative from questions of adjudicative jurisdiction. Causes of action have been treated as "transitory" — that is, although created by one sovereign they might be enforced by another. There are special substantive areas, however, in which this is not true; that is, in which a court will only enforce its own state's laws. We have already noted in the discussion of international law that federal courts may dismiss claims based on foreign country law because of lack of subject matter jurisdiction. More dependent on specific underlying substantive policies, however, are the examples described below. The next three chapters deal with criminal jurisdiction, jurisdiction over domestic relations disputes, and jurisdiction to tax.

Chapter 11
CRIMINAL JURISDICTION

Criminal jurisdiction, unlike its civil counterpart, is based on an offense against the state itself, rather than on a dispute arising between two or more parties to a particular transaction. In criminal cases the state claims that the defendant has injured the state as well as any victim of the crime, and that the state has a right to seek redress for its injury. Because no individual state can claim to represent the rights of other states, punishment of criminal offenses must be instituted by the sovereign against which the offense was committed. This fundamental difference in state interests between civil and criminal jurisdiction has produced several differences between the jurisdictional rules used in civil cases and those used in a criminal context. This chapter first sets out the major distinctions between civil and criminal jurisdictional rules. It then analyzes them in greater depth, showing how the potential conflict between states, or between the federal government and the states, justifies the different treatment.

Criminal jurisdiction is distinctive in three respects: the scope of legislative jurisdiction, the scope of adjudicative jurisdiction, and the peculiar interaction between legislative and adjudicative jurisdiction. First, legislative jurisdiction is distinctive in criminal cases because it continues to be largely dominated by territorial notions of jurisdiction. As we have seen, in civil cases territorialism has been modified by analysis of state interests, so that a state may apply its civil law to events in which the state has an interest independent of whether the events occurred within state borders. Yet even in states rejecting the *First Restatement* for civil cases, the traditional territorialist view is virtually universal in criminal cases. Second, adjudicative jurisdiction in the criminal context also continues to be dominated by territorialist notions even more rigid than those applied in criminal choice of law. A forum court has personal jurisdiction over a criminal defendant if and only if the defendant is physically present within the state. In civil cases, by contrast, personal jurisdiction does not depend on physical presence, but has been replaced by minimum contacts analysis. Third, criminal law conflates the two inquiries of legislative and adjudicative jurisdiction into one. In criminal cases, the state is both a party — granted standing to prosecute by statute — and the adjudicatory forum — given jurisdiction to decide criminal cases brought by the state against alleged criminals. Because one state cannot validly involve the other's interest as a party in redressing an injury, states do not enforce one another's criminal laws. Once it is determined that the criminal law of another state will be applied, the forum court dismisses the case. Dismissal is not, of course, automatic in civil cases.

Once the state court has jurisdiction over a criminal defendant, furthermore, its power to conduct the prosecution without interference is given extraordinary deference. For example, federal courts are reluctant to intervene in state criminal prosecutions. Federal courts have thus declined to entertain constitutional challenges to state criminal statutes when a state proceeding is pending.[1] Again, this is contrary to the general rule that federal and state courts may have concurrent jurisdiction. Further, the federal system is likewise thought to have an unusually strong interest in exclusive control over criminal prosecutions brought under federal law. This policy underlies the grant of exclusive jurisdiction over federal criminal actions to federal courts,[2] despite the fact that in civil matters federal jurisdiction is typically vested concurrently with state jurisdiction.

These differences between criminal jurisdiction and civil jurisdiction are firmly established, although they potentially produce odd disparities between cases involving similar sorts of offenses. Fraud, for example, could give rise to either civil or criminal litigation. Assume, for instance, that Adams, a resident of State A, defrauds Baxter in State B. Baxter is a resident of State B. If the wrong is deemed civil, Baxter may sue Adams in State A, since State A has general personal jurisdiction over Adams. State A may apply either State B's law or its own, depending on its choice-of-law rules and the relevant constitutional limitations. Alternatively, Baxter could sue Adams in State B, since State B would have specific personal jurisdiction over Adams. State B may apply either State A's law or its own.

In a criminal action arising out of the same fraudulent transaction, the result would be different. The traditional view is that Adams may be sued only in State B, and then only if State B can obtain the physical presence of Adams within its borders, perhaps by requesting interstate rendition of Adams. State B will apply only its own law. State A may not constitutionally prosecute Adams under its own laws for a crime committed entirely out-of-state. And in the event that State A determines that its own law does not apply, the case will be dismissed rather than adjudicated under the law of State B in a State A forum. Similarly, in the federal/state system, each court refrains from involvement in the enforcement of the criminal laws of the other.

While apparently peculiar, this pattern makes more sense than might at first appear. We start with the distinctive territorial character of criminal choice of law rules.

---

1. Younger v. Harris, 401 U.S. 37 (1971) (federal courts will not enjoin ongoing state criminal proceedings, except under extraordinary circumstances where danger to constitutional rights is great and immediate). See also the discussion of federal abstention, *supra* ch. 4, sec. IIB.

2. 18 U.S.C. § 3231.

I. *Legislative Jurisdiction*

The first distinction between civil and criminal jurisdiction concerns the continuing importance of territorialist reasoning in determining the interstate scope of legislation. Traditionally, the common law limited the legislative criminal jurisdiction of the states to their territorial boundaries.[3] The common law thus required that the "gist" or "gravamen" of the offense occur within the territorial boundaries of the forum state.[4] This requirement resembles the *First Restatement*'s last-act doctrine for torts, in its focus on the location of a single element in the transaction as uniquely relevant to the choice-of-law problem. Further, the development of particularized rules to deal with specific crimes parallels the *First Restatement*'s specified rules for defamation, poisoning, and other sorts of tort claims. Traditionally, jurisdiction to prosecute a murder belonged to the forum where the act took effect, as opposed to the state where the criminal conduct began, or the victim expired.[5] Thus if a murderer stood just over the border of State A, and fired his gun into State B, where the victim was struck by the bullet, State B would be the only state with jurisdiction to prosecute, even if the victim eventually staggered into State A to die. Bigamy, under a similar rule, was punishable in the state where the marriage was celebrated, rather than in the state of marital domicile.[6] While there were departures from such rules,[7] no one seemed to doubt that the general enterprise of formulating such rules was sound.

---

3. Discussions of the history of legislative criminal jurisdiction include George, *Extraterritorial Application of Penal Legislation*, 64 MICH. L. REV. 609, 621-23 (1966); Levitt, *Jurisdiction over Crimes*, 16 J. CRIM. L. & CRIMINOLOGY 316, 331-32 (1925); Perkins, *The Territorial Principle in Criminal Law*, 22 HASTINGS L.J. 1155, 1163 (1971); Rothenberg, *Extraterritorial Legislative Jurisdiction and the State Criminal Law*, 38 TEX. L. REV. 763, 773 (1960); Comment, *Jurisdiction Over Interstate Felony Murder*, 50 U. CHI. L. REV. 1431, 1433-36 (1983). *See also* Corr, *Criminal Procedure and the Conflict of Laws*, 73 GEORGETOWN L.J. 1217 (1985).

4. Levitt, *supra* note 3, at 337-38; Comment, *supra* note 3, at 1434.

5. Comment, *supra* note 3, at 1434 n.22; *see also* W. LAFAVE & A. SCOTT, CRIMINAL LAW 118 (1972) (hereinafter cited as LAFAVE & SCOTT).

6. Comment, *supra* note 3, at 1434 n.22.

7. For example, inchoate crimes, such as attempt and conspiracy, are particularly difficult to locate geographically. Some jurisdictions hold that a criminal attempt may be prosecuted wherever a substantial step was taken, even though the actual crime was completed in another state. *See, e.g.,* Commonwealth v. Neubauer, 142 Pa. Super. 528, 16 A.2d 450 (1940) (defendant could be prosecuted in Pennsylvania for attempted extortion, even though extorted payment was made in Ohio). The majority of jurisdictions, however, hold that an attempt must be prosecuted where the completed crime would have taken place. *See, e.g.,* State v. Snow, 84 A. 1063 (N.J. 1912) (attempted voter fraud must be punished where voter registration would have taken place); *see generally* LAFAVE & SCOTT, *supra* note 5, at 120: "[P]erhaps the most sensible view is that the attempt has the same situs as the completed offense would have had if the defendant were successful."

However, as time passed and travel and communications between states improved, interstate crimes became more frequent and more complicated, and courts developed escape devices to mitigate the rigors of these inflexible rules. First, to ensure that at least one forum had jurisdiction, legal fictions gradually relaxed the common-law rules. For example, the notion of constructive presence was developed to confer jurisdiction over conspiracy resulting in a death in state even though the defendant had never set foot in the state.[8] The Supreme Court upheld jurisdiction based on constructive presence against constitutional challenge in *Hyde v. United States,* stating that if a crime is "consummated [within a given jurisdiction,] it may be punished by an exercise of jurisdiction; that is, a person committing it may be brought to trial and condemnation."[9]

Other fictions include the "new offense" doctrine in larceny cases (a new theft occurs as the defendant crosses the state's border),[10] and the "continuing offense" rule, which expands the period of time in which a crime is supposedly committed. Typically applied when a single element of the crime occurs in the forum state after commission of all the other elements elsewhere, the continuing offense rule gives the forum state jurisdiction if a murder victim dies there, or libelous material is published there.[11] It was also possible to reinterpret an offense as one of omission rather than commission. One commits a crime when one fails or omits to conform actions to the law, such as failure to return property,[12] or to pay child support.[13] These omissions might then constitute a basis for jurisdiction in the state where the omission occurred.

Several state legislatures have abolished these common-law rules by enacting statutes that confer jurisdiction over interstate crimes. These

---

8. *See also* Comment, *supra* note 3, at 1435 n.25 citing Commonwealth v. Thomas, 189 A.2d 255, 258-59 (Pa. 1963); Simpson v. State, 17 S.E. 984, 985 (Ga. 1893); Johns v. State, 19 Ind. 421, 428-29 (1862); State v. Wyckoff, 31 N.J.L. 65, 68 (Sup. Ct. 1864).

9. 225 U.S. 347, 362-63 (1912).

10. Comment, *supra* note 3, at 1435 n.26 citing State v. Underwood, 49 Me. 181, 182-83 (1858); Worthington v. State, 58 Md. 403, 409-10 (1882). *See also* LaFave & Scott, *supra* note 5, at 119-20.

11. Comment, *supra* note 3, at 1435-36 & n.27, citing Newlon v. Bennett, 112 N.W.2d 884 (Iowa), *cert. denied,* 369 U.S. 658 (1962); Commonwealth v. Macloon, 101 Mass. 1 (1869), *overruled,* Commonwealth v. Lewis, 409 N.E.2d 771 (Mass.), *cert. denied sub nom.* Phillips v. Massachusetts, 450 U.S. 929 (1981); Commonwealth v. Blanding, 20 Mass. 304 (1825).

12. State v. Scofield, 438 P.2d 776 (Ariz. 1968) (embezzlement prosecution for failure to return rental car within ten days after expiration of rental agreement is punishable in state where car was rented, even though defendant left state before agreement expired).

13. Poindexter v. State, 137 Tenn. 386, 390, 193 S.W. 126, 129 (1917) (because purpose of child support statute is to punish the father, venue is proper in county where father resides).

statutes typically grant jurisdiction over crimes committed "in whole or in part"[14] within the state. There has been much debate over how much of the crime must be committed within the state to justify application of its law to the entire crime. Many states, in interpreting the legislative grant of jurisdiction over interstate crimes, have followed Justice Cardozo's opinion for the New York Court of Appeals in *People v. Werblow:*[15]

> We think a crime is not committed either wholly or partly in this state, unless the act within this state is so related to the crime that if nothing more had followed, it would amount to an attempt.[16]

According to this formulation, mere preparation would not be sufficient to justify applying the state's criminal law. Although Cardozo did not explain why attempt should be the threshold, it seems clear that the law of attempt provides an adequate basis for invocation of criminal legislative jurisdiction.

A second statutory development is known as impact territoriality. The basic territorial thrust of the analysis remained unchanged, but the focus was not on where events took place but on where their consequences were felt. As Justice Holmes stated in *Strassheim v. Daily,*

> Acts done outside a jurisdiction, but intended to produce and producing detrimental effects within it, justify a State in punishing the cause of the harm as if [the actor] had been present at the effect. . . .[17]

Of course, some common-law rules had also used location of the harmful consequences as the relevant test.[18] Impact territoriality statutes, however, carried this concept a step further in holding that detrimental consequences within the jurisdiction might function as an alternative independent basis for jurisdiction even when the common-law rule focused on a different contact. Particularly when combined with Cardozo's attempt test, statutory modifications of traditional jurisdictional rules vastly expanded state jurisdiction over crimes with multistate elements.

---

14. *See, e.g.,* Cal. Penal Code § 27 (West Supp. 1986).

15. 241 N.Y. 55, 148 N.E. 786 (1925).

16. 241 N.Y. at 61, 148 N.E. at 789; *see, e.g.,* People v. Buffum, 40 Cal. 2d 709, 712, 256 P.2d 317, 320 (1953) (following *Werblow* and other cases that have held that states may validly prosecute multistate crimes if acts done within state are sufficient to amount to crime of attempt). Rothenberg, *supra* note 3, at 776-80 offers a careful analysis of both *Werblow* and *Buffum.*

17. 221 U.S. 280, 285 (1911).

18. *See,* Levitt, *supra* note 3, at 333: "[S]ome courts have decided that the death of the victim is the gist of the offense [of murder]. . . . It has been held that the [crime of abortion] is committed in the place where the instruments or drugs which are to produce the abortion are used; and also that the abortion occurs where the fetus is discharged." (citations omitted).

These strategies for enlarging the forum's legislative jurisdiction resemble the devices used to enlarge legislative jurisdiction in the civil context, such as long-arm statutes.[19] It is striking, however, that in criminal law territorialist thinking has remained a powerful force, while the civil law has largely abandoned territoriality by adopting the "modern" approaches to choice of law. In particular, the domiciliary focus that pervades modern choice of law in civil cases has had little impact on criminal jurisdiction. Although in certain criminal cases involving constitutional claims, the Supreme Court has recognized the relevance of domiciliary (as opposed to territorial) connecting factors, the uses of domiciliary contacts in criminal cases remain severely circumscribed.

The case that best exemplifies the limited reliance on domiciliary factors in the criminal context is *Skiriotes v. Florida*.[20] In that case, the Supreme Court explicitly authorized the extraterritorial application of state criminal law to residents of the state, at least when there is no conflict with another sovereign's criminal law. The Court upheld Florida's conviction of one of its residents for violating Florida's criminal statute prohibiting certain forms of sponge harvesting, even though the defendant took the sponges from waters outside the territory of Florida and the United States.

> If the United States may control the conduct of its citizens upon the high seas we see no reasons why the State of Florida may not likewise govern the conduct of its citizens upon the high seas with respect to matters in which the State has a legitimate interest and where there is no conflict with acts of Congress.[21]

Skiriotes and comparable cases[22] have led one observer to conclude that criminal jurisdiction extends to (1) the territorial boundaries of the state, (2) the protection of identifiable interests with some nexus to the state, and (3) the occurrence of activities outside the state when performed by state residents.[23]

It is not clear, however, whether the cases should be read so broadly. In particular, it is uncertain whether each of these bases is sufficient when standing alone. In *Skiriotes,* for example, the state arguably had an interest in protecting the local sponge fishing industry, in addition to regulating the activities of a local domiciliary. Furthermore, the

---

19. For a discussion of long-arm statutes, see ch. 1.

20. 313 U.S. 69 (1941).

21. *Id.* at 77.

22. *See* George, *supra* note 3, at 633-35 (discussing cases upholding interstate compacts that provide concurrent jurisdiction in more than one state over large bodies of water).

23. *Id.* at 634-35.

defendant's actions did not take place within another state, which might have raised a claim that the prosecution interfered with the other state's interests. Finally, a more recent case, *Bigelow v. Virginia*,[24] casts some doubt on a state's authority to regulate the activities of residents while in other states.

Bigelow dealt with the conviction of a Virginia newspaper editor for publishing an advertisement for a New York abortion referral service. The advertisement in the Virginia newspaper stated that abortions were legal in New York and that there was no residency requirement, and gave an address and telephone number for obtaining information about placements in New York hospitals. During the pendency of the litigation, *Roe v. Wade* was decided, holding that women in the first trimester of pregnancy have a constitutional right to abortion.[25] Although the Court in *Bigelow* apparently assumed that state regulation of commercial health care advertising would be valid,[26] it held the Virginia statute invalid as applied to multistate cases:

> [T]he placement services advertised in appellant's newspaper were legally provided in New York at that time. The Virginia Legislature would not have regulated the advertiser's activity in New York, and obviously could not have proscribed the activity in that State. . . . Neither could Virginia prevent its residents from traveling to New York to obtain those services or . . . prosecute them for going there. . . .
> A State does not acquire power or supervision over the internal affairs of another State merely because the welfare and health of its own citizens may be affected when they travel to that State.[27]

The dissent would have adopted a more explicit analysis of the state's interests in regulating its citizens:

> Virginia's interest in this statute lies in preventing commercial exploitation of the health needs of its citizens. So long as the statute bans commercial advertising by publications within the State, the extraterritorial location at which the services are actually provided does not diminish that interest.[28]

The dissent also relied upon Justice Holmes' language in *Strassheim,* quoted earlier, concerning the state's interest in regulating activities that have an impact within the state.[29]

---

24. 421 U.S. 809 (1975).

25. 410 U.S. 113 (1973).

26. *Bigelow,* 421 U.S. at 824 n.9 ("We, of course, have no occasion to comment here on whatever constitutional issues, if any, may be raised with respect to these statutes.").

27. *Id.* at 822-24.

28. *Id.* at 836 (Rehnquist, J., dissenting).

29. *Id.* at 834-35 n.2 (Rehnquist, J., dissenting).

There are several ways to reconcile *Bigelow* with *Skiriotes*. One would be the simple fact that *Bigelow* involved conduct in another state, while *Skiriotes* involved conduct on the open seas. As just noted, *Bigelow* for this reason raises problems of interference with other sovereigns which *Skiriotes* does not pose. Another possibility lies in the fact that *Skiriotes* did not condone regulation of out-of-staters. The *Bigelow* dictum may simply stand for the proposition that commercial health care providers in other states are not subject to regulation by Virginia. This does not speak to the issue of Virginia's right to regulate the conduct of its own citizens. While the *Bigelow* Court did note that Virginia might not prohibit Virginians from travelling to New York and there obtaining abortions, this may be more a function of the right to travel and to obtain an abortion than of the limits on extraterritorial assertion of state power. At any rate, the casual and brief nature of the *Bigelow* treatment of the issue necessarily leaves it open to differences of opinion.

Whether *Skiriotes, Bigelow,* or both are aberrations, it is clear that neither case fully embodies the modern interest analysis used in civil cases. While *Skiriotes* uses domiciliary connecting factors, it does so with an eye to justifying the application of a law that burdens local domiciliaries. It does not impose local law on an individual not domiciled within the state in order to benefit a local domiciliary. The dissent in *Bigelow* comes closer to adopting interest analysis, arguing that a state has a right to protect the welfare of local citizens. Yet even the dissent notes the relevance of certain territorial factors, such as the deliberate placement of an advertisement in the local newspapers.[30]

At least one lower court opinion has rejected the idea that mere residence of the injured party would give rise to a right to apply local criminal law, even in a setting where the alternative forum is another country and not another state.[31] The conclusion seems inescapable that, whatever inroads interest analysis has made in civil cases, the analysis in criminal cases is still a modified form of territorialism.

---

30. *Id.* at 836 (Rehnquist, J., dissenting): "So long as the statute bans commercial advertising by publications within the State, the extraterritorial location at which the services are actually provided does not diminish [the state's] interest."

31. United States v. Columba-Colella, 604 F.2d 356 (5th Cir. 1979) (United States courts do not have jurisdiction to prosecute Mexican defendant who received goods in Mexico that had been stolen in Texas). *See also* ch. 10, sec. IIB2, note 47.

II. Adjudicative Jurisdiction

A state court may assert personal jurisdiction over a criminal defendant if and only if the defendant is physically present in the state at the time of trial.[32] If the defendant is not physically present, the forum state may request interstate extradition[33] from the executive of the asylum state,[34] by alleging that the defendant committed a crime in the demanding state. Furthermore, physical presence is an adequate basis for jurisdiction even when that presence is merely transient; indeed, jurisdiction has been upheld even when the physical presence is the result of physical coercion such as kidnapping.[35] That mere presence is a necessary and sufficient condition for jurisdiction suggests that the power theory of personal jurisdiction, like the jurisdiction upheld in the early civil case, *Pennoyer v. Neff*,[36] still applies in criminal proceedings. If a state can find the defendant within its borders, *Pennoyer* holds, it has the power to adjudicate any case against him.

The power theory of personal jurisdiction has been replaced in civil jurisdiction by a minimum contacts standard, based on notions of "fair play and substantial justice."[37] The Supreme Court has stated that this minimum contacts test should be applied to all types of civil jurisdiction, regardless of historically established conventions to the contrary.[38] Despite the sweeping application of minimum contacts in civil cases, the minimum contacts analysis is not required in criminal jurisdiction.[39]

---

32. E. STIMSON, CONFLICT OF CRIMINAL LAWS 3, 24-25 (1936).
33. U.S. CONST. art. IV, § 2, cl. 2 provides:

> A person charged in any State with Treason, Felony, or other Crime, who shall flee from Justice, and be found in another State, shall on Demand of the executive Authority of the State from which he fled, be delivered up, to be removed to the State having Jurisdiction of the Crime.

See also Murphy, *Revising Domestic Extradition Law,* 131 U. PA. L. REV. 1063 (1983).
34. The asylum state is the state where the defendant is found.
35. Frisbie v. Collins, 342 U.S. 519 (1952) (forcible abduction of criminal defendant from one state to another to secure physical presence does not undermine criminal jurisdiction); Pettibone v. Nichols, 203 U.S. 192 (1906) (same); Mahon v. Justice, 127 U.S. 700 (1888) (criminal defendant has no constitutional or statutory right to be returned to state from which he was abducted); Ker v. Illinois, 119 U.S. 436 (1886) (same).
36. 95 U.S. 714 (1877).
37. International Shoe Co. v. Washington, 326 U.S. 310, 320 (1945).
38. Shaffer v. Heitner, 433 U.S. 186, 212 (1977).
39. Howells v. McKibben, 281 N.W.2d 154, 158 n.8 (Minn. 1979) (minimum contacts analysis does not apply in criminal cases) (citing State v. McCormick, 273 N.W.2d 624, 628 (Minn. 1978)). Our research has not revealed any criminal case applying minimum contacts analysis.

It is easy enough to see why presence might be a *necessary* condition for criminal jurisdiction. In civil cases, a default judgment may be rendered if a defendant fails to make an appearance. Default judgments would be highly suspect in criminal cases, however, given that the sixth amendment right to confrontation guarantees the defendant's right to be present and to participate at all stages of trial absent the defendant's abusive misconduct.[40] When the defendant cannot be brought before the court through voluntary appearance, normal processes of arrest, or interstate rendition, the trial ought not to proceed until the defendant's presence can be secured.

Although mere presence logically may furnish the necessary condition for jurisdiction, it is not clear that it should also be considered a sufficient condition. For example, in the civil context it is uncertain whether mere presence remains an adequate basis for jurisdiction after *Shaffer v. Heitner.*[41] Further, states typically decline to exercise civil jurisdiction over defendants brought into the state through trickery or force.[42] As noted above, the same is not true for criminal jurisdiction. Moreover, even if a minimum contacts analysis could be satisfied by mere presence, this fact cannot account for the lack of judicial interest in whether minimum contacts exist in a given case, or for the persistent belief that the minimum contacts standard is simply not pertinent in the criminal context.[43] The fourteenth amendment applies to crimi-

---

40. *See* Illinois v. Allen, 397 U.S. 337, 342-43 (1970) (defendant's obstreperous and contumacious conduct justifies removal from trial proceedings); Shields v. United States, 273 U.S. 583, 588-89 (1927) (defendant in criminal case generally has right to be present from time jury is impaneled until verdict); Lewis v. United States, 146 U.S. 370, 372 (1892) ("A leading principle that pervades the entire law of criminal procedure is that, after indictment found, nothing shall be done in the absence of the prisoner."); Hopt v. Utah, 110 U.S. 574, 579 (1884) ("[I]t was not within the power of the accused or his counsel to dispense with the statutory requirement as to his personal presence at trial. . . . [I]t was error . . . to permit the trial of the challenges to take place in the absence of the accused."). Indeed, there is some suggestion that the defendant cannot waive the right to be present when the state has an interest in the defendant's presence. *See* United States v. Fitzpatrick, 437 F.2d 19, 27 (2d Cir. 1970) (upholding denial of motion to waive right to be present where defendant's identification a focal point of trial). However, if a defendant who has been released on bail voluntarily disappears in the midst of the trial, the absence is deemed an effective waiver of the right to be present. Taylor v. United States, 414 U.S. 17 (1973).

41. 433 U.S. 186 (1977). *See* ch. 1.

42. *See, e.g.,* Titus v. Superior Court, 23 Cal. App. 3d 792, 796, 100 Cal. Rptr. 477, 482 (1972) (court has "authority to refuse to exercise judicial jurisdiction if the basis of that jurisdiction, i.e., the physical presence of the [defendant] in this state, has been obtained by fraud or unlawful force); Zenker v. Zenker, 72 N.W.2d 809, 816 (Neb. 1955) (husband could collaterally attack divorce decree because his presence in decreeing state was fraudulently induced by wife); Oden Optical Co. v. Optique Du Mond Ltd., 598 S.W.2d 456 (1980); *see also* ch. 1, sec. IIA2b (transient presence).

43. *See supra* note 39.

nal cases,[44] and the minimum contacts standard is considered a consequence of that amendment's guarantee of due process of law. Why, then, does not the minimum contacts analysis apply to criminal jurisdiction?

The most plausible account of the divergence in due process analysis between civil and criminal cases points to the constitutional protections of venue and vicinage, which may render minimum contacts analysis superfluous. The venue provision of the Constitution prescribes the place of criminal trials:

> [T]he trial of all Crimes . . . shall be held in the State where said crimes shall have been committed.[45]

The sixth amendment is commonly called the "vicinage" requirement, because it requires the jury to be drawn from the vicinity of the crime:

> [T]he accused shall enjoy the right to a . . . trial by impartial jury of the state and district wherein the crime shall have been committed.[46]

In theory, then, minimum contacts would exist in every case in which these constitutional protections were satisfied. Venue and vicinage in criminal cases can be understood as the constitutional counterparts to minimum contacts in civil cases.

Constitutional historians have identified policies underlying the venue and vicinage requirements that are similar to those underlying the minimum contacts test.[47] The venue provision, for example, was

---

44. The due process clause of the fourteenth amendment has long been held to require "fundamental fairness" in state criminal cases. The only question has been the extent to which the fourteenth amendment incorporated the Bill of Rights. *See, e.g.,* Benton v. Maryland, 395 U.S. 784 (1969) (holding that the double jeopardy prohibition of the fifth amendment is enforceable against the states through the fourteenth amendment); Malloy v. Hogan, 378 U.S. 1 (1964) (fifth amendment privilege against self-incrimination was incorporated by fourteenth amendment).

45. U.S. CONST. art. III, § 2, cl. 3.

46. U.S. CONST. amend. VI.

47. The colonists misinterpreted history, mistakenly claiming a right from time immemorial to trial in the vicinity of a crime: "[T]he respective colonies are entitled to the common law of England, and more especially to the great and inestimable privilege of being tried by peers of the vicinage, according to the course of that law." Resolution 5 of the Declaration of Rights, Continental Congress (1774). Yet as one scholar has noted:

> In England, trial in the county in which the crime was committed was never thought of as a fundamental right. Parliament ha[d] enacted many statutes authorizing trial in counties other than the one in which the crime was committed . . . . The colonists seem to have regarded what was a mere rule of convenience as a fundamental right of Englishmen.

E. STIMSON, CONFLICT OF CRIMINAL LAWS 27-29 (1936).

intended to protect the accused from defending in an inconvenient forum.[48] The colonists objected to the long and dangerous journey back to England to be tried for crimes (especially violating revenue laws and encouraging riots) alleged to have been committed in the colonies. Thus, the Declaration of Independence indicted King George III "for transporting us beyond seas to be tried for pretended offenses."[49]

The Framers assumed that in most cases the place in which the crime was committed and the defendant's place of residence would be the same.[50] Thus the defendant would have the benefit of local counsel, friends and relatives nearby, and acquaintance with the prosecutor, jurors, and witnesses. While the place of residence and the place of the crime would not always be the same, the place of the crime would at least be the most convenient setting for the defendant to prepare and present a defense. The victim, the witnesses, and the tangible evidence of the crime would all be found in the vicinity of the crime. Furthermore, the venue requirement would limit government forum shopping.[51]

The vicinage requirement was intended to serve similar purposes. Requiring a local jury limits the ability of the federal government to "jury-shop."[52] Vicinage also protects the defendant from the tyranny of a centralized government, because the jury interprets federal crimes in accordance with local community values and standards.[53]

The Supreme Court has recognized these forum non conveniens purposes of the venue and vicinage clauses in criminal change of venue cases. In *United States v. Johnson,* the Court stated:

> [S]uch leeway [allowing Congress to determine venue over continuing offenses] not only opens the door to needless hardship to an accused by prosecution remote from home and from appropriate facilities for defense. It also leads to the appearance of abuses, if not to abuses, in the selection of what may be deemed a tribunal favorable to the prosecution. . . . [T]here must be balanced against the inconvenience of transporting the Government's witnesses to trial . . . the serious hardship of defending prosecutions in places remote from home including the accused's difficulties, financial and otherwise, . . . of marshalling his witnesses.[54]

---

48. "By limiting venue, the colonists and constitutional [drafters] apparently intended to insure that an accused would usually be prosecuted for criminal conduct at [the accused's] place of residence." Kershen, *Vicinage,* 29 OKLA. L. REV. 801, 808 & n.19 (1976) (citing Travis v. United States, 364 U.S. 631 (1961)).
49. The Declaration of Independence, para. 21 (U.S. 1776).
50. Kershen, *supra* note 48, at 808-811.
51. *Id.* at 810-11.
52. *Id.* at 838.
53. *Id.* at 839-40.
54. 323 U.S. 273, 275, 278 (1944).

Further, in *Travis v. United States,* the Court

> start[ed] with the assumption that . . . the residence of petitioner, might offer conveniences and advantages to him which a trial in [another state] might lack. We are also aware that venue and vicinage provisions in Acts of Congress should not be so freely construed as to give the Government the choice of "a tribunal favorable" to it.[55]

Although in disagreement with the majority about whether venue was appropriate on the facts of *Travis,* the dissent agreed that preventing inconvenience to the defense was the underlying motivation for the constitutional protection.[56]

Although the emphasis on convenience to the defendant is appealing, there are difficulties with the notion that the venue and vicinage requirements in the criminal context are equivalent to minimum contacts analysis in civil law. First, the venue requirement does not apply to the states.[57] In civil cases, on the other hand, fair play and substantial justice are due process requirements, and apply to all assertions of civil jurisdiction, state or federal. However, most state constitutions contain their own venue and/or vicinage requirement.[58] Recognition of those rights would, of course, be a matter of state law, leaving open the possibility of different standards developing in different states.

Further, the concepts of venue and vicinage might have somewhat different content in criminal than minimum contacts analysis does in civil cases; the requirements are not functional equivalents. Courts could arguably assert criminal jurisdiction in cases in which they would refuse personal jurisdiction if they were civil, and vice versa. The jurisdictional analysis, therefore, would depend on whether the act is characterized as criminal or civil. This is not because criminal actions necessarily deal with different types of conduct than civil of-

---

55. 364 U.S. 631, 634 (1961) (citing *Johnson,* 323 U.S. at 275).

56. *Id.* at 640 (Harlan, J., dissenting) (provision for trial in vicinity of crime is safeguard against unfairness and hardship of prosecution in remote place).

57. Nashville C. & S.L. Ry. v. Alabama, 128 U.S. 96, 101 (1888) (art. III. venue requirement applies only to federal courts). The sixth amendment vicinage requirement, however, may well have been incorporated through the fourteenth amendment. In Duncan v. Louisiana, 391 U.S. 145, 149 (1968), the Court held that "trial by jury is fundamental to the American scheme of justice," and applied the jury right to the states. No case, however, has explicitly held that a vicinage requirement is attached to the jury right as applied to the states. *See* RESTATEMENT (TENTATIVE DRAFT No. 6) FOREIGN RELATIONS LAW § 422 Reporters' Notes 2 (1985). It seems likely that such a vicinage requirement would be held to be a part of the jury right incorporated by the due process clause. And since at any rate no state could empanel jurors from out-of-state, the issue is unlikely to arise.

58. *See, e.g.,* CONN. CONST. § 8; TENN. CONST. art. I, § 9.

fenses. Often, similar conduct could be involved. Compare the treatment, for example, of criminal child neglect and detainment,[59] with civil paternity and nonsupport,[60] or the treatment of civil and criminal libel.[61]

The potential for different treatment arises from the relative importance of demonstrating purposefulness and foreseeability. In the civil context, foreseeability of being haled into a specific forum has been a crucial element in the minimum contacts analysis.[62] By contrast, in one well known criminal jurisdiction case, *United States v. Hyde*,[63] foreseeability was not deemed important enough to address. Given the heightened mens rea requirement in criminal cases,[64] this result seems ironic. One would expect that criminal jurisdiction would be more narrowly construed than its civil counterpart. Unless the Court is willing to develop a foreseeability test for criminal jurisdiction, anomalous results will follow. For example, if the defendant sells spoiled meat to the complainant, who unpredictably takes it to another state, eats it and becomes ill, jurisdiction in the second state could depend on whether a criminal or civil action is lodged.

A final possible explanation for the difference between the criminal and civil jurisdictional standards points to the fact that states characteristically decline to adjudicate criminal cases in which the criminal law of another state supplies the pertinent rule of decision. Since applicability of local law is a prerequisite to the assertion of criminal adjudicative jurisdiction, there must be some contacts with the forum for the state to assert jurisdiction. It can be argued, therefore, that this safeguard, like the venue and vicinage requirements, protects defendants from an inconvenient choice of forum. This argument, obviously, does not hold in the case of a federal defendant, who will be subject to

---

59. State v. McCormick, 273 N.W.2d 624 (Minn. 1978) (state may not criminally prosecute defendant father for detaining his children outside state borders, when all relevant acts took place in another state).

60. Howells v. McKibben, 281 N.W.2d 154 (Minn. 1979) (state may validly assert personal jurisdiction over alleged father in paternity suit, even though illegitimate child was conceived out-of-state).

61. Buckley v. Beaumont Enter., 232 F. Supp. 986 (E.D. La. 1964) (rules of venue for criminal prosecution of libel do not apply to civil libel actions).

62. *See* ch. 1, sec. IIA.

63. 225 U.S. 347 (1912).

64. In common-law crimes, criminal intent is a necessary element of guilt. LaFave & Scott, *supra* note 5, at 192. Many state legislatures recently have enacted specific strict liability criminal statutes that do not require intent, merely knowledge of the act. *Id.* at 218-23. But these statutes prohibit conduct that causes grave harm to the public, thus suggesting negligence simply from the gravity of the resulting harm. Criminal punishment for negligence generally requires a greater degree of negligence than tort law. *Id.* at 209-14.

federal law everywhere in the nation, but might nevertheless wish to protest an inconvenient forum. However, the minimum contacts standard would not help federal defendants to any greater degree, since Congress can provide nationwide service of process. Further, federal defendants are protected by the venue requirement. More important, however, this analysis begs the real question. Explaining the difference between civil and criminal jurisdiction in terms of the different treatment criminal cases receive, fails to answer the underlying question: why do states refuse to apply one another's criminal laws?

III. The Connection Between Legislative and Adjudicative Jurisdiction

The classic relationship between legislative and adjudicative jurisdiction in the criminal context is summed up in Chief Justice Marshall's famous statement: "the Courts of no country execute the penal laws of another."[65] Although this statement referred to international law, the Supreme Court in the 1892 case of *Huntington v. Attrill*[66] applied this rule to the states holding that penal state judgments are not enforceable by sister states. The Court traced the origin of the doctrine to Blackstone's report of Chief Justice De Gray's statement that "[c]rimes are in their nature local, and jurisdiction of crimes is local. . . . But personal injuries are of a transitory nature."[67] This concept of locality no longer applies to tax judgments,[68] and probably not to criminal judgments, either. Indeed, the courts of one state have often recognized factual findings in the criminal proceedings of another state.[69] The requirement of local enforcement of criminal substantive law, however, has never been seriously questioned.

As *Huntington* indicates, the ban on foreign enforcement of penal laws is grounded in the perception that penal actions are not "transitory." A cause of action presumably is transitory if it is portable. For example, it is sometimes said that causes of action for real property are not transitory. They are governed by the "local action rule," which

---

65. The Antelope, 23 U.S. (10 Wheat.) 66, 123 (1825) (dictum).
66. 146 U.S. 657, 669 (1892):

> Crimes and offenses against the laws of any State can only be defined, prosecuted and pardoned by the sovereign authority of that State; and the authorities, legislative, executive or judicial, of other States take no action with regard to Them, except by way of extradition to surrender offenders to the State where laws they have violated, and whose peace they have broken.

67. *Id.* at 669 (quoting 2 W. BLACKSTONE, COMMENTARIES 1055, 1058).
68. Milwaukee County v. M.E. White Co., 296 U.S. 268, 271 (1935) ("[t]he obligation to pay taxes is not penal" and thus civil jurisdictional rules apply).
69. *See* ch. 5, sec. IIIB.

holds that they cannot be enforced except in the area where the land is located.[70] It remains to be seen whether penal laws necessarily have a peculiar relationship to their jurisdiction of origin.

A. THE RULE AGAINST FOREIGN ENFORCEMENT OF PENAL LAWS

At the outset, it is important to note that traditional statements of the rule against foreign enforcement of penal laws extend well beyond typical criminal prosecutions. The principle applies to all "penal" laws, a term that encompasses certain types of civil as well as criminal actions. Roughly speaking, certain civil causes of action are designed to compensate the injured plaintiff, and other types are designed to punish the wrongdoing defendant. The latter sort are characterized as "penal," and courts have refused to enforce such penal claims.[71] Read broadly, this category might include actions for treble damages, punitive damage claims, or causes of action for technical infractions of local corporation statutes.[72] In the federal/state area the Supreme Court has invalidated on supremacy clause grounds state refusal to enforce federal "penal" civil actions that confer jurisdiction on state courts.[73] But it has not yet extended this reasoning to interstate relations. States, apparently, may validly choose not to enforce each other's penal civil laws, even though they owe the federal government that degree of deference.

Although the penal law exception is sometimes analogized to the public policy exception to application of a foreign law repugnant to local values,[74] it is clear that they are distinct. If a cause of action is characterized as penal, it will be unenforceable even if the forum state has the identical rule of law. The public policy exception in conflicts analysis, on the other hand, denies enforcement only where the substance of the law is abhorrent to local standards of justice.

---

70. R. WEINTRAUB, COMMENTARY ON THE CONFLICT OF LAWS 221 (2d ed. 1980).

71. *See, e.g.,* Gardner v. Rumsey, 196 P. 941, 944-45 (Okla. 1921) (refusing to enforce Arkansas statute that created personal liability against officers of Arkansas corporation who fail to comply with filing requirements as "penal" law). *See also* Kutner, *Judicial Identification of "Penal Laws" in the Conflict of Laws,* 31 OKLA. L. REV. 590 (1978); Leflar, *Extrastate Enforcement of Penal and Governmental Claims,* 46 HARV. L. REV. 193 (1932).

72. Paper Prod. Co. v. Doggrell, 261 S.W.2d 127 (Tenn. 1953) (Arkansas law imposing personal liability on corporate officers who do not file incorporation certificate with county clerk is penal).

73. *Cf.* Testa v. Katt, 330 U.S. 386 (1947). In *Testa,* the Supreme Court rejected an attempt by the Rhode Island Supreme Court to refuse to enforce a federal act providing for treble damages. Rhode Island had deemed the federal act "penal" and therefore not properly brought in state court. The U.S. Supreme Court reversed.

74. *See Paper Prod. Co.,* 261 S.W.2d at 129 (Arkansas rule is both contrary to public policy of Tennessee and penal in nature). *See also* ch. 4, sec. IB.

Several traditional justifications for the refusal to apply the penal laws of other states apply to both the civil and the criminal versions of the rule; others apply only to the latter. The consequence is that nonenforcement can be more persuasively justified in criminal than in "penal" civil cases. In civil cases, moreover, the full faith and credit clause requires that states not discriminate against one another's laws.[75] Thus any decision not to enforce a civil law must overcome full faith and credit objections. Dismissal of criminal actions, in contrast, has not been challenged on these grounds. This raises the question whether, if such a challenge were raised, the dismissals would be constitutionally justifiable.

B. LOCAL ACTIONS ARE OF PECULIARLY LOCAL INTEREST

Proponents of both the civil and criminal versions of the rule against enforcing foreign penal laws argue that several policies justify its continued application. First, if the purpose of the action is a public one (i.e., deterrence of wrongdoing as opposed to private compensation) the state that created the cause of action ought arguably to bear the expense of enforcing it. Dockets, after all, may be too crowded to accommodate enforcement proceedings that are uniquely of interest to the state that created them. Conversely, the state of origin may have such a strong interest in its law that it would be intrusive for a foreign forum to entertain the action. The local community, it might be said, has an interest in local enforcement of matters of local concern.[76]

Whether this argument justifies automatic dismissal of foreign penal claims is doubtful. The argument resembles the considerations brought to bear on a typical motion to dismiss on forum non conveniens grounds.[77] As this doctrine indicates, even in civil cases a forum might legitimately be disinterested in a cause of action that arose elsewhere. This similarity suggests that the jurisdictional differences between penal and other claims are not as great as might appear. The policies cited do not establish the need for an irrebuttable presumption of inconvenience for penal claims, in place of the discretionary analysis applied in civil, non-punitive cases.

---

75. *See supra* ch. 4, sec. IB.

76. *See generally* Murphy, *supra* note 33, at 1087 ("criminal trials in the locus of the crime serve significant therapeutic needs of the community . . . provid[ing] a substitute for the natural human reactions of outrage, protest and some form of vengeful self-help").

77. *See* ch. 4, sec. IB.

C. LOCAL ENFORCEMENT IS CONVENIENT FOR BOTH PROSECUTION AND DEFENSE

The second reason typically cited for the nonenforcement of foreign penal laws is convenience to the defendant in litigating the case where the cause of action arose.[78] The convenience rationale does not necessarily distinguish civil from criminal causes of action; it is usually more convenient in civil cases, for example, to bring witnesses and evidence to a trial where the cause of action arose than to a trial located elsewhere. But the full faith and credit clause prohibits irrebuttable presumptions based on the geographical source of the legal claim in the civil context.[79] This explanation by itself, therefore, is not complete.

In situations where the action is truly a criminal prosecution, as opposed to a civil "penal" action, however, an irrebuttable presumption is justifiable, because the state, rather than a private plaintiff, is the moving party. Clearly, the state is able to provide a local forum whenever local litigation is constitutionally appropriate. Interstate extradition of criminal defendants has been cited as one justification underlying the penal law rule.[80] Because there is no need to provide a forum for foreign causes of action out of the fear that no other forum will be available, proponents of the penal law rule argue, states should not be required to enforce each other's criminal statutes. From the point of view of the state as plaintiff, moreover, it is unlikely that it will ever be more convenient to prosecute an action outside state borders. Only private plaintiffs need the flexibility of a transitory cause of action. Thus, while the rule limits the prosecutor's choice of forum, it limits that choice to the one most likely to be favorable to the state.

Furthermore, as the policies underlying the venue and vicinage requirements suggest, this forum is also likely to be relatively advantageous to the defendant. The place where the cause of action arose should be a convenient place to present evidence and witnesses. Thus,

---

78. *See supra* sec. II.

79. *See* ch. 4, sec.IB. Admittedly, it is usually more convenient to litigate where the cause of action arose. But in certain circumstances, it may happen that another forum is more convenient. For instance, in Hughes v. Fetter, 341 U.S. 609 (1951), the cause of action arose outside the forum state, but the suit was brought in the forum state where both parties were domiciled. Thus, the transitory nature of the cause of action reflects the occasional practical need of the plaintiff to litigate elsewhere than where the cause of action arose. In fact, the state in which the cause of action arises may lack a long-arm statute, thus compelling the plaintiff to seek remedy elsewhere. *See also* Wells v. Simon Abrasive Co., 345 U.S. 514 (1953).

80. *See* Leflar, *Extrastate Enforcement of Penal and Governmental Claims,* 46 HARV. L. REV. 193, 200-01 (1932) (interstate rendition has made penal law rule a practicable one in America).

the defendant usually has no greater interest in imposing the litigation upon foreign courts than does the prosecutor.[81] In fact, it is to the defendant's advantage that the prosecutor's choice of forum be strictly limited. Whatever the merits of forum shopping in civil cases, the threat posed by forum shopping to the rights of criminal defendants is obvious. As the venue and vicinage discussion suggested,[82] prosecutorial discretion in the choice of forum has long been perceived as undermining the right to a fair trial. In short, none of the policy considerations that motivate us to characterize civil actions as transitory applies in the context of criminal prosecutions.

D. PRACTICAL DIFFICULTIES OF FOREIGN ENFORCEMENT

Other consequences also follow from the fact that in a criminal prosecution the prosecuting party is the state. While the prosecuting state itself is unlikely to prefer conducting litigation in another state, it might, in theory, be content to have a foreign forum use its own prosecutorial apparatus to litigate a criminal case. Indeed, it is difficult to imagine how the creating state might litigate in another state's courts *without* bringing to bear that other state's prosecutorial apparatus. Under this theory, State A would prosecute a cause of action in its own courts, under State B's laws and on its behalf. Although this scenario seemingly offers a plausible structure for the enforcement of penal laws in foreign forums, the practical difficulties it raises are staggering.

Consider the example of plea bargaining. Most criminal charges are settled by negotiated pleas.[83] Would State A have the authority to negotiate a plea with the defendant that would bind State B? Since plea bargaining relieves congested dockets,[84] it would seem that State A ought to have control over whether the case proceeds to trial; State B's preference not to accept the plea bargain might only reflect the fact

---

81. However, trying a crime in the place of its commission can cause problems of pretrial publicity that may result in a jury prejudiced against the defendant. *See, e.g.,* Irvin v. Dowd, 366 U.S. 717 (1961) (pretrial publicity about defendant prejudiced jury against him).

82. *See supra* sec. II.

83. "Excluding those cases that are disposed of by a post-arraignment *nolle prosequi* or a successful defense motion . . . 70 to 90 percent of the remaining felony cases are resolved by a guilty plea in most jurisdictions." Y. KAMISAR, W. LAFAVE & J. ISRAEL, MODERN CRIMINAL PROCEDURE 22 (5th ed. 1980) (footnote omitted).

84. *See id.* at 1222-24, citing Burger, C.J., "Address at the American Bar Association Annual Convention," N.Y. Times, Aug. 11, 1970, at 24, col. 4; *see also* Santabello v. New York, 404 U.S. 257, 260-61 (1971) ("If every criminal charge were subjected to a full-scale trial, the States and the Federal Government would need to multiply by many times the number of judges and court facilities.").

that it could have its law enforced without bearing the costs of the litigation. Similar problems would arise if the case proceeded to trial, under the sole litigation control of State A, but under State B's law. If the result were an acquittal, would this bind State B under principles of either collateral estoppel or double jeopardy?[85] Would State B really want to relinquish control over the litigation process if it were to be bound by the results? These considerations suggest that it is deference to the interests of the other state, and not discrimination against it, that underlies the dismissal of the other state's criminal claims.

This conclusion is reinforced by consideration of the problem of remedies. If the remedy is a fine, which state gets the money? Is it fair for State A to get it, considering that the offense was an offense against the people of State B? On the other hand, is it fair for State B to take the fine, thereby denying to State A recompense for the costs of prosecution? The opposite problem arises when the remedy is imprisonment, which results in a net drain rather than a net gain. Who bears the cost of imprisonment? If State B pays the bill, it seems that it ought to have more control over the decision that the defendant will be imprisoned: it should control the sentencing stage, at least. If, on the other hand, State A, as the site of trial, is also the site of imprisonment, one wonders why the taxpayers of State A should incur the costs of imprisonment on behalf of the people of State B.

Similar remedial problems would exist if federal courts entertained state criminal actions, which they typically do not.[86] Indeed, to a minor degree these remedial issues exist when federal courts entertain cases challenging criminal prosecutions initiated by states, such as a defendant's suit in federal court to protest a state's criminal law or procedures. Such cases are considerably different from removing the criminal case to federal court. A federal court can intervene only on behalf of the defendant, not the state, because federal courts have no power to institute a remedy on the state's behalf. The one-sidedness of the remedy that federal courts are equipped to offer may account for federal reluctance to intervene in situations where the state has manifested an interest in securing a criminal judgment.[87] In the federal/state context,

---

85. Double jeopardy does not bar two sovereigns from each prosecuting a defendant for the same criminal act when that act transgresses the laws of both sovereigns. In effect, by one act that crosses state boundaries the defendant has committed two offenses. Heath v. Alabama, 106 S. Ct. 433, 437 (1985).

86. Except for one relatively minor exception, there is no federal district court jurisdiction over state criminal cases. See ch. 2, sec. IIC. Cf. 42 U.S.C. §§ 1983, 1985, 1986.

87. See Brilmayer & Lee, *State Sovereignty and the Two Faces of Federalism,* 60 Notre Dame L. Rev. 833, 859 (1985) (remedial structure of federal courts uniquely advantageous to state criminal defendants).

it is also worth mentioning that Congress has granted exclusive juris-diction over federal crimes to federal courts.[88] This separation mani-fests, again, the judgment that criminal actions belong in a sovereign's own courts.

Overall, absent some agreement between State A and State B about how these formidable conflicts should be resolved, dismissal is a proper response to other sovereign's criminal cases. As indicated earlier, the prohibition against entertaining other state's "penal" civil actions is more troublesome. The principle may simply be an outgrowth of an apparent but misleading similarity to criminal prosecutions. It may, in the alternative, reflect a disinclination to expend judicial resources to enforce another state's policies, a disinclination of dubious constitu-tionality.

Conclusion

Both theoretical and practical considerations support the continued vitality of territoriality in criminal jurisdiction. Unlike civil jurisdic-tion, the unique nature of criminal law makes concepts of locality especially powerful — and virtually insurmountable practical difficul-ties entailed in extra-state enforcement of criminal law ensure that territorial factors will remain controlling in both legislative and adju-dicative criminal jurisdiction.

---

88. 18 U.S.C. §§ 241, 242, 245.

Chapter 12

JURISDICTION OVER DOMESTIC RELATIONS

The law of domestic relations, sometimes called family law, governs legal familial relationships such as marriage, divorce, child custody, alimony and child support. Jurisdiction, choice of law and judgments take on new dimensions when the subject is domestic relations. For example, the federal judiciary refuses to include most domestic relations cases within its original jurisdiction, even when diversity jurisdiction would otherwise exist.[1] Domestic relations cases are, however, included in the Supreme Court's appellate jurisdiction.[2] As a result, state courts adjudicate family disputes in the first instance.

Even though federal courts decline to take domestic relations cases, federal constitutional principles pertaining to jurisdictional issues, such as due process and full faith and credit, apply to them with full force.[3] The operation of these principles in the domestic relations realm has produced curious results. For example, while two consenting adults need only be present within a state to become married pursuant to the laws of that state, at least one of the parties must be domiciled within a state to secure a divorce.[4] If the divorce only eliminates the marital status, the divorcing state need not have personal jurisdiction over the defendant-spouse.[5] However, if there is no personal jurisdiction over the defendant-spouse and if the divorce purports to determine alimony, property division, child support or child custody, it is only valid insofar as it terminates the marital status, not as to any money or custody judgment.[6] With child custody, constitutional law seems to require personal jurisdiction over the custody contestants, but not necessarily over the children.[7] State statutes, however, require only that the state rendering a custody award be the "home state" of the child; the statutes do not require personal jurisdiction over the custody contestants.[8]

While these quirks of domestic relations jurisdiction seem to suggest that the jurisdictional principles developed in other areas of law do not apply to domestic relations cases, this is not really true. The principles of jurisdiction do indeed apply — but not straightforwardly. Several factors account for these idiosyncrasies. Most of the constitutional precedents in domestic relations jurisdiction were developed under the

---

1. *See* sec. I, *infra.*
2. *See* sec. I, *infra.*
3. *See, e.g.,* sec. IIB3, *infra* (recognition of judgments).
4. *See* sec. IIB1.
5. *Id.*
6. *See* sec. IIC1 (divisible divorce).
7. *Id.*
8. Sec. IID1 (Uniform Child Custody Jurisdiction Act).

older regime of jurisdictional theory in which the distinction between *in rem* and *in personam* jurisdiction still had meaning, the power theory of jurisdiction held sway, and the *First Restatement of Conflicts of Laws* still applied.[9] While courts have passed this stage of jurisdictional theory in other areas of law, the subject of domestic relations is so imbued with tradition that change in domestic relations jurisdiction has been slow.

I. Federal Jurisdiction

Federal courts claim to lack original subject matter jurisdiction over domestic relations controversies. Federal courts decline, therefore, to hear domestic relations cases in the first instance, even if the parties are diverse. This exception to federal diversity jurisdiction dates back to the 1859 diversity case of *Barber v. Barber*,[10] when the Court announced in dictum, "[w]e disclaim altogether any jurisdiction in the courts of the United States upon the subject of divorce, or for the allowance of alimony, either as an original proceeding in chancery or as an incident to divorce *a vinculo*, or to one from bed and board." In 1890, the Court explained its denial of jurisdiction over domestic relations more fully in *In re Burrus*, a federal habeas corpus action to obtain custody of a child:[11] "The whole subject of the domestic relations of husband and wife, parent and child, belongs to the laws of the States and not to the laws of the United States." While *Burrus* might have been interpreted as a statement that there was simply no federal substantive law governing domestic relations, and thus no habeas (or federal question) jurisdiction over cases involving solely domestic relations, later cases interpreted the rule far more broadly, describing it as "indubitable"[12] and "long-established"[13] that "the Courts of the United States have no jurisdiction over divorce."[14]

The original justification for this seemingly arbitrary denial of jurisdiction was the argument that the equity jurisdiction of the courts was intended by the Framers of the Constitution to extend only so far as the equity jurisdiction of the Court of Chancery in England. The jurisdiction so conferred did not include jurisdiction over "infants, lunatics, or idiots."[15] And it was asserted that matrimonial matters were handled exclusively by the English ecclesiastical courts and the Parlia-

---

9. *See* ch. 1 & ch. 7, sec. I.
10. 62 U.S. (21 How.) 582, 584 (1859).
11. 136 U.S. 586, 593-94 (1890).
12. Simms v. Simms, 175 U.S. 162, 167 (1899).
13. De La Rama v. De La Rama, 201 U.S. 303, 307 (1906).
14. Ohio ex rel. Popovici v. Agur, 28 U.S. 379, 383 (1930).
15. Fontain v. Ravenel, 58 U.S. (17 How.) 369, 393 (1855).

ment. More prosaically, it was also explained that divorce cases did not meet the literal requirements for diversity jurisdiction because "the husband and wife cannot usually be citizens of different states so long as the marriage relation continues"[16] — based on the doctrine that a wife could not acquire a domicile separate from her husband.

In the 1968 case of *Spindel v. Spindel*,[17] Judge Weinstein challenged the assumption that English courts of chancery did not handle matrimonial matters, and argued that the earlier cases actually showed that federal courts have the constitutional power to hear domestic cases. He gave two reasons: (1) the Supreme Court had approved cases in which federal courts in the U.S. territories had adjudicated matters of domestic relations;[18] and (2) those cases denying jurisdiction were simply interpreting the diversity statute's reference to cases in "equity," while article III extends to all cases and controversies, not merely to cases in law or equity.[19] Judge Weinstein also correctly pointed out that the earlier cases conflated the idea that there was no federal legislative jurisdiction over domestic relations with the question whether there was also no federal judicial jurisdiction. Judicial jurisdiction could, of course, be based on diversity even where substantive law claims arose under state law, as with torts or contracts.[20] True or not, however, Judge Weinstein's views were not adopted even by the Second Circuit, which argued that whatever the scope of article III, Congress had not conferred jurisdiction to hear domestic relations cases on the federal courts under the diversity statute.[21]

A more contemporary explanation for the domestic relations exception to diversity jurisdiction is that it is not a jurisdictional question but a form of abstention, a *Burford*-type rationale. *Burford v. Sun Oil Co.*[22] stands for the proposition that abstention should be used to avoid needless conflict with a state's administration of its own affairs. Abstention is appropriate where the issues involved in the case are a "specialized aspect of a complicated regulatory system of local law which should be left to the local administrative bodies and courts."[23]

---

16. *De La Rama,* 201 U.S. at 303.

17. 283 F. Supp. 797 (E.D.N.Y. 1968).

18. *Id.* at 804; *see, e.g.,* Maynard v. Hill, 125 U.S. 190 (1888).

19. *Id.* at 801. The concerns of *Barber* and *In re Burrus, supra,* were directed at delimiting the confines of equity jurisdiction. Even if they meant to interpret the constitutional language, if federal jurisdiction extends to all cases and controversies, not just to cases in law or equity, then the limits of equity jurisdiction are irrelevant as a constitutional matter.

20. *Id.* at 804-05.

21. Phillips, Nizer, Benjamin, Krim & Ballon v. Rosenstiel, 490 F.2d 509, 514 (2d Cir. 1973).

22. 319 U.S. 315 (1943). *See* discussion in ch. 4, sec. IIC.

23. C. WRIGHT, THE LAW OF FEDERAL COURTS 308 (4th ed. 1983).

Because the federal courts — and Congress — have always abstained from domestic relations, the states have developed intricate rules governing family law, and state courts have developed expertise in this specialized area. Indeed, some states have specialized "family courts." Therefore, it is argued, domestic relations is a logical category for a *Burford*-type abstention, and even when they have jurisdiction, federal courts should "abstain for reasons of comity and common sense" — not to mention overcrowded federal dockets — from deciding such cases, which are "better handled" by state courts.[24] However, these arguments for abstention could logically be applied to *any* area of law — tort law, for example — into which federal law has not yet intruded. Yet torts cases are routinely heard in federal courts under diversity jurisdiction, applying state law.

The peculiar deference federal courts accord to states in family cases may be due largely to the nature of domestic relations law. Domestic relations cases are usually emotionally charged; and substantive family law lacks clearly delineated standards. Because the cases are highly fact-specific, it is difficult to develop clear-cut principles. Family law has also been heavily imbued, historically, with moral and religious overtones. Under the circumstances, federal courts have carved a special exception for domestic relations cases (and for probate cases as well)[25] from federal diversity jurisdiction so as not to intrude into the cultural norms of the states.

This is not to say that domestic relations cases are never heard by lower federal courts. Federal courts will exercise original jurisdiction, under federal question jurisdiction, to ensure that state rules do not unconstitutionally impinge on protected individual liberties. Hence, in some circumstances, a party may challenge the constitutionality of a state domestic relations statute in federal district court. In *Sosna v. Iowa*,[26] for example, the named plaintiff's divorce litigation had been dismissed in Iowa state court because she had not been a resident of the state for a year. Instead of appealing, she brought a separate class action in federal district court, alleging that the statute violated the equal protection and due process guarantees of the Constitution. The court exercised its jurisdiction and upheld the statute's constitutionality.[27] Interestingly, while the Supreme Court did not discuss the do-

---

24. Armstrong v. Armstrong, 508 F.2d 348, 350 (1st Cir. 1974).
25. *See* C. WRIGHT, *supra* note 23, at § 25.
26. 419 U.S. 393 (1975).
27. The Supreme Court did note, however, that the suit might have been barred by the eleventh amendment or sovereign immunity because the state of Iowa was a party. *Id.* at 396 n.2. The Court held, though, that under the Iowa law the state consents to suit and waives any defense of sovereign immunity by appearing and defending.

mestic relations exception to diversity, the Court cited *Barber* and its progeny as a rationale for deference to the state's legislative policy decisions.[28]

Even under its federal question jurisdiction, however, the lower federal courts do not necessarily hear constitutional domestic relations cases. In *Barbier v. Governor, State of New Jersey*[29], for example, a divorced father challenged a state child-custody statute as a denial of equal protection because the statute gave unfair advantage to women. The plaintiff brought the federal challenge while the custody dispute was pending appeal in state court. The federal court dismissed the suit for want of jurisdiction on the grounds that: (1) because the suit was really against his former spouse, the suit against the state was hypothetical, offering no case or controversy; (2) the state courts could apply a saving construction to the statute; (3) the U.S. District Courts do not sit as appellate courts to state courts; and (4) it would contradict the principles of res judicata to institute a federal action pending state appeal. Barbier's appropriate remedy was to raise his constitutional challenge in state court and appeal to the Supreme Court. Again, this suggests the deference that is afforded the state court system when it comes to questions of domestic relations. For much the same reasons, it has been held that constitutional attack on a state court child-custody judgment through a federal habeas proceeding would represent an impermissible and unwarranted interference with the state judicial system,[30] even though state habeas corpus may be available within the state to resolve a custody dispute.[31]

Finally, even the exception to diversity jurisdiction has in some respects been narrowly construed. It has been clear since the seminal case of *Barber* — despite its influential dictum denying jurisdiction as a general rule — that lower federal courts may be available to *enforce* some types of state-court domestic relations judgments. Thus, district courts will enforce state-court alimony judgments, if they are final,[32] as well as judgments providing for payment of child support.[33] Similarly, lower federal courts enforce written prejudgment separation agreements that provide for support payments during separation[34] — so long

---

28. 419 U.S. at 404.

29. 475 F. Supp. 127 (D.N.J. 1979).

30. Lehman v. Lycoming County Children's Servs. Agency, 458 U.S. 502 (1982).

31. H. CLARK, DOMESTIC RELATIONS § 17.7 at 598 (1968).

32. C. WRIGHT, *supra* note 23, at 145 & n.12 (citing Crouch v. Crouch, 566 F.2d 486 (5th Cir. 1978); Harrison v. Harrison, 214 F.2d 571 (4th Cir. 1954), *cert. denied,* 348 U.S. 896; Davis v. Davis, 452 F. Supp. 44 (E.D. Pa. 1978)).

33. *See, e.g.,* Zimmerman v. Zimmerman, 395 F. Supp. 719 (E.D. Pa. 1975).

34. *See, e.g.,* Crouch v. Crouch, 566 F.2d at 486.

as they do not also involve continuing questions of child custody, divorce, alimony, and so on.[35] Interestingly, federal courts have even enforced unwritten agreements between unmarried couples for lifetime support — so-called "palimony" suits — even though this in essence amounts to adjudicating such rights in the first instance.[36] The theory is that all of these types of permissible actions are simply contract suits, which a federal court is competent to adjudge. When the court will be called upon to make a judgment about family status, however, or perhaps more accurately, when the family status question will be one of particular interest to the state (as general contractual relationships or relationships of persons not married to each other are considered not to be),[37] then the federal court will defer to the state system to adjudicate the case.

While lower federal court jurisdiction over domestic relations disputes is generally not available, the Supreme Court does include within its appellate jurisdiction certain such cases.[38] Pursuant to 28 U.S.C. § 1257, the Court will hear domestic relations cases upon appeal from final judgments of the highest state court subject, of course, to all of the limitations on the Court's appellate jurisdiction — including the existence of some federal element to the case.[39] Thus, the Supreme Court has entertained constitutional challenges, on appeal from state courts, of state statutes governing adoption[40] and alimony.[41] The Court has heard yet other constitutional challenges to state domestic relations statutes under its certiorari jurisdiction, under which it has reviewed state court judgments on such issues as child custody statutes and statutes terminating parental rights.[42] Finally, the Supreme Court may also have occasion to address domestic relations issues in review-

---

35. *See, e.g.,* Solomon v. Solomon, 566 F.2d 1018 (3d Cir. 1975).

36. *See, e.g.,* Anastasi v. Anastasi, 532 F. Supp. 720 (D. N.J. 1982).

37. *See* Haddock v. Haddock, 201 U.S. 562 (1906).

38. *See, e.g.,* Simms v. Simms, 175 U.S. 162, 167-68 (1899).

39. For a discussion of the Supreme Court's appellate jurisdiction, see ch. 2, sec. IIIB.

40. *See, e.g.,* Caban v. Mohammed, 441 U.S. 380 (1979) (appeal on equal protection challenge to N.Y. adoption statute); Quilloin v. Walcott, 434 U.S. 246 (1979) (appeal challenging adoption statute on equal protection and due process grounds).

41. *See, e.g.,* Orr v. Orr, 440 U.S. 268 (1979) (appeal challenging alimony statute on equal protection grounds).

42. Santosky v. Kramer, 455 U.S. 745 (1982) (cert. granted to consider due process requirements for termination of parental rights); Webb v. Webb, 451 U.S. 493 (1981) (cert. granted to consider full faith and credit requirements of two conflicting custody awards rendered under the Uniform Child Custody Jurisdiction Act); Stanley v. Illinois, 405 U.S. 645 (1972) (cert. granted to consider due process requirements before termination of parental rights); Halvey v. Halvey, 330 U.S. 610 (1947) (cert. granted to consider full faith and credit problems of two state's child custody awards).

ing judgments of federal appellate courts, for example on the question *whether* federal habeas may be used to obtain custody of a child[43] — the very question presented in the early case of *Burrus*.

II. State Court Jurisdiction

Because federal courts for the most part refuse to become involved in domestic relations cases, the difficult task falls to state courts and legislatures. States, having different customs, traditions, and values, have different laws concerning domestic relations. For example, state law varies as to the minimum age of consent to marry, as to the degree of consanguinity that would prevent marriage, as to whether parties must have grounds for divorce, and as to presumptions created to determine child custody. If people travel across state lines, or move to separate states, they may thereby obtain different rights and duties flowing from the same legal relationship. The outcome of any controversy regarding a relationship — for example, divorce — may vary depending upon where suit is brought. Indeed, a relationship may be recognized in one state but not another.

Because there is no federal law of domestic relations,[44] uniformity and consistency across state lines typically is lacking in the field. Recognizing the need for uniformity — and reciprocity — many state legislatures have adopted their own modified versions of uniform family relations statutes.[45] But the states rarely all enact a uniform or model act without alteration, and not all states enact such statutes. Therefore, a domestic relations case is affected not only by the law of the states in which the plaintiff and defendant reside, but also by the law of any other state that might have a significant connection to the relationship at issue, such as the law of the state in which the parties were domiciled before they separated (the state of marital domicile).

The general principles of state jurisdiction (personal and subject matter), of choice of law, and of judgments (res judicata, collateral attack, and full faith and credit) have been discussed in earlier chapters. These apply to domestic relations cases as to any civil suits, but

---

43. *See, e.g.,* Lehman v. Lycoming County Children's Servs. Agency, 458 U.S. 502 (1982) (cert. granted to consider constitutionality of federal habeas corpus in child custody dispute).

44. Recently, however, Congress has entered the field with, for example, Title XX of the Social Security Act regarding child protective services and foster care and amendments to the IRC to allow deduction from wages to pay child support. The Foster Care and Adoption Assistance Act, 42 U.S.C. §§ 670-676 (Supp. 1985), and the Parental Kidnapping Prevention Act, 28 U.S.C. § 1738(A).

45. *E.g.,* Uniform Child Custody Jurisdiction Act, 9A U.L.A. (1979); Uniform Marriage and Divorce Act, 9 U.L.A.; Uniform Parentage Act, 9A U.L.A.; and Uniform Reciprocal Enforcement of Support Act, 9A U.L.A.

with important modifications. By and large, the states manifest the same tendency as the federal courts in declining to entertain actions brought under other sovereigns' domestic relations laws, thus preserving the intimate link between legislative and adjudicative jurisdiction in this area of substantive law. The remainder of this chapter will focus on the particular jurisdictional problems created by domestic relations, in terms of both state-legislative and state-adjudicative jurisdiction. Each section will distinguish personal jurisdiction, choice of law, and judgments for the four typical state domestic relations suits: marriage; termination of marriage (divorce); alimony and property division; and child custody and child support.

A. Marriage

1. Jurisdiction

Most state statutes authorize the marriage of any two consenting adults present in the state who meet certain personal character requirements. To marry, the two persons must be of opposite sex, not too closely related by blood or marriage, not married to anyone else, of a certain minimum age, and physically capable of consummating a marriage; the marriage, in addition, must be solemnized by a qualified person.[46] The connections with the state that are necessary to authorize marriage are much more tenuous than are necessary for divorce. For example, to marry there is no minimum residency requirement, although a six-week residency is the minimum some states require for divorce. Perhaps this is because both parties to a marriage have necessarily, by their joint presence in the state, consented to the authority.

2. Choice of Law

Choice-of-law problems arise in marital cases when more than one state has an interest in the validity of a particular marriage. For example, assume that two parties, at least one of whom is domiciled in State X, travel to State Y to get married because their marriage is forbidden in State X. After marrying they return to State X and establish a marital domicile. At a later point, one of them challenges the validity of that marriage. This might happen, for instance, where one spouse seeks to terminate the marriage, but would rather claim that the marriage was invalid from the start than get divorced, because if their marriage was never valid there can be no claim for support and there is no marital property to divide. Under State X's marriage law their marriage is invalid, in State Y's it is valid. Which law governs?

---

46. *See* Uniform Marriage and Divorce Act, 9 U.L.A., §§ 206-208 (1979).

State X will hold a marriage celebrated in State Y valid, if the marriage is valid under State Y law, unless the marriage falls into one of two exceptions. First, a state court will invalidate a marriage when the legislature of State X has expressly stated its intent to prohibit such an extraterritorial marriage of its domiciliaries. For example, State X might statutorily prohibit a domiciliary of State X from availing herself of any other state's marriage laws if her intent is to evade a specific marriage law of State X.[47]

Second, a court of State X will invalidate a foreign marriage if the marriage profoundly contradicts an important public policy of State X such as the prohibition of marriage between uncle and niece.[48] To invalidate the marriage on public policy grounds the marriage must deeply offend the court's sensibilities such that the court views the union with horror. Usually, the public policy exception is triggered only if State X criminally punishes the type of marriage secured in State Y. For example, most states do not on these grounds recognize marriages of a minor even if it may have been valid in State Y.[49]

3. Judgments

Analytically, a marriage could be viewed as a judgment by the state in which the marriage was performed. While the power of the state to authorize marriages is generally considered an exercise of its legislative jurisdiction, once a marriage relationship is created, in many ways it resembles a judgment more closely than a contract, since it requires the state's sanction for its validity and implicates many of the state's keenest interests. Perhaps this is the reason that so much credence is lent to the law of the state in which the marriage was performed. However, in practice, marriages are not viewed as judgments and it does not appear that a forum state's refusal to recognize an extraterritorial marriage has ever been attacked on the grounds that the forum state has failed to give full faith and credit to the "public Acts, Records and judicial proceedings of every other State."[50] In general, marriages are actually treated, and enforced, as a contract rather than as a judgment. Presumably, if an actual judgment is rendered as to the validity of a marriage, it will be respected in other states in the same manner as any other sort of judgment.

---

47. *See* R. WEINTRAUB, COMMENTARY ON CONFLICTS OF LAWS § 5.1A at 223 & n.6 (1980).
48. *Id.* at 223-224; *but cf.* In re May's Estate, 305 N.Y. 486, 114 N.E.2d 4 (1953).
49. *See* R. WEINTRAUB, *supra* note 47, at § 5.1A at 224 n.7 (statutory rape).
50. U.S. CONST. art. IV, § 1.

B. Divorce

1. Jurisdiction

Domicile is the pertinent factor in determining a state court's power to grant a divorce, distinguishing divorce from virtually any other field except probate.[51] The general rule was set down in *Williams v. North Carolina (Williams I)*.[52] The Supreme Court there held that in order for a court to have jurisdiction to grant a simple divorce (one affecting only the marital status and not affecting any marital property, alimony, or child support or custody) one of the parties to the divorce must be domiciled in the forum state. The court need not have personal jurisdiction over the other party, and the other party need not appear.[53] This doctrine seems, in many ways, a remarkable one:

> The petitioner's domicile alone is a sufficient constitutional basis for divorce jurisdiction even though the marriage was not celebrated in the forum, the spouses never lived there as husband and wife, none of the facts on which the divorce is based occurred in the forum, and even though the other spouse does not appear in the action and there is no other basis for in personam jurisdiction over the absent spouse.[54]

Thus, the defendant might have *no* contacts with the forum state, yet the judgment would still be entitled to full faith and credit — contrary to all modern theories of jurisdiction. Even under traditional principles of jurisdiction,[55] such a judgment, rendered where the court lacks jurisdiction over the defendant-spouse, would only be permissible where the basis of the jurisdiction is in rem — based on the court's power over the *thing* sought to be adjudicated. Yet a decision that one spouse may be divorced in one state necessarily has certain extraterritorial effects on the other spouse, and the Supreme Court early rejected this theory.[56] The action must therefore be in personam. However, if divorce is in personam, based on the court's power to determine the parties' status, not only would jurisdiction over the defendant be required but domicile of the moving party would be irrelevant. Thus, under traditional principles of jurisdiction, divorce jurisdiction is an anomaly.

The basic rationale for the theory, and the explanation for its emphasis on domicile, may be that divorce jurisdiction is necessary to protect the state's interest in determining the status of its domiciliaries. This

---

51. *See* Restatement (Second) of the Conflict of Laws, § 260 (1971).
52. 317 U.S. 287 (1942).
53. *Id.* at 298-99.
54. R.Weintraub, *supra* note 47, at § 5.2A at 229 (footnote omitted).
55. *See* ch. 1, sec. I.
56. *See Williams I,* 317 U.S. at 303-04.

interest prevails even though the divorce may adversely affect the interests of the state of marital domicile, which may have stricter divorce laws, as well as the interests of the absent spouse. The real underpinnings of the rule, perhaps, lie in the Supreme Court's recognition that refusing to allow broad extraterritorial effect of divorce judgments could create serious harm to "innocent people," the children that may be deemed illegitimate in a subsequent marriage which would be found polygamous.[57]

This is not to say that there are no protections for the defendant-spouse. Where the plaintiff seeks an ex parte divorce, without the presence of the defendant, due process provides certain minimal protections to that spouse, albeit not in the form of a requirement of personal jurisdiction. In such cases, the defendant-spouse must be given adequate notice of the pending divorce.[58] Process can be served or notice mailed to the defendant-spouse out of state, and service by publication may be adequate if the defendant's whereabouts are unknown. But the plaintiff-spouse must exercise due diligence in attempting to notify the absent spouse.[59]

In addition, while domicile is a constitutional minimum for divorce jurisdiction, states may add jurisdictional requirements. For example, Louisiana has required, with some exceptions, that the grounds for divorce must occur in Louisiana or while Louisiana was the marital domicile.[60] New Hampshire has required that the acts or activities constituting grounds for divorce must have occurred while the plaintiff-spouse was domiciled in New Hampshire.[61] Moreover, the statutory requirements for a divorce based on domicile alone also vary, since states have varying residency requirements.[62] The result is that divorce jurisdiction turns to a great degree on the particular state's law.

2. Choice of Law

As a practical matter, if a court takes jurisdiction over a divorce action, it applies its own state's law. Just as with criminal law,[63] it is not immediately obvious why a state taking jurisdiction cannot apply the divorce law of another state. A state could, for example, apply the

57. *Id.* at 317 U.S. at 295-96.
58. R. WEINTRAUB, *supra* note 47, at § 5.6A at 229.
59. R. CASAD, JURISDICTION IN CIVIL ACTIONS 9-12 & nn. 62, 63 (1983); R. WEINTRAUB, *supra* note 47, at § 5.2A at 229 & n. 33.
60. R. WEINTRAUB, *supra* note 47, at § 5.2A at 229 n.32 (citing La. Code Civ. Proc. Art. 10(A)(7)).
61. *Id.* (discussing New Hampshire Law).
62. *See* Sosna v. Iowa, 419 U.S. 393, 404-05 (1975).
63. *See* Chapter 11.

law of the marital domicile — the state in which the parties were domiciled while they held themselves out as married. That state's interest in the continuation of the marital relationship might be equally important to that of the current domiciliary state of the plaintiff. However, there are few or no cases applying a foreign state's divorce law, although at least one state's statute grants the authority to apply a foreign state's divorce law. Kentucky allows its courts to award a divorce based either upon Kentucky law or upon the law of the state in which the grounds for divorce occurred.[64] Interestingly, the Supreme Court has, in the context of addressing a state's power to apply its own divorce laws, raised (and rejected) the argument that the full faith and credit clause requires a state to defer to the divorce *statutes* of another state, finding that the state of marital domicile cannot be said to have a greater interest in the form state's domiciliaries than the forum state itself.[65]

3. Judgments

As *Williams I* established, a divorce granted by the state of domicile of one of the spouses is entitled to full faith and credit in every other state, provided due process has been satisfied.[66] However, this doctrine was modified somewhat by the holding in *Williams II*, based on the same facts, that a divorce decree may be successfully attacked in another state by demonstrating that the divorcing state was not in fact the domicile of the plaintiff-spouse.[67] Under this rule, however, the burden rests upon the challenging party to demonstrate that the divorcing state was not the domicile of the original plaintiff; and the divorce decree is entitled to the presumption that it was awarded under proper jurisdiction.[68] A court may not, moreover, reopen the question of jurisdiction if it were fully and fairly litigated by all parties in the initial divorce proceeding.[69]

Williams II came about in the following way. *Williams I* had involved a man and woman who were each married to separate spouses in North Carolina. They went to Nevada, divorced their respective spouses and married each other, returned to North Carolina, and were convicted of bigamy. In *Williams I*, the Supreme Court had reversed their convictions on the ground that the divorce decree was entitled to full faith and credit. On retrial, the North Carolina courts again con-

---

64. Ky. Rev. Stat. Ann. § 403.035(2); R. CASAD, *supra* note 59, at 9-15.
65. *Williams I*, 317 U.S. at 293-95.
66. *Id.* at 303.
67. Williams v. North Carolina (Williams II), 325 U.S. 226 (1945).
68. *Id.* at 233-34; *see also* Cook v. Cook, 342 U.S. 126, 128 (1951).
69. Davis v. Davis, 305 U.S. 32 (1938); Sherrer v. Sherrer, 334 U.S. 343 (1948).

victed them, this time on the basis that the divorces were invalid and not entitled to full faith and credit because the divorcing parties were not actually domiciled in Nevada.

On this occasion, the Supreme Court upheld the convictions, holding that although the Nevada court had found the parties domiciled in Nevada, there was sufficient evidence for the North Carolina court to find that the parties never relinquished their North Carolina domicile. This case seems somewhat in tension with *Williams I*, in that it allows the marital domicile state's interest in what it considers to be its domiciliaries to trump the forum state's interest in what it has similarly found to be its domiciliaries. On the other hand, the rule is essentially in accord with the general principle that only valid judgments are entitled to full faith and credit, and that it is the foreign state's duty to ensure the validity of the judgment. The state of North Carolina, after all, had not been party to the original divorce proceeding. On the same day that *Williams II* was decided, the Court addressed another case involving a Nevada divorce, in which a private plaintiff sought to use the divorce affirmatively to invalidate a support order. Again, the Court upheld the state's right to find no domicile in Nevada, thereby extending the right to attack a divorce collaterally to the absent party against whom the ex parte divorce was obtained.[70]

If both parties appear in the divorce proceedings, the divorce is bilateral, not ex parte. After a bilateral divorce, neither party may attack the divorce collaterally by challenging the finding of domicile unless the state in which the divorce was granted would allow the attack. Indeed, after a bilateral divorce, *no one else* (including a child of the divorced parents and a second spouse of one of the divorced parties) may attack the divorce collaterally:[71]

> If the defendant spouse appeared in the Florida proceedings and contested the issue of the wife's domicile, . . . or appeared and admitted her Florida domicile, . . . or was personally served in the divorce state, . . . he would be barred from attacking the decree collaterally; and so would a stranger to the Florida proceedings . . . .[72]

The theory behind this principle seems to be that just as an objection to personal jurisdiction may be waived by consent, a jurisdictional objection to a divorce based on lack of domicile may also be waived by the

---

70. Esenwein v. Commonwealth, 325 U.S. 279 (1945).

71. *See* R. WEINTRAUB, *supra* note 47, at § 5.2D at 237-38. Some scholars suggest that the state of the marital domicile, unlike individuals, is not barred from attacking the bilateral divorce in order to assert some compelling state interest, e.g., for child support. *Id.* at § 5.20 at 240 & n.74.

72. Cook v. Cook, 342 U.S. at 127-28 (citations omitted).

party's opportunity — and failure to — adjudicate it initially. For the same reason that basic fairness has been provided to the parties, it is also held that even if the divorce is ex parte, anyone attacking the divorce collaterally is estopped if the challenging party is deemed to have consented to or benefited from the divorce.[73] Thus, the absent party who remarries cannot attack the divorce, nor can his or her second spouse if the second spouse had knowledge of the circumstances of the divorce.[74]

Once a divorce decree has been successfully attacked and declared invalid in another state, must the state that granted the divorce in the first place give full faith and credit to the foreign state's judgment invalidating the divorce? The answer should probably be yes, because the last-in-time rule holds that the most recent judgment on an issue is the one entitled to full faith and credit.[75] However, in the Nevada case of *Colby v. Colby*,[76] the court refused to give full faith and credit to a Maryland decree invalidating a Nevada divorce, and the Supreme Court denied certiorari.[77] Thus, the question remains unanswered.

C. ALIMONY, CHILD SUPPORT AND PROPERTY DIVISION

1. Jurisdiction

While a state may change the parties' marital status without having jurisdiction over the defendant, a state court must still have jurisdiction over both parties in order to enter a valid and enforceable award pertaining to alimony, child support or property division.[78] Therefore, if the money judgment is entered in connection with a divorce, the court must have jurisdiction over both parties *and* be the domicile of one of the parties. Both of these factors are necessary in order to satisfy the special jurisdictional requirement for divorce jurisdiction — domicile — while also fulfilling the jurisdictional requirements for typical civil actions that result in personal financial liability.

The traditional means of obtaining personal jurisdiction apply in domestic relations. Thus, personal jurisdiction over the defendant may be obtained by the appearance of the defendant,[79] service while the

---

73. H. CLARK, *supra* note 31, at § 11.3.
74. *Id.*
75. See ch. 5, sec. IIB.
76. 78 Nev. 150, 369 P.2d 1019 (1962).
77. 371 U.S. 888 (1962).
78. *See* Armstrong v. Armstrong, 350 U.S. 568, 579-80 (1956) (Brode, J., concurring); RESTATEMENT (SECOND) CONFLICT OF LAWS § 77(1) (1971).
79. *See* Sherrer v. Sherrer, 334 U.S. 343, 348 (1948).

defendant is present in the state,[80] or domicile of the defendant in forum state.[81] In addition, application of a long-arm statute can create personal jurisdiction.[82] Most important, the forum state has sufficient contacts to exercise long-arm jurisdiction over a defendant-spouse who has left the state if that state is the last state of marital domicile.[83] In fact, some states hold that only if the forum is the last state of marital domicile will that state have sufficient contacts to exercise long-arm jurisdiction over the defendant,[84] even if the suit for spouse support, child support, or property division is not part of a divorce action.[85] Continued residence by the plaintiff is considered to be necessary to ensure that the forum state has strong enough interest in the litigation to justify affording the plaintiff a forum.

However, other states exercise long-arm jurisdiction over a defendant-spouse and render money judgments in connection with a divorce if the grounds for divorce occurred in the state.[86] In addition, even if the court does not otherwise have personal jurisdiction over the defendant, any property he or she has in the state might nevertheless serve as a contact that may create jurisdiction over the defendant in an action for division of that property.[87] But the mere fact that the plaintiff-spouse and children live in the forum state is not sufficient contact

---

80. See Sutton v. Lieb, 342 U.S. 402, 408 (1952). However, service while defendant is present in the state may not confer jurisdiction if the presence is obtained by fraud. Compare Hammet v. Hammet, 424 N.Y.S.2d 913, 914-15 (App. Div. 1980) (defendant's presence in New York for a weekend held voluntary and sufficient for valid service of process because presence not obtained by fraud or deceit of spouse) with Zenker v. Zenker, 72 N.W.2d 809, 818 (Neb. 1955) (husband's presence in Colorado, induced by wife's request to sign papers for real estate transaction, held involuntary so husband not collaterally estopped from challenging Colorado divorce).

81. See generally Milliken v. Meyer, 311 U.S. 457, 462 (1940).

82. See generally R. WEINTRAUB, supra note 47, at § 4.20; see, e.g., State ex rel. Oklahoma v. Griggs, 625 P.2d 660, 663-665, modified, 628 P.2d 791 (Ore. 1981); Von Ohlsen v. Von Ohlsen, 406 A.2d 393, 394 (1979); Mizner v. Mizner, 439 P.2d 679, 680-81 (Nev.), cert. denied, 393 U.S. 847 (1968).

83. See R. WEINTRAUB, supra note 47, at § 4.20 at 175-76. A number of states have long-arm statutes with specific provisions conferring jurisdiction if the forum state is the last state of marital domicile, see Kan. Stat. Ann. § 60-308(b) (1983); see also Ill. Ann. Stat. Ch. 110, § 17(1)(e); Wis. Stat. Ann. § 262.05(11). See also Prybolsky v. Prybolsky, 430 A.2d 804, 807 (Del. 1981) (interprets "doing business" in the state to include establishing the last marital domicile in the state).

84. See, e.g., Corcoran v. Corcoran, 353 So. 2d 805, 809 (Ala. Ct. Cir. App. 1978).

85. Kendall v. Kendall, 585 P.2d 978, 981 (Kan. 1978); Dillon v. Dillon, 176 N.W.2d 362, 370-71 (Wis. 1970).

86. See, e.g., Haymond v. Haymond, 377 N.E.2d 563 (Ill. 1978).

87. See Shaffer v. Heitner, 433 U.S. 186, 207-08 (1977) (jurisdiction usually permissible where property is the underlying source of the dispute). Cf. Vanderbilt v. Vanderbilt, 354 U.S. 416, 418 n.6 (1957) (pre-Shaffer case where jurisdiction obtained by sequestering property).

between the state and the defendant-spouse to confer personal jurisdiction over the defendant-spouse for any judgment against him or her.[88]

What happens when a state has jurisdiction to enter an ex parte divorce, based on the plaintiff's domicile, but does not have the personal jurisdiction over the defendant to enable it to divide the spouses' property or fix financial obligations? This was the question the Court addressed in *Estin v. Estin.*[89] In that case, the wife obtained legal separation and award of permanent alimony in New York while New York had personal jurisdiction over the husband. The husband then went to Nevada and obtained a divorce that granted the wife no alimony. The wife was not personally served nor did she appear in the Nevada proceedings. The husband stopped paying alimony pursuant to the Nevada decree and the wife sued in New York to enforce New York's support order. The Supreme Court held that full faith and credit required enforcement of the Nevada divorce decree but also allowed enforcement of the New York support order:

> The result in this situation is to make the divorce divisible — to give effect to the Nevada decree insofar as it affects marital status and to make it ineffective on the issue of alimony. It accommodates the interests of both Nevada and New York in this broken marriage by restricting each State to the matters of her dominant concern.[90]

In *Estin,* the "divisible divorce" involved a support order preceding the ex parte divorce. In *Vanderbilt v. Vanderbilt,*[91] the Court decided that *after* an ex parte divorce is awarded by one state, another state may award spousal support without violating full faith and credit. The court reasoned that the first state, Nevada, that granted the ex parte divorce did not have jurisdiction over the defendant-spouse, and thus could not extinguish her right to spousal support conferred upon her by the state of her domicile, New York.[92] Again, the state deciding the support issue was required to have jurisdiction over the defendant-spouse. It is not clear why a court that terminates only the marital status need not have jurisdiction over the defendant-spouse, while a court which determines his or her financial liabilities from that marriage must have such jurisdiction. Presumably, this reflects a policy that marriage, but not financial responsibilities, should be terminable at will by either party.

---

88. Kulko v. Superior Court, 436 U.S. 84, 93-94 (1978).
89. 334 U.S. 541 (1948).
90. *Id.* at 549.
91. 354 U.S. 416 (1957).
92. *Id.* at 418.

2. Choice of Law

In enunciating the doctrine of "divisible divorce," the Supreme Court emphasized that the state in which a spouse seeking support is domiciled has a legitimate interest in the support of the spouse: "The problem of her [or his] livelihood and support is plainly a matter in which her [or his] community ha[s] a legitimate interest."[93]

At least one court has interpreted this as an indication that the law of defendant-spouse's domicile is the proper choice of law in determining a right to support following an ex parte divorce, even though that law is not the law of the forum.[94] However, the choice of law as to spousal support will generally be between the state in which the supportable spouse is domiciled (or was domiciled at the time of the divorce) and the law of the state in which the supporting spouse is domiciled, typically the forum state. Usually the forum state applies its own law, especially when the spousal support award is in conjunction with a bilateral divorce.

States are somewhat more inclined to apply a foreign state's law to a division of marital property. In *Scheuler v. Scheuler,*[95] for example, the Louisiana court interpreted a federal statute's mandate to apply its own law in dividing military retirement benefits on divorce as authorizing it to apply its own choice-of-law rules, which required application of Wyoming's law as the marital domicile state. Similarly, in *Anderson v. Anderson,*[96] the District of Columbia court was willing to apply another state's law to the division of property. It applied Maryland law to govern the division of real estate located in Maryland, although it decided the alimony and attorneys fee questions under District of Columbia law. The *Anderson* case might be thought to be a vestige of the *First Restatement,* under which states are considered to have a unique interest in property located within its borders. Its reliance on *Williams v. Williams,*[97] however, another case in which the District of Columbia courts applied Maryland's real property laws, makes clear that it was based on weighing the relative strength of the state interests served.

If a state in which a spouse is domiciled at the time of a divorce has an interest in his or her support, logically it could also be thought that a state in which an offspring of the marriage is domiciled at the time of the divorce would have a similar interest in the child's support. Thus,

---

93. *Estin,* 344 U.S. at 547.

94. *See* Portnoy v. Portnoy, 401 P.2d 249, 250 (Nev. 1965) (affirms application of California's alimony law as law of place of wife's domicile at time of ex parte divorce).

95. 460 So. 2d 1120, 1122-23 (La. Ct. App. 1985).

96. 449 A.2d 334, 335 (D.C. 1982).

97. 390 A.2d 4, 5-6 (D.C. 1978).

it might be expected that a forum state would be willing to apply the child-support law of the state in which the child is domiciled, or was domiciled at the time of the divorce or child-custody determination. However, there are apparently no cases applying a foreign state's child-support law. This may be due to the circumstance that in all states the amount of child support is heavily determined by equity and trial courts have great discretion in its determination, so that choice of child-support law would make little difference to the outcome. Choice of law, indeed, pales into insignificance in such cases. The problem in this area is not usually the amount of the award, but the failure to pay. We turn to these problems concerning judgments next.

3. Judgments

In general, any judgment awarding the payment of money, including alimony, property division or child support, is subject to successful collateral attack and is not entitled to recognition and enforcement if the court rendering the decree lacked personal jurisdiction over the parties. The requirements of due process and full faith and credit apply with equal force to money judgments in domestic relations as to other money judgments.

Two special judgments problems arise in the context of domestic relations. One relates to the old doctrine of the "land taboo." Even if a divorcing court has personal jurisdiction over the defendant, an order purporting directly to transfer ownership of real property located outside the forum state need not be enforced by the state in which the property is located.[98] Many states do at their discretion, however, enforce such foreign states' property settlements, even though the property is located outside the divorcing state.[99]

A more serious problem is that alimony and support decrees are often modifiable; for example, an order for monthly alimony payments may be modified upon a showing of changed circumstances. Thus, the court must determine whether the judgment ought to be enforced is a "final judgment," entitled to full faith and credit, or is a modifiable nonfinal award. Awards are modifiable only if the rendering state's law or decree announces them as such.[100] Enforcing states are not compelled by full faith and credit to enforce future installments or past installments that are modifiable under the decreeing state's law.[101]

---

98. Fall v. Eastin, 215 U.S. 1, 9 (1909).

99. *See, e.g.,* Varone v. Varone, 359 F.2d 769 (7th Cir. 1966); McElreath v. McElreath, 345 S.W.2d 722 (Tex. 1961); Weesner v. Weesner, 95 N.W.2d 682 (Neb. 1959); Gately v. Gately, 316 F.2d 585 (7th Cir. 1963).

100. *See* Yarborough v. Yarborough, 290 U.S. 202, 209 (1933).

101. *See* Halvey v. Halvey, 330 U.S. 610, 614-15 (1947); Sistare v. Sistare, 218 U.S. 17 (1910).

However, past due or accrued installments that, under the law of the decreeing state, are no longer modifiable, are "final" judgments entitled to full faith and credit.[102]

Although not required to enforce modifiable judgments, a state, at its discretion, may enforce it as it stands or may consider modifying it.[103] The question then arises, under whose law shall the award be modified — the rendering state's or the enforcing state's? The answer lies at the discretion of the enforcing state and its choice-of-law rules, even though the rendering state has, under its continuing jurisdiction, an interest in the modification of its decree. The enforcing state in such cases might modify the award pursuant to the decreeing state's modification principles, although it could also, theoretically at least, adopt the modifiable award as its own and modify it pursuant to its own law.[104]

4. Uniform Reciprocal Enforcement of Support Act: An Exception

The Uniform Reciprocal Enforcement of Support Act (URESA), which has been adopted in some form by every state,[105] provides important exceptions to general rules for spousal support and child support. Generally, the Act allows an "obligee,"[106] that is, any person, state or political subdivision to whom a duty of support is owed, to file a complaint in his or her home state, called the "initiating state,"[107] alleging the identification and location of the "obligor,"[108] the person from whom support is sought.[109] If a court in the initiating state determines that the complaint sets forth facts that may establish a duty to support and that another court (the "responding state" or "responding court")[110] may have jurisdiction over an obligor or his or her property, the initiat-

---

102. *See* Barber v. Barber, 323 U.S. 77, 86 (1944); *Sistare,* 218 U.S. at 16-17.

103. *See Halvey,* 330 U.S. at 615.

104. *See, e.g.,* Worthley v. Worthley, 283 P.2d 19, 25 (Cal. 1955) (en banc) (holding foreign support order modifiable by law of foreign sovereign). For a discussion of the obligation to apply the rendering state's res judicata rules, see ch. 5, sec. IIA.

105. 9A U.L.A. (1968 Revised Act and 1950 Act) (1979 & 1985 Supp.) ("URESA" or "Act"). The 1950 Act was adopted by all states and jurisdictions of the United States; by 1985 33 states had adopted the 1968 Revised Act. The substantive provisions of the two Acts are largely the same; the 1968 Act makes technical revisions to the enforcement mechanisms. URESA, 9A U.L.A. Prefatory Note (1979 & Supp. 1985); *see generally* W. BROCKELBANK & F. INFANSTO, INTERSTATE ENFORCEMENT OF FAMILY SUPPORT (1971).

106. URESA § 2(f).

107. *Id.* at § 2(d).

108. *Id.* § 2(g).

109. *Id.* § 11.

110. *Id.* § 2(l).

ing state certifies the complaint and transfers it to the responding state.[111] The responding state appoints counsel,[112] allocates other resources needed to locate the obligor or his or her property, and prosecutes the support action.[113] The obligee need not leave his or her home state to obtain support.[114] If the responding state has jurisdiction over the obligor,[115] then after notice and opportunity for hearing[116] the state determines the duty to support[117] pursuant to its own law,[118] and enforces its support order.[119] Additionally, the obligee may register a foreign support order in a forum state.[120] The forum state's court then appoints an attorney,[121] and enforces the foreign order as if the order were its own.[122]

The purpose of the Act is to provide dependent spouses and children with an expedient means of securing support from liable persons residing in other states.[123] The Act is also intended to lessen the state's responsibility to support dependent spouses and children by compelling liable parties to pay family support, independent of where that party may travel to escape liability.[124] To achieve these ends, however, states enacting URESA relinquish many of the rights afforded them by the full faith and credit clause. Specifically, they lose the right to have their law applied to their dependent domiciliaries and to have their judgments enforced and modified pursuant to their own law. We now examine how URESA affects jurisdiction, choice of law, and judgments, respectively.

a. Jurisdiction

In an action brought under URESA, a responding state must have jurisdiction over the defendant[125] pursuant to the responding state's

---

111. *Id.* § 14.

112. *Id.* § 12.

113. *Id.* §§ 17-19.

114. *See, e.g.,* Hodge v. Maith, 435 So.2d 387, 389 (Fla. Dist. Ct. App. 1983); O'Halloran v. O'Halloran, 580 S.W.2d 870, 873 (Tex. Civ. App. 1979).

115. *See* URESA §§ 14 and 18.

116. *Id.* §§ 20-23.

117. *Id.* § 24.

118. *Id.* § 7.

119. *Id.* § 26.

120. *Id.* §§ 36-37, 39.

121. *Id.* § 38.

122. *Id.* § 40(a).

123. *See, e.g.,* Paredes v. Paredes, 454 N.E.2d 1014, 1017 (Ill. App. Ct. 1983), Banks v. McMorris, 121 Cal. Rptr. 185, 189 (Ct. App. 1975), *cert. denied,* 423 U.S. 871 (1975).

124. *See* Government of The Virgin Islands v. Lorillard, 242 F. Supp. 1021, 1022 (D.V.I. 1965).

125. URESA §§ 14, 18.

procedural law[126] before it can award support or enforce a foreign state's support order. However, the responding state need not have jurisdiction over the obligee. An obligor may not therefore counterclaim for divorce, child custody, or visitation, because URESA does not confer jurisdiction over the obligee nor require the obligee to enter an appearance; thus, she or he is not deemed to have consented to the jurisdiction of the responding court.[127]

b. Choice of Law

The state in which a supportable spouse or child is domiciled has a legitimate interest in the domiciliary's support. In a non-URESA action, therefore, the law of the dependent person's state may be applied to support actions whether the action is brought in the dependent's home state or another state.

If an action is brought under URESA, however, the responding state applies the law of the state where the obligor was present during the period for which support is sought, presumptively the responding state.[128] The authors of URESA justify this choice of law, premised upon the mere presence of the obligor, on the grounds that the state in which the obligor is located has a legitimate interest in forcing that resident to support his or her dependents, wherever they may be found.[129] By enacting URESA, the authors argue, the legislature declares that its support law applies to all its resident obligors. However, the state also relinquishes its interest in the application of its law to its resident *obligees*. This relinquishment must be justified by the need expeditiously to extract support from foreign obligors.

c. Judgments

In order to ensure that URESA judgments will be fully enforceable, URESA not only authorizes the issuing state to enforce it but also allows the obligee to register a foreign support award with a responding state.[130] The foreign award is then treated as if it were the responding state's award, subject to the same procedures and defenses as a support order of the responding state.[131] The obligor has the same de-

---

126. *See, e.g.,* Pousson v. Superior Court, 332 P.2d 766, 767-68 (Cal. App. 1958).

127. *See, e.g.,* Ibach v. Ibach, 600 P.2d 1370, 1373 (Ariz. 1979) (en banc); Register v. Kandlbinder, 216 S.E.2d 647, 648 (Ga. Ct. App. 1975); Simpson v. Simpson, 247 So. 2d 792, 793 (Fla. 1971); State ex rel. Schwartz v. Buder, 315 S.W.2d 867, 869-70 (Mo. Ct. App. 1958).

128. URESA § 7.

129. W. BROCKELBANK & F. INFANSTO, *supra* note 105, at 31.

130. URESA § 36.

131. *Id.* § 40(a).

fenses as she or he has in an action to enforce a foreign money judgment.[132] This creates the potential for forfeiting the state's interest in the integrity of its judgments, because an award which was not modifiable in the rendering state could become modifiable, and a modifiable award could be modified pursuant to different standards in a responding state. In fact, however, courts generally interpret the registration provisions as authorization to apply their own procedures, but with any modification made pursuant to the rendering state's law.[133] Although the issue is not settled, it may arguably violate full faith and credit to modify a foreign state's judgment pursuant to the enforcing state's law.[134]

Furthermore, to the extent that two awards are at odds (perhaps because the obligee chose not to register the foreign award, and instead relitigated support),[135] URESA allows states to ignore the last-in-time rule. State B's award does not nullify State A's previous award because State B's award under URESA is believed to be in addition to other remedies available to an obligee.[136] Any amount paid, however, is credited against all awards for the same time period.[137] A responding state is also prohibited from staying a proceeding simply because another action is pending elsewhere. Again, the state's concern with obtaining support payments expeditiously has apparently overridden concerns about forum shopping.

D. CHILD CUSTODY

Child custody disputes, perhaps more than any other area of law, involve emotional and hotly contested battles in which there are often no right answers. No wonder that the federal courts decline to get involved! The most significant problem in this area is that all too often

---

132. *Id.* § 40(c).

133. *See, e.g.,* Creed v. Schultz, 196 Cal. Rptr. 252, 257 (Ct. App. 1983) (modification pursuant to rendering state's law); Walzer v. Walzer, 376 A.2d 414, 418-19 (Conn. 1977) (same). *Cf.* State ex rel. Greeble v. Endsley, 379 N.E.2d 440, 441 (Ind. 1978) (applying its own venue rules to enforcement of registered support order); State on Behalf of McDonnell v. McCutcheon, 337 N.W.2d 645, 651 & n.6 (Minn. 1983) (leaving open question of whose law would apply in modification of registered award).

134. *Cf.* Oglesby v. Oglesby, 510 P.2d 1106, 1107-08 (Utah 1973) (entrance of support order under URESA in one state does not modify preexisting support order in another, which is still entitled to full faith and credit). Another constitutional challenge to URESA is that it is an interstate compact without congressional approval. Courts have held URESA does not violate the compact clause, U.S. CONST. art. I, § 10, cl. 3. *See, e.g.,* Fraser v. Fraser, 415 A.2d 1304, 1305-06 (R.I. 1980); Ivey v. Ayers, 301 S.W.2d 790, 794-95 (Mo. 1957).

135. URESA § 31.

136. *See id.* § 3.

137. *Id.* § 31.

the losing contestant takes the child/ren into another jurisdiction to seek a more sympathetic forum in which to re-adjudicate custody.[138] Because (as we shall see) the Supreme Court's interpretation of the constitutional requirements of the full faith and credit accorded child custody decrees has left children inadequately protected from this danger, all fifty states and the District of Columbia have enacted the Uniform Child Custody Jurisdiction Act (UCCJA),[139] and Congress has enacted the Parental Kidnapping Prevention Act of 1980 (PKPA).[140] These acts regulate state court jurisdiction over child custody disputes and the full faith and credit to be accorded to foreign states' custody decrees.

1. Jurisdiction

Jurisdiction to determine child custody is somewhat confused because state statutory law does not comport precisely with Supreme Court decisions. In *May v. Anderson*,[141] the Court held that a child custody decree, even if rendered by the state in which the children are domiciled, was not entitled to full faith and credit unless the rendering court had personal jurisdiction over the other parent in the custody dispute. In *Kulko v. Superior Court*,[142] furthermore, the Supreme Court held that due process requires personal jurisdiction over the defendant in an action to modify a child custody agreement and to increase the defendant's child support obligations. *Kulko* admittedly focused on the child-support element of the action; had the action been one only for child custody, the result might have been different. But *Kulko* arguably reiterates *May*'s holding that personal jurisdiction over the defendant in a custody contest is required by due process.

State statutes following the Uniform Child Custody Jurisdiction Act (UCCJA), on the other hand, confer jurisdiction based on the "home state" of the child/ren:[143] that is, the state in which the child has lived

---

138. *See* Commissioners' Prefatory Note, Uniform Child Custody Jurisdiction Act (UCCJA), 9 U.L.A. 111-12 (1979).

139. 9 U.L.A. 111-70 (1979 & Supp. 1985).

140. 28 U.S.C. § 1738A (1982). For the international aspects of jurisdictional and conflicts of laws problems in child custody disputes, see UCCJA § 23, 9 U.L.A. 167 (1979); Convention on the Civil Aspects of International Child Abduction, Oct. 25, 1980, Hague Conference on Private International Law, reprinted in 15 FAM. L.Q. 149, 149-63 (1981); Middleton v. Middleton, 314 S.E.2d 362 (Va. 1984) (discussing effect of English custody proceeding in Virginia proceedings).

141. 345 U.S. 528 (1953).

142. 436 U.S. 84 (1978).

143. UCCJA § 3, 9 U.L.A. 122-23, provides in full:

(a) A court of this State which is competent to decide child custody matters has

for the last six consecutive months.[144] Personal jurisdiction over the defendant contestant is not required by the Act,[145] although the defendant must be provided with notice and an opportunity to be heard.[146] The drafting commission noted that "[t]here is no requirement for technical personal jurisdiction, on the theory that custody determinations, as distinguished from support actions . . ., are proceedings in rem or proceedings affecting status."[147]

The UCCJA was drafted after *May* was decided but before *Kulko*. The drafters decided to interpret *May* within the confines of full faith and credit. Relying on Frankfurter's concurrence, they decided that *May* allowed, but did not require, states to decline to enforce foreign custody decrees rendered without personal jurisdiction over the custody contestants. Accordingly, by adopting the UCCJA, the state legislatures exercised their discretion under *May* and directed their courts to accord such judgments full faith and credit.[148]

If, however, due process, not just full faith and credit, requires personal jurisdiction over the contestants, then the state may not waive

---

jurisdiction to make a child custody determination by initial or modification decree if:

(1) this State (i) is the home state of the child at the time of commencement of the proceeding, or (ii) had been the child's home state within 6 months before commencement of the proceeding and the child is absent from this State because of his removal or retention by a person claiming his custody or for other reasons, and a parent or person acting as parent continues to live in this State; or

(2) it is in the best interest of the child that a court of this State assume jurisdiction because (i) the child and his parents, or the child and at least one contestant, have a significant connection with this State, and (ii) there is available in this State substantial evidence concerning the child's present or future care, protection, training, and personal relationships; or

(3) the child is physically present in this State and (i) the child has been abandoned or (ii) it is necessary in an emergency to protect the child because he has been subjected to or threatened with mistreatment or abuse or is otherwise neglected [or dependent]; or

(4) (i) it appears that no other state would have jurisdiction under prerequisites substantially in accordance with paragraphs (1), (2), or (3), or another state has declined to exercise jurisdiction on the ground that this State is the more appropriate forum to determine the custody of the child, and (ii) it is in the best interest of the child that this court assume jurisdiction.

(b) Except under paragraphs (3) and (4) of subsection (a), physical presence in this State of the child, or of the child and one of the contestants, is not alone sufficient to confer jurisdiction on a court of this State to make a child custody determination.

(c) Physical presence of the child, when desirable, is not a prerequisite for jurisdiction to determine his custody.

See also Parental Kidnapping Prevention Act of 1980 (PKPA), 28 U.S.C. § 1738A.

144. UCCJA § 2(5), 9 U.L.A. 119.

145. *See id.,* Commissioners' Note § 12, 9 U.L.A. 150.

146. *See id.,* §§ 4, 5, 9 U.L.A. 129-31.

147. *Id.* Commissioners' Note § 12, 9 U.L.A. 150.

148. *See* Bodenheimer, *The Uniform Child Custody Jurisdiction Act: A Legislative Remedy for Children Caught in the Conflicts of Laws,* 22 VAND. L. REV. 1207, 1232 (1969).

the contestant's right to personal jurisdiction by enacting UCCJA. A custody award rendered pursuant to the UCCJA without personal jurisdiction over the contestants might successfully be appealed or attacked collaterally for lack of due process. At least one state, nonetheless, has held since *Kulko* that the minimum contacts necessary to confer personal jurisdiction over an absent party are not required to adjudicate custody under the UCCJA because "custody is in effect an adjudication of a child's status, which falls under the status exception of *Shaffer v. Heitner.*"[149]

Custody arguably is not a status. Unlike paternity, maternity, and legitimacy, which may represent a status relationship, custody is arguably a right, namely a right to exercise parental control. Thus, child custody might not fall under any "status exception" to minimum contacts analysis. However, there may be several avenues other than the usual minimum contacts analysis by which to obtain personal jurisdiction. One is to argue that the home state of the child has *specific* personal jurisdiction over the absent contestant to adjudicate custody. Given the home state's interests in the child, the relationship between the contestant and the child may be a sufficiently significant contact to confer specific personal jurisdiction over the absent custody contestant. Another is to argue that substantial fairness to the out-of-state contestant requires only notice of the pendency of litigation. The reason would be that the home state of the child is not an unexpected forum, and if the absent contestant cannot afford to appear the forum has the discretion under the UCCJA to order one party to pay the travel expenses of the absent party.[150] Neither of these arguments is particularly convincing in light of the holding in *Kulko,* where the forum had an interest in support for locally domiciled children and had afforded notice of the litigation. A further defense of the statute might rest on

---

149. In re Marriage of Hudson, 434 N.E.2d 107, 117 (Ind. Ct. App.) (referring to Shaffer v. Heitner, 433 U.S. 186 (1977)), *cert. denied sub nom* Hudson v. Hudson, 459 U.S. 1202 (1982). The Indiana court continued:

> After concluding the minimum contact standard of *International Shoe* applied to *in personam* and *in rem* actions alike, the Court cautioned: "We do not suggest that jurisdictional doctrines other than those discussed in text, such as the particularized rules governing adjudications of status, are inconsistent with the standard of fairness." *Shaffer v. Heitner, supra,* 433 U.S. at 208 n.30.[14]
> [14] Furthermore, the Supreme Court has apparently recognized the unique nature of similar proceedings and the concomitant necessity for specialized jurisdictional rules in *Stanley v. Illinois* (1972) 405 U.S. 645, . . . where notice by publication was held sufficient to terminate the rights of an unwed father when personal service could not be obtained. In fact, at least one commentator has suggested *Stanley v. Illinois* overruled *May "sub silentio."* H. CLARK, CASES AND PROBLEMS ON DOMESTIC RELATIONS 673 (2d ed. 1974).

Hudson, 434 N.E.2d at 119.
150. Section 11(c), 9 U.L.A. 148.

the fact of the adoption of the statute by the home state of the supporting parent. By adopting the statute, that state might be consenting to a local person's amenability to suit at the domicile of the children. Such consent might be upheld[151] on the grounds that the supporting parent has no legitimate objection to assertion of his or her own state's authority. Finally, now that much of the UCCJA has been incorporated into federal law, the constitutional problems may have evaporated because Congress can establish nationwide service of process.[152]

Another sort of jurisdictional problem arises in child-custody disputes in which several fora may have jurisdiction. Before the UCCJA, four jurisdictions potentially could entertain a child-custody dispute: the state in which the child is domiciled; the state in which the child is present; and the two states having jurisdiction over the contestants (usually the mother and father). A problem of concurrent jurisdiction, with its concomitant problem of inconsistent judgments (exacerbated when judgments are not accorded full faith and credit), left the child and custody contestants without the certainty and security of a single, final, consistent and enforceable judgment.

The UCCJA attempted to remedy the problem of concurrent jurisdiction by conferring jurisdiction upon the one best forum among competing fora: the state with maximum, not just minimum contacts.[153] The Act thus specifies that the home state of the child exercise jurisdiction.[154] Yet it also recognizes concurrent jurisdiction in certain limited cases. It allows another state to exercise jurisdiction if it is in the best interest of the child,[155] or if the child is present in the state and abandoned or threatened by abuse,[156] or if no other state will take jurisdiction.[157] Thus, despite best efforts, the Act fails to eliminate concurrent jurisdiction.

---

151. Cf. New York v. O'Neill, 359 U.S. 1 (1958).

152. 28 U.S.C. § 2361, see C. WRIGHT, supra note 23, at 498, R.CASAD, supra note 59, at § 5.03[2] at 5-20-22.

153. "The interest of the child is served when the forum has optional access to relevant evidence about the child and family. There must be maximum rather than minimum contact with the state." UCCJA, Commissioners' Note § 3, 9 U.L.A. at 124.

154. Id. § 3(a)(1), 9 U.L.A. 122.

155. Id. § 3(a)(2), 9 U.L.A. 122.

156. Id. § 3(a)(3), 9 U.L.A. 122.

157. Id. § 3(a)(4), 9 U.L.A. 122.

The problem of concurrent initial jurisdiction is supposed to be resolved by the priority-in-time[158] or the inconvenient forum principle,[159] aided by interstate judicial communication and cooperation.[160] Once a court has exercised its jurisdiction, the Act requires other states to defer to the first state until that initial forum no longer has the requisite contacts to maintain jurisdiction.[161] While the Act has reduced the problems of concurrent jurisdiction, it has not eliminated them.[162] In part, this is because the Act relies on the good faith and discretion of competing fora to give deference to competitors and cooperate with them; the UCCJA does not specifically confer power on one state to prohibit another state from exercising jurisdiction.[163] The problem of concurrent initial jurisdiction is exacerbated when under the UCCJA one state may take jurisdiction over another state's custody decree and modify it. This is a problem we address below.

2. Choice of Law

Every state in the nation theoretically has adopted the same standard by which to determine initially who shall be given custody of a child: the best interest of the child.[164] However, the meaning of "best interest of the child" varies from state to state and from judge to judge. Some states have statutes enumerating factors to be considered when judging the best interest of the child, and each state has judicial opinions attempting to clarify the standard.[165] Yet the standard is so amor-

---

158. *Id.* § 6, 9 U.L.A. 134. Section 6 generally provides that if one state has already taken jurisdiction over custody proceedings, another state shall not exercise its jurisdiction, unless the proceedings have been stayed in the first state. *See also* Vanneck v. Vanneck, 404 N.E.2d 1278 (N.Y. 1980) (New York court should defer adjudicating custody dispute where custody proceedings in Connecticut already had commenced).

159. UCCJA § 7, 9 U.L.A. 137-38; Bodenheimer, *supra* note 148, at 1218. Section 7 instructs any court that has jurisdiction over a custody dispute to decline to exercise its jurisdiction if it is an inconvenient forum or if another forum would be more appropriate. *Cf.* In re Marriage of Ben-Yehoshu, 91 Cal. App. 3d 259, 154 Cal. Rptr. 80 (1979) (California court cannot enter custody decree because children did not have significant relationship to state and another forum had maximum contacts).

160. UCCJA §§ 19-22, 9 U.L.A. 162-67.

161. *Id.* § 14, 9 U.L.A. 153-54.

162. *See* Webb v. Webb, 451 U.S. 493 (1981) (inconsistent custody judgments of Florida and Georgia made under UCCJA left unresolved because party failed to raise below the full faith and credit argument).

163. *Cf.* Vanneck v. Vanneck, 404 N.E.2d 1278, 1280 (N.Y. 1980) (power of New York court to enjoin custody action in another forum, if it exists at all, derives from New York court's authority over divorce, and not from UCCJA).

164. Wexler, *Rethinking the Modification of Child Custody Decrees*, 94 YALE L.J. 757, 779 & n. 87 (1985).

165. For example, some states have a "primary caretaker rule" that presumes it is in the child's best interest to award custody to the person who has been primarily

phous that it allows judges great leeway to impart their own individual values. Thus, in theory it perhaps should make no difference which law is applied because the law is the same virtually everywhere. In practice, however, it makes a great difference not only which law the judge applies but also which judge applies the law.

Upon an initial custody determination, the forum applies its own law.[166] The maximum contacts necessary to confer jurisdiction under the UCCJA also justify application of the forum's law. Choice-of-law problems are confronted, however, when a contestant requests a court to modify a foreign custody decree. Analytically, this presents a two-tiered problem: (1) the choice of law governing whether to modify the original decree; and (2) the choice of law governing to whom to award custody. Courts, however, do not address the second problem; they assume because the "best interest of the child" standard is the same everywhere, that they are not confronted with a conflict of underlying substantive law.[167] Instead their choice-of-law attention has focused upon the first question.

Choice of law governing whether to modify the decree is a problem of increasing interest to scholars. Professor Joan Wexler has identified three standards governing whether to modify the decree:

> One [standard] permits modification if there is a substantial change in circumstances that makes a modification in the child's best interest. An even more flexible test allows modification if it is in the child's best interest regardless of whether there has been any change in circumstances since the initial award. A third standard permits modification only consensually or upon a showing of serious harm to the child.[168]

---

responsible for the child's care. *See, e.g.,* Garska v. McCoy, 278 S.E.2d 357 (W. Va. 1981). Some states had subscribed to the "tender years" doctrine, under which the custody of very young children was granted to their mother, but states have abandoned that doctrine in recent years. *See, e.g.,* Johnson v. Johnson, 564 P.2d 71 (Alaska 1977), *cert. denied,* 434 U.S. 1048 (1978). Furthermore, some states have a statutory preference for joint or shared custody. *See* Cal. Civ. Code § 4600.5 (West Supp. 1986); 23 Pa. Cons. Stat. Ann. § 1002 (Purdon Supp. 1983).

166. We have identified only one potential exception to this rule: where custody and/or adoption is the subject of a contract. *See* Smith v. Green, 480 P.2d 437 (Or. Ct. App. 1971) (court looks to law governing contract and then to its own law to determine whether enforcement would violate forum's public policy). This exception may grow wider if surrogate parenting gains popularity.

167. One might also argue that if the court has sufficient contacts to modify an award, it has sufficient interest to apply its own law. However, modifying a decree and entering an initial decree are not the same. Full faith and credit argues that a court should modify a foreign state custody decree only to the extent the award is modifiable in the foreign state. *See* Halvey v. Halvey, 330 U.S. 610, 614-15 (1947); *see also* Ford v. Ford, 371 U.S. 187 (1962) (South Carolina courts not bound by Virginia custody agreement and dismissal of suit because Virginia agreement not res judicata in Virginia).

168. Wexler, *supra* note 164, at 760-61.

Obviously, the choice-of-law issue here may determine whether a custody order will be modified. Because the later two tests are fairly recent, however, courts have not yet confronted this choice-of-law problem.

Most likely, the choice of law on modification standards will be determined by the full faith and credit to be afforded the foreign state's judgment. If the foreign state's judgment is accorded full faith and credit, its custody award should be modified pursuant to the rendering state's modification standard. If, however, the foreign state's judgment is adopted as the modifying state's order (as are child-support orders under URESA), then the modifying state might modify the order pursuant to its own standard. This could occur where the other state no longer has jurisdiction over the dispute.

States will probably disagree about whether to apply a foreign state's child custody modification standards just as they have disagreed about whether to apply a foreign state's child *support* modification standards.[169] The likely result is that children and their custodians will have neither the certainty and security of a non-modifiable, final custody judgments, nor the certainty of a single standard by which the custody award may be modified. If society's goal is to provide children with stability, security, and continuity,[170] it is important to make custody awards enforceable in other states, an issue to which we now turn.

3. Judgments

The Supreme Court has specifically reserved for decision the question whether full faith and credit applies to custody decrees.[171] The general rule, however, is that a state may modify a foreign custody decree if the decree was modifiable in the rendering state.[172] Because custody decrees are virtually always modifiable, this means that no state is required to enforce the terms of the custody decree of a foreign state. This is tantamount to declaring that custody decrees are never final and hence not entitled to the protections of full faith and credit. Prior to adoption of the UCCJA, states could afford foreign decrees full faith and credit at their discretion. The UCCJA now obligates states to enforce foreign custody decrees.

The UCCJA and its federal counterpart, the Parental Kidnapping Prevention Act, allow states to modify a foreign custody decree in only two instances, namely when (1) the enforcing state has jurisdiction,

---

169. *See* sec. C *supra.*

170. *See* Bodenheimer, *supra* note 148, at 1208-09.

171. Ford v. Ford, 371 U.S. 187, 192 (1962); Kovacs v. Brewer, 356 U.S. 604, 607 (1958); New York ex rel. Halvey v. Halvey, 330 U.S. 610, 615-16 (1947).

172. *Kovacs,* 356 U.S. at 607; *Halvey,* 330 U.S. at 614.

and (2) the rendering state does not have jurisdiction or has declined to exercise its jurisdiction.[173] This power is broader than it might at first appear. First, modification includes the right to reverse the initial award completely. Furthermore, deciding when a foreign state has declined to exercise jurisdiction is a determination made by the enforcing state. At least one court has held that, if a rendering state has refused to modify a custody decree in accordance with the child's best interest (as determined by the enforcing state), the rendering state has declined to exercise its jurisdiction under the PKPA.[174] Consequently, an "enforcing" state having jurisdiction may, at its discretion, modify or reverse a foreign state's custody award. In practice, then, despite UCCJA and PKPA, child custody awards are not recognized or enforced as final judgments under the full faith and credit clause. Because children are, therefore, denied the security of knowing with certainty who will be their custodial parent, it can be argued that the current rules are not in the "best interest" of children.[175] Professor Wexler has thus suggested that "[n]o custodial modification should be allowed . . . unless the child is seriously endangered."[176]

Conclusion

As in criminal law, the jurisdictional doctrines surrounding domestic relations are idiosyncratic in several respects. Domestic relations law is assumed to be of peculiar interest to the states. Thus, for instance, federal courts decline to become involved in domestic relations problems. Similarly, state adjudicative jurisdiction and state legislative jurisdiction typically go hand in hand, so that for a state to entertain a case typically means that it will apply its own law. The decision as to whether to adjudicate and apply local law in domestic relations cases, however, fits less comfortably within traditional legal doctrine than does the state's exercise of criminal jurisdiction. The latter is still straightforwardly territorial, whereas domestic relations law is dominated by domiciliary contacts and state interests.

The reason, perhaps, lies in the ongoing nature of familial relations. A state that is confronted with a continuing familial problem on the part of one of its domiciliaries is unlikely to care that certain other aspects of the case occurred elsewhere. Why should a state be denied the right to intervene simply because earlier events, such as the mar-

---

173. PKPA, 28 U.S.C. § 1738A(f); UCCJA § 14, 9 U.L.A. 153-54.

174. E.E.B. v. D.A., 446 A.2d 871 (N.J. 1982).

175. *See* Wexler, *supra* note 164, at 784-803 (reviewing available social science data and concluding that compelling policy reasons exist for adopting stricter standard for custody modification).

176. *Id.* at 782.

riage itself or the previous marital domicile, were located in another state? The important focus is instead on the ongoing consequences of the legal relationship. Such a focus does not sit well with the traditional territorialist orientation towards vested rights, which emphasized certainty at the expense of flexibility.

The pendulum may now have swung the other way, at least in the child custody context. The child's need for certainty is reflected in statutory developments such as the UCCJA and PKPA. One expects that the substantive tension between certainty and flexibility will require continual readjustment in domestic relations, and that it will continue to be reflected in the relevant jurisdictional doctrines.

Chapter 13

JURISDICTION TO TAX

The power to tax has been called "the power to destroy."[1] In determining who is permitted to wield this sword, courts balance the government's need for revenue against the restrictions placed by taxation on persons and free trade. The power to tax has also been called "an incident of sovereignty . . . co-extensive with that to which it is an incident. All subjects over which the sovereign power of a state extends, are objects of taxation; but those over which it does not extend, are, upon the soundest principles, exempt from taxation."[2] This chapter examines the jurisdiction to tax within our federal system of government.

Jurisdiction to tax is similar to other topics addressed here in Part III in that adjudicative and legislative jurisdiction are highly dependent upon one another. For one thing, the legislative jurisdiction needed to apply a tax virtually always supplies an adequate nexus for adjudicative authority.[3] Furthermore, at common law, other states typically declined to enforce one another's tax laws,[4] although this has been altered in most states by statute.[5] The reasons for this refusal are presumably similar to those relied upon in the criminal context;[6] the state, as party, has a paramount interest in enforcement, which is best served by suit in its own courts. Furthermore, other states are less inclined to perform what is basically a free public service to the taxing state. And as with both criminal and domestic relations law, federal courts are reluctant to become involved with administration of state taxing schemes.[7] While this refusal to adjudicate other state's tax claims has not been recently reviewed by the Supreme Court,[8] it has at least become clear that full faith and credit is owing once the claim has been reduced to judgment.[9]

Throughout this book, we have illustrated the fundamental tensions caused by allocating power between the state and federal governments and between the states as coexistent sovereigns. These tensions are

---

1. McCulloch v. Maryland, 17 U.S. (4 Wheat.) 316, 431 (1819).
2. *Id.* at 429.
3. *See, e.g.,* International Shoe Co. v. Washington, 326 U.S. 310 (1945).
4. *See generally* Leflar, *Out-of-State Collection of State and Local Taxes,* 20 VAND. L. REV. 443 (1976).
5. By 1981, 44 states had adopted reciprocal statutes for enforcing tax laws. E. SCOLES & P. HAY, CONFLICT OF LAWS 77 n.5 (1982).
6. Chapter 11, sec. III.
7. Fair Assessment in Real Estate Ass'n v. McNary, 454 U.S. 100 (1981).
8. The Court did address the issue, upholding the refusal to enforce, in Wisconsin v. Pelican Ins. Co., 127 U.S. 265, 292 (1888).
9. Milwaukee County v. M.E. White, 296 U.S. 268 (1935).

particularly well illustrated by issues surrounding jurisdiction to tax. The concurrent jurisdiction of the federal and state governments to tax is especially problematic because the party who benefits from the assertion of jurisdiction is the government itself, which will therefore generally be predisposed to exercise jurisdiction whenever possible. This often results in the multiple taxation of a single transaction, either by more than one state, or by both the state and federal governments.

The concurrent exercise of jurisdiction to tax arises in essentially two contexts. First, two governmental units may have alternative means of taxing the same transaction. For example, in the taxation of intangible property, one state may tax on the basis of the owner's domicile and another because the taxpayer conducted business within the state with respect to the intangible property. Both of these assertions of jurisdiction would be legitimate, although together they result in multiple taxation. A more problematic exercise of concurrent jurisdiction occurs when two states purport to use the same means of asserting jurisdiction over the transaction and yet both states attempt to exercise this taxing authority. Both states, for instance, might agree that domicile is the requisite nexus for taxation of an estate; but each might claim to be the state of domicile.

In the usual choice-of-law context, areas of potentially concurrent jurisdiction are resolved so that only one state ultimately prevails. If Adams sues Baxter, then the forum decides which law to apply and full faith and credit guarantees that other states respect the determination. Where Alabama sues Baxter to collect a tax, however, the entry of a judgment applying Alabama law does not preclude taxation by another state. For one thing, that other state may use a different nexus for taxation, so that Baxter must meet a second tax liability. Even if the other state uses the same nexus, however, it is not bound by a judgment to which it was not party. Thus, if Florida and Alabama both agree that domicile is the relevant connecting factor, they may disagree about where Baxter was domiciled and Baxter will not be protected by full faith and credit. Such issues make jurisdiction to tax an unusually intricate, and fascinating, topic.

This chapter begins by briefly outlining the power of the federal government to tax. It then describes state taxing policies and analyzes the restrictions placed on state jurisdiction to tax by the Constitution and federal law. Finally, a particularly complex issue — the taxation of multistate enterprises — is analyzed according to these principles.

376

I. Jurisdiction of the United States Federal Income Tax

The United States Constitution limits federal taxation in several respects. The purpose of all federal taxes must be to provide for defense, for the general welfare or to pay debts.[10] The federal government may not tax articles exported from one state to another.[11] Moreover, all indirect taxes — that is, all taxes, such as sales taxes, that are passed on from the original party taxed to a third party — must be uniform.[12] As ratified in 1787, the Constitution also required that all direct taxes be apportioned among the several states according to population.[13] In 1895, the Supreme Court held that this provision prohibited a federal income tax.[14] This ruling led to the passage of the sixteenth amendment in 1913 authorizing a federal income tax "without apportionment among the states, and without regard to any census or enumeration."[15] Ever since, federal income taxation has provided the primary source of revenue for the national government.

Federal power to tax the states is unclear. The validity of federal taxation of states varies according to the concepts of sovereignty employed to analyze the overall relationship between the federal and state governments.[16] For example, the primary theory used to explain this relationship during the early part of this century was a notion of dual sovereignty. This led to the idea that states should be immune from federal taxation as quasi-independent sovereigns.[17] The legal analysis of federalism has changed over the last fifty years, however. In the 1930s,[18] the Supreme Court held that the states were immune from federal taxation only to the extent that those taxes would place an actual burden on public activities. In *Garcia v. San Antonio Metropolitan Transit Authority*,[19] furthermore, the Court recently validated federal regulation of essential state governmental functions.[20] It remains

---

10. U.S. CONST. art. 1, § 8, cl. 1.

11. U.S. CONST. art. 1, § 9, cl. 5.

12. U.S. CONST. art. 1, § 8, cl. 1.

13. U.S. CONST. art. 1, § 9, cl. 4.

14. Pollock v. Farmers' Loan & Trust Co., 158 U.S. 601 (1895).

15. U.S. CONST. amend. XVI.

16. For a discussion of different concepts of sovereignty in Supreme Court decisions on state taxation, see L. TRIBE, AMERICAN CONSTITUTIONAL LAW 303-04 n.15 (1978).

17. Collector v. Day, 78 U.S. (11 Wall.) 113, 125 (1871): "[T]he means and instrumentalities employed for carrying on the operations of [state] governments, for preserving their existence, and fulfilling the high and responsible duties assigned to them in the Constitution, should be left free and unimpaired, should not be liable to be crippled . . . by the taxing power of another government."

18. Helvering v. Gerhardt, 304 U.S. 405 (1938).

19. 105 S. Ct. 1005 (1985).

20. *Id.* at 1019. In *Garcia,* the Court held that the states' continued role in the federal system is guaranteed by the federal structure itself, rather than by any externally imposed limits on the commerce power.

to be seen whether this decision will have any implications for state immunity from federal taxation.

The jurisdictional reach of the federal government's taxing power is broad. Legal persons within its reach can be divided into two groups for analytical purposes: those with unlimited and those with limited liability. Those subject to unlimited liability include citizens of the United States, resident alien individuals, domestic corporations, and domestic trusts and estates. These persons are generally subject to tax on their entire income, wherever earned, and therefore must pay United States federal income tax on their world-wide income. Pursuant to statute, however, in certain circumstances a citizen living abroad may be partially exempt from tax on earned income from foreign sources.[21]

Persons subject to limited liability are nonresident alien individuals, foreign corporations, and foreign trusts and estates. These persons are taxed only on income from sources within the United States.[22] Thus, they are taxed on all their income from the United States if they are engaged in trade or business here. Otherwise, they are taxed on "fixed or determinable annual or periodical" income from United States sources, such as dividend income.[23]

The Supreme Court has interpreted these jurisdictional rules expansively, resulting in broad federal discretion to exercise its taxing power.[24] There is, therefore, extensive overlap between state and federal power to tax. This concurrent jurisdiction allows double tax liability for the average American citizen. With federal tax rates relatively low, as they are today, this may seem satisfactory. However, as little as forty years ago, double liability subjected individuals to taxation at a rate higher than their total income. This led to the federal income tax deduction for state and local taxes.[25]

II. State Jurisdiction to Tax

Throughout our national history, the coordination of taxes between the state and federal levels and between the several states has been a problem. When disputes over taxation reach the courts, the judiciary

---

21. I.R.C. § 931 (1985). HARVARD UNIVERSITY, TAXATION IN THE UNITED STATES 351 (1963) (hereinafter cited as TAXATION IN THE UNITED STATES).

22. I.R.C. §§ 371-79 (1985). *See* TAXATION IN THE UNITED STATES, *supra* note 21, at 1090 n.14. Citizens of all United States possessions except Puerto Rico are considered nonresident aliens. I.R.C. § 932(a) (1985).

23. *See* TAXATION IN THE UNITED STATES, *supra* note 21, at 32.

24. Recently, a number of grass roots movements have questioned this broad authority. *See, e.g.,* Tax Brief, Barristers' Inn School of Common Law. The gist of their argument is that the sixteenth amendment was never properly ratified.

25. I.R.C. § 164 (1985).

must balance the needs of the individual states to raise revenue against those of the other states, and the legitimate concerns of the nation as a whole. These issues of the proper balance of power between federal and state governments cut to the core of "our federalism."

The depth of the problems caused by concurrent tax jurisdiction is illustrated by the fact that all fifty states have the sovereign power to tax. The tensions in concurrent federal/state jurisdiction are exacerbated on the state/state level, where several states may vie for access to tax dollars. The limits placed on state power by the Supreme Court, in light of the federal structure of our government, generally fall into three categories: (1) insufficiency of nexus between the state's legitimate interests and the tax imposed, (2) discrimination in nature or effect of the tax, and (3) preemption of the states by federal policy. These three categories form a general framework for analyzing federal limitations on state taxes.

The next section gives a general overview of state taxing methods. The principle restraints placed on the states' jurisdiction to tax by the federal constitution and congressional statute are then outlined. In the final section, the special problems involved in state taxation of multistate entities are considered.

A. An Overview of State Taxing Methods[26]

Traditionally, two important distinctions have been made in state taxation. The first is between direct and indirect taxes. Direct taxes are those collected from the persons expected to bear the burden. Indirect taxes, on the other hand, are shifted from the taxpayer to a third party. For example, when a producer of goods is taxed on their production he generally passes on the additional cost to the buyer. Income taxes, however, are borne by the person that makes the tax payment. The second common distinction is between specific versus ad valorem methods of levying taxes. Specific taxes are applied at a fixed rate per physical item. Ad valorem taxes are paid at a percentage of value. Although specific taxes are easier to calculate, ad valorem taxes are much more common, and are considered fairer because they are more closely related to consumer expenditures.

Although the means used by states to tax their citizens vary greatly, some general observations can be made. Taxing methods fall largely into three categories: wealth, consumption, and income taxes.

---

26. This section gives a brief synopsis of the various means by which states impose taxes. It is not meant to be exclusive or exhaustive; it merely acquaints the reader with the basics of state taxation.

1. Wealth Taxes

Wealth taxes are applied to aggregations of monies or possessions, and are generally assessed against real property, estates and recently also capital stock transfers. Today, wealth taxes are not an important part of state tax revenue. During most of the history of the nation, however, the property tax was the most important revenue source in the United States.[27]

Property taxes are applied exclusively at the state and local levels. In recent years, many states have replaced property taxes with other methods of revenue collection. Property taxes are an "in rem" levy; they are imposed against the property itself rather than the owners. The tax is imposed on the gross value of the property and generally is a proportional tax. Most commonly the tax applies either to real property alone or real property plus some types of tangible property. Intangible property is generally excluded.

Many states have moved away from reliance on property taxes, in part because of the method by which they were collected. State governments did not assess and collect property tax through state officials. Instead, states required local governments to collect a given amount of property tax. This method generated insufficient revenue, as well as being cumbersome and expensive for local governments, and most states have therefore discontinued the property tax. Property taxes were a mere 1.8% of total state tax collections in 1974,[28] and are now primarily local taxes.[29]

Death taxes are also a small part of state tax revenue — in 1973 they provided a mere 2.1% of total state tax collections.[30] Death taxes are of two types — estate and inheritance. An estate tax is imposed upon the entire estate, less deductions, without regard to the number of heirs. The rate is generally progressive — that is, the rate increases as the total size of the estate increases.[31] Estate taxes are usually applied at the federal level. Inheritance taxes, on the other hand, are imposed on the individual shares received by the various beneficiaries, and are levied by most states.[32] The number and amount of exemptions as well as the tax rate imposed vary with the relationship of the beneficiary to

---

27. J. MAXWELL & J. ARINSON, FINANCING STATE AND LOCAL GOVERNMENTS 134 (2d ed. 1977) (hereinafter cited as MAXWELL & ARINSON).

28. *Id.* at 135.

29. Local taxes are not the focus of this chapter. Of course, they are also required to meet constitutional requirements.

30. MAXWELL & ARINSON, *supra* note 27, at 127.

31. J. DUE, GOVERNMENT FINANCE: ECONOMICS OF THE PUBLIC SECTOR 94 (4th ed. 1968).

32. *Id.*

the decedent. Direct heirs generally have low rates and high exemptions. The progressivity of the rates works separately on each bequest.[33]

Capital stock taxes are taxes placed upon, or measured by, corporate capital. A majority of states impose some form of capital stock tax. Various names, such as "Corporate Transfer Tax" or "Corporate Business Tax," are used to describe these taxes.[34] The purpose of a capital stock tax is taxation of corporations at approximately the real economic value of the firm. A general property tax is insufficient to meet this goal, because the actual value of a firm is usually higher than the value of its property alone.

Capital stock taxes measure the value of a firm by a variety of techniques. These methods can be grouped together into two broad categories. One category of basis, called the "capital account" basis, looks only to the firm's capital account. This is a statement of the authorized, issued or outstanding capital. The second valuation method measures the corporation's "capital value" as reflected in the historical earning capacity of the corporation as a going concern. Therefore, it includes earned surplus in the tax base, and has generally been more controversial than capital account valuation.[35]

After the tax base is calculated by some variation of these methods, a tax is levied based upon the value of the corporation's capital, as opposed to its property. Capital stock taxes are generally annually-recurring levies.[36]

In summary, wealth taxes are applied as a percentage levy against accumulated wealth. For the most part, wealth taxes are regressive, because they have a greater impact on people in lower income brackets. For example, a low- or middle-income family generally spends a higher percentage of its total income on a house. Lower-income families thus have less ability to pay a property tax on the house. This unfairness has led many states to eliminate most wealth taxes as a source of income.

2. Consumption Taxes

Consumption taxes are generally added on at the retail level and take the form of selective sales taxes and general sales taxes. Often referred to as excise taxes, selective sales taxes are generally of two types; benefit taxes and sumptuary taxes. Benefit taxes, such as motor

33. *Id.*
34. P. HARTMAN, FEDERAL LIMITS ON STATE AND LOCAL TAXATION (1981) (hereinafter cited as HARTMAN).
35. *Id.* at 64.
36. *Id.*

fuel taxes, are considered a quid pro quo for public highway services. The costs of these services should be paid by the one who receives the benefits.[37] In 1981, taxes collected from motor fuel and motor vehicle licenses equalled 15.4 billion dollars. This was 10.3% of the total sales tax collected.[38] Sumptuary or "sin" taxes, on the other hand, punish consumers for purchasing certain items, such as alcohol and tobacco.[39]

The general retail sales tax has only become a major revenue source since World War II, but recently has become the second largest source of state tax revenue. In 1981, it produced 31% of tax revenue with a yield of 46.4 billion dollars, compared with 1932, when the retail sales tax produced only 7 million or .4% of total state tax revenues.[40] The increase in use of the retail sales tax as a revenue source has provoked widespread criticism, primarily because it is a regressive tax. Persons at a lower income level consume a higher portion of their income, and therefore pay a proportionally higher tax.

Generally applied as a percentage of the sales price, the extent of the regression depends upon the breadth of the sales tax base. Many states exempt necessities such as medicine and food, thus reducing the regressivity of the tax because lower income bracket individuals spend more of their income on these items. The ultimate nature of the tax remains regressive, however.

3. Income Taxes

The unfairness of regressive taxation has led states to enact a progressive income tax. Individual and corporate income taxes are currently the leading source of state tax revenue. In 1981, they produced 55 billion dollars in state tax revenue or 36.7% of the total revenue collected, compared with 1932, when they produced a mere 153 million dollars, or 8% of state revenues.[41]

The individual income tax is a direct tax, based on an individual's taxable income. Net income is gross income minus the expenses of earning that income. Most states allow deductions for certain types of expenditures, such as medical expenses, and an allowance for the taxpayer and his or her dependents. After the deductions are taken, one reaches "taxable income," and the rate structure is then applied to the taxable income. In the United States, rate structures tend to be progressive and thus tax individuals at a higher rate as their income level

---

37. *Id.* at 100.
38. J. HELLERSTEIN, STATE TAXATION: CORPORATE INCOME & FRANCHISE TAXES 6 (1983 & Supp. 1985) (hereinafter cited as HELLERSTEIN).
39. *Id.*
40. *Id.* at 5-6.
41. *Id.*

rises. Income taxes are generally considered the preferred form of tax, since they are based on ability to pay.

The corporate state income tax started in 1911 with the Wisconsin tax.[42] By 1973, forty-five states had a corporate income tax.[43] Thirty-two states imposed these taxes at flat rates and thirteen applied rates graduated for income levels.[44] Corporate income taxes produce an average of 8% of total state tax revenues.[45] Variations between the states are considerable, however.

The question of what constitutes corporate income has been answered by the different states in a variety of ways. The majority of states simply apply the federal standard. Conformity with federal standards means that the state secures the benefits of federal enforcement at little or no expense.[46] All payments of state corporate income taxes are deductible by corporations from their income in computing federal taxable income.[47] A minority of states, however, define income differently than the federal government. This creates obvious compliance problems. The biggest problem caused by the state corporate income tax is the allocation of interstate income.[48] The constitutional questions raised by the taxation of multi-state corporate income will be discussed at the end of this chapter.

4. State Uniformity and Equality Provisions

Many state constitutions contain provisions requiring taxes to be equal, uniform or both. These self-imposed provisions limit their power to tax unequally. This creates severe taxing problems because, as discussed above, the fairest of taxes, in economic terms, is an unequal or progressive tax.

In analyzing the way the uniformity provisions actually affect the states' ability to tax, the most important current issue is that of income taxes. As the revenue requirements of government have expanded, the states' need for new methods of taxation also have increased. Many states have looked to taxation of income as a revenue source. Whether income taxes are subject to uniformity provisions often depends on whether the tax is classified as a property tax.

---

42. MAXWELL & ARINSON, *supra* note 27, at 115.
43. *Id.* at 116.
44. *Id.*
45. *Id.*
46. Special Committee on State Taxation of Interstate Commerce of the House Judiciary Committee, State Taxation of Interstate Commerce 88:2 (1964).
47. I.R.C. § 164 (1985).
48. MAXWELL & ARINSON, *supra* note 27, at 117.

The debate over this issue began in Massachusetts in 1915. In a landmark decision, the Supreme Judicial Court held that a tax on income from property is a property tax and thus would be subject to state uniformity requirements. Therefore, a graduated tax would violate the state constitution.[49] Three years later, Missouri held that an income tax is not a property tax and thus is not covered by the state's uniformity and equality clause.[50] The analyses in these cases formed the foundation for the debate as more and more states tried to impose income taxes. Many courts classified income taxes as excises and construed their states' uniformity provisions as only applicable to property taxes.[51] Other courts relied on the notion that an income tax does not constitute a tax on property in the "constitutional" sense.[52]

Although this issue is far from settled, the recent trend is to sustain net income taxes, including graduated taxes, under various rationales. But Illinois, New Hampshire, Massachusetts, Pennsylvania, and Washington still maintain that these taxes violate state constitutional requirements of uniformity.[53] In other states these decisions have been overruled by constitutional amendments that authorize graduated income taxes.[54] Forty-one states and the District of Columbia currently impose broad-based personal income taxes.[55]

B. Federal Limitations on the State Taxing Authority

The maintenance of an appropriate balance of power among the states and between the states and the federal government is essential to the operation of our federal system of government. Judicial review of state taxing policies is imperative because there is no political check on the power of a state to tax those not represented in its legislature. The standard by which state laws are judged find their source both in the Constitution and federal statutes.

1. Constitutional Limits

The principal constitutional limitations on state taxing power are found in the (a) due process clause, (b) commerce clause, (c) equal

---

49. Opinion of the Justices, 220 Mass. 613, 108 N.E. 570 (1915).

50. Ludlow-Saylor Wire Co. v. Wollbrinck, 275 Mo. 339, 205 S.W. 196 (1918).

51. *See, e.g.,* Miles v. Department of Treasury, 209 Ind. 172, 199 N.E. 372 (1935).

52. Featherstone v. Norman, 170 Ga. 370, 384, 153 S.E. 58, 65 (1930) (income is not property for tax purposes, although it can validly be called property in a broader sense).

53. HELLERSTEIN, *supra* note 38, at 34.

54. *See, e.g.,* ALA. CONST. amend. 24; KY. CONST. § 174; WIS. CONST. art. VIII, § 1.

55. HELLERSTEIN, *supra* note 38, at 34. Generally, corporate income taxes are less seriously scrutinized than personal income taxes.

protection clause, (d) privileges and immunities clause, and (e) import-export clause. Justice Brennan has aptly summarized the situation:

> Because there are [50] states and much of the Nation's commercial activity is carried on by enterprises having contacts with more States than one, a common and continuing problem of constitutional interpretation has been that of adjusting the demands of individual States to regulate and tax these enterprises in light of the multistate nature of our federation.[56]

a. The Due Process Clause

The fourteenth amendment prohibits the states from depriving any person of property without due process of law.[57] A taxed activity must bear a rational relationship to the taxing state for it to be consistent with the due process clause. The issue is "whether the state has given anything for which it can ask return."[58] Due process thus requires "some definite link, some minimum connection, between a state and the person, property or transaction it seeks to tax."[59] It is, of course, for the Supreme Court to decide when this standard has been met.[60]

The Court has delineated different due process guidelines for tangible and intangible property, because the states' power to tax tangible as opposed to intangible property is understood to have different bases. These bases are analogous to the concepts of in rem and personal adjudicative jurisdiction. Jurisdiction to tax tangible property is treated similarly to pre-*Shaffer* in rem jurisdiction.[61] That is, if tangible property is located within the state, the state has an absolute right to levy a tax on the property. In contrast, taxation of intangible property requires a case-by-case showing of nexus between the state and the property, similar to the traditional analysis applied to assertions of personal jurisdiction.

The state where real property and other tangibles are located has exclusive power to tax the property.[62] This exclusivity of home state taxing power is premised upon the protections offered by the taxing state to the property. The nature of the protections are "so narrowly

---

56. Allied Stores of Ohio, Inc. v. Bowers, 358 U.S. 522, 532 (1959) (Brennan, J., concurring).

57. U.S. CONST. amend. XIV, § 1.

58. Standard Pressed Steel Co. v. Department of Revenue, 419 U.S. 560, 562 (1975) (citing Wisconsin v. J.C. Penney Co., 311 U.S. 435, 444 (1940)).

59. Miller Bros. v. Maryland, 347 U.S. 340, 344-45 (1954).

60. *Id.*

61. *See* ch. 1, sec. IIA1.

62. Curry v. McCanless, 307 U.S. 357, 363 (1939).

restricted to the state in whose territory the physical property is located as to set practical limits to taxation by others."[63] Other states are without jurisdiction because those states "can afford no substantial protection to the rights taxed."[64] Thus, the analysis of jurisdiction to tax real property is premised upon the relationship between the taxing state and the property itself.[65]

Intangible property has been described by the Supreme Court as relationships between persons, natural or corporate, that the law recognizes, attaching to them certain sanctions that the courts will enforce.[66] As such, intangibles themselves have no physical location. Therefore, jurisdiction to tax intangibles requires that the state have a sufficient nexus with the person who has a legal interest in the intangible. Domicile is always a sufficient nexus,[67] the rationale being that since the state protects the person he or she therefore has a duty to contribute to the support of the government.[68] Although all states except North Carolina agree that a person may have only one domicile at a time, occasionally more than one state claims that the taxpayer is domiciled there.[69] The problem may arise because states define domicile differently, and two states thus may legitimately claim that pursuant to their law the taxpayer is domiciled in that state. In the alternative, two states may apply the same standard but reach different conclusions based on their view of the facts. There are no established constitutional barriers to multiple taxation of intangible property.[70]

Domicile of an owner, moreover, is not the exclusive means of gaining jurisdiction to tax intangible property. When a taxpayer conducts business with respect to intangibles, so as to avail itself of the benefits and protections of the laws of another state, that state may also tax the intangible property.[71] Consequently, various states other than the state of the owner's domicile may have a sufficient nexus with the intangibles to constitutionally tax them.[72] This produces another po-

---

63. *Id.* at 364.

64. *Id.*

65. Where tangibles have not acquired a permanent situs outside the domiciliary state, the state of domicile of persons having interests in the tangibles retains jurisdiction to tax. Central R.R. v. Pennsylvania, 370 U.S. 607, 611-612 (1962).

66. State Tax Comm'n v. Aldrich, 316 U.S. 174, 178 (1942) (citing Curry v. McCanless, 307 U.S. at 366).

67. Curry v. McCanless, 307 U.S. at 367. Income from land is regarded as an intangible and as such may be taxed by the domiciliary state. New York ex rel. Cohn v. Graves, 300 U.S. 308 (1937).

68. HARTMAN, *supra* note 34 at 51; *see also* Cory v. White, 457 U.S. 85, 99 (1982) (Powell, J., dissenting); Curry v. McCanless, 307 U.S. at 365-66.

69. Curry v. McCanless, 307 U.S. at 366.

70. *Id.* at 368.

71. *Id.*

72. *Id.*

tential double taxation. The due process clause does not make a tax unconstitutional merely because it creates a multiple tax burden.[73]

Litigation between California and Texas over the right to tax the estate of Howard Hughes highlights the inadequacies of the federal structure in eliminating multiple taxation of intangibles. Estate taxes may only be imposed by the state of domicile. In this case, the estate included corporate stock valued at 370 million dollars. Both California and Texas claimed that Hughes was domiciled there at the time of his death.

When the case reached the Supreme Court,[74] Justice White's majority opinion held that the Federal Interpleader Act does not provide a jurisdictional basis for resolving inconsistent domicile-based death tax claims by state officials. The Court refused to adjudicate the issue of domicile, holding that a statutory interpleader action brought by a taxpayer or his representative against the taxing officials of two states was a suit against the states, and thus barred by the eleventh amendment.[75]

In a later action, *California v. Texas*,[76] California alleged that the combined state and federal taxes exceeded the Hughes estate, and again asked the Court to decide whether Hughes was domiciled in California or Texas at the time of his death. The Court took original jurisdiction premised upon the claim that the estate was not enough to pay the taxes. This meant the interests of the states were necessarily in conflict with one another, so that the suit was between two states. Shortly thereafter, the Supreme Court appointed a Special Master, who arranged settlement of the case. No finding of domicile was made.

By accepting original jurisdiction in *California v. Texas,* the Supreme Court indicated that it may be willing to resolve the issue of domicile, but only if an estate is insufficient to pay the tax claims against it. This is little comfort to the heirs of an estate that is sufficient to meet the double tax burden. The Federal Interpleader Act is the only procedural remedy that a decedent's estate could invoke to resolve the issue of domicile where the estate is sufficient to pay the tax.[77] This remedy, however, has been foreclosed by the Supreme Court.

---

73. *Id.* at 372-73.

74. Cory v. White, 457 U.S. 85 (1982).

75. *Id.* at 91. See Note, *Supreme Court Decisions in Taxation: 1981 Term,* 36 Tax Law. 421, 468-79 (1983) for an analysis of why *Cory* may have been improperly decided.

76. California v. Texas (II), 457 U.S. 164 (1982) (per curiam).

77. *Cf.* Note, *Section 1983 in State Court: A Remedy for Unconstitutional State Taxation,* 95 Yale L.J. 414 (1985) (arguing that 42 U.S.C. § 1983 should provide relief from unconstitutional taxation in the state courts); Note, *Due Process Limits on State*

b. The Commerce Clause

The commerce clause grants Congress the power to regulate commerce among the states, with foreign nations, and with the Indian Tribes.[78] The courts have held that this power preempts the states' ability to tax certain activities. The commerce clause limits state taxing authority to the extent that the tax is an undue burden on the national economy.[79]

The Supreme Court first invalidated a state tax on commerce clause grounds in 1827.[80] Since that time, the Court has shifted its position a number of times concerning the extent to which the commerce clause limits the states' power to tax interstate and foreign commerce.[81] The Court itself has recognized the unreliable and confused state of the law.[82] The resulting judicial application of constitutional principles to specific state statutes leaves much room for controversy, and provides few precise rules for the states in the exercise of their indispensable power of taxation.[83]

The most fertile areas for conflict between the interests of the state and federal governments have been in the field of interstate commerce. The Framers of the Constitution entrusted Congress with the power to regulate interstate and foreign commerce in order to assure free trade within the national economy.[84] Formerly, the commerce clause was interpreted as providing immunity from taxation of interstate activity. This "free trade immunity" from taxation reflected a desire to promote interstate trade.[85] Federal policies thus preempted state authority.

Estate Taxation: An Analogy to the State Corporate Income Tax, 94 YALE L.J. 1229 (1985) (arguing that the constitutional limits on state taxation of income provides a useful framework for analyzing estate tax issues).

78. U.S. CONST. art. 1, § 8, cl. 3.

79. *See* Complete Auto Transit, Inc. v. Brady, 430 U.S. 274, 279 (1977) (taxes may not discriminate against interstate commerce).

80. Brown v. Maryland, 25 U.S. (12 Wheat.) 419 (1827).

81. *See* Hellerstein, *Foreword — State Taxation Under the Commerce Clause: An Historical Perspective,* 29 VAND. L. REV. 335, 335-39 (1976). *Compare* Spector Motor Serv., Inc. v. O'Connor, 340 U.S. 602 (1950) (a state tax on the privilege of doing business in the state is per se unconstitutional when it is applied to interstate commerce), *with* Complete Auto Transit, Inc. v. Brady, 430 U.S. 274 (1977) (taxpayer must show that the tax is somehow unfair, overruling *Spector*).

82. Northwestern States Portland Cement Co. v. Minnesota, 358 U.S. 450, 457 (1959).

83. For example, in Northwestern States Portland Cement Co. v. Minnesota, 358 U.S. 450 (1959), the Supreme Court upheld state taxation of exclusively interstate operations of a foreign corporation, requiring only that the tax be nondiscriminatory and fairly apportioned — both notoriously vague requirements.

84. Smith v. Turner, 48 U.S. (7 How.) 283, 394 (1849) (Opinion of McLean, J.).

85. Complete Auto Transit, Inc. v. Brady, 430 U.S. 274, 278 (1977) (citing Freeman v. Hewitt, 329 U.S. 249, 252 (1946)):

After decades of basing its commerce clause decisions upon abstract concepts with little basis in reality,[86] the Court in 1977 changed its focus to the effects of the tax on interstate commerce. In *Complete Auto Transit, Inc. v. Brady*,[87] the Court sustained a tax imposed directly on the privilege of engaging in interstate commerce. *Complete Auto Transit* upheld a Mississippi tax on the privilege of doing business in the state that was applied to a foreign corporation transporting vehicles that were manufactured elsewhere to dealers in Mississippi. In upholding the tax, the Court rejected the notion that the privilege of engaging in interstate commerce should automatically be immune from state taxation. Rather, the Court focused the legislation's affect on interstate commerce.[88]

The Court set forth a four-part test for determining when the commerce clause provides immunity from state taxation.[89] The taxpayer in *Auto Transit* failed all four parts of this standard, because it had not claimed: (1) that the taxed activity was not sufficiently connected with the taxing state to justify the tax; or (2) that the tax was not fairly related to the benefits provided the taxpayer; or (3) that the tax discriminated against interstate commerce; or (4) that the tax was not fairly apportioned.[90] This new test moved away from a preemption analysis. The first two parts resemble the due process inquiry into sufficient nexus, while the third exemplifies a traditional commerce clause concern: preventing discrimination. It is well settled that a state may not discriminate against interstate commerce by providing a direct commercial advantage to local business.[91]

[T]he Commerce Clause was not merely an authorization to Congress to enact laws for the protection and encouragement of commerce among the States, but by its own force created an area of trade free from interference by the States. In short, the Commerce Clause even without implementing legislation by Congress is a limitation upon the power of the States. . . . This limitation on State power . . . does not merely forbid a State to single out interstate commerce for hostile action. A State is also precluded from taking any action which may fairly be deemed to have the effect of impeding the free flow of trade between States. It is immaterial that local commerce is subjected to a similar encumbrance.

86. *See* Spector Motor Serv., Inc. v. O'Connor, 340 U.S. 602, 608 (1950): "Even though the financial burden on interstate commerce might be the same, the question whether a state may validly make interstate commerce pay its way depends first of all upon the constitutional channel though which it attempts to do so." *Cf.* Railway Express Agency, Inc. v. Virginia, 347 U.S. 359 (1954) (Virginia statute deemed unconstitutional because phrased in terms of privileges). Railway Express Agency, Inc. v. Virginia, 358 U.S. 434 (1958) (Virginia statute upheld when changed to read "franchise tax").

87. 430 U.S. 274 (1977).

88. *Id.* at 288-89.

89. *Id.* at 287.

90. *Id.*

91. *Id. See also* Japan Line, Ltd. v. County of Los Angeles, 441 U.S. 434, 445-46 (1979).

Two years after its decision in *Auto Transit,* the Court was faced with a case of state property taxation of *foreign* commerce where duplicative taxation existed in the home country. In *Japan Line, Ltd. v. County of Los Angeles,*[92] the Court determined that a different and more complicated inquiry is mandated for foreign commerce. Not only must the tax meet the four requirements of *Auto Transit,* but two additional considerations come into play. Also relevant to state taxation of foreign entities are: (1) whether the tax, notwithstanding its apportionment, creates a substantial risk of international tax multiplication; and (2) whether the tax prevents the federal government from "speaking with one voice when regulating commercial relations with foreign governments."[93] If the challenged tax interferes with either of these precepts, it is invalid.

The tax in *Japan Line* violated both of these standards. It created more than the risk of multiple taxation; it imposed actual multiple tax burdens to which domestic commerce was immune. The opinion leaves open the question whether the mere risk of multiple taxation is enough to defeat a tax. Moreover, the Court held that the tax interfered with foreign affairs powers of the federal government. Balancing the competing needs of the states for taxes against the need for beneficial international trade relations, the Court held in favor of international trade.[94] This factor re-introduces preemption analysis as an important element of limits on state taxation.

c. The Equal Protection Clause

The equal protection clause of the fourteenth amendment provides that no state shall "deny to any person within its jurisdiction the equal protection of the laws."[95] Although equal protection does limit state and local taxing powers, in fact it has not been used regularly to defeat taxes.[96] Theoretically, the equal protection clause prohibits taxes that are discriminatory in cause or effect. The Supreme Court, however, has been liberal in its grant of state authority to classify for tax reasons.[97] States may make any "reasonable" classification for tax purposes.

---

92. *Id.*

93. *Id.* at 451. *But cf.* Wardair Canada, Inc. v. Florida Dep't of Revenue, 54 U.S.L.W. 4687 (6-18-86) (state tax on airline fuel not invalid under foreign commerce clause).

94. *Id.*

95. U.S. CONST. amend. XIV, § 1.

96. *See* Sholley, *Equal Protection in Tax Legislation,* 24 VA. L. REV. 388, 414-16 (1938).

97. HARTMAN, *supra* note 34, at 132.

The Court first applied the equal protection clause to state taxation in 1890, holding that the equal protection clause "was not intended to compel the State to impose an iron rule of equal taxation."[98] A state is thus permitted to adjust "its system of taxation in all proper and reasonable ways so long as they proceed within reasonable limits."[99] The Court has continued to allow the states wide discretion in taxation decisions.

It has explained the logic behind this broad grant of authority to classify as follows:

> Traditionally, classification has been a device for fitting tax programs to local needs and usages in order to achieve an equitable distribution of the tax burden. It has, because of this, been pointed out that in taxation, even more than in other fields, legislators possess the greatest freedom in classification. . . . The burden is on the one attacking the legislative arrangement to negative every conceivable basis which might support it.[100]

But there is a point beyond which the state cannot proceed. In *Allied Stores of Ohio v. Bowers,* the Court declared "[t]he State must proceed upon a rational basis and may not resort to a classification that is palpably arbitrary . . . [and the] classification 'must rest upon some ground of difference having a fair and substantial relation to the object of the legislation.'"[101]

In *Metropolitan Life Insurance Co. v. Ward,* the most recent equal protection challenge to a state tax, the Court struck down an Alabama

---

98. Bells Gap R.R. v. Pennsylvania, 134 U.S. 232, 237 (1890).
99. *Id.*
100. Madden v. Kentucky, 309 U.S. 83, 88 (1940) (citations omitted).
101. 358 U.S. 522, 527 (1959) (quoting Royster Guano Co. v. Virginia, 253 U.S. 412, 415 (1920)). The most controversial classification is the distinction between corporations and other forms of business. In 1973, the Supreme Court held that the advantages of doing business as a corporation justify separately classifying corporations for tax purposes. In Lehnhausen v. Lake Shore Parts Co., 410 U.S. 356 (1973), the Court recognized significant advantages attaching to the corporate form, including: (1) the continuity of business, (2) the ease of property interest transfer, (3) the advantage of separating ownership and control, and (4) limited liability. *Id.* at 362 (quoting Flint v. Stone Tracy Co., 220 U.S. 107, 161-62 (1911).
A tax that differentiates between corporations based on size is called the "chain store" tax. Beyond raising revenue, the tax is designed to equalize the economic advantages between chain stores and the sole proprietor. The Court has upheld a chain store tax against commerce clause, due process and equal protection arguments. Great Atl. & Pac. Tea Co. v. Grosjean, 301 U.S. 412 (1937). In approving a state tax for stores within its borders in proportion to the total number of stores in the chain, wherever located, the Court stated that "Taxation may be made the implement of the exercise of the state's police power; and proper and reasonable discrimination between classes to promote fair competitive conditions and to equalize economic advantages is therefore lawful." *Id.* at 426.

statute that taxed out-of-state insurance companies at a higher rate than domestic insurance companies.[102] The statute levied a tax of 3% on life insurance premiums, and 4% on property and casualty premiums paid to out-of-state companies, but charged domestic companies only a 1% tax on all premiums. The statute allowed out-of-state companies to reduce their tax liability by investing in assets in Alabama, but never to a point of equality with domestic companies.[103]

The Court held that encouraging the formation of new insurance companies and the investment by foreign insurance companies in Alabama assets are not legitimate state purposes when pursued through a discriminatory scheme. Justice Powell, writing for a 5-4 majority, stated that Alabama's tax penalty on foreign businesses "constitutes the very sort of parochial discrimination that the Equal Protection Clause was intended to prevent."[104] In a strong dissent, Justice O'Connor argued that the ruling threatens "the freedom of both state and federal legislative bodies to fashion appropriate classifications in economic legislation."[105] Despite the recent holding in *Ward*, however, the Court is likely to remain hesitant to strike down state tax classifications on equal protection grounds.

d. The Privileges and Immunity Clauses

The Constitution contains two clauses that protect the privileges and immunities of "citizens."[106] As interpreted by the Supreme Court, the privileges and immunities clause of the fourteenth amendment provides no protection against discriminatory state taxation.[107] Article IV, § 2 provides that: "The Citizens of each state shall be entitled to all Privileges and Immunities of Citizens in the several States." The "interstate privileges and immunities clause," as it is commonly known, has been interpreted as an instrument of national union. In the landmark case *Toomer v. Witsell,* for example, the Court stated that:

---

102. Metropolitan Life Ins. Co. v. Ward, 105 S. Ct. 1676 (1985).

103. *Id.*

104. *Id.* at 1681-82. The case was decided on equal protection rather than the commerce clause grounds, because insurance transactions have been specifically excluded from protection under the commerce clause by the McCarran-Ferguson Act, 15 U.S.C. §§ 1011-1015 (1976). 105 S. Ct. at 1683.

105. *Id.* at 1684 (O'Connor, J., dissenting).

106. U.S. CONST. art. IV, § 2, cl. 1; amend. XIV, § 1. Corporations are not regarded as citizens for purposes of standing under either clause. Blake v. McClung, 172 U.S. 239 (1898).

107. *See generally* Slaughterhouse Cases, 83 U.S. 36 (1873); G. GUNTHER, CASES AND MATERIALS ON CONSTITUTIONAL LAW 473-75 (10th ed. 1980); HARTMAN, *supra* note 34.

The primary purpose of this clause . . . was to help fuse into one Nation a collection of independent, sovereign States. [] In line with this underlying purpose, it was long ago decided that one of the privileges which the clause guarantees to citizens of State A is that of doing business in State B on terms of substantial equality with the citizens of that State.[108]

In that case, the challenged statute charged nonresidents one hundred times more than residents for the same fishing license. While the Court agreed that the state could charge a different fee sufficient to make up for other taxes paid by residents for conservation, it stressed that the fee virtually excluded nonresidents from fishing in the restricted zone.[109]

According to *Toomer*, discrimination against nonresidents is constitutional when: (1) the activity of the nonresidents is the cause of the evil that the state seeks to remedy by legislation; and (2) the discrimination against nonresidents bears a "reasonable relationship" to the problem presented by the nonresident.[110]

e. The Import-Export Clause

The United States Constitution provides:

No State shall, without the Consent of the Congress, lay any Imposts or Duties on Imports or Exports, except what may be absolutely necessary for executing its inspection Laws, and the net Produce of all Duties and Imposts, laid by any State on Imports or Exports, shall be for the Use of the Treasury of the United States; and all such Laws shall be subject to the Revision and Control of the Congress.[111]

The Court has recently made a major shift in its analysis of import and export taxation under this clause. Previously, even nondiscriminatory taxes were prohibited on goods as long as they retained their character of imports — that is, as long as they remained in their shipping cases.[112] In the 1976 decision in *Michelin Tire Corp. v. Wages*,[113] however, the Court held that the import-export clause does not bar a state-imposed nondiscriminatory property tax on goods imported and held for sale. The state in *Michelin* argued that the import-export clause proscribes only "imposts" or "duties." The Court, however, decided that the Framers sought to accomplish three basic goals through the clause:

---

108. 334 U.S. 385, 395-96 (1948).
109. *Id.*
110. *Id.*
111. U.S. Const. art. I, § 10, cl. 2.
112. *See* Low v. Austin, 80 U.S. (13 Wall.) 29, 33 (1871).
113. 423 U.S. 276 (1976).

The Federal government must speak with one voice when regulating commercial relations with foreign governments, and tariffs, which might affect foreign relations, could not be implemented by the States consistently with that exclusive power.[114]

Further, the Framers intended that import revenues would be a major source of federal funds, and that the states should not be permitted to divert import revenues from the federal government.[115] Finally, the Framers feared that

> harmony among the States might be disturbed unless seaboard States, with their crucial ports of entry, were prohibited from levying taxes on citizens of other States by taxing goods merely flowing through their ports to the other States not situated as favorably geographically.[116]

The Court in *Michelin* concluded that a nondiscriminatory property tax did not run counter to any of these policies underlying the clause, since the goods involved, although imported, were no longer in transit, but were held for sale within the state.

Two years after *Michelin* was decided, the Court followed the same reasoning to sustain a business and occupation tax applied to stevedoring.[117] The stevedoring consisted of loading and unloading foreign cargo. The tax was attached to gross receipts, all of which were attributable to services performed within the state imposing the tax. Although many questions remain about the future application of this standard to varying fact patterns, one may safely conclude that the underlying historical analysis will prevail.

In addition to constitutional restrictions on state taxing power, Congress has also enacted legislation controlling the power of the states to tax. The next section will briefly review the congressional role in delineating the states' jurisdiction to tax.

2. Statutory Limits

It is well settled that Congress has the power to displace or expand the states' power to tax. Indeed, the Supreme Court has often hinted that it would like Congress to play a more active role in certain areas of state taxation, such as a multistate corporate income tax. Justice Frankfurter first argued for the extension of congressional power over interstate commerce to control over state taxation in *Northwestern States Portland Cement Co. v. Minnesota*:

---

114. *Id.* at 285.

115. *Id.*

116. *Id.* at 285-86.

117. Department of Revenue v. Association of Washington Stevedoring Cos., 435 U.S. 734 (1978).

The problem [state taxation of interstate commerce] calls for solution by devising a congressional policy. Congress alone can provide for a full and thorough canvassing of the multitudinous and intricate factors which compose the problem of the taxing freedom of the States and the needed limits on such state taxing power.[118]

On the whole, however, Congress has not taken the initiative in shaping state taxing policy.

The *Northwestern States* decision, which upheld a non-discriminatory, fairly apportioned tax on multistate corporate income, provoked an exception to this congressional reluctance.[119] In response to intense lobbying by corporations, Congress passed Public Law 86-272, which mandates minimum jurisdictional standards before states may impose such taxes. Public Law 86-272 prohibits state taxation of businesses that confine their in-state activities to solicitation of orders for merchandise that will be shipped from out-of-state locations.[120]

In fact, the barrier imposed by Public Law 86-272 offers little protection to taxation of large multistate corporations for two reasons. First, because of their size it is difficult for them to limit their activities in each state to mere solicitation. Secondly, if at all possible on the facts before it, the Court has held that a corporation's activities meets the standard. Decisions following the enactment of Public Law 86-272 have upheld the imposition of state taxes on protected sales activities, if accompanied by even minimal unprotected activity, or by the presence of property in the state.[121] Since the enactment of Public Law 86-272, Congress has not passed a major state tax bill.[122]

C. State Taxation of Multistate Corporate Income: An Illustrative Application

Thus far we have considered the types of taxes and the various restrictions placed on state taxing authority separately. This section integrates the two concepts in the most controversial area of state taxation — that is, the taxation of multistate income.

During the nineteenth century, the states were restricted in their ability to tax multistate income. Applying an indirect-direct test, the Supreme Court only allowed the states to tax local activities that had an "indirect" effect on interstate commerce.[123] As the economy became

---

118. 358 U.S. 450, 476 (Frankfurter, J., dissenting).

119. *Id.* at 450.

120. 15 U.S.C. § 381(a) (1976).

121. *See* Corrigan, *Interstate Corporate Income — Recent Revolutions and a Modern Response,* 29 Vand. L. Rev. 423, 427 n.7 (1976), and cases cited therein.

122. *See* Hellerstein, *supra* note 81, at 339-41.

123. Postal Tel. Cable Co. v. Adams, 155 U.S. 688 (1895); United States Glue Co. v. Town of Oak Creek, 247 U.S. 321 (1918).

more sophisticated, however, the Court recognized the states' needs to tax multistate income. This led a shift in 1938 to the "multiple burdens" doctrine.[124] Under this standard, a state tax is permitted on multistate income unless it subjects an interstate activity to a burden not equally imposed upon local activities. Not infrequently, however, lower courts continued to apply the old indirect-direct burdens test.

This led to the landmark case of *Northwestern States Portland Cement Co. v. Minnesota,*[125] where the Supreme Court explicitly held that a state could impose a fairly apportioned nondiscriminatory tax on interstate commerce. More recently, in *Standard Pressed Steel Co. v. Department of Revenue,*[126] the Court upheld Washington's imposition of a gross receipts tax on a corporation whose only contact with the state was a resident engineer and occasional visits by other personnel. In practice, therefore, the courts have generally deferred to the states to develop their own taxing formulae for multistate income. The Supreme Court has invalidated state taxing formulas only when an actual burden on interstate commerce has been proven by the corporation challenging the tax.[127]

The result is that different states have different methods of taxing multistate income,[128] producing under- and over-taxation of multijurisdictional entities.[129] This lack of uniformity is a serious problem. A consistent and uniform system is possible only at the federal level — Congress or the courts would have to institute a mandatory state taxing method. But the Court has stated that if anyone is to impose a specific taxing formula on the states, it should be Congress.[130] Congress, however, has failed to enact any requirement of uniformity in state taxation of multistate income.

Under the present system, therefore, any challenge to a state tax must be on constitutional grounds. The Court has developed a four-part test for determining whether a state tax violates the due process or commerce clause. The test requires that: (1) a substantial nexus must exist between the business activity and the state, (2) the tax must be fairly apportioned, (3) the tax must be fairly related to services

124. Western Live Stock v. Bureau of Revenue, 303 U.S. 250 (1938).
125. 358 U.S. 450 (1959).
126. 419 U.S. 560 (1975).
127. General Motors Corp. v. Washington, 377 U.S. 436, 441 (1964).
128. The primary methods of taxing corporate income are separate accounting, specific allocation and formula apportionment. For a discussion of the problems associated with taxing methods, see Corrigan, *supra* note 121, at 429-36.
129. *See generally* Hellerstein, *supra* note 81.
130. J.D. Adams Mfg. Co. v. Storen, 304 U.S. 307, 327 (1938) (Black, J., dissenting in part).

provided by the state, and (4) the tax must not discriminate against interstate commerce.[131]

The substantial nexus criterion requires that the state have some minimum connection with the taxed activity.[132] Although phrased in terms of minimum contacts, the taxation standard is far easier to satisfy than the minimum contacts test in adjudicative jurisdiction. For one thing, unlike the minimum contacts standard for personal jurisdiction, contacts are aggregated whenever unity of ownership or management exists between separate entities.[133] Essentially, the standard only requires that a benefit of some sort be derived from the state.[134] For example, in *Butler Brothers v. McColgan,* California taxed a portion of an Illinois corporation's income based upon unity of management with a California distributor. The Court upheld the tax even though the distributor had in fact lost money that year.[135]

The second requirement is that the tax be fairly apportioned.[136] In the absence of congressional apportionment rules, however, "the Court has allowed the states wide latitude in the selection and application of apportionment rules."[137] Thus, a constitutionally acceptable apportionment formula may be based on gross sales; location of tangible assets in the state or by an averaging of payroll, sales and tangible properties.[138] This gives the states substantial discretion to apportion multistate income as they see fit.

The third requirement, the "fairly related" test, does not require that the amount of the tax bear a reasonable relationship to the value of services provided by the state. Instead it requires only that the measure of the tax be "reasonably related" to the corporation's contact with the state "since it is the activities or presence of the taxpayer in the state that may properly be made to bear a 'just share of the state tax burden.'"[139] The cases suggest that whenever the state provides the

---

131. *See* Japan Line, Ltd. v. County of Los Angeles, 441 U.S. 434, 444-45 (1979); Department of Revenue v. Association of Washington Stevedoring Cos., 435 U.S. 734, 751 (1978); Complete Auto Transit, Inc. v. Brady, 430 U.S. 274, 279 (1977).

132. Complete Auto Transit, Inc. v. Brady, 430 U.S. at 287; Miller Bros. v. Maryland, 347 U.S. 340, 344-45 (1954).

133. 315 U.S. 501 (1942).

134. Northwestern States Portland Cement Co. v. Minnesota, 358 U.S. at 462.

135. 315 U.S. 501 (1942).

136. *See* cases cited *supra* note 131.

137. Mobil Oil Corp. v. Commissioner of Taxes, 445 U.S. 425, 452 (1980) (Stevens, J., dissenting) (citing Moorman Mfg. Co. v. Bair, 437 U.S. 267, 278-80 (1978)).

138. *Id.* at 453 (Stevens, J., dissenting).

139. Commonwealth Edison Co. v. Montana, 453 U.S. 609, 626 (1981) (quoting Western Live Stock v. Bureau of Revenue, 303 U.S. 250, 254 (1938)).

taxpayer with "the benefits of a trained work force and the advantages of a civilized society," the "fairly related" standard is satisfied.[140]

The final criterion is that the tax be nondiscriminatory. Here the court has been more vigilant, prohibiting states from imposing a greater burden on interstate activities than on intrastate activities.[141] Therefore, if a tax is discriminatory in cause or effect, it is deemed unconstitutional.[142]

In summary, state taxation of multistate income produces both theoretical and practical problems. Neither the judiciary nor Congress, however, has developed a more uniform system. The result is a confused and often unfair system with different taxing standards and methods applied in the different states.

Conclusion

The preservation of the federal system mandates that the powers to tax asserted by the state and federal governments be brought into harmony. The inherent conflicts of interest that exist both between the states and between the states and the federal government requires limiting state jurisdiction to tax.

There are two sources of federal limits on state taxation. Constitutional provisions such as the due process clause, commerce clause, equal protection clause, privileges and immunities clause and the import-export clause all limit state taxing power. Further, although Congress has the power to limit the states' jurisdiction to tax through legislation, this power has rarely been utilized. Most of the problems created by state taxation of multistate income have never been resolved. It seems unlikely that there will be a solution to these problems in the near future.

---

140. Japan Line, Ltd. v. County of Los Angeles, 441 U.S. at 445.
141. Northwestern States Portland Cement Co. v. Minnesota, 358 U.S. at 462.
142. Halliburton Oil Well Cementing Co. v. Minnesota, 373 U.S. 64 (1959) (invalidating tax on goods imported from out-of-state where no tax was placed on goods produced within state boundaries).

Table of Cases

Index

A

C

J

L

INDEX

414

S

T

415